BEST ANCH
of the
INSIDE PASSAGE

SECOND EDITION

ANNE VIPOND

WILLIAM KELLY

BRITISH COLUMBIA'S SOUTH & CENTRAL COAST

FROM VICTORIA TO BELLA BELLA

**OCEAN
CRUISE
GUIDES**

Published by: Ocean Cruise Guides Ltd.
325 English Bluff Road
Delta, BC V4M 2M9
Phone: (604) 948-0594
Email: info@oceancruiseguides.com

Editor: Duart Snow
Copy Editor: Katharine Dawe
Contributing Editors: Mike Woodward, Michael DeFreitas
Cartography: OCG, John Kelly
Design: Ocean Cruise Guides Ltd
Publisher: William Kelly

Photos: Front Cover, Fury Island. Page III, Long Harbour, Saltspring Island. Page IV, Handfield Bay. Back cover, Green Island, Kendrick Island

Printed in China

Library and Archives Canada Cataloguing in Publication

Vipond, Anne, 1957-, author
        Best anchorages of the Inside Passage : from the Gulf Islands to Fitz Hugh Sound / Anne Vipond, William Kelly. -- 2nd edition.

Includes index.
ISBN 978-1-927747-01-8

1. Boats and boating--British Columbia--Pacific Coast--Guidebooks.
2. Boats and boating--Inside Passage--Guidebooks.
3. Pacific Coast (B.C.)-- Guidebooks.
4. Inside Passage--Guidebooks.
I. Kelly, William, 1951-, author II. Title.

GV776.15.B7V56 2013   797.109711'31
C2013-907142-3

Authors' Acknowledgements

We would like to thank the many people who have supported and assisted us over the years. Bill Wolferstan has been an inspiration to us, as boaters and as writers. Bob Hale has been a welcome presence in our boating lives and in the boating community at large. Mike Woodward has generously shared his expertise on piloting the south coast's numerous tidal passes. And Fred Suthern has been a steadfast friend and advisor.

We also thank the many boaters we have met at anchorages, marinas, boat shows and elsewhere, for sharing their personal experiences with us and for offering encouragement to keep writing about the B.C. coast. And we thank the various editors who have published our articles over the years, most notably those who have spent time at the helm of *Pacific Yachting* magazine, namely Paul Burkhart, John Shinnick, Simon Hill, Peter Robson, Dale Miller and Duart Snow, who has moved over to the bridge of *Canadian Yachting West*.

Bill Kelly & Anne Vipond
Tsawwassen, B.C.

For notices of updates or corrections, please visit our web site: oceancruiseguides.com and click on the Best Anchorages page.
If you have any comments, suggestions or updates regarding the contents of this book, please write or email us.

This book is dedicated to Reid and John, and to the memory of Tuck.

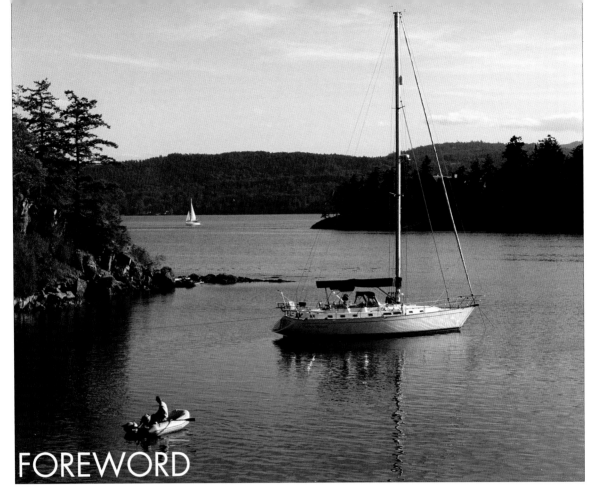

FOREWORD

The best cruising guides speak from the heart as well as the mind. They present the facts – how to get there, what is there – the vital details about the safety and suitability of different anchorages, and so on. But they also need to convey stories and impressions that help you to decide whether you should visit these places in the first place. Anne Vipond and Bill Kelly have considerable experience in providing both, having explored the Inside Passage for nearly three decades in their 35-foot sloop *Sway*. They have written countless authoritative articles on coastal cruising since the early 1980s.

Their book *Best Anchorages of the Inside Passage* is designed to assist small boat operators voyaging between Victoria and Bella Bella with over 250 carefully selected anchorage locations, many of which are finely detailed through illustrations, maps and summary pros and cons. In a most comprehensive and entertaining manner, they answer the important questions: What is there and how do you get there? And, why go? Their first-hand local knowledge provides valuable insight into the intricacies of navigating a safe course through tidal passes and into a variety of rock-bound anchorages.

Most important, they also have a native-born sympathy for the local history, flora, fauna, culture and geography of the places they describe. Reading through these descriptions I can only repeat what Miles Smeeton said in his foreword to my first cruising guide on the Gulf Islands: "For those who have already experienced their peace, it will bring back memories to be enjoyed and sometimes perhaps they will wonder, why they ever went away."

Bill Wolferstan
Victoria, B.C.

Authors' Note
After thirty years spent cruising the B.C. coast in our Spencer 35, we decided to sell *Sway*. We now cruise in a Tayana 48 named *Perfect Bound,* and although some of our favourite gunkholes feel a bit tighter in a larger boat, we're rediscovering old haunts and finding new places to drop the hook.

CONTENTS

Darby Channel

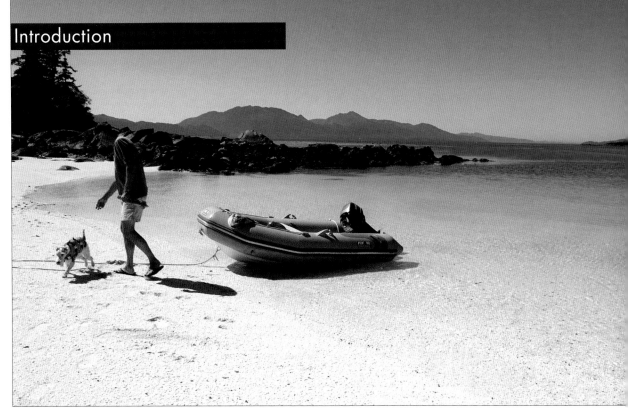

There are many scenic waterways in this world, but there is only one Inside Passage. Stretching northward from Puget Sound in Washington State to Skagway in Southeast Alaska, this vast and intricate coastline of winding channels and forested islands is unsurpassed in both beauty and accessibility for boaters. The Canadian portion of the Inside Passage spans 500 nautical miles, from the southern tip of Vancouver Island to the exposed waters of Dixon Entrance, where the border runs between British Columbia and Alaska.

This cruising guide covers the southern half of B.C.'s inside waters, the area that lies between Vancouver Island and the mainland coast, as well as B.C.'s central coast between Cape Caution and Bella Bella. Included in this guide is information on the marinas and ports we have pulled into while wandering up and down the coast, but the emphasis is on anchorages.

It's the anchorages that inspire us. We have been exploring the coastal waters of B.C. for over three decades, yet it seems we would need several lifetimes to visit every potential anchorage along the way. Some areas in fact have only recently been charted and many anchorages remain unnamed.

Finding new anchorages is relatively easy when cruising the Inside Passage's myriad of islands and inlets. More difficult was choosing, for this guidebook, our favourite anchorages from the many beautiful and sheltered spots we have called home for the night. Fluctuating factors can colour a person's perception of an anchorage – the weather, the people you meet while there, your own state of mind at the time. Yet, some anchorages provide the haven we all seek and these become, however briefly, the places we enjoy revisiting, even if only in our memories.

Whether tucked into a craggy cove or hidden at the head of a glassy fjord, there are so many fine anchorages along our coast that, whatever your vessel, you will be sure to find one or two that are special. It may be small and unnamed, or a place unremarkable except that it provided shelter in a storm. Or perhaps it was an anchorage that offered a clear view onto the nature and wildness of our coast. Remoteness and seclusion certainly help make an anchorage special, but this guidebook covers the popular destinations as well. We never tire of returning to our old favourites or of discovering new places. This, for us, is the joy of boating.

Anne Vipond and Bill Kelly

Fury Island

Although sheltered from the open Pacific Ocean, the intricate waterways of the Inside Passage present numerous challenges. Significant tides create strong currents in passes and channels, and local winds can produce steep, choppy seas in the straits. These waters demand an understanding of the elements that make up weather and sea conditions. While some factors are more predictable than others, the ever-changing nature of weather and the sea is what makes cruising along the Inside Passage a fascinating adventure.

Seamanship means being prepared for any contingency and making sure every item on your vessel has been checked and is in good working order. Being prepared also means having Canadian Hydrographic Service (CHS) charts, tide tables and Sailing Directions on board for safe navigation of the intricate waterways of the B.C. coast. The CHS Symbols, Abbreviations and Terms booklet (available online) also helps interpret charts and assists in gaining insight to an anchorage. An anchorage is influenced by many factors including the seabed, the topography of the surrounding land, sometimes even shoreside structures, all of which are included in CHS charts.

Things can go wrong for even the most experienced skipper and keeping this in mind helps. Halyards jam, bad fuel gets onboard and deadheads find you. Perhaps the most important thing to control during an out-of-control situation is yourself. Panicked thinking is common during a crisis on the water and is not easy to suppress. We've found there is usually more time to respond during a critical situation than there seems to be and that most boats can handle the range of weather conditions of the Inside Passage in summer. The test, as always, is the response of the crew.

CHS charts are superb – accurate and well inked with definitive colours and text.

Weather and Sea Conditions

Weather systems flow in a west-to-east direction in the northern hemisphere, giving the west coast of North America the moderating effects of the Pacific Ocean throughout the year. In winter, wet and windy weather prevails along the Pacific Northwest coast, its mountainous shoreline a catch-basin for offshore storms from the Gulf of Alaska. Precipitation that falls as snow on mountain slopes rarely remains more than a few days in low-lying areas of B.C.'s south coast.

Summer weather in the North Pacific is dominated by a subtropical high which brings reduced precipitation and increased sunshine. Autumn is a transitional season when the North Pacific High gradually shrinks and the relatively light breezes of summer are replaced with winter storms generated by the Aleutian Low. At any time of year, winds along the sheltered Inside Passage are less intense than those on the open Pacific.

Summer winds are generally light to moderate and seas range from calm to choppy. Wind conditions are highly localized due to the mountainous topography and twisting channels, with acceleration off capes and headlands, and strong outflow winds near large inlets. Generally speaking, winds blow strongest on the north coast and lose their velocity as they move south until they reach Juan de Fuca Strait, where strong westerlies are common.

The waterways of the Inside Passage are sheltered from ocean swells, but local hazards include steep, choppy seas, fog and tidal currents. One of the most challenging bodies of water of the Inside Passage is the Strait of Georgia, where very steep seas can be encountered during large tides along the eastern side of the strait south of Vancouver. This results from one of the largest rivers in North America, the Fraser River, emptying its waters into the strait. Johnstone Strait has also gained notoriety for its strong afternoon westerlies which, when opposing an ebbing tide, can whip up large, steep seas. There have been times when afternoon westerlies have persisted for weeks in this strait, and if you are determined to make progress north, a good strategy is to get underway before dawn, or travel in the evening or at night.

In summer, sea fog occurs anywhere there are upwellings of cold water. This dense fog is frequently encountered in Juan de Fuca Strait and Queen Charlotte Strait. Also called advection fog, sea fog occurs when warm, moist maritime air blows onshore across colder coastal water that has been brought to the surface by upwellings. These upwellings are caused either by tidal currents being deflected upward from an irregular sea bottom or by wind pushing away the surface water to allow deeper, colder water to rise to the surface. Sea fog drifts inland on onshore breezes and will drift to the head of even the longest inlets, lingering through the day.

Radiation-type fog occurs on clear cold nights when the land cools, causing water droplets to condense onto fine particles suspended in the warmer air. This type of fog is most dense at sunrise and slowly burns off with daytime heating. Radiation fog begins in September and lasts through February, occurring throughout the Strait of Georgia and adjacent waterways where visibility is reduced to a half-mile on about 20 days per year. In specific areas, such as the Fraser River estuary, where the river's relatively low temperature contributes to the cooling process, up to 60 days per year can be fog-ridden.

The Canadian Coast Guard issues a continuous marine weather broadcast on the VHF weather channel and this should be monitored before leaving port. If you are travelling in poor visibility, it is a good idea to contact the traffic channels maintained by the Coast Guard along the Strait of Georgia and Johnstone Strait. This excellent service alerts commercial vessels of your presence and is very helpful in areas of large-vessel activity, such as Active Pass and the traffic lanes of the Strait of Georgia. See this book's 'Cruising Essentials' for VHF channels for Coast Guard traffic.

Other Hazards

Drifting logs and other debris are a common hazard in B.C. waters, especially following a spring tide or a storm. Seaborne material tends to collect along tide lines and is easy to spot. Harder to avoid are logs lying in the troughs of large waves and deadheads – which are logs standing upright in the water with just a few inches protruding above the surface. Keep a constant lookout for debris while underway.

Boats anchored at Port McNeill wait for the sea fog to lift in Queen Charlotte Strait.

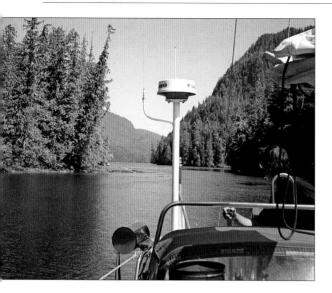

Looking back at notorious Hopetown Passage

Tides, Currents and Passes

The waters of the Inside Passage are greatly affected by tides, and current from tides is encountered in the many passes, channels and straits. It's not uncommon for anchorages to experience remnant current, although not usually more than one or 2 knots. Tides rise and fall twice a day (referred to as semidiurnal or mixed) with one a higher high water and one a lower low water variation as shown in the tide tables. Tides, caused by the gravitational pull on the earth's water by the sun and moon, move water from the Pacific Ocean into mainland inlets and back again, forcing current to flow around both ends of Vancouver Island. The ocean current enters southern waters through Juan de Fuca Strait, and northern waters through Queen Charlotte Strait, which results in tides flooding north in the Strait of Georgia and south in Johnstone Strait and Discovery Passage.

The size of tides is related to the phases of the moon and its position with the sun. Approximately twice a month, during a new moon and a full moon, the difference between high water and low water reaches a maximum (usually about 10 to 15 feet at Point Atkinson) and this is referred to as a spring tide. The cycle then reverses itself and each day for one week the tide range becomes smaller until the difference between high and low water can be as little as 3 feet (a neap tide).

Coastal British Columbia's complex topography of islands and channels creates localized tide and current conditions, and makes the annual Canadian Hydrographic Service's Tide and Current Tables an indispensable reference for boaters cruising the Inside Passage.

Safely transiting any tidal pass is simple if done at or near slack water, which is the time span when the tide turns from one direction to another. The CHS Tide and Current Tables contain the times of turn to flood and to ebb, and maximum rates of current, for all the major passes. Local weather conditions and the amount of land drainage can sometimes cause a discrepancy in the predicted time versus actual time of slack water, but generally speaking the CHS Tide and Current Tables are very reliable. When calculating slack water, be sure to add an hour in summer for daylight saving time.

Missing slack water is a reality when cruising the Inside Passage, and transiting a pass before or after slack – when current and turbulence will be encountered – becomes less daunting with experience. Smaller passes without obstructions or fast currents can be taken with a wider window, and an example of this is Chatham Channel near Johnstone Strait. A wide-open pass without obstructions (such as Seymour Narrows or Hole in the Wall) can be navigated safely on some amount of positive or pushing current during the beginning or end of a tide. A narrow or intricate pass with hazards (such as Whiterock Passage or Booker Lagoon Passage) is best transited against current or at slack and not when the current is pushing you. Going with the current in large passes saves time and, if done carefully, can work well in improving distance for the day.

Sometimes you may find yourself entering a pass that is experiencing more current than you expected. If such is the case, stay away from whirlpools or areas of heavy turbulence and steer toward the tongue (the flat, quiet part) of the current where there is usually deeper water.

Detailed information on each of the passes is contained in applicable chapters of this book.

Anchoring

Anchoring is often a source of anxiety for new boaters but it needn't be. Although good anchoring practise comes with experience, it starts with safe anchoring tackle and a skeptical view of all anchorages. As wryly noted in *Oceanography and Seamanship* by William Van Dorn, anchoring is not ordinarily regarded as an emergency procedure but perhaps it should be. Few subjects inspire more opinions in boaters than anchors and how best to set them. After 30 years of cruising the Inside Passage and the Gulf of Alaska, we've seen there are many ways to stay safely anchored, but the common thread with experienced skippers is to install the largest (heaviest) ground tackle practical and make sure the bitter end is attached to the boat.

CHS team measuring current with an inflatable at Hole in the Wall pass.

Measuring Tides & Currents

The harmonic nature of tides and currents wasn't fully understood until the late 19th century when Dr. A.T. Doodson at the Tidal Institute of Liverpool completed years of study involving complex calculus and algebra. Doodson's method of harmonic analysis, based on a long series of measurements of the tide or current at a particular location, was a remarkable improvement over previous methods and still stands as the accepted principle of tidal prediction to this day.

More recently, and much closer to home, a research scientist at the Institute of Ocean Sciences in Sidney, Mike Foreman, introduced digital computation to the process of harmonic analysis. Modern predictions by the Canadian Hydrographic Society are based on Foreman's routines, but the quality of the predictions are only as good as the series of measurements necessary to derive the local tidal constituents. Typically, a tide station or pass needs a complete year of measurements at one-hour intervals to give oceanographers a complete picture on which to base predictions.

British Columbia's first tide-recording stations were established in the 1890s, and the first tide tables for B.C.'s southwest coast were published in 1901, but attempts to improve predictions of the passes really got underway after World War II. CHS field workers would often set up a fixed transit and float poles with flags through the pass to determine current speed. On one occasion, baby bottles with lights inside were used to gauge Gabriola Passage during night observations.

CHS also uses submerged buoys to measure the current over the long periods needed for harmonic analysis, as well as boats, which were first used in the late 1970s.

In the 1980s, rigid-bottom inflatables became the workhorse of CHS field workers. Their design – based on U.K. rescue vessels – provided a stable platform for CHS workers to maneuver in the passes without losing control in the strong eddies. Working in pairs, the coxswain's job is to hold position while the other team member keeps track of speed and judges the quality of the measurement. According to oceanographer Mike Woodward, "We'd often just sit in a pass – seemingly stuck in one place for a long time. I've wondered how many other vessels have given up after seeing what appears to be our failure to get through the contrary current."

Michael Woodward, a pioneer of tide & current research

Mariners plying the many passes along the British Columbia coast have detailed information at their fingertips on tides and currents, thanks to research conducted by the Canadian Hydrographic Service (CHS). Many of the passes were thoroughly researched in the 1980s and much of the key data was assembled by Mike Woodward of Victoria. Mike learned sailing from his father Jack who also taught him some of the competitive advantages of playing the currents off Cadboro Bay. Years later, after completing a degree in physics (Toronto, 1974), he found a job with CHS in Current Surveys where he was involved in all aspects of currents to assist the navigation of the various passes.

Mike spent some 20 years studying tidal streams in the narrow passes of the B.C. coast. He developed a unique methodology, spanning measurement technology, field surveys, and computer models, to produce year-long continuous data records of currents in many of our turbulent tidal rapids. This data was then analyzed to establish current predictions for ten key locations that are now included in the Tide and Current Tables: Porlier Pass, Gabriola Pass, Dodd Narrows, Sechelt Rapids, Beazley Pass, Hole-in-the-Wall, Gillard Passage, Arran Rapids, Quatsino Narrows and Nakwakto Rapids. He also used current meters (see photo page 178) to study and analyze tidal streams in Race Passage, Weynton Passage and Scott Channel that resulted in daily predictions for these locations in the Current Tables.

Mike retired from CHS in 2000.

Mike Woodward when he worked at CHS.

CQR shows its holding power – with only partial burial into a rocky bottom, this 45-pound anchor was able to kedge off a grounded 6-ton boat.

Modern anchors are designed to dig into the seabed and bury themselves quickly, with the result that most have tremendous holding power. Notwithstanding anchor holding tests from various sources, most anchors will hold a vessel if they are sized properly for the boat, are allowed to set and are given adequate scope. We have owned a variety of anchors, including a CQR, Delta, Bruce and Danforth, and all have performed well.

The debate of all-chain versus chain-and-rope continues unabated. Many mariners swear by an all-chain rode and it seems an equal number stand by a rope-and-chain combination. It really depends on boat size, with larger vessels having the stronger case for an all-chain rode because the weight of the tackle (and winch) at the vessel's bow has less impact on sea handling and trim. On our previous boat, a 35-foot sailboat, we used a 45-pound CQR with 24 feet of 3/8-inch BBB chain shackled to 500 feet of 5/8-inch abrasion-resistant nylon line. We had consistently good results with this tackle for many years. On our new boat, which is much heavier, we still have a CQR, at 60 pounds, but now have an all chain 3/8-inch BBB rode. Both the CQR plow-type anchor and the Bruce anchor work well for our coast because of their ability to penetrate into the variety of sea beds. The new spade-type anchors, such as the Rocna and Manson, would probably perform equally well and are known to be quick setting.

Most anchor manufacturers have recommended anchor weights for boat length and for uses such as lunch anchor, working anchor and storm anchor. Cruisers should take the storm-anchor weight to be the standard for cruising in B.C. which, depending on the anchor, is about one and a half to two pounds for every foot of waterline.

Bow and stern cleats need to be well secured with backing plates or heavy stainless washers to ensure the cleat holds in emergency use, such as securing a tow line. If you lack confidence in your bow cleats and decide to replace them, choose large, heavy stainless steel or solid bronze cleats with a high saddle. The Herreshoff cleat is an excellent example that allows numerous lines to be attached.

As we get older, our interest in anchor winches increases proportionally. There are some very advanced and efficient winches being manufactured which operate electrically or hydraulically. On sailboats, mast-mounted winches can be used and offer the advantage of being at waist-height when you're manually cranking up the anchor.

Testing the Bottom

Because every anchorage has different material for its seabed, the holding ability can vary greatly. Although some bottoms are rocky or pebbled and others have kelp or eel grass, almost all are a mud-based mix of material. South of Campbell River, where there is less kelp, the bottom is invariably mud mixed with sand, crushed shell or, occasionally, clay. **Ganges Harbour** and **Long Harbour** on Saltspring Island have such a mix of mud and clay, which makes for superb holding power. Some anchorages north of Discovery Passage have thickets of bull kelp which can be difficult or impossible for some anchors to penetrate. Anchorages with rocks or stones and those with heavy kelp bottoms are usually not great for holding but there are exceptions. Port Neville's west shore is notorious for kelp yet, once past the stuff, we've found the holding ground to be quite good. Many anchorages have been home to recent logging operations and debris is often scattered about the seabed. The worst leftovers are lengths of steel cable which, if hooked onto, can be the last a skipper sees of their anchor. Decaying branches, stumps, abandoned crab pots and other matter can foul any anchor and turn an otherwise good anchorage into a bad memory.

One way you can obtain a feel of the bottom is by snubbing the rode on a short scope (2 or 2.5 to 1) as the anchor drags along the seabed. If the anchor is bouncing, the ground may have a mix of large stones or rock. If the anchor line swings back and forth and the anchor is not sure if it wants to hold, the bottom could be soft mud and needs more scope. If the rode has a jerking and sliding feel, like the anchor is trying to set on a conveyor belt, it might be in a kelp bed or perhaps hard sand and rock. For most mud bottoms, if the hook is having trouble setting, letting out a few feet more of line (to a minimum of 3 to 1) will usually help it set properly. You can check the set by slowly applying more engine power in reverse.

There are situations, in soft mud for example, where the holding may start out poor but improve as the anchor worries its way down into a thicker bottom. This is the case at **Walker Island Group** in Queen Charlotte Strait where the top strata of soft mud and kelp lies over a thicker mix of mud and shell. If you have concerns about the set or the bottom, be extra vigilant for an overnight stay. Check land bearings regularly and keep in mind there is no honour lost in simply re-anchoring, which is best done before darkness falls.

The surrounding terrain will affect local wind speed and direction, and what might appear to be a well-protected anchorage could turn out to be a wind tunnel under certain conditions. An example of this is **Boot Cove** on Saturna Island, where southerly winds accelerate off the steep cliff-like northwest side of the cove. At other anchorages, winds are usually redirected by a steep shoreline and a good example is **Russell Island**, where south winds defect away from the anchorage lying in its lee.

Keep in mind that when winds reach gale force or stronger, almost all anchorages will get some gusts. If the wind strength is forecast to be severe, consider a line to a windward shore and pull yourself in as close to the lee of the land as is safely possible. Also, remember that an anchorage might be well protected from wind on one point of the compass but may be quite breezy should the wind shift by just a few degrees, which is often the case when an anchorage is narrow, such as **Princess Cove** on Wallace Island.

Finding a spot to anchor in tight situations can be intimidating, especially under the territorial glares of other boaters. Study the chart before entering an unfamiliar anchorage and take your time deciding where you want to drop the hook. Inexperienced boaters tend to cluster with other boats and sometimes miss a better anchoring opportunity in another part of the bay. Tying a line to shore in a crowded anchorage is a prudent solution when current or crosswind is not an issue. If all other boats have done the same, it usually is the best course for the next arriving boater.

The anchoring routine should begin with a slow approach into the anchorage, checking the depth with the chart to reach a spot clear of other boats. Bring the boat slowly to the position you want to be once the anchor has set and take visual bearings while drifting forward to the point where the anchor will be lowered – usually a distance of four to five

Bull Kelp

Bull kelp, which thrives in shallow areas of strong tidal current, tells boaters many things. A type of seaweed, its long, rubbery stem is rooted to the sea bottom in depths reaching 30 feet (HW) and its long fronds float at the surface, held there by a ball-shaped float that is kept inflated by trapped gases, the result of rapid photosynthesis. Bull kelp grows rapidly during the summer and alerts boaters to the presence of underwater shoals and reefs. Also, if there is current, the direction and speed are indicated by the plant's fronds flowing with the current away from the inflated float.

If current is pushing the float underwater, the stream is likely flowing faster than 3 knots. If the float remains above the water but the blades are flowing straight out, then the current will be about 2 knots or less. If the blades appear to be gently flowing in opposite directions or are at an angle to the orientation of the pass, you know you are at or near slack. In narrow passes, a distinct open channel clear of kelp usually indicates deeper water. Bull kelp should always be seen as a sign of danger and be given a wide berth. Bull kelp sometimes comes adrift during storms and collects in large clumps with other debris (logs, branches, etc.) along the edges of tidelines and should also be avoided.

BOTTOMS UP

An anchorage's bottom material varies and is an important consideration when setting the hook. Mud is the medium that makes up most anchorages and its mix with other material will determine holding power. CHS charts indicate the type of bottom for most anchorages but sometimes there is a bit of guesswork involved for the skipper. The foreshore may give some idea of the type of bottom below or a sample from the bottom might be obtained using a small anchor with the tip smeared in grease. Here in descending order is our view of the best mix for holding bottom:

Mud with clay – sets like wet cement. Can be difficult to retrieve anchor, with large chunks sticking to the anchor.

Sticky mud with sand – grit of sand helps lock anchor, streaks of mud remain on anchor as it comes up. All anchors set very well in this.

Thick mud with sand or broken shell – anchor sinks well into this and buries deep. Great holding.

Mud / mud sand – most burying anchors do well in this bottom. Generally good holding.

Sand with mud – an all-sand anchorage is rare along the Inside Passage and most sandy bottoms (such as Sidney spit) still have some mud and broken shell mixed in. Holding usually is good. Hard sand will be difficult to penetrate for some anchors.

Soft mud – a good burying anchor will hold here, but this is not the best medium for many hooks.

Mud and kelp – can be good although the sharp point of a CQR, Delta or a spade-type anchor may be the only anchor able to penetrate well.

Sand and gravel – not easy to penetrate and not usually good holding.

Soft mud and rock – anchors may have a tough time staying set, rocks can foul the anchor and holding is fair at best.

Gravel and rock – tough to penetrate and holding usually only fair.

Soft mud over a hard layer – not uncommon along Inside Passage. Holding is fair at best.

Oozy mud and rock – one of the poorest bottoms. A good burying anchor such as a CQR, Rocna or Bruce will be your only hope here.

times the depth. Lower the anchor after the reverse gear has stopped the boat and started pulling the boat slowly back, as this ensures the chain is lying clear of the anchor and the anchor shank is in line with the bow of the boat. Once the anchor has touched bottom, keep a slight tension to ease the point into the seabed and let out more rode to at least 3:1 scope. Securely set the anchor by slowly bringing the engine in reverse to a quarter to half-speed throttle.

When calculating the amount of line to let out, account for the rise and fall of the tide and the height of your vessel's freeboard. Also, be aware of the swinging circles of nearby boats. Set your anchor in line with vessels already at anchor and be sure you have enough water underneath your vessel for your entire swinging circle! Although some experts extol the benefits of anchoring with large scopes of 6:1 or 7:1, this is rarely practical in most of the tight anchorages of the Inside Passage and 3:1 scope is the norm. However if there is room enough and conditions are windy, or expected to be, letting out 4:1 or 5:1 is good insurance. Also, in a roadstead anchorage or a large bay where your vessel is exposed to swell or wave action, letting out more rode in windy conditions is the wise course.

Although the urge is to go to the shallow part of a bay close to shore, it's usually better to drop the hook in deeper water especially in an unfamiliar anchor-age, to give yourself more room if you need to let out line. Deeper water also provides better shock absorption for the ground tackle because the longer rode presents greater resistance to being straightened in deep water. Three-to-one scope in 45 feet (15 m) is better than 3:1 in 15 feet (5 m). Another benefit of deeper water is that wave action is less pronounced in bad conditions and the surge strain on the anchor will be reduced. Sometimes, however, the conditions in a specific cove call for a stern anchor or line to pull into a lee to create a secure and comfortable mooring closer to shore. Most anchorages covered in this book will be in depths less than 50 feet (16 m).

At some popular marine park anchorages, where space is limited, yoiu can tie a stern line to one of the shoreside ring bolts, if available. At many anchorages, tying your stern line to a tree trunk is your only option. When tying a stern line ashore, our method is to secure the stern line first, then power slowly forward to drop the anchor, while paying out the stern line. Once the anchor is down, we pull back on the stern line using the boat's inertia to set the hook.

Some anchorages have foul bottoms, such as those where logging operations have taken place, and a tripline is a prudent step to ensure retrieval of the anchor. Most anchors allow a line to be attached at the fluke end of the shank which, when pulled, easily disengages the anchor.

Best Anchorages Map Symbols:

Indicates Main Anchorage:

Temporary / Conditional:

Suitable for large vessels (75-150'):

Indicates Waypoint location: Ⓦ

ANCHORING ETIQUETTE

With more boats visting more anchorages, conditions can sometimes become tense and a pristine cove can soon resemble a parking lot. But even in crowded conditions, if civility is the rule, the experience can still be pleasant and so herein is our brief primer in anchoring etiquette.

1) When entering an anchorage with boats already at anchor, enter at a slow speed, less than 5 knots.

2) Try not to anchor upwind of other boats unless there is plenty of room giving at least five boat lengths (200 feet) to the boat behind after you have anchored. This will give you room if the wind picks up and more scope is needed.

3) Do not anchor closer than at least three boat lengths between yourself and other vessels. If the boat has a different type of rode than yours, make that five boat lengths. Give other boaters space.

4) If you intend to raft, keep well away from other vessels and give five boat lengths swinging room.

5) Music or parties should be moved below decks after 11 pm. Loud music in a quiet anchorage is really showing yourself to be a neophyte.

6) Buzzing around in a dinghy or jet ski within an anchorage is also bad form.

7) The last boat in is the first required to re-anchor if boats are swinging too close.

In summer, when the weather is settled, we all like to raft with other boats. The problem with rafts is that if something goes wrong, like a strong wind coming up in the night, each boat tugs and strains to its own rhythm, putting strain on the ground tackle. More prudent, but less fun, is to anchor off and visit friends' vessels by dinghy.

Mooring to a log boom is always a little risky as a tug may arrive anytime – such as the middle of the night – to move the logs elsewhere. We rarely tie to log booms, but when we do, we thread our lines to the boom stick chains and double these back to a cleat to allow for a quick release and departure.

The Engine

Whether your boat is power or sail, maintaining a reliable engine is critical, especially when powering against current and wind in the narrow channels of the Inside Passage. North of Campbell River, there are few opportunities to repair boats and obtain parts until you reach Port Hardy or Port McNeill. Before leaving on your trip, if you suspect something is amiss with your engine, a sample of its oil can be tested at an oil analysis laboratory. The results of this analysis will give you a picture of the state of your engine – for example, copper in the oil might indicate the connecting rod bearings are wearing out. If you use an outboard engine, have a mechanic service it before you leave.

We've always followed the manual for our engine's maintenance schedule, religiously changing the oil and filter (usually every 50 to 100 hours of running) and keeping the fuel clean with regular fuel filter changes. When cruising we wipe down the engine every day or two and inspect all wiring and hoses to ensure nothing has been jarred loose by a bumpy passage.

Not all marinas supply fuel, so it's critical to know your daily fuel consumption and fuel levels when planning each leg of your trip. This is especially true north of Campbell River, where fuel supply is limited.

Note: Throughout 'The Anchorages' section of this book, references to numbered islands means the island is labeled on the relevant chart to indicate height (in metres) above high water.

The anchorage nightmares are made of. We were trapped here for 2 days along the Alaska Peninsula in 40- to 50-knot winds. With 400 feet of line out, the CQR held but the rode was badly chafed.

HMS Plumper in Port Harvey during a British surveying expedition in May 1860.

A Look Back at Pilotage

Explorers of the 18th century were constantly expanding the frontiers of ocean and coastal navigation. A knack for pilotage meant a successful career in the navy, as was proven by James Cook, whose three Pacific voyages earned him lasting acclaim as the Great Navigator.

George Vancouver, who served on Cook's last two voyages, proved himself a worthy successor to his famous mentor. While Cook often made running surveys of the coastlines he was sweeping past, Vancouver was sent to the Pacific Northwest to conduct a detailed survey of the coastal mainland from Juan de Fuca Strait to Cook Inlet in Alaska. Vancouver's painstaking delineation of our intricate coastline is considered one of the most demanding surveys ever undertaken. He and his men spent three summers (1792-94) on the B.C. and Alaska coasts, departing each fall for the Sandwich Islands (Hawaii), then returning the following spring to resume the survey. This lengthy voyage, which began and ended in England, took four and a half years to complete and covered 65,000 nautical miles, making it the longest continuous sailing expedition in history.

Aids to coastal navigation in the 18th century lagged behind those being developed for ocean navigation. Deviation of the magnetic compass was by then understood and the sextant, a refinement of the quadrant, was an accurate measuring instrument at sea. The most recent breakthrough was the chronometer, which allowed ocean navigators to determine longitude without making complex calculations based on lunar observations. But this state-of-the-art equipment was of limited use when a ship entered uncharted coastal waters. This was when pilotage skills became critical.

The term 'pilotage' derives from the Dutch word *peillood* which means 'sounding lead', the measuring device of Vancouver's day. Attached to a hemp line was a 7-lb lead weight, its lower end cap-shaped to hold a pressed lump of tallow, which, when dragged across the bottom, picked up whatever was down there – sand, mud, shell or, if the tallow came up clean, rock. A 25-fathom line was marked at standard intervals with pieces of leather, cord or cloth, their different textures allowing the leadsman to feel the marks in the dark. Experience and skill were needed to take soundings with this hand line. The leadsman, hanging from the forechains by a bight of line, would swing the lead over and over, then heave it far ahead of the ship so that it was straight below when the bow glided over it.

For deeper waters, a 100-fathom line with a heavier lead was used. With the ship hove to, a 14-lb weight was carried forward, its line leading aft along the weather side and held in coils at regular intervals by seamen. The heavy lead was cast at the order "heave." When the leadsman was sure the weight hadn't touched bottom, he would release his section of line and call to the next man abaft who in turn would release his coil once he was sure the lead had not yet touched, and so on down the line until the lead hit bottom. A sounding rod was used in shallow water when the bottom could be poked.

Vancouver made running surveys of the California, Oregon and Washington coastlines. However, upon reaching Juan de Fuca Strait, he realized he would have to continue the survey in the ships' boats because of the labyrinth of islands and inlets facing him. This meant finding safe anchorages for the two ships, then setting off in open boats for two or three weeks of shoreline surveying. Vancouver and his officers headed the survey teams, sailing or rowing up the many inlets in search of an inland waterway. On shore they took angles of headlands and drew sketches, these findings later plotted on a master chart.

Vancouver's disciplined approach saw him and his officers take frequent and multiple sets of lunar observations to determine the longitude, and the chronometers were constantly monitored. Even so, Vancouver's longitudinal readings were slightly east of actual bearings – a situation he became aware of when he reached Nootka Sound at the end of his first survey season. He decided to carry on with this slightly-to-the-east orientation rather than alter all of his surveying to this point.

Vancouver's search for an inland waterway was of course futile but his survey laid the groundwork for further detailed charting in the 19th century, when Britain extensively surveyed all of her Empire's distant coastlines. The seminal charts produced by Captain Vancouver and his officers were, at the time, unequalled in detail and accuracy, and are the basis for today's charts of coastal British Columbia and Alaska. For Vancouver and his men, their daunting survey was a nervewracking test of seamanship and pilotage skills. One can't help but marvel at their accomplishment.

Although Captain George Vancouver brought a number of chronometers (one shown here) for his survey of the Inside Passage, he preferred lunar observations to determine longitude.

Place Names

The natives who first inhabited the B.C. coast had their own names in place when European explorers began filling their charts with new ones. Politicians, naval heroes, winning racehorses and faraway women have all been honoured with place names, not to mention Captain Pender's Skye Terrier, Connis, for whom a point of land was named.

We used to cruise with a Scottish terrier, and even though Tuck cruised extensively along the B.C. coast, spending most of his 14 years living aboard and travelling by boat, we would no doubt have a hard time convincing the Geographical Names Board of Canada to officially name a cove after him. The criteria for bestowing new place names have changed since pioneer days, but anyone can submit a name proposal by first visiting the B.C. provincial government's Property, Titles and Maps website for guidelines.

Even sea captains of the Royal Navy can be thwarted in their attempts to bestow place names. Captain Richards tried to honour Rear Admiral Baynes by changing Saltspring Island's name to Admiral Island in 1859. The earlier name, bestowed when some Hudson's Bay Company officers found springs of brine on the island, remained in common use however. So, in 1905, the Geographic Board of Canada adopted Saltspring Island as its official name.

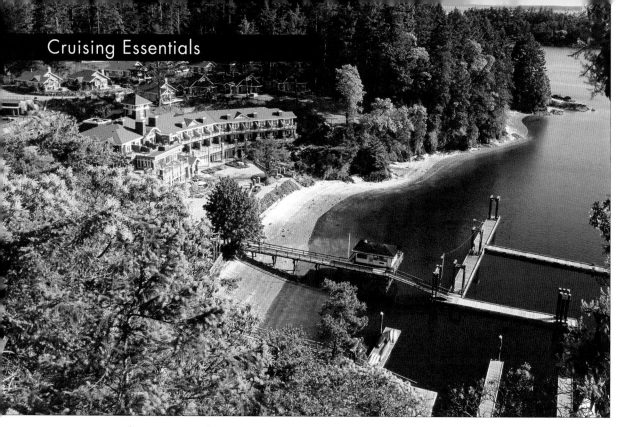

Customs Clearance / Ports of Entry

American boaters arriving in Canadian waters can clear customs by calling the Canada Customs Telephone Reporting Centre (1-888-226-7277) from the phone provided at one of numerous Marine Reporting Sites. These reporting sites include the customs dock in Victoria's Inner Harbour and the Oak Bay Marina. In the Sidney area, telephone reporting sites are located at Port of Sidney Marina, Van Isle Marina (Tsehum Harbour) and Canoe Cove Marina. In the southern Gulf Islands, Bedwell Harbour on South Pender Island is a popular port of entry (location of Poets Cove Marina) where boats can obtain customs clearance from May 1 through September 30 (a Nexus Pass is required from October through April). A telephone reporting site is also located in the Nanaimo Boat Basin – E Dock.

CANPASS holders can also clear Canada Customs in Ganges, Saltspring Island (at the public float); Port Browning, Pender Island; Cabbage Island; Horton Bay and Miners Bay, Mayne Island; Montague Harbour Marina, Galiano Island; and Steveston Harbour Authority on the Fraser River. Canada Customs Telephone Reporting Centre is contacted at 1-888-CANPASS (226-7277). CANPASS permit holders must call this number at least 30 minutes before arriving (but not more than four hours ahead of time) and inform a customs offi-

Canada Customs can be cleared in summer at Bedwell Harbour, beside Poets Cove Marina.

cer of your estimated arrival time and destination.

For more information on customs clearance regulations or applying for a CANPASS, visit the Canada Border Services Agency website at www.cbsa-asfc.gc.ca or write to the Customs Processing Centre, 28 – 176 Street, Surrey BC V3S 9R9, telephone 604-535-9346.

American boaters returning stateside should check with current customs regulations to ensure re-entry guidelines are followed.

Holding Tanks / No-Discharge Zones

A number of popular anchorages along B.C.'s inner coast fall within the Canada Shipping Act's Pleasure Craft Sewage Pollution Prevention Regulations. In accordance with these regulations, pleasure craft visiting these anchorages are required to be fitted with a holding tank if their vessel has a built-in toilet. Vessels without fitted toilets can use portable toilets, which can be emptied via suction wand at a pump-out station or emptied ashore if a pump-out facility is not available. Details regarding holding tanks and approved piping systems can be viewed on Transport

Canada's website at www.tc.gc.ca. Pump-out stations are concentrated in southern waters, at marinas and harbour authorities in and around Sidney, Ganges, Nanaimo, Vancouver, Howe Sound, Pender Harbour, Comox and Campbell River.

The sewage pollution prevention regulations require zero discharge overboard in the following anchorages:

Montague Harbour, Galiano Island;

Pilot Bay, Gabriola Island;

Smuggler Cove;

Prideaux Haven;

Roscoe Bay, West Redonda Island;

Squirrel Cove, Cortes Bay, Mansons Landing, Gorge Harbour and Carrington Bay, Cortes Island.

It's also against park regulations to discharge sewage in Princess Cove or Conover Cove at Wallace Island.

It makes good sense not to pump sewage overboard in busy anchorages, especially ones near beaches or swimming areas, or in anchorages with low tidal flushing. Many boaters wait until they are in a strait or large channel, well away from shore, before discharging effluent.

Insects

In summer, flies and mosquitoes can be a nuisance. Porthole screens are recommended, as is mosquito netting placed over opened hatch covers on hot summer nights to allow air ventilation while keeping the bugs out. Mosquito coils are a good way to keep insects away while you lounge outside in the cockpit, and sprigs of fresh lavender or mint are also effective. Dark-coloured dodgers attract bugs more than do light-coloured dodgers.

When hiking ashore, your best defense against mosquitoes is to wear long pants and a light-coloured top with long sleeves. Apply insect repellent to your face, neck and hands. Small children and pregnant women should use non-DEET repellent or one containing a low concentration of DEET. Upon returning to the boat, wash off all repellents with soap and water. Also, avoid wearing cologne or any scent that will attract insects. If you don't want to wear repellent, another option is to wear a sheet of fabric softener under your cap, letting it drape over the back of your neck, or to simply pull a sheet of fabric softener through your belt loop.

Long pants and a hat will also protect you from wood ticks, which are small, spider-like insects that bite into the skin and feed on blood, possibly passing on one of many diseases they can carry, including Lyme disease. After a hike in a forest, check any exposed part of your body, such as the back of your neck, for ticks. Prompt removal of a tick will prevent any infection and is best done with tweezers, gently pulling the parasite straight out and taking care not to crush it. Afterwards, wash the area with soap and water, then apply an antiseptic.

VHF Channels

During times of poor visibility, or when approaching busy passes, you may alert Vessel Traffic Services of your presence and intentions. In Victoria use Channel 11, which covers the waters between Juan de Fuca Strait in the south, and Ballenas Island to the north. Victoria Traffic also uses Channel 74 east of Sand Heads. Near the entrance to Burrard Inlet and north of Iona Island, use Channel 12 for Vancouver Traffic. North of Ballenas Island, contact Comox Traffic on Channel 71. To communicate with the Coast Guard in a non-life-threatening situation, use Channel 22A. Use Channel 16 for distress or as a calling channel only. To communicate with other recreational vessels use channels 06, 67, 68, 69, 72 and 73. Contact marinas using Channel 66A.

Wi-Fi and Cellular Coverage

Wi-Fi is available at numerous marinas and resorts up and down the coast. Contact your destination marinas beforehand to confirm connections. Wi-Fi hotspots can be found in and near the major ports.

Cell coverage along the B.C. coast varies from one provider to the other. Telus and Rogers both provide coverage maps on their websites. The best reception will be near airports and larger communities while reception is spotty to non-existent in remote fjords and inlets. A cell booster for your boat will improve transmission and reception of both voice and data connections. A cell booster consists of an external antenna, cell amplifier and internal connection point.

Marine Parks

Marine Parks dot the B.C. coastline and are generally more concentrated in southern waters. Facilities vary from park to park and can include floats, mooring buoys, dinghy docks, campsites, hiking trails, picnic shelters and freshwater pumps. Many others remain, for the most part, undeveloped.

There is no fee for anchoring a boat in a provincial marine park but there is an overnight fee for tying to a buoy and for mooring at a float. (There is no charge for using a dinghy dock.) In Pirates Cove there is a charge for mooring to a stern tie ring. Although marine parks are open year round, user fees are collected only from May 1 through September 30 (www.env.gov.bc.ca/bcparks/). A

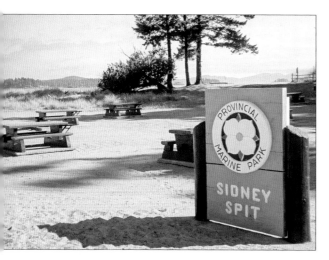

Sidney Spit Marine Park, now administered by Parks Canada, has extensive visitor facilities.

number of former provincial marine parks are now administered by Parks Canada (see page 52) as the Gulf Islands National Park Reserve (www.pc.gc.ca).

Pets on Board

For years we cruised with a Scottish terrier and his needs included daily walks ashore. Most healthy dogs are quite happy with two visits ashore – one in the morning, the other in the late afternoon or evening. This routine melds nicely with coastal cruising and we appreciated the fact that Tuck's urgings prompted us to head ashore at every anchorage we visited, come rain or shine, and discover things we might otherwise have missed.

Be alert to potential wildlife you might encounter when walking your dog, which should be kept on a leash if you're hiking a forest trail in a northern anchorage. Often called 'bear bait', an unleashed dog is also a magnet for wolves.

Dogs should always be inspected for ticks immediately after a walk in the forest. Run your hands over your dog's back and if you feel a hard little bump, part the fur to see if it's a tick embedded in the skin. Removal can be done with tweezers, gently pulling the tick straight out.

U.S. boaters entering Canada with a dog or cat are required to carry written confirmation from a veterinarian that the pet is vaccinated against rabies.

Provisioning

Most communities of the south coast are well served by local stores situated near the marinas. In the major ports, local supermarkets will usually provide complimentary taxi service back to the docks. At marina resorts, a general store is often part of the facilities, and its selection will vary. Some are well stocked with fresh produce and dairy products, and a liquor off-licence, while others are not. Credit cards are widely accepted at coastal resorts and in all the large centres.

When cruising the Gulf Islands, good places to stock up on groceries and other items include Sidney, Ganges and Nanaimo. In Vancouver, Granville Island is a great place to shop for fresh produce and baked goods. Along the Sunshine Coast, one of the best reprovisioning ports is Pender Harbour, at Madeira Park. For boaters venturing north of the passes, Campbell River is a good place to shop when taking the 'main route' of Discovery Passage, while the 'back route' is serviced by several small ports, including Blind Channel where the resort's general store sells freshly baked bread. At the north end of Vancouver Island, several ports are excellent for reprovisioning, including Port McNeill, Alert Bay and Port Hardy. North of Cape Caution, reprovisioning ports include Dawsons Landing in Rivers Inlet and the Shearwater Resort near Bella Bella.

Public Docks and Shore Access

What used to be called government docks, easily recognizable by their red railings and maintained by the federal Government of Canada, are now community docks run by local authorities. The public is still welcome at these docks, but the moorage rates and services provided (traditionally, fresh water on the docks and garbage disposal at the top of the ramp) vary from harbour to harbour. In Canada, foreshore up to the high water mark is, with rare exceptions, public property.

Reference Materials

The best investment any boater can make is the purchase of up-to-date nautical charts – the larger the scale, the better. The **Canadian Hydrographic Service** produces beautiful charts with good detail and these add to the adventure of boating. U.S. boaters should be aware that Canadian charts are drawn to more conservative standards and minimum depths are shown relative to 'lowest normal tides' as compared with U.S. charts which define lower low water as an averaged value of low water. To calculate water depth using CHS charts and tide tables, add the predicted tide height for the time in the area you are cruising to the datum shown on the local chart. If you're using electronic charts instead of paper charts, these must meet chart carriage requirements. For a list of manufacturers licenced to use CHS chart data in their value-added digital products, visit the CHS website at www.charts.gc.ca/copyright.

In addition to carrying the appropriate charts, boaters should have CHS's annual Tide and Current Tables (Volumes 5 , 6 and 7 apply to the areas covered in this book) as well as the Sailing Directions for the British Columbia Coast (South Portion), which covers waters up to Cape Caution. If you're planning to venture past Cape Caution, you'll also need the North Portion, Volume II. Equipped with the tide tables, Sailing Directions (SD) and charts, you can explore every mile of our coast and find your own special anchorages. The SD, in addition to offering excellent information on currents, regional weather and local hazards, also provides advice on approaches to sounds and passes, suggestions for anchoring, and contains distance tables and weather statistics for many ports along the Inside Passage.

To supplement these essential reference materials are the numerous cruising guides, available at most chandleries. All are helpful and they often complement one another with their varying approaches on how to cruise this complex coastline.

Bill Wolferstan set the standard for cruising guides in the 1970s and '80s with his *Cruising Guides* in three volumes covering the *Gulf Islands, Sunshine Coast* and *Desolation Sound*. His seminal guides remain informative and capture the atmosphere of each destination. John Chappell's *Cruising Beyond Desolation Sound*, published in the late 1970s, contained his first-hand insight into anchorages north of Campbell River but is, like Wolferstan's guides, now out of print.

Peter Vassilopoulos, a long-time B.C. boater and contributor to Pacific Yachting magazine, publishes a series of popular guidebooks, including *Docks and Destinations* – which provides up-to-date information on marinas, fuel and moorage facilities throughout the coastal waters of British Columbia and Washington State. Peter also has written useful guidebooks covering anchorages and marine parks, from the Gulf Islands up to Seymour Inlet.

In their insightful book *Cruising the Secret Coast,* Jennifer and James Hamilton provide detailed information about some of the Inside Passage's less-travelled waterways, such as the upper reaches of Smith Sound and the intricate waters of Kildidt Sound and Queens Sound.

Don and Reanne Douglass's **Exploring** series of guidebooks are an exhaustive study of anchorages up and down the coast and add greatly to the Sailing Directions. Also helpful are the **Dreamspeaker Cruising Guides** by Anne and Laurence Yeadon-Jones, which cover B.C.'s southern waters.

Mark Bunzel's popular *Waggoner Cruising Guide* is a single-volume pilot companion, updated annually, with comprehensive coverage of marinas and anchorages from Seattle to Ketchikan. **Pacific Yachting** magazine publishes an annual boating services directory, *Boaters Blue Pages and Marina Guide*, which is inserted in the February issue.

Safety on the Water

If you're new to boating, it is prudent to take a few courses. The Competency of Operators of Pleasure Craft Regulations, enforced by the Canadian Coast Guard, require operators of motorized pleasure craft to have proof of competency on board at all times. However, cruising boaters should have experience and knowledge far beyond this basic competency, and the best-known supplier of these courses is the Power Squadron, in both Canada and the United States. The Power Squadron's basic Boating Course provides in-depth boat operation and safety training, and teaches you the skills of plotting and navigation. This course also delves into weather, tides, currents and anchoring. For information on Transport Canada's boating regulation requirements, visit www.boatingsafety.gc.ca.

Sportfishing Licences

B.C. is well known for its excellent sportfishing. Before catching finfish or harvesting shellfish in local waters, all recreational fishermen must obtain an annual B.C. Tidal Waters Sports Fishing Licence, available at marinas and sporting goods stores. The accompanying B.C. Tidal Waters Sport Fishing Guide contains details on species, openings, restricted fishing areas and possession limits. In summer, localized algae blooms known as 'red tide' will occasionally result in dangerous concentrations of paralytic shellfish poisoning (PSP) in oysters, clams, mussels and other filter-feeding shellfish. Check for any PSP closures on their website at www-comm. pac.dfo-mpo.gc.ca.

A humble rock cod holds a fascination for kids.

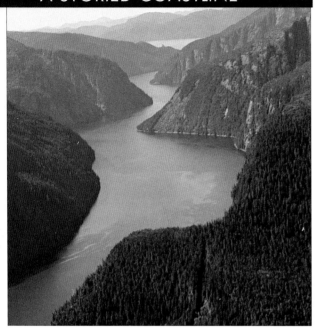

The Prehistoric Coast

Boaters who explore the remote inlets of British Columbia's Inside Passage can likely envision this immense coastline as it would have looked long ago. The overwhelming aspect of these meandering, mountain-bounded waterways is the dominance of nature – that relentless force that creates, destroys and rejuvenates, measuring time in millennia while pockets of human habitation come and go like wisps of fog.

Until recently, it was widely believed that the first human inhabitants came to North America by land, crossing from Siberia to Alaska and into the continent's interior via an ice-free corridor called the Bering land bridge, or Beringia. New evidence suggests the first arrivals may have come not by land, but by sea, working their way around the Pacific Rim and using as stepping stones the ice-free coastal refuges that had been exposed by retreating glaciers.

When the last great ice age drew to a close some 15,000 years ago and the glaciers began staging their retreat, these giant bulldozers of ice left behind U-shaped valleys that would eventually become the channels and fjords of the Inside Passage. Early inhabitants established village sites near the food-rich shorelines, where lush lowlands and intertidal zones were a habitat for waterfowl and edible greens, such as fireweeds and sea asparagus. Clams were gathered from shellfish beds, and sea lions were hunted in local waters. Salmon, caught in traps and weirs, were a major food source.

When coastal lands were first relieved of the massive weight of the ice fields, widescale uplifting took place and sea levels dropped. Today's underwater banks in Hecate Strait and Queen Charlotte Sound became exposed as islands, and the Haida Gwaii archipelago – parts of which remained free of ice throughout the last ice age – became a single land mass, twice as large as it is today.

Over time, growing torrents of glacial meltwater from further inland swelled the oceans and turned valleys into waterways. This rise in sea level brought the 'great flood' referred to in Haida mythology, when sea levels rose as much as 50 feet (15 m) above today's levels. Entire villages were submerged, including one at Montague Harbour in the Gulf Islands where scuba divers performed an undersea archaeological excavation and retrieved artifacts over 6,000 years old.

Sea levels eventually stablilized, and permanent villages began to dot the coastline as it exists today. Evidence of prehistoric habitation can be seen along the foreshore of many anchorages in the form of stone boat skids and fish traps. Most obvious, however, are the patches of clamshell beach – ancient kitchen middens – that are found throughout south coastal waters. A midden is an ancient refuse dump of shells and bones which, over time, is crushed and compressed into a beach several yards deep. The shell in a midden neutralizes the acid in the soil, preserving ancient tools and artifacts such as antler carvings and stone bowls engraved with human and animal figures.

The aboriginal people of British Columbia were once called Indians but they now refer to themselves collectively as First Nations. It is also appropriate to refer to these peoples as aboriginal, native or indigenous. The lands they occupy are called Indian Reserves ('IR' on CHS charts).

The First Nations' traditional languages were oral, not written, which is why there is often a variation in the spelling of words and names. Early explorers, attempting to phonetically record what they were hearing, gave certain groups erroneous names. For instance, the Nootka were called such by Captain Cook, but they prefer to be known as the Nuu-chah-nulth or simply the West Coast peoples. The Southern Kwakiutl are now called Kwakwaka'wakw – 'those who speak Kwakwala.' Groups living in the Strait of Georgia basin no longer collectively refer to themselves as Coast Salish (the language family to which they belong) but have reverted to traditional names for specific groups within the area.

The natives living on the southern Gulf Islands and south end of Vancouver Island are collectively referred to as the 'People of the Straits,' i.e. Strait of

Juan de Fuca and Strait of Georgia. These straits were their 'rivers' and migrating salmon were caught in shallow reefs near shore. Nets were anchored by lashing them with twine to beached boulders, and the fishermen would return to specific salmon sites year after year, century upon century.

The northern Gulf Islands were inhabited by the Hul'qumi'num, 'Those Who Speak the Same Language', with individual groups including the Malahat, Cowichan and Snuneymux (Nanaimo). These peoples fished salmon in the Cowichan, Chemainus and Nanaimo rivers of Vancouver Island using fish weirs stretched from bank to bank where the salmon, crowded into enclosures, would be scooped or speared. In Cowichan Gap (Porlier Pass), the Chemainus hunted the Steller sea lion. Each summer entire villages travelled by canoe across the Strait of Georgia to fish for salmon in the lower reaches of the Fraser River.

While salmon was a major food source for coastal settlements up and down the coast, the inhabitants of Kingcome Inlet were known as the Tsawatainuk, 'People with Eulachon.' This long, silvery fish, also called oolichan, was valued as a food source and for its oil, which could be used as a condiment, preservative and medicine.

With the establishment of permanent coastal villages, the various groups began marking out their territories and protecting them through warfare. The northern tribes would travel hundreds of miles in their canoes to conduct raids on southern villages and capture slaves. Warrior chiefs were the village leaders, their family crests displayed on totem poles carved from logs of red cedar and erected as frontal and interior poles of their post-and-beam houses.

Sometimes serving as territory markers were petroglyphs (pecked or scratched into foreshore rocks) and pictographs, which were drawn with ochre on rock walls. These images depicted animals, humans and supernatural beings. Shamans, who could foretell events and cure sickness, were important members of these prehistoric societies. Also respected were the souls of other living creatures, for it was believed that animals had the ability to transform themselves into humans.

Native mythology explains the creation of the universe and the evolution of humanity in terms of transformation. Raven was a supernatural trickster and transformer who accidentally released the sun and stars and who, upon opening a clamshell, released the first humans. Anthropologists and archaeologists take a more scientific approach to

Opposite, mainland fjords were formed by glacial action. Above, a prehistoric midden lies at the head of Echo Bay on Gilford Island.

Canoes were carved from huge cedar logs, then steamed to soften the wood and allow the sides to be spread. Separate prow and stern pieces were added and the hull torched to harden the wood before sanding. Above, artist Alan Nakano's depiction of Haida seafarers.

evolution, but all agree that however the early inhabitants may have arrived at our shores, their modern descendants can claim ancestral ties rooted in antiquity, when stands of cedar and spruce first appeared along the water's edge.

The Discovered Coast

The legend of Juan de Fuca Strait was once a source of great speculation among European cartographers, who referred to it the Strait of Anian – a possible northwest passage. The entrance to this mysterious waterway reputedly was first sighted by the Greek mariner Juan de Fuca while he explored the North Pacific for Spain in 1592. When the English sea captain Charles W. Barkley arrived on a trading expedition in 1787, he named the strait for Juan de Fuca. But it wasn't until the summer of 1792, when British and Spanish survey expeditions made a thorough exploration of the waters lying beyond Juan de Fuca Strait, that the Strait of Anian legend was finally laid to rest and the Inside Passage was revealed to the outside world.

The 18th century was a great era of naval exploration. Russian explorers – led by Vitus Bering – set off from Siberia to find out what lay to the east, while Spanish, French and British ships ventured into the Pacific's northern waters in search of the elusive Northwest Passage. They were also pursuing knowledge during this Age of Enlightenment, with naval commanders such as Britain's Cook, France's La Perouse and Spain's Malaspina all leading scientific expeditions to the New World. The logbooks of these and other commanders provide a wealth of information on the native cultures that thrived at this time of First Contact.The natives were truly impressed with the white-winged sailing ships that magically appeared on the horizon. Captains were honoured guests at the homes of village chiefs and, in a show of reciprocal hospitality, ship's tours were often held for high-ranking members of a village.

The Spanish explored much of the Pacific Northwest in the mid-to-late 1700s but were secretive about their discoveries. When the journals of Captain Cook's final voyage (1776-79) were published in 1783, merchant ships began flocking to these northern waters in pursuit of sea otter pelts, which fetched a phenomenal price in China.

As more and more ships frequented the coast, many of the natives became wary and, at times, openly hostile. Captain Vancouver's men reported incidents in which they were approached, while in open boats, by canoes filled with armed natives intent on pillage. A few shots fired over their heads would prompt them to unstring their bows and arrows, and offer them in trade. The British sailors gladly exchanged items of barter for weapons, since this was the easiest way to disarm the natives.

Spain, whose colonial empire had long encompassed the Pacific coastlines of the Americas, was aware of the steady increase in fur trade traffic and grew worried about its holdings in the Pacific Northwest. Nootka Sound, Spain's northernmost outpost on the west side of Vancouver Island, had become alarmingly busy with the comings and goings of British and American fur-trading ships. As a result, Alejandro Malaspina was sent north from Acapulco in 1791 to investigate the situation and check out the persistent rumours regarding Juan de Fuca Strait and the Northwest Passage.

Several Spanish expeditions had preceded Malaspina's, including one led by Juan Perez in 1774 in which he sighted the northern end of the Queen Charlottes (Haida Gwaii) and another in 1789 when Esteban Jose Martinez led an expedition to Nootka Sound, sparking a dispute with Great Britain over territorial rights. In 1790, the Spanish sent more soldiers to Nootka Sound to build a permanent fort and settlement while Manuel Quimper explored Juan de Fuca Strait. After wintering in Nootka Sound, the Spanish continued their explorations the next summer, with Francisco Eliza and Jose Maria Narvaez becoming the first Europeans to enter the Strait of Georgia aboard the small schooner *Santa Saturnina*.

Upon returning to Acapulco, Malaspina recommended a continuation of these surveys, and in the spring of 1792 two small schooners commanded by Dionisio Galiano and Cayetano Valdes headed up the coast from Acapulco. A British expedition of two ships, commanded by George Vancouver, had left England the previous spring, wintered in Hawaii, and was now on its way to the Pacific Northwest. All were in the hunt for the elusive Northwest Passage.

Captain Vancouver was also on a diplomatic mission, with instructions to stop at Nootka Sound to take possession of the harbour, as agreed upon in a treaty signed by England and Spain. For the first time in almost 300 years, Spain had formally acknowledged another nation's trading rights in the

Above, early 17th-century map clearly showing 'El Streto d'Anian' – The Strait of Anian – in top left corner. Below, Captain Vancouver's overview chart showing 'Quadra and Vancouver Island.'

Right, marine artist John Horton's well-known painting of Captain Vancouver's ships in Desolation Sound called 'I Name This Place Desolation Sound.'

Discovery aground in Queen Charlotte Strait.

North Pacific. Vancouver's first goal, however, was to explore the legendary Juan de Fuca Strait and disprove, once and for all, the existence of a Northwest Passage.

When Vancouver arrived on our coast in April 1792, few explorers had ventured into the twisting and treacherous channels of the Inside Passage, with fur-trading ships preferring to call at native villages that bordered the open Pacific. Vancouver's task was to explore and map every mainland inlet as far north as Cook Inlet at the top of the Gulf of Alaska.

Much of Vancouver's surveying work was done in open boats, with crewmen drawing on the oars from dawn until dusk and sometimes well into the night. They pitched tents on shore and the men on watch cooked the next day's food over open fires. If the forest above the high-water mark was impenetrable, they were forced to sleep in the boats – something the men detested. A few preferred taking their chances on shore, where a rising tide swamped them more than once. On one occasion an oarsman was so tired he didn't wake up and was floating away when roused by his companions.

The men dined on such mainstays as portable soup (similar to today's bouillon cubes), peas, wheat and oatmeal. To add variety to their fare, they hunted ducks, crows and cormorants. They also shot deer whenever they sighted them. While enjoying a picnic lunch of venison pasty in Puget Sound, Vancouver's men were approached by some Coast Salish natives who thought these strange white men were eating human flesh. The natives conveyed their repugnance by throwing the offered venison on the ground. Vancouver's officers had to show them the deer carcass before the natives were convinced they weren't in the company of cannibals.

When the ships lay at anchor for a few weeks, a brewery was set up on shore to make beer by boiling pine sprouts or spruce sprigs in water and molasses, then fermenting this mixture with dried yeast. The men also collected oysters, clams, berries and nettles on shore, but they soon discovered it was easier to obtain fresh salmon by bartering with the region's residents than trying to catch these elusive fish with their seine nets. Copper was a popular item of trade, highly valued by the Kwakwaka'wakw (Kwakiutl), whose territory extended from Quadra Island to Cape Caution. Kwakwaka'wakw artisans would shape this malleable metal into elaborately decorated shields which became the ultimate symbol of wealth at potlatch feasts and were often broken into pieces to distribute among the guests as a "non-perishable representation of perishable wealth."

Captain Vancouver made only a brief visit to the harbour that would one day be the site of a major city bearing his name. Settlements of the Squamish Nation were located here when Vancouver sailed his ship's boats past the future site of Stanley Park into Burrard Inlet to survey the surrounding shores. In seamanlike fashion, he ordered that the boats proceed "under an easy sail" as a welcoming party of natives paddled out to greet these strange-looking visitors. An exchange of goods (salmon for iron) took place on the run as the British survey boats sailed toward the head of the mountain-enclosed inlet in search of an inland waterway. It was not to be found so, after spending a night camped on shore, the British sailors left at dawn.

In his journals Captain Vancouver frequently mentions the lofty barrier of mountains and snow that frustrated his efforts at finding an inland waterway. The coastal mountains weren't his only source of frustration. He didn't realize Spain had also dispatched ships to explore these waters and thought he was the first European to venture into the Inside Passage. However, Galiano and Valdes had been exploring the Gulf Islands while Vancouver and his officers were exploring the mainland inlets, and when Vancouver returned from a survey of Jervis Inlet to see the *Mexicana* and *Sutil* anchored off Point Grey, it was an unwelcome surprise. His orders were to be cordial to the Spanish, and the names English Bay and Spanish Banks commemorate this encounter.

Together, the four ships proceeded up the Strait of Georgia (initially called Gulf of Georgia by Vancouver upon entering it) to Desolation Sound – a name Vancouver bestowed on the area because of its gloomy weather, poor fishing and few inhabitants. The ships anchored in Teakerne Arm and

Vancouver's officers set off in boats to explore the mainland shore. Lieutenant James Johnstone led a party of men through the 'back route' of the Inside Passage, where the natives helped with ropes when the sailors had to haul their boats through the rapids. While Johnstone's party was exploring Frederick Arm and Phillips Arm, some natives fled into the forest at the sight of these strange-looking white men, who left some trinkets – a token of friendliness – in the canoes left abandoned on shore.

Johnstone's first clue to the existence of Vancouver Island came while he and his men were camped on shore in Loughborough Inlet. During the night they were unexpectedly swamped by a tide that was rising several hours earlier than in the Strait of Georgia. This meant the tide was coming in through a northern entrance and this revelation diverted Johnstone's attention from tracing the continental shoreline to locating a seaward passage at the top of Vancouver Island.

He followed Sunderland Channel into the strait that would bear his name and rowed all the way to Pine Island for an unobstructed view of the open waters of the Pacific Ocean. Johnstone and his men were exhausted and hungry by the time they backtracked 130 miles to the ships at anchor in Desolation Sound, but they had found a navigable channel to the ocean.

Top, John Horton's painting of Vancouver's ship Discovery undergoing repairs in Restoration Bay. Above, theatrical dances were performed at ceremonial potlatch gatherings.

Upon Johnstone's return, Captain Vancouver bid adieu to Galiano and Valdes and headed for Discovery Passage where they observed the tidal currents from Menzies Bay before proceeding through Seymour Narrows.

It took Captain Vancouver and his officers three summers to survey the entire Inside Passage. His search for an inland waterway was of course futile, but his painstaking exploration of nearly every main-land inlet produced marine charts of remarkable accuracy and laid the groundwork for further detailed charting in the 19th century when Great Britain extensively surveyed all of her empire's distant coastlines.

The lucrative trade in sea otter pelts thrived until the 1820s, and during its peak years, from 1790 to 1812, as many as two dozen merchant ships were on the coast, obtaining tens of thousands of pelts from the natives in exchange for European goods, including iron tools with which they enhanced their wood-working and carving. As their artistry flowered, so too did their ceremonial traditions, which became ever more elaborate. Kwakwaka'wakw potlatch events were the most flamboyant of all the native groups, their theatrical dances performed with elaborate props and costumes, especially masks. All of the First Nations societies and their existing territories would soon be threatened, however, by the arrival of European settlers drawn to the rich resources of the B.C. coast.

The Working Coast

The Inside Passage has always been a land of plenty. Its maritime climate and abundance of salmon supported a large concentration of native inhabitants long before European seafarers began venturing into these waters in search of sea otters.

The Russians called it 'soft gold' – the thick, lustrous fur coat that keeps these marine mammals warm and buoyant in frigid waters. Once inhabiting coastal kelp beds from Alaska to California, the sea otter was hunted ruthlessly by fur traders who could sell these pelts on world markets for 10 times the price of a beaver skin. After the sea otter was hunted to near-extinction, the merchant ships plying coastal waters turned their sights on beaver pelts.

The Hudson's Bay Company of Great Britain had been working its way westward across the continent in pursuit of beaver pelts when, in 1821, it merged with the competing Northwest Company's operations west of the Rockies. The HBC began building trading posts on the banks of strategic rivers to intercept the beaver skins being brought by natives from the interior. Fort Vancouver was built in 1825 on the Columbia, Fort Langley in 1827 on the Fraser, Fort Simpson in 1831 near the mouth of the Nass, and Fort McLoughlin (Bella Bella) in 1833 on the edge of Queen Charlotte Sound. In 1836, the SS *Beaver* – the first steamship to work the Inside Passage – arrived at Fort Vancouver and was used by the HBC to supply its trading posts, collect furs and explore the coast. (The vessel was sold in 1874 and operated as a coastal freighter and towboat until it was wrecked off Stanley Park's Prospect Point in 1888.)

To counter encroachment of the fur trade by American traders from the east coast (known as 'Boston Men') the Hudson's Bay Company sought to regain its monopoly by forming a naval department that hired American skippers (veterans of the coastal trade) to shadow the Boston ships and outbid American traders. As their profits dwindled, the Boston men gradually withdrew from the fur trade and turned to whaling.

Meanwhile, an influx of American settlers into Oregon Territory (which included the modern state of Washington) was creating pressure on Great Britain to withdraw from this jointly occupied region. In anticipation of an impending border settlement, the HBC built Fort Victoria in 1843 to replace Fort Vancouver on the Columbia River as its trading headquarters on the west coast. Three years later, the Oregon Treaty fixed the boundary between

A replica of Lady Washington, a ship that played a major role in the fur trade.

B.C. and the U.S. to lie along the 49th parallel before it dipped south of Vancouver Island. (The line that wove through the Gulf Islands and the San Juans remained in dispute until it was resolved by international arbitration in 1872.)

To encourage colonization of its territory, Great Britain issued the HBC proprietary rights to Vancouver Island (declared a crown colony in 1849) and chief factor James Douglas, who had overseen construction of Fort Victoria, took charge of company operations. Appointed governor of Vancouver Island in 1851, Douglas soon purchased the Saanich Peninsula (with the exception of village sites and potato patches) from the local natives in exchange for 371 blankets. A town sprang up south of Fort Victoria around James Bay, and the outlying area became farmland as white settlers arrived. A natural meadow where the Coast Salish had traditionally harvested camas was set aside as a park reserve that would eventually become Beacon Hill Park, named for the navigational range markers atop its hill.

The HBC also established Fort Rupert in Beaver Harbour in 1849 after coal deposits were discovered there. Mining ceased a few years later, when the HBC found coal deposits more conveniently situated at Nanaimo. There a wooden military bastion was built in 1853 to protect settlers who came from England and Scotland to work in the local coal mines. They called their new home Colville Town, but the native name was Nanaimo, which means 'big strong tribe' in reference to the five First Nations villages located in the area. Acting on information provided by the natives, the HBC soon opened another mine on Newcastle Island across the harbour from Nanaimo. But it was gold, not coal, that caused a sudden surge in the region's white population.

When word leaked out of gold deposits on the upper Fraser, a stampede of prospectors converged on the area in the spring of 1858. Most were American, numbering some 30,000, and they arrived at Victoria by steamboat, then caught a boat across the Strait of Georgia to the mouth of the Fraser River, where gold was found on the gravel bars

Top right, cannon firing ceremonies take place daily in summer beside Nanaimo's historic Bastion. Middle right, Fisgard Lighthouse at the entrance to Esquimalt Harbour is a National Historic site. Built in 1860, it was the first lighthouse on the B.C. coast. Bottom right, a steamship docks at Knox Bay on West Thurlow Island, where a major logging camp once operated.

Tale of the Beaver

The SS *Beaver* was a famous steamship employed by the Hudson's Bay Company during the fur trade. She also served as a survey ship, freighter, passenger vessel and tugboat. The *Beaver* met her end in 1888 at the entrance to Burrard Inlet when the departing steamship was gripped not by tidal rips and back eddies but by a sense of panic in the crew when they realized their liquor supply had been left behind in port. They turned the ship sharply around and grounded her off Prospect Point. She was still there a few years later when the new CPR luxury liner Empress of India stopped in Vancouver on her maiden voyage.

Left, the Beaver hard on the rocks.

below Hope and all the way up the Fraser Canyon. To protect its lumber and mining interests and prevent any land grabbing, Great Britain declared the mainland a separate colony, with New Westminster the point of entry. This new colony was later merged with Vancouver Island to form British Columbia and, in 1868, Victoria became the capital.

The Fraser gold rush was short-lived but other newcomers – many of whom hailed from the British Isles – began exploiting the region's natural resources. Small steam- or water-powered sawmills were soon operating up and down the coast, and in 1861 a British sea captain named Edward Stamp built B.C.'s first export sawmill in Alberni Inlet. He briefly operated another mill in Port Neville before opening Hastings Mill in 1867 on the south shore of Burrard Inlet, around which grew the settlement of Granville (now the City of Vancouver). A.P. Allison, a London-born logger who worked at a sawmill in Chemainus before starting his own logging company, opened a shingle mill at Greene Point Rapids in 1908 and sent the first cargo of B.C. shingles through the Panama Canal in 1914.

Salmon canning became another thriving industry, thanks to a new industrial process that could produce very thin, uniform sheets of metal for making cans. By 1881 there were 10 salmon canneries on the Fraser River, concentrated in Steveston and Ladner. Others opened on the north coast, at Rivers Inlet, Namu and on the Skeena and Nass rivers. Initially the bulk of the salmon was supplied by native fisher-

Above left, a cannery once operated at Blind Channel. Left, an Alan Nakano painting of a fish-buying boat on the Fraser River.

men, but by 1900 the salmon fishing fleet was dominated by Japanese and Europeans. Inside the canneries, the processing lines were manned by Chinese workers and aboriginal women.

In 1889, the Union Steamship Company was established to service remote coastal settlements, many of which were built on floats and could move from one sheltered cove to another. Initially these logging camps were collections of bunkhouses, cook shacks and equipment sheds, but with the growing number of women in the camps – hired to cook or accompanying their husbands – tidy floathomes became a common sight. Picket fences, split from cedar, would prevent small children from falling in the water, and some floats were large enough to hold a garden. The logging camp at Simoon Sound evolved into a floating village with a store, community hall, post office and school.

Settlements built on land included Blind Channel on West Thurlow Island, where a sawmill was built in 1910. The surrounding forest was hand-logged by nine lumbermen who would fell a tree with axes while standing on springboards wedged into tree trunks. The timber was hauled out by oxen along skid trails to the mill. The community became a centre for nearby logging camps, with a hotel and dock built to accommodate the Union Steamship boats that called regularly with freight and passengers. A one-room schoolhouse at Blind Channel served the area and children not living on West Thurlow Island were rowed to school by their mothers.

By 1918 the population at Blind Channel had soared to 120, with a cannery and shingle mill in operation. The mill's boiler usually had enough steam left at the end of the day to power a generator that lit everyone's home with a recent invention called the light bulb. A gas engine provided auxiliary power on Saturday nights when the dance hall was lit. Loggers from nearby camps would descend on Blind Channel and forget their worries as they kicked up their heels and "skidded the ladies across the floor."

Other vessels plying coastal waters were the mission boats of the Methodist and Anglican churches, which travelled to these isolated camps and villages to provide medical care and assistance. Some missionaries focused on the aboriginal people, whose

Top right, the old pulpstones on Newcastle Island are a reminder of the coast's pioneering past, as is the abandoned steam donkey once used by loggers in Thompson Sound (bottom right).

local populations had been decimated by diseases such as influenza and smallpox, to which they had no immunity. By 1890, newcomers outnumbered the aboriginal population, and native villages were being abandoned as the survivors of epidemics moved to central locations to be closer to commercial fishing.

In the summer of 1898, Emily Carr visited her missionary sister in Ucluelet and her fascination with aboriginal subjects began. While sketching scenes of the local Nuu-Chah-Nulth (Nootka), she was given the name Klee Wyck – The One Who Laughs. In pursuit of her art, Carr travelled up and down the coast, visiting remote villages with the aid of native guides, and her paintings captured both a disappearing way of life and the primeval power of a northern rainforest.

While the native populations continued to decline through the 1920s, the city of Vancouver was steadily growing. Bowen Island was transformed from a logging and farming community into a holiday resort in 1920 when the Union Steamship Company bought property at Snug Cove, including the local hotel. In summer, day-trippers came by the hundreds from Vancouver to enjoy company picnics and dances in the pavilion.

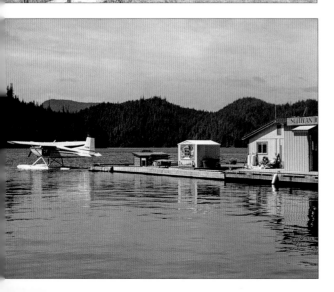

In 1931 the Canadian Pacific Railway (CPR) bought Newcastle Island near Nanaimo and the island, the site of a coal mine, sandstone quarry, saltery and shipyard, was transformed into a holiday resort. An old ship was permanently docked in Mark Bay as a floating hotel and on summer weekends as many as 1,500 steamship passengers would arrive for the day from Vancouver. They came to enjoy such facilities as a dance pavilion, tea house, picnic areas, change houses, soccer field and wading pool. World War II brought an end to these pleasure excursions as ships were diverted by the war effort.

Following Japan's attack on Pearl Harbor, blackouts went into effect and the coast darkened. Lighthouses were covered, vessels travelling at night couldn't use running lights and no weather reports were issued. People of Japanese descent living on the coast were relocated to the interior and their fishing vessels were impounded.

To protect against potential Japanese invasion, flying boat stations (in addition to the existing one at Jericho Beach) were established at Ucluelet, Alliford Bay in Skidegate Inlet, Seal Cove near Prince Rupert, Coal Harbour in Quatsino Sound and Bella Bella. A reserve unit of fishermen within the Royal Canadian Navy was formed to patrol the coast; these 42 boats and 975 men were dubbed the Gumboot Navy. Yorke Island, at the junction of Johnstone Strait and Sunderland Channel, became a military outpost designed to detect and destroy any enemy ships approaching Vancouver from the north with its searchlight and 6" turret guns.

Yorke Island never came under attack and the last firing practice took place on August 10, 1945. The troops were coming home, the Gumboot Navy had disbanded and the B.C. coast, like the rest of the world, was entering a new era.

The Recreational Coast

At the start of the 20th century, coastal B.C. was a place of abundance with seemingly unlimited raw resources. Thick stands of high-grade timber covered the mountain slopes and pristine rivers swelled with spawning salmon. Lumber and coal barons grew rich by logging and mining the land, while fishing ports thrived along the coast, their canneries busy each summer as boat after boat unloaded its catch.

Top to bottom, Sullivan Bay's heritage buildings; Billy Proctor's museum near Echo Bay; the floatplane dock at Sullivan Bay.

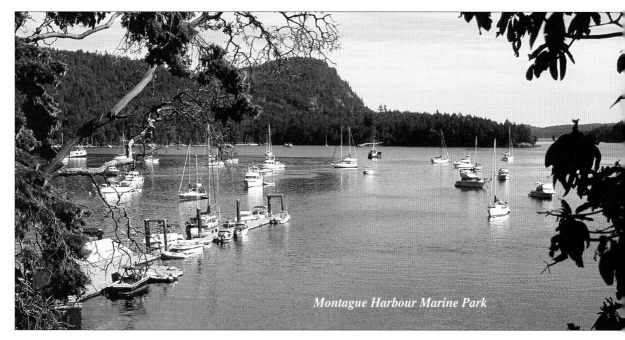

Montague Harbour Marine Park

When Muriel Wylie Blanchett, author of *The Curve of Time*, spent her summers cruising the Inside Passage with her young children in the 1930s, she was ahead of her time. Most vessels then plying these waters were pursuing commerce – fishing, logging, mining or servicing the coastal communities centred around these activities. Recreational boating as we know it didn't burgeon until after World War II, when mass production of fibreglass boats and an increase in leisure time and spending power made yachting a pastime everyone could enjoy.

The war brought other changes. A shortage of skilled tree fallers on the coast during the war years spurred the development of gasoline-powered saws. Following the war, improved machinery, centralization of sawmilling operations and the use of floatplanes to fly logging crews in and out of camps all contributed to the decline of coastal logging communities. In 1945 the floating village at Claydon Bay was towed to Sullivan Bay, where the string of buildings included a store and post office servicing what was, until the mid-1950s, the busiest floatplane base on the coast. Several of the original buildings remain as part of the Sullivan Bay Marine Resort.

Until the 1960s, Minstrel Island had been a popular watering hole and steamer stop with a general store and hotel where hand-loggers gathered to drink beer when they weren't felling trees in 'The Jungle' – as the maze of islands at the mouth of Knight Inlet was then called.

Blind Channel was another former logging community that transformed itself into a marine resort, its revival dating to 1969 when the Richter family, cruising the coast in their small boat, pulled up to a lonely dock and noticed a 'For Sale' sign on the store. Within months the family sold their Vancouver home and, with entrepreneurial vision and hard work, created a summertime mecca for recreational boaters.

Echo Bay on Gilford Island is one of the area's few year-round floathome communities, where the marinas serve boaters each summer and a marine park is located at the head of the bay.

Sportfishing also increased in popularity following World War II. April Point Lodge on Quadra Island, established in 1945 by the Peterson family of San Francisco, soon became a popular retreat for celebrities, as did the famous Painter's Lodge near Campbell River. When the latter burned in 1985, it was replaced with a new facility.

Production of canned salmon, which peaked in the 1920s, began to consolidate during the Depression and the closure of canneries accelerated after the war when freezing technology was introduced. Namu's cannery remained in operation until 1969. By then, surviving plants had centralized at Prince Rupert and in the Vancouver area.

While industry on the coast was consolidating at major centres following World War II, recreational boaters were venturing farther afield, exploring the coast and marvelling not at the resource potential but at the scenic beauty of our coast. To preserve as much pristine and historic property as possible, the provincial government began establishing marine parks. Involved in the selection process was the Council of B.C. Yacht Clubs, which was formed in

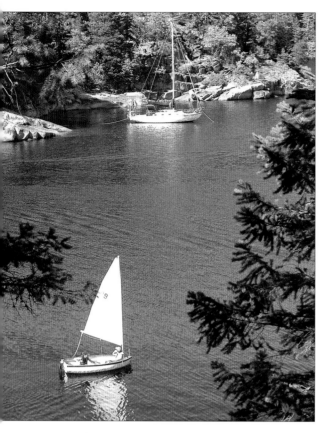

Above, a summer's afternoon at Hardy Island Marine Park. Below, an aerial view of Rebecca Spit Marine Park on Quadra Island.

1958 to represent the interests of recreational boaters in consultations regarding potential parks. Montague Harbour was designated B.C.'s first marine park in 1959, and since then dozens more have been established, including joint acquisitions by the federal and provincial governments under the Pacific Marine Heritage Legacy program. The diverse list of small craft anchorages now protected by park status is inspiring to any recreational boater intent on exploring the Inside Passage. In the Gulf Islands alone, boaters can enjoy a rich variety of easily accessible destinations that encompass beautiful beaches, forest trails and places of historical interest.

Farther north, the parks increase in size, often encompassing several islands and anchorages within their boundaries. Many are undeveloped, dominated by dense forests. North America's Pacific forest belt has the heaviest stands of trees in the world, and about a quarter of this temperate rainforest is found in B.C. The forest industry, the province's largest industrial sector, came under heavy criticism in the final decades of the 20th century for its practice of clear-cut logging, and environmentalists waged a much-publicized war in the woods with the forestry companies.

The province's environmental movement began back in the 1950s when Roderick Haig-Brown and other conservationists protested the building of a hydroelectric dam on Buttle and Campbell Lakes for fear the rising waters would destroy valuable wildlife habitat in Strathcona Park. Since then, the preservation of wilderness areas has propelled a growing environmental movement represented by a variety of organizations. Of direct benefit to boaters is the BC Marine Parks Forever Society, established in 1989 by the Council of B.C. Yacht Clubs to raise money and assist BC Parks in establishing new marine parks.

Other organizations working to preserve the coastal wilderness include the Nature Conservancy of Canada – a private, not-for-profit organization created in 1962 that raises funds to acquire properties across the country and preserve their biodiversity for future generations. Specific plant and animal species have also gained protection through the establishment of ecological reserves.

In Johnstone Strait the Robson Bight Ecological Reserve protects killer whales that come to rub against rounded pebbles covering the sea bottom near shore. These whales feed on the salmon that have traditionally travelled in huge runs along the strait. The early pioneers would boast that the fishing was so plentiful they could cross a stream on the back of spawning salmon. However, decades of overfishing, along with the destruction of salmon habitat, have contributed to dwindling salmon stocks, with some on the verge of extinction.

The proliferation of fish farms is no solace. These salt-water net pens used for raising Atlantic salmon began appearing on the coast in the mid-1970s, despite concerns by environmentalists and commercial fishers that escaped salmon would transmit diseases and weaken wild salmon stocks. Also of concern are the declining southern populations of killer whales, their dwindling numbers blamed in part on pollutants in the water. Meanwhile, the Fraser River watershed is being cleaned up through upgrades of sewage-treatment plants and the reduction of toxic discharges by pulp and wood mills. Such measures may allow the southern resident killer-whale population to stabilize and ultimately increase.

Past grievances have also been addressed. In 1988 a formal apology was made by the federal government to the Japanese Canadians who were relocated to internment camps during World War II, with compensation offered to those whose property, including fishing boats, was seized. Amends have also been made to the First Nations people, whose potlatch ceremonies were once banned by the federal government. Many of the seized artifacts were eventually returned and are now displayed at local band museums, such as the U'mista Cultural Centre in Alert Bay, a Kwakwaka'wakw fishing village on Cormorant Island.

Much has changed since the days when our early pioneers travelled the coast by boat. There were no marinas then (the word 'marina' was not even part of the vernacular prior to World War II), let alone marine parks and sportfishing lodges. But the primeval mystique of the Inside Passage endures, drawing boaters to its labyrinth of channels, islands and mountain-bounded inlets. A marine highway travelled by vessels ranging from one-man kayaks to cruise ships carrying 2,000-plus passengers, the Inside Passage is indisputably one of the most beautiful and storied coastlines in the world.

Artists, Authors & Adventurers

The first artists to inhabit the B.C. coast were the aboriginal people, whose miniature works of art have been found preserved deep within the compacted layers of shell middens. Less permanent is the art form many of us readily associate with the Pacific Northwest – the totem pole.

Made from the trunks of massive red cedars, totem poles were the most monumental of all native artworks. Master carvers were commissioned to sculpt a pole with crests (totems) representing the

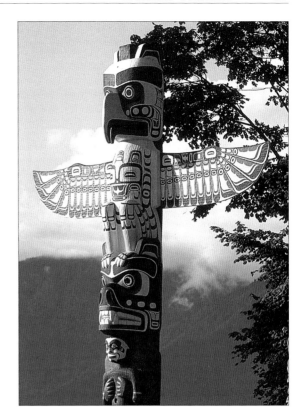

A thunderbird crowns one of numerous totem poles on display in Vancouver's Stanley Park.

clan and family to which the pole owner belonged. The average lifespan of a totem pole exposed to the elements is about 60 years before wood decay causes it to topple. When this happens, according to traditional beliefs, the pole's spirit departs and the fallen pole is left to return to nature. However, anthropologists concerned about their preservation began removing totem poles from abandoned village sites at the turn of the last century, and in the 1950s the Totem Pole Preservation Committee at the University of British Columbia's Museum of Anthropology (MOA) in Vancouver, rescued and restored poles that were slowly rotting.

The Irish-born 'Indian painter' Paul Kane arrived in local waters in 1847, embarking by canoe on a sketching trip to southern Vancouver Island and the Gulf Islands. Sea conditions in Juan de Fuca Strait on his 11-hour crossing by canoe from Port Angeles to Fort Victoria are vividly described in his diary:

"The wind increased to a perfect gale, and blowing against an ebb tide caused a heavy swell. We were obliged to keep one man constantly bailing to prevent our being swamped. The Indians on board commenced one of their wild chants, which increased to a perfect yell whenever a wave larger

*Top, 'Kwakiutl House' by Emily Carr, Vancouver
Art Gallery. Above, 'Indian Houses at Alert Bay'
by E.J. Hughes, National Gallery of Canada.*

than the rest approached; this was accompanied with
blowing and spitting against the wind as if they were
in angry contention with the evil spirit of the storm.
It was altogether a scene of the most wild and intense
excitement: the mountainous waves roaming round
our little canoe as if to engulph us every moment, the
wind howling over our heads, and the yelling
Indians, made it actually terrific...It was with the
greatest anxiety that I watched each coming wave as
it came thundering down, and I must confess that I
felt considerable fear as to the event. However, we
arrived safely."

Seasickness was Emily Carr's constant companion when native guides were delivering her to remote
villages along the coast. At times the natives were
suspicious of her motives, but more often they were

her friends and protectors. She observed the way
they survived hand in hand with nature as they
built fires on damp beaches and skillfully paddled
their canoes through steep waves.

Emily Carr confesses in her book *Klee Wyck*
that to the natives she was but a child, "ignorant
about the wild things which they knew so well."
She did, however, master the natural elements in
her boldly interpretive paintings, eventually gaining recognition as one of Canada's greatest paint-
ers. Among her famous works is a 1912 painting
entitled *War Canoes, Alert Bay*. A permanent collection of her paintings is displayed at the
Vancouver Art Gallery.

Another west coast artist whose paintings are
now highly valued was Edward John Hughes.
Born in North Vancouver in 1913 and raised in
Nanaimo, E. J. Hughes worked as a war artist
during World War II. A reclusive artist whose
paintings are held in galleries and private collections around the world, Hughes lived in Duncan
on Vancouver Island from 1959 until his death in
2007. His oil paintings include *Echo Bay,
Gilford Island* (1963) and *Departure from
Nanaimo* (1964).

One of the best-known figures of west coast
literature is the late Jim Spilsbury, a gifted
raconteur, painter and photographer whose tal-
ents have been captured in several books published by Harbour Publishing. *Spilsbury's Coast*
is an anecdotal recounting of his life on the
coast, co-written with Howard White, and
Spilsbury's collection of photographs is featured
in *Spilsbury's Album* along with entertaining
reminiscences of the people and places he came to
know along the coast.

Of all the books written about boating in B.C.
waters, one that remains on the bestseller list year
after year is *The Curve of Time* by Muriel Wylie
Blanchet. This coastal classic, written by Wylie
Blanchet in her final years and published after her
death in 1961, is found on the bookshelf of many a
boater who wanders the same watery channels as the
crew of Caprice did in the 1930s.

Time was not measured in minutes and hours for
Wylie Blanchet during those long-ago summers she
spent on the B.C. coast in her 25-foot cabin cruiser.
She and her five children got up with the sun and
spent their days exploring secluded anchorages and
visiting abandoned native villages. For meals, they
caught fish or baked beans and bread. They bathed
in lakes and washed their clothes in streams. Their
world was small in terms of cabin space and conve-
niences, but it was a world of their own making,

filled with grand scenery and endless adventures.

It is still possible to explore many of the same anchorages and to step ashore at the same remote village sites for a look back along the curve of time – back to the days when dugout canoes once lined the clamshell beaches and rows of cedar-planked houses, fronted by totem poles, overlooked the waterfront.

Understanding Native Art

The late Bill Reid, of Haida and Scots-American ancestry, is credited with reviving West Coast native art and reintroducing it to the world. His famous sculptures include *The Black Canoe*, which is the centrepiece of the Canadian embassy in Washington, DC. A second casting, *The Jade Canoe*, stands in the departure hall of Vancouver's International Airport. His *Killer Whale* bronze sits outside the entrance to the Vancouver Aquarium, and his massive yellow cedar carving *The Raven and The First Men* is housed at the University of British Columbia's Museum of Anthropology.

Haida art is highly regarded for its classsical purity, but the basic components of northwest native art are shared by all groups, In drawings and paintings, the form line defines the shape of the figure being portrayed. Its flowing outline varies in thickness and is usually painted black, with the figure's secondary features in red. Black and red are the traditional colours of native art. Red was made from ochre (a clay-like mineral) ground to a powder and turned into a paste with the addition of a binding agent such as oil from salmon eggs. Black came from charcoal, graphite or lignite. With the introduction of commercial paints, artists began experimenting with non-traditional colours; however, much of their work is still done in the original colours. The Kwakwaka'wakw (Kwakiutl) traditionally used more colours than the northern artists, adding green, white and yellow to their palettes.

Another basic component is the ovoid – an oval that is pushed out of shape to fit inside the form lines. An ovoid can represent a face, eyes, major joints or simply fill in empty spaces. The U form is used to help contour the figure, fill in spaces or represent features such as feathers. The S form is also used in a variety of ways, such as joining elements, filling in space or

representing part of a leg or arm. The four basic design elements – form lines, ovoids, U forms and S forms – are closely assembled to create other shapes in the spaces between them.

Split figures (mirror images) are also widely used, as are transformation figures (i.e. half human/half animal). The basic elements of a figure are sometimes dismantled and rearranged to fit inside a given shape, such as a blanket, hat or spoon. The key to recognizing the figures portrayed in native art is to learn a few of their dominant features.

For example, a raven has a long, straight beak whereas an eagle has a shorter, hooked beak. The legendary Thunderbird – a crest used only by the most powerful and prestigious chiefs – is always portrayed with outstretched wings and a sharply recurved upper beak. A bear will have flared nostrils, clawed paws and sharp teeth, sometimes with its tongue hanging out. The beaver has two large front teeth and a cross-hatched tail. The wolf is often shown standing on all four legs whereas the bear and beaver are usually sitting upright.

One of the easiest motifs to recognize is the killer whale, frequently portrayed in an arched position with a tall dorsal fin protruding from its back and two saw-like rows of teeth in its mouth. The moon, an exclusive crest of high-ranking Haida chiefs, is round with a face in the centre. The sun is similar to the moon but with long rays projecting from the outer circle. Human figures are also part of native art and those wearing high-crowned hats atop a totem pole are watchmen.

Kwakwaka'wakw art is recognized by its abundance of small elements and the protruding beaks, fins and wings that are added to totem poles whereas Haida poles and other objects are minimallly altered by shallow carvings that blend with the basic shape. Coast Salish natives used no crest system, so their art traditionally depicted animal and human figures rather than clan emblems. They are noted for their excellent weaving and basketry as well as their carved spindle whorls. The Cowichans on Vancouver Island still employ traditional methods when making their famous sweaters.

Above, Bill Reid's 'Killer Whale' outside the Vancouver Aquarium.

Winter Point, Saturna Island

Plant and animal life thrives along the Inside Passage, where temperate rainforests flourish in the maritime climate and saltwater wetlands provide a nutrient-rich habitat for waterbirds and other species. Pacific salmon travel these waters, destined to spawn in the streams where they were born unless they are thwarted by one of the region's fish-eating predators – humans, marine mammals, eagles or bears.

Boaters might find themselves escorted unexpectedly by a pod of Dall's porpoises or Pacific white-sided dolphins – nautical daredevils which will dart and dive and leap in the bow wave of any

moving vessel, from a small pleasure craft to an 80,000-ton cruise ship. Harbour seals and California sea lions are common sights, fishing in the passes or hauling out on rocky outcroppings.

Conifers dominate the forested coastline. They are perfectly adapted to the region's cool, wet winters, able to gather sunlight and grow almost year-round, whereas deciduous hardwoods grow only when their leaves are out. A notable exception to the dense rainforests dominating the B.C. coast is the rain-shadow belt on southeastern Vancouver Island and the Gulf Islands. Here the habitat is warmer and dryer, and the vegetation more complex.

Wildflowers and Shrubs

Spring, when the world is in bloom, is the best time to enjoy the coastal wildflowers of southern B.C. The air is sweet with the scent of rain-drenched vegetation and shoreside trails lead hikers past the intoxicating scent of new spruce shoots. Uninhabited islets, in particular, are a delight to explore. Pink-hued wildflowers such as nodding onion and sea blush grow in profusion, the latter blanketing grassy bluffs, while bluebells grow from rock crevices.

Other indigenous species include the common camas, identified by its purple-blue star-like flower. Native people of the southern straits traditionally used the region's bulbous plants for food, and the common camas was one of these, although great care had to be taken to distinguish it from the poisonous bulbs and leaves of a similar lily called meadow death-camas. The only way to tell the two types apart is by their flowers – those of the death-camas are cream-coloured. The Salish of

Above left, camas is a wildflower that thrives on pristine islets, often alongside sea blush (left).

southern Vancouver Island would weed death-camas from their cultivated beds of common camas, which they harvested during or soon after flowering so as not to confuse them with the death-camas. Only the large bulbs were dug up, while the smaller ones were left to grow. The harvested bulbs were steamed in large pits for a day or more until they were cooked, then served at feasts or sun-dried for storage.

When Europeans arrived they introduced new plant species, sometimes inadvertently importing their seeds in crop seed or straw packing. Others were purposely cultivated. Scotch broom, which grows in golden-yellow abundance along roadsides, was introduced by a Scottish sea captain in 1850. He acquired some seeds while visiting the British consul in the Sandwich Islands (Hawaii) and brought these to Sooke for planting. An invasive shrub, Scotch broom quickly colonized most of southern Vancouver Island and the Gulf Islands, sometimes to the detriment of local flora. Scotch broom's flowers, pods and seeds (which resemble small peas) are toxic and can be poisonous if eaten by children. The shrub's usefulness was as a source of twigs to be bunched into brooms.

Beach pea grows along the edge of sand-and-gravel beaches, while lupine grows in a variety of habitats, its tall spires thick with pea-like flowers that are usually blue or purple. The large-leaved lupine is commonly seen along southern shores while the Nootka lupine thrives in estuarine marshes of the north coast where grizzly bears feed on their roots. One plant found the entire length of the B.C. coast is fireweed, its bright rosy-pink petals blooming on stalks that grow four feet high. Fireweed grows in thick patches on recently logged or burned land and in meadows, thickets and along river bars.

A Walk in the Forest

The dense and complex forests of coastal B.C. form some of the world's most impressive examples of temperate rainforest. Rarely struck by catastrophic fires, the trees of these coastal rainforests have been slowly replaced on an individual basis, creating a many-canopied forest with a dense shrubby understorey and an abundance of lichens, mosses and ferns growing at the base of trees, up their trunks and on top of decaying logs. Individual trees may be as old as 1,000 years, and the forests themselves are even older. Species such as the western red cedar found refuge in northern California during the last ice age, then moved northward as the glaciers retreated.

Western red cedar, B.C.'s official tree, was called the 'tree of life' by the Kwakwaka'wakw and is considered the cornerstone of Northwest Coast native culture. The tree's rot-resistant wood is straight-grained and easily split, making it the perfect material for everything from house planks and posts to baskets and bentwood boxes. Thriving in moist-to-wet soil and tolerant of shade, the western red cedar's massive trunk (2 to 8 feet in diameter) reaches heights of 150 to 200 feet and bears soft, shiny needles that grow in splayed clusters from branches that droop slightly then turn upward.

Yellow cedar (also known as cypress) grows at higher elevations and is smaller than the western red cedar, reaching heights of 60 to 130 feet, with flattened branches that hang downward. Its inner bark is yellowish and its tough, straight-grained wood was used by Northwest Coast peoples to make a variety of implements, including paddles and bows.

The forest trails at Blind Channel

Above, the massive trunk of a Western red cedar.
Below, the peeling bark of an arbutus.

The Sitka spruce grows quickly (up to 3 feet per year), reaches an average height of 160 feet, and has a trunk of 3 to 5 feet in diameter. Its branches project at an upward angle from its straight trunk, giving the tree a conical crown, and its spiky green needles are a deep green. In B.C., the Sitka spruce grows at low to middle elevations with the oldest forests occurring in low terraces of river floodplains.

The Western hemlock is a tall, slender tree with branches that droop slightly and twigs that contain two rows of needles which are flat and soft. With an average height of 100 to 150 feet and a trunk diameter of two to four feet, this tree is tolerant of shade and often sprouts up among the faster-growing Sitka spruce. The Western hemlock is more prevalent on B.C.'s north coast than the south coast, and will grow only in soil with significant organic content. Few plants can grow beneath the thick canopy of the Western hemlock, which forms the densest forest canopy of any tree species in this region.

Douglas fir is one of the tallest trees known (over 200 feet) and can live for over 1,000 years. The tree's slightly drooping branches bear flat needles that grow in two rows, and its extremely thick bark provides protection from moderate surface fires. Douglas fir naturally establishes on moist sites following a fire, but also grows in dry, open forests and is found throughout the south coast region, predominantly on the east side of Vancouver Island and the mainland opposite.

The Douglas fir began appearing in our region about 7,000 years ago, and was first described by Dr. Archibald Menzies, the naturalist with Captain George Vancouver's expedition to our coast in the 1790s. The species is named for the Scottish botanist David Douglas, who explored the Pacific Northwest in the 1820s. Douglas was called 'the Grass Man' by the aboriginal people who respected him for his knowledge of the wilderness. The tall cylindrical trunk of the Douglas fir made it a favourite with loggers, and the wood is used extensively in construction. The popularity of the tree has been its downfall, with few of the giant specimens still standing.

Shore pine is common along the immediate coast, its trunk often crooked and its crown irregular. Its branches bear needles that grow in pairs, and hanging from the tip of each branch is a cluster of small pollen cones and an egg-shaped seed cone. This highly adaptable tree is tolerant of sea spray and low-nutrient soil.

The arbutus (madrona) is a broadleaf evergreen found in the south coast's rain-shadow forests. It grows on dry, sunny sites at low to middle elevations, and often shares its habitat with the Douglas fir and Garry oak. Arbutus trees are easy to identify with their smooth, twisting limbs covered in red bark which begins to peel off in August. The broad leaves are a dark shiny green, and in spring the branches are adorned with sprays of white blossoms.

Garry Oak, the only oak native to B.C., is found on southern Vancouver Island and the adjacent Gulf Islands. Named for Nicholas Garry of the Hudson's Bay Company, the Garry Oak can be seen growing on dry rocky bluffs, its light-green leaves sprouting from gnarled branches covered with light-grey bark.

Providing splashes of colour in fall is the bigleaf maple, its deeply lobed leaves turning brilliant yellow before falling to the ground. The trunk and main branches of the bigleaf maple are often covered with a moss layer so thick that other tree roots can sprout and grow as 'canopy roots'.

Carpeting the forest floors are over 700 mosses and about 40 species of ferns, the latter needing abundant moisture for reproduction. Skunk cabbage is also found in wet areas, near streams and bogs, and is easy to spot, with its yellow, tulip-shaped inner leaf and large outer leaves. These leaves are eaten by deer and geese, and were widely used by First Nations people to wrap salmon for baking and for lining berry baskets. Slugs, often seen lying on a trail, feed at night on roots and plants. The largest in B.C. (and second-largest in the world) is the banana slug, so named for its yellow-green colour with brown or black spots.

Salal is plentiful, growing in thickets, its branches of waxy evergreen leaves shipped to florists worldwide for use in cut-flower bouquets. The salal's small purple berries appear in mid- to late summer and have long been a common part of the native people's diet. Devil's club, a broadleaf plant related to ginseng, was used as a medicine and protective agent by the area's First Nations people. The inner bark of the roots and stems was boiled in water, making a tea used to treat various ailments. The plant's bright red berries are a favourite food for bears, but its tough, prickly spines can inflict bad scratches on bare-legged hikers.

Land Mammals

Northern coastal forests are home to a variety of animals, including bears. Black bears live on the B.C. mainland, Vancouver Island and the Discovery Islands, while grizzlies roam the mainland's mountainous backcountry, appearing at remote inlets when salmon are returning to their natal streams and rivers.

Most bears avoid humans but not all are timid – some lose their natural fear if they learn to associate humans with food. Small dogs are 'bear bait' so pet

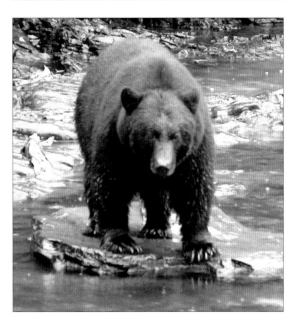

Above, a black bear feeds on spawning salmon.
Top, skunk cabbage. Middle, Devil's club.

Above, grizzly bears are found at the head of mainland inlets along salmon streams. Below, the shells of an oyster, cockle and butter clam.

sea asparagus

sea urchins

owners must be extra careful. If you decide to hike inland, remember that salmon streams and berry patches attract bears. Watch for bear scat and if you come across a decaying animal carcass, it's probably some bear's food cache and you should leave the area immediately or risk becoming part of the picnic.

The best way to avoid encountering a bear is by being noisy. Talking, singing and jingling bells are better than silence, but the most effective warning is an air horn. Any bear in the area is sure to hear its piercing blast, ensuring you won't come face to face with a surprised and therefore dangerous bear. Should you encounter a bear, back away very slowly without making eye contact, which the bear perceives as aggression. Never turn and run. Very few people suffer bear attacks and most can be avoided by taking a few sensible precautions.

A grizzly (a sub-species of brown bear) can be identified by its large size and distinctive shoulder hump. Its fur can range in colour from blond to black with varying shades of brown and gray in between. At 200 to 600 pounds, black bears are smaller than grizzlies (which weigh 300 to 1,500 pounds) and are usually jet-black or brown with a brown-yellow muzzle.

Another forest predator to be aware of is the cougar, a solitary predator that hunts deer and small game. Also called mountain lion, this large member of the cat family will rarely attack humans, but when it does, small children are most vulnerable. Cougars are known to stalk and attack from behind and if one is approaching, you are better off acting aggressively using rocks or a large stick to defend yourself. Maintain eye contact, try to make yourself appear as large as possible and do not run or turn your back.

Wolves also inhabit coastal forests, with transient grey wolves often swimming from island to island. Resident wolf packs, which number about a dozen, have been seen with increasing regularity on several Discovery Islands, most notably Cortes Island. Wolves are naturally secretive and avoid people unless they become habituated. Should you be approached by a wolf or pack of wolves, wave your arms to appear larger and slowly back away. Throw rocks and sticks if necessary.

It's always best to hike with at least one other person, keep any dogs leashed, carry an airhorn, and never let small children wander off.

The Intertidal Zone

There is much to explore along the foreshore of an anchorage where tidal pools contain a microcosm of marine life, including tiny shore crabs. Sea stars, which prey on crabs, barnacles, clams and mussels, are often found high and dry, clinging to foreshore rocks with stiff arms that contain rows of feet on their undersides. Brightly coloured sea anemones attach themselves to rocks and look like rounded lumps of jelly when the tide recedes and they retract into themselves to conserve moisture.

The native people harvested much of their food from the foreshore, where clams feed on microscopic plants and animals that they filter from the water through their siphons (necks). These bivalve filter-feeders, along with cockles, oysters, scallops and mussels, are susceptible to harmful blooms of algae, commonly called red tide. When shellfish ingest large quantities of this toxic algae, the poison becomes concentrated. When it is ingested by seabirds and mammals (including humans), this toxin will cause paralytic shellfish poisoning.

Eelgrass, a ribbon-like vascular plant, grows in the lowest intertidal zone and the sub-tidal zone, usually along sheltered shores where Dungeness crab can be found hiding in beds of eelgrass. Eelgrass was traditionally eaten fresh or dried into cakes for winter food; the Kwakwaka'wakw dined on eelgrass at special feasts, while the Haida preferred eelgrass with herring spawn attached to the leaves.

Sea asparagus, or pickleweed, grows along the foreshore and is harvested commercially just before summer flowering for use in salads. If you pick sea asparagus in summer, the plant's excessive saltiness can be diminished by boiling it several times in fresh water with a pinch of sugar until tender.

Bull kelp, a type of seaweed, grows throughout the summer in thick beds from the sea bottom. Its long, hollow, rubbery stem ends at the water's surface with a cylindrical float and long brown fronds that trail across the water, their direction an indicator of any tidal current (see page 13 for more on kelp and current). A variety of marine life finds shelter in kelp beds, including sea urchins, which feed on this iodine-rich plant. Sea urchins consumed vast kelp forests along the Inside Passage after the sea otter, which feeds on sea urchins, was hunted nearly to extinction in the early 1800s.

Jellyfish are not a fish but, like sea anemones, an invertebrate. They swim by pulsing their bodies and they absorb oxygen from the water. Suspended from the edges of its saucer-shaped body are tentacles. The jellyfish protects itself with small stinging cells which can cause discomfort if touched. (A drop or two of alcohol will soothe a jellyfish sting – bar scotch works well.)

At night, water disturbed by the oars of a dinghy will sometimes produce tiny sparkles that look like phosphorescence. They are, however, caused by bioluminescence which is the production of light by living organisms. Certain marine algae, called dinoflagellates, produce light only when disturbed, triggering the change of chemical energy to light.

Birds

Sooner or later most boaters become casual birders. With so many opportunities to see birds while out on the water, it's a fairly effortless hobby. Who hasn't awoken in an anchorage to a medley of bird calls – eagles chittering, kingfishers chattering, gulls mewing. To hear the haunting laugh of a loon in a northern anchorage is one of those moments that make boating such a rewarding pastime.

Coastal B.C. is part of the Pacific Flyway, a migratory route for millions of birds, and the region's river estuaries and tidal passes provide a rich habitat for the many waterbirds that winter in local waters. The Fraser River Delta is one of the largest and most important estuaries on North America's west coast, its marshes and mud flats supporting more waterfowl, shorebirds and gulls than

A bald eagle swoops down to snatch a salmon with its powerful talons.

anywhere else in Canada. Birds congregate near food sources, and the mouth of the Fraser River is a prime feeding area due to upwelling caused by the mixing of saltwater and fresh water. Upwellings of cold water bring plankton and small fish to the surface, and this phenomenon also occurs in channels and passes, such as Active Pass, where strong tidal currents are deflected over underwater ridges.

Bald eagles are often seen fishing in passes, using their keen eyesight, speed and sharp talons to pluck salmon from the water. A high-soaring eagle, with a wingspan of 6 to 8 feet, can spot a fish from over a mile away and can dive from the sky at 100 miles per hour. Eagles, which mate for life, build their nests in the tallest trees of their territory and close to the water. Juvenile eagles retain their ragged

plumage until the age of five, when they attain the distinctive markings of a mature bald eagle, including the snowy white head feathers for which the bird is named.

Although they are birds of prey, eagles are also scavengers and each winter, from October through February, they gather by the thousands at the head of Howe Sound to feed on spawning salmon along the Lower Squamish River. Eagles also gather each December along the shores of Northumberland Channel near Nanaimo in anticipation of the Pacific herring spawn in February and March.

The coast is home to many species of duck. These include **dabbling ducks**, who feed at the water's surface or by dipping their heads and bodies until only their tail is protruding from the water. Dabblers include the well-known mallard, the drake (male) sporting an emerald green head and chestnut chest. Other dabbler species are the teal, northern pintail, widgeon and wood duck.

Diving ducks, as the name implies, completely submerge when feeding. Scoters, goldeneye and bufflehead are diving ducks, as are scaup and harlequin. Mergansers are nicknamed 'sawbills' due to their long, tapering bills lined with sharp 'teeth' for grabbing fish. A mother merganser will carry her brood of newborn chicks on her back as she swims near shore.

Shorebirds include the black oystercatcher, which has a long orange beak with which it pries open shellfish. The feet of the pigeon guillemot, an alcid, are also bright orange and quite a sight when this black seabird runs across the surface of the water, gaining speed for take-off.

Gulls are buoyant swimmers and strong fliers. Their long, pointed wings allow them to glide and soar and set down lightly upon the water. Cormorants, which enter the water only to feed, are often seen perched on rocks or buoys, their wings spread out to dry. **Loons**, on the other hand, remain mostly in the water and come ashore only to nest, for they cannot walk on land and they cannot fly during moult. Swimming is their specialty and their heavy bodies are designed for diving.

The largest seabird colony in the Strait of Georgia is on Mandarte Island, known locally as Bare Island, which lies off the northeast side of Sidney Island and is private property, owned by the East Saanich First

Top left, oystercatchers can be seen on reefs and outcroppings at low tide. Middle left, common mergansers. Bottom left, coho salmon is a favourite catch of sportsfishermen.

Nation. More than 8,000 birds nest on this barren island, their numbers building over the summer, with a sizeable flock remaining throughout the winter. Scientists have been studying birds here since the 1950s and have identified more than 100 species. It is the largest seabird breeding colony in B.C. for double-crested and pelagic cormorants, glaucous-winged gulls and pigeon guillemots. It is also a major nesting site for rhinoceros auklets and tufted puffins. The lagoon at the south end of Sidney Spit Marine Park is a productive feeding ground for these birds and others, including great blue herons.

Pacific Salmon

The life cycle of a Pacific salmon makes a fascinating tale. Salmon spawn in fresh water, usually streams, where they spend varying lengths of time depending on the species. Some juveniles migrate directly to saltwater while others linger in river estuaries where they grow and adapt to the mix of fresh and saltwater habitats. Depending on the species, salmon will spend one to 7 years in the open ocean before returning to their natal streams to spawn.

Salmon struggle against incredible odds to return to the stream of their birth. If a fish makes it past the sport and commercial fisheries, there will be other predators, such as bears and eagles, waiting along stream banks to make a meal of these weary fish. Salmon often have to leap up waterfalls and swim against rushing currents to return to their spawning grounds. Once there, the females dig nests in the gravel and lay their eggs while their male partners release milt which fertilizes the eggs. All Pacific salmon spawn only once, then die. Most salmon spawn in late summer or fall.

There are five species of salmon: king (chinook) is the largest; silver (coho) is prized by sportfishermen; red (sockeye), with its rich red meat, is the highest-priced commercial salmon; pink (humpy) is the most common and an important commercial fish for the canneries; and chum (dog) salmon, when smoked, is a tasty delicacy.

A specific salmon stock – often identified by the name of its spawning stream – is lost forever once its spawning stream is destroyed, and this loss of biodiversity means there are fewer genetic types to deal successfully with future vagaries of the environment. Hatcheries, which recreate a spawning habitat of gravel covered with clear, still, shallow water, have become a substitute for rejuvenating salmon stocks but the survival rate of hatchery fish has been declining.

One of the biggest threats to salmon survival appears to be climate change. A rise of just a few degrees in water temperature causes a salmon's metabolic rate to increase and forces it to expend valuable energy needed to swim upstream. Fish and other cold-blooded animals can't regulate their body temperatures like mammals, and salmon are particularly susceptible because they spend most of their lives near the ocean surface.

Marine Mammals

One of the most thrilling sights while cruising is to see a plume of mist rise from the water, indicating the presence of a whale. Several species of whale thrive along the B.C. coast, including killer whales and, in summer, humpback whales. Called cetaceans and found in all the world's oceans, whales vary greatly in size. The smallest are dolphins and porpoises. **Killer whales** (orcas) are the largest member of the *Delphinidae* family of toothed whales. Male

Above, the killer whale has a distinctive dorsal fin.
Below, a dall porpoise skims the water's surface.

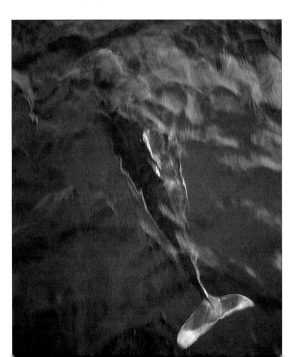

orcas can reach 30 feet and live for about 30 years, while females, who average 23 feet in length, live for about 50 years, sometimes longer. The male is distinguished from the female by his tall, straight dorsal fin (up to 6 feet high on mature males). Females give birth to single calves following a gestation period of 15 months.

A killer whale's most distinctive features are its prominent dorsal fin and the white marking just behind it, called a saddle patch. Scientists who observe killer whales in B.C. waters have developed a database in which regularly sighted pods and their members – identified by individual markings – are given reference names. Every killer whale belongs to a pod – the extended family group into which it was born. Each sub-group within a pod consists of a mature cow and her progeny of all ages. Mature males likely mate with females of other pods, but they always return to their own pod and remain with it until death.

Resident pods, with up to 50 members, form the largest groups, remaining near established salmon runs along inshore waters. Transient pods form smaller groups and travel a wider area in search for food, preying primarily on marine mammals such as seals and sea lions. It was because of their swift, ferocious attacks on their warm-blooded prey that killer whales, whose mouths hold more than four dozen sharp teeth, were once feared by humans.

Killer whales can swim for long distances at a cruising speed of about 7 knots, but can accelerate dramatically when attacking prey or leaping from the water. Resident pods communicate with high-pitched sounds that can be heard on hydrophones. These vocalizations include sonar-like clicks, squeaks and whistles. Transient pods remain silent, so as not to alert potential prey of their presence.

Dall porpoises are sometimes confused with killer whales because their black-and-white colouring is similar. However, Dall porpoises are much shorter (about 7 feet long) and stockier in shape, and their

dorsal fin is topped with white. They are the world's fastest marine mammals, reaching speeds of 30 miles per hour. Travelling in groups of a half-dozen or more, they swim just beneath the surface of the water, kicking up splashes, called rooster tails, when they leap partially out of the water. These social creatures love to ride the bow wave of a moving vessel and will perform dazzling, crisscross maneuvers in which two pairs race toward the bow, one from either side, only to veer off at the last moment to prevent a collision. Their split-second reflexes and swiftness allow them to dart through the water and turn quickly.

Also playful and sociable is the **Pacific white-sided dolphin**, which travels in large groups (115 members on average). Like the Dall porpoise, white-sided dolphins are attracted to the bow waves of moving vessels. Slightly longer than the Dall porpoise, these dolphins are black with a white belly and a hooked dorsal fin. During the fall mating season, they indulge in wild acrobatics, leaping with abandon in front of large vessels and cruise ships.

Baleen whales are also sighted along B.C.'s Inside Passage. These toothless whales feed on schooling fish, plankton and other small organisms, which they catch by swimming with their mouths wide open. When the whale closes its mouth, it raises its tongue to force the scooped water out the sides where the bristles of its baleen plates trap the food.

The **humpback whale** is a filter feeder and, although large in size, is an acrobatic whale that performs breaches, flipper-slaps and deep dives. This surface activity and close-to-shore feeding by the humpback made it an easy target for commercial whalers in the 19th century. By the time humpbacks in the Pacific were protected in 1966, their numbers had dwindled to a few thousand from an estimated high of 125,000. However, their numbers are rebounding and sightings outside coastal Alaska, the main summer feeding grounds of Pacific humpbacks, are increasing. In recent years, humpbacks have been sighted regularly in Juan de Fuca Strait, northern **Johnstone Strait, Dixon Entrance** and **Fitz Hugh Sound**, where summer sightings are a daily occurrence. In late summer and fall, humpbacks have been observed in eastern Queen Charlotte Strait feeding on dense schools of herring. As winter approaches, humpbacks head to the warm waters of Hawaii or Mexico to mate and give birth.

Adult humpbacks are, on average, 45 feet long and weight up to 40 tons. Their large flippers provide maneuverability and the pleats on the sides of their mouths can create a pouch large enough to hold six

Pacific white-sided dolphins in Knight Inlet

adult humans. When feeding, a humpback blows columns of bubbles that create a ring around a school of fish, which it then lunges at with its mouth wide open. Sea birds, attracted by the water disturbance, feed on the krill and herring swimming to the surface.

Humpbacks are not aggressive but they are unpredictable and seem unaware of vessels in their vicinity, so boaters should be alert to any signs of whale activity or risk colliding with one of these gentle giants.

The **minke**, another filter feeder that frequents inshore waters, is considerably smaller than the humpback. Measuring 20 to 30 feet in length and weighing up to 10 tons, minkes travel alone and are much more elusive than the humpback, surfacing to breathe and lunge-feed through schools of fish.

Seals and **sea lions** (which are a type of seal) are widespread in B.C. coastal waters. These fin-footed marine mammals have a thick layer of fat beneath their hair-covered skin and spend much of their time in the water. Unlike whales, however, who never leave the water, seals and sea lions will haul out onto rocky islets, sandbars and mudflats to rest, breed and give birth. In most instances, a seal pup lying alone on a beach has not been abandoned but is waiting for its mother to return, so it should be left alone. Sea lions gather in colonies to breed, with mature males assembling harems. Seals and sea lions live for about 30 years and feed on fish.

Most common in southern waters is the Pacific harbour seal, recognized by its mottled white-black-brown colouring, with males approaching 6 feet in length. California sea lions breed in B.C.'s southern waters in fall and winter. They appear black when wet and are smaller than the tawny-coloured Steller sea lion; male Steller sea lions weigh up to 2,400 pounds and their main rookeries are found in northern waters.

Otters belong to the weasel family and are kept warm not by blubber but by a thick coat of fur. The endangered sea otter is not found in the inside waters of B.C., but the smaller river otter is often seen scampering along the foreshore of an anchorage or swimming near shore. Not considered a marine mammal because it is also found in lakes and rivers, the river otter makes its home on land and, with webbed feet, is agile on land and in the water. Males reach 4 feet in length and weigh up to 25 pounds. River otters are very sociable and playful, and have been observed sliding headfirst on their bellies down mudbanks into the water.

Top to bottom, a humpback whale displays its fluked tail before doing a deep dive; the sea otter has the densest fur coat of any mammal; sea lions haul out at a northern rookery.

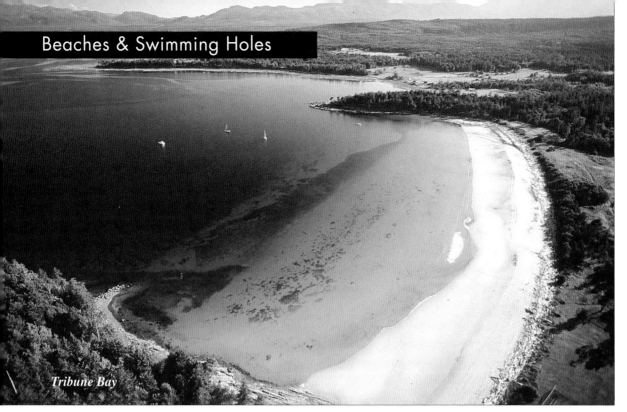

Tribune Bay

When the sun shines, the beach beckons. Boaters cruising B.C.'s south coast can enjoy a variety of beaches, ranging from stretches of fine sand to half-moon slivers of white shell. Those made of sand originated some 10,000 years ago when glaciers retreated and left behind drift deposits of ground-up sand, gravel and clay. Remnants of these glacial outwash plains are the beaches into which we now like to sink our toes.

More abundant are the white-shell beaches. These were not naturally formed but created in prehistoric times by the area's early inhabitants. The empty clam and mussel shells they would toss into heaps were, over time, crushed and compressed into beaches several yards deep. Archaeological digs have taken place at a number of these middens but the general public is not allowed to disturb them. We can, however, enjoy them as foreshore beaches on which to picnic or go for a swim.

Some of the best swimming spots are found in the northern Strait of Georgia, where currents are generally weak and variable, resulting in relatively warm water. Good spots for swimming can be found in protected bays and coves where the surface water isn't disrupted by vigorous tidal mixing and may be further warmed by a sandy beach or rock foreshore during a rising tide.

And then, of course, there are the lakes. Mariners have, for centuries, delighted in the discovery of a freshwater lake near the head of an anchorage. The early explorers washed their clothes and bathed in this clean water, but modern mariners are more likely to head ashore with pure pleasure in mind as they hike to the nearest lake for a swim. (The use of soap and shampoo is not allowed in marine park lakes.) Numerous anchorages have trails leading inland to a lake in which you can take a dip.

These are some of the beaches and lakes we have enjoyed along B.C.'s Inside Passage.

Sandy Beaches:
Sidney Spit, Sidney Island
Buccaneer Bay, Thormanby Islands
Sandy Island Marine Park
Tribune Bay, Hornby Island
Spilsbury Point, Hernando Island
West Beach and North Beach, Calvert Island

Middens:
Russell Island Marine Park
Cabbage Island Marine Park
Hawkins Island
Montague Harbour Marine Park
Matilpi
Burdwood Group
Insect Island
Blunden Harbour
Fury Island, Penrose Island Marine Park

Freshwater Lakes:
Tenedos Bay (Unwin Lake)
Roscoe Bay (Black Lake)
Teakerne Arm (Cassel Lake)
Small Inlet / Waiatt Bay (Newton Lake)
Turnbull Cove (Huaskin Lake)

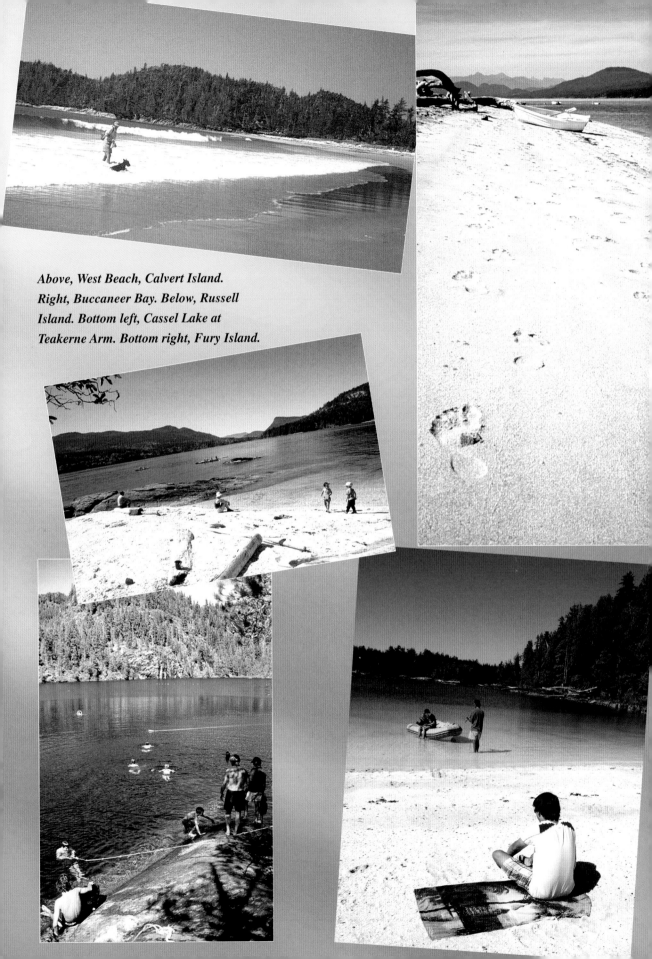

Above, West Beach, Calvert Island.
Right, Buccaneer Bay. Below, Russell
Island. Bottom left, Cassel Lake at
Teakerne Arm. Bottom right, Fury Island.

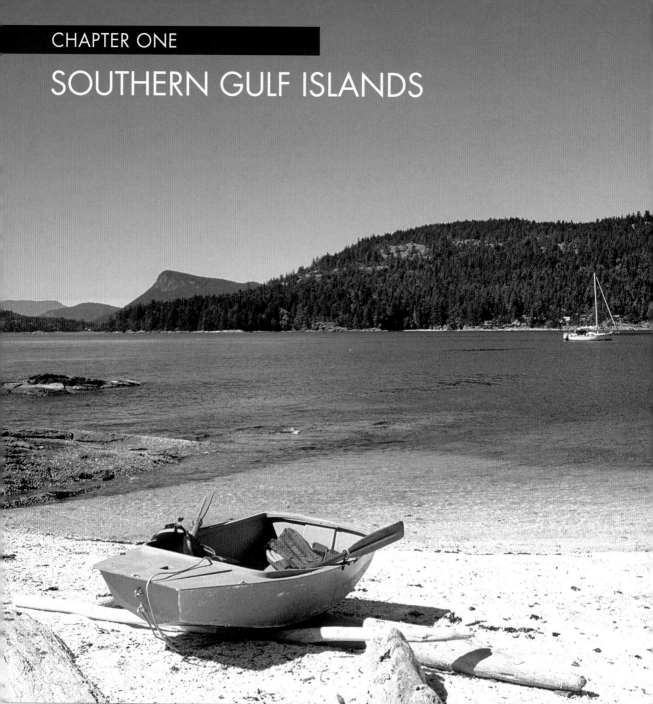

Bordered by dark green conifers, the golden hilltops of the Gulf Islands roll down to a sheltered sea. When heaving a dinghy onto a clamshell beach – for the first time or the hundredth – you can't help but be struck by the beauty of these islands, where deer wander freely and narrow roads weave past fenced pastures on their way to the water's edge. The final bend of a leafy lane often reveals yet another snug cove or secure harbour where boaters can find refuge, recreation and, perhaps, a moment of reflection.

Nestled in the lee of Vancouver Island and named the Gulf Islands when the Strait of Georgia was referred to as a 'gulf', these sheltered islands enjoy a temperate climate – warm and dry in summer, cool and wet in winter. With a decent heater on board, you can cruise these islands year-round and each season brings refreshing changes – from the bright bustle of summer to the solitude of winter when shorebirds are your only company in an otherwise deserted cove. The shoulder seasons of spring and fall are ideal times to cruise the Gulf Islands – the weather is changeable

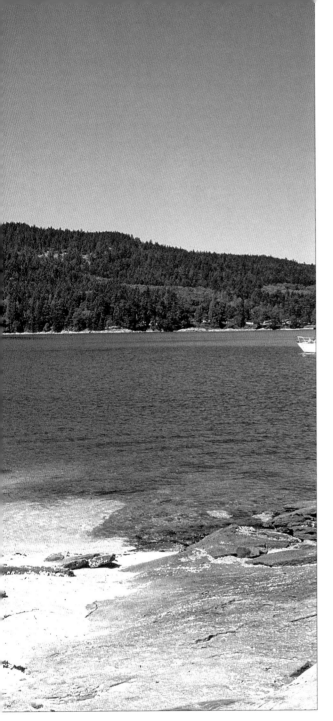

Beautiful midden beach fronts Russell Island.

but the anchorages are quiet. In spring the arbutus trees are in blossom and tiny wildflowers blanket the green meadows. By mid-summer, drought conditions often exist on the islands, with green fields turned to flaxen gold. Fall brings cool nights and morning fog, but this is when the islands are their most beautiful, the shorelines warmed by the coppery tones of berried arbutus and maple leaves that have turned mustard yellow and plum red.

Charts and Publications:

Use charts 3440, 3441 and 3442. Large-scale charts include 3412 for Victoria harbour and 3473 for Active Pass and Montague Harbour. Chart 3477 contains South Pender Island and the north end of Saturna Island. Chartbook 3313 has good detail and covers Gulf Islands to Nanaimo. Use Volume One of the CHS Sailing Directions for the BC Coast, South Portion, and the Canadian Tide and Current Tables, Vol. 5.

The Gulf Islands are ideal for recreational boating with their network of protected anchorages, marine parks, full-service marinas and meandering channels waiting to be explored. The islands' relatively calm waters appeal to powerboaters, while sailors can take advantage of breezes that funnel up or down the various channels, including a summertime thermal wind that often pipes up in the afternoon, allowing for a leisurely sail from one anchorage to the next.

Gulf Islands National Park Reserve

In May 2003, Canada's 40th national park was established in the Gulf Islands. This new park reserve encompasses various islands and numerous islets within its boundary, which extends southeastward from Active Pass and the southern shores of Saltspring Island to the Canada/U.S. border that runs along Boundary Pass and Haro Strait.

Forming much of this new national park were existing provincial parks – Beaumont, Cabbage Island, Princess Margaret, Winter Cove, Sidney Spit, D'Arcy Island and Isle De Lis – along with additional waterfront properties acquired by the Pacific Marine Heritage Legacy, a federal/provincial partnership program established to protect a network of marine and coastal areas along the B.C. coast. Facilities vary and often include a dinghy dock and mooring buoys (free for day use until 3:00 pm , after which an overnight fee is charged).

Winter Cove Marine Park on Saturna Island is part of the Gulf Islands National Park Reserve.

The park encompasses nearly half of Saturna Island – the least developed of the large Gulf Islands – where PMHL acquisitions, ecological reserves and Crown land combine to form the largest parcel of land within the park reserve. In addition, all Crown islets lying within the park boundaries are part of the Gulf Islands National Park Reserve. Many of these are nesting sites for seabirds or haul outs for marine mammals, so visitors should be mindful of their sensitive ecosystems.

The southern Gulf Islands were considered a candidate for national park status for a variety of reasons, including their natural beauty and a mild year-round climate, unique in Canada, which allows a variety of plants and animals to flourish. The mix of vegetation includes arbutus, Garry oak, western red cedar and broadleaf maple, while animals living in this habitat include the Townsend's chipmunk, Douglas squirrel and black-tailed deer.

Boaters have long appreciated the gentle nature of these islands, where a walk ashore poses no risk of encountering a hungry bear or cougar, although a western spotted skunk could be lurking in the bushes. Despite their location within easy cruising distance of three large urban centres – Vancouver, Victoria and Seattle – the Gulf Islands have retained much of their pastoral charm. This was another reason for establishing a national park before the islands succumbed to population and development pressures.

For more information, visit www.pc.gc.ca or write to Gulf Islands National Park Reserve of Canada, 2220 Harbour Road, Sidney, BC V8L 2P6.

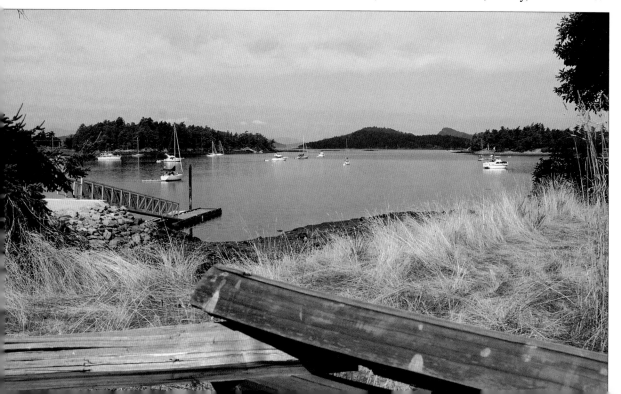

Cruising the Gulf Islands

Prevailing winds in the Strait of Georgia and Juan de Fuca Strait are moderated in the Gulf Islands by the buffer provided by various islands. Most important, these anchorages are not subject to the large seas generated by wind blowing across long stretches of open water. The climate is often described as 'Mediterranean' in summer with one big difference. Once you are in the Gulf Islands, you are never far from a safe anchorage.

Anchorages have mud seabeds and often with a mix of clay, sand and shell. Most anchors set well in this combination of material, although we did have one unusual experience in Selby Cove when our 45-pound CQR was actually bouncing over a mud-and-shell bottom. Perplexed, we hauled the brute up to discover a large clam shell had been neatly pierced in the centre by the point of the plough, defeating the anchor's burying action.

Many anchorages in the Gulf Islands have some current generated by tides but this is rarely a problem. Winter Cove, Sidney Spit, Horton Bay and Russell Island – all have current in the one- to 2-knot range. Tide tables should be consulted when anchoring to allow for variations in depth when anchoring.

Prevailing summertime winds in the Gulf Islands follow two general patterns. Up to South Pender Island, a SW breeze blowing in from Juan de Fuca Strait is the norm during the day and usually dies down in the evening. North of the Penders, northwesterlies prevail as winds adhere to the orientation of Trincomali Channel.

Tides and Currents

For many recreational boaters, the Gulf Islands offer an introduction to the numerous tidal passes you will encounter throughout B.C. waters. A flood tide rushes around both ends of Vancouver Island and in the Gulf Islands the flood current comes from the Strait of Juan de Fuca, flowing through the constricted channels of the Gulf Islands on its way to Georgia Strait. Conversely, an ebb tide brings the water rushing back through the Gulf Islands on its way seaward through the Strait of Juan de Fuca.

Boundary Pass

This eastern entrance to Haro Strait separates the Gulf Islands from the American San Juan Islands to the south and is not an especially tricky pass as long as the wind is not too strong against the current. The international border between Canada and the United States lies along Boundary Pass, which is part of the main shipping route, so it's prudent to cross at right angles and make the transit as quickly as possible. Westbound ships rounding East Point can very quickly be on a collision course with you.

This is a wide pass – over 2 1/2 miles – but currents can exceed 5 knots. On large floods, tide rips and overfalls form off the north end of Patos Island, and tremendous turbulence also forms in the reefs

East Point Lighthouse is a National Historic Site, its fog alarm building recently restored as an interpretive centre for visitors.

Bluffs Park on Galiano Island provides an eagle's eye view of the western entrance to Active Pass.

and shoal water extending from Tumbo Island and East Point on Saturna Island, the main turning point for flood currents entering the Strait of Georgia via Haro Strait. When wind is against tide, large, steep seas will form south and east of East Point. During an ebb, the current sets onto this reef, as the captain of the barque *Rosenfeld* discovered in 1886 when his vessel, in tow from Nanaimo, ran on the rock now bearing the ship's name.

East Point on Saturna Island was widely considered the most dangerous point on the shipping route between Vancouver and Victoria until a fog horn was installed in 1939. The original lighthouse, erected in 1888, was replaced in 1967 with a modern house and skeleton tower. Killer whales (orcas) are frequently sighted in the waters off East Point from May to November, and we have been accompanied by Pacific white-sided dolphins when crossing Boundary Pass.

John Passage

John Passage, lying between Coal and Goudge Islands, is the recommended pass when departing Sidney for points north. Currents through here can run at up to 4 knots but the hazards are obvious – the shallow shelf in the middle of the pass is marked with a day beacon and the reef at the S end is either visible or has wash breaking over the top.

Active Pass

This is the main pass for commercial and recreational vessels heading in and out of the Gulf Islands. It is an S-shaped channel, complicated by the regular transits of large, wave-generating car ferries. These ferries, often travelling at speeds of 10 knots or more in the pass, can kick up a lot of wash and must be given the right of way. Some pleasure boaters avoid Active Pass because of this ferry traffic, but they are missing a beautiful channel abundant with wildlife, towering bluffs and impressive hydraulics. It is also a forgiving pass in the sense that currents aren't usually excessive and there are ways to work the back eddies if you have missed slack.

That aside, Active Pass is a challenging stretch of water and requires a skipper to be on full alert from beginning to end. The ferry traffic is almost constant and the recreational boater should never obstruct or impede the course of a ferry in these restricted waters. Check for approaching ferries both visually and on VHF. The large ferries travelling between Tsawwassen and Swartz Bay usually arrive in Active Pass at the same time. They announce their arrival at Active Pass on Channel 16 but you can also contact Victoria Traffic on Channel 11 to receive details on ferries or other large vessels approaching the pass.

Pass tip sheet – Active Pass

Location: East Entrance: 48°53.06'N, 123°18.00'W just east of U47.
Maximum Flow: Flood, 8 knots. Ebb, 7 knots.
Slack: 15 minutes on large tides.
Anchorages: Westbound, Whaler Bay and Sturdies Bay. Eastbound, Village Bay.
Hazards: Ferry traffic. Heavy tide-rips near Gossip Island, Fairway Bank and near Lion Islets on flood with a NW wind. Whirlpools and tide rips south of Mary Anne Point.
Key to safe transit: Arrive at or close to slack, be alert for ferry traffic, monitor channel 11 or 16 and keep to the starboard side of channel.

Although your arrival should be at slack for this pass, we have found ourselves arriving at the Georgia Strait entrance when a flood is already well underway. Over the years we've watched fish boats and other craft use the back eddies to get through and we too have employed this method. When inbound, we motor between Fairway Bank and the green can buoy at the S end of Gossip Shoals. We stay within a cable of the buoy, keeping close to it and the Galiano Island shoreline as we make our way toward Mary Anne Point. Once around this point, we normally are able to make our way through the pass, keeping to the Galiano Island side. However, during strong floods the current is strong at Matthews Point and we sometimes have to cross over to Lord Point on Mayne Island. We work close along that shore until arriving at the large kelp bed E of Helen Point where we cross back over to the Galiano Island side to continue through the pass.

The area from Helen Point to Collinson Point is where the current is strongest on a flood (up to 7 knots on the Mayne Island side) and where you may be tempted to turn up the engine revs to get free. If it looks dicey or the current appears too strong, you can turn around and drift back into Georgeson Bay to wait for the current to slacken. In our 30 years of transiting this pass, we've only had to do this once.

Stream direction in the pass: From Enterprise Reef in Trincomali Channel, flood currents rapidly gain speed near Helen Point. The stream makes a beeline to the bluffs on the opposite Galiano shore where it turns 90 degrees to starboard. When this stream combines with ferry wash, there can be tremendous overfalls and rips in the area west of Matthews Point.

A Spirit Class BC Ferry heads for Helen Point.

This main stream sets close to Matthews Point (a dangerous area during strong flood tides) and races to Reserve Point, where it makes another course change toward Laura Point. As it approaches Laura Point, the current splits, with some of the stream turning right into Miners Bay while most of the water goes out into Georgia Strait. The stream that turns into Miners Bay creates a clockwise flow of water – a flywheel – which continues well after the flood has ended and often slows the onset of the ebb. This flywheel can cause severe rips where it meets the main stream in the area SE of Mary Anne Point. The spinning direction changes with the ebb to become counterclockwise.

The flood current generates a large back eddy on both sides of the pass from Mary Anne Point into the Strait of Georgia. If you're bucking a flood, the Galiano Island side of the pass should be favoured, for it has less turbulence than the Mayne Island side, and the back eddy can be taken up to and around Mary Anne Point. If the current is too strong here, you can cross over to the Mayne Island side and wait in Naylor Bay or Miners Bay for slack.

An ebb current is generally less turbulent, although ferry wash will continue to be a problem for small recreational boats throughout the pass. Generally speaking, rips are not as bad during ebbs.

If you don't want to transit Active Pass after a late-evening crossing of Georgia Strait or need a spot to wait for slack water, there is a useable anchorage in Whaler Bay just inside the reefs at Cain Point. Further into the bay is a public dock which may or may not have space but be aware that the water is very shallow near the dock. Miners Bay is another possible overnight location, either at anchor or at the government dock (both of which will be bumpy). ***See map for detail.***

For information on Porlier Pass, Dodd Narrows and Gabriola Passage, please see Chapter 2.

THE ANCHORAGES
Sidney Spit 1 Marine Park

Some of the best swimming beaches in the Gulf Islands are found at this marine park. Shaped like a South Seas atoll, but consisting of fine sand rather than crushed coral, Sidney Spit extends nearly a mile from the north end of Sidney Island. Understandably popular with boaters, kayakers and campers, the park is also serviced by a summertime passenger ferry from Sidney.

The beach on the SW side of the bay is especially pretty with clean fine sand, and the anchorage here is usually less crowded than the anchorage near the dinghy dock. However, this side of the bay is popular with locals from Sidney and occasional-

Main dock at Sidney Spit Marine Park with mooring buoys to the right of dock.

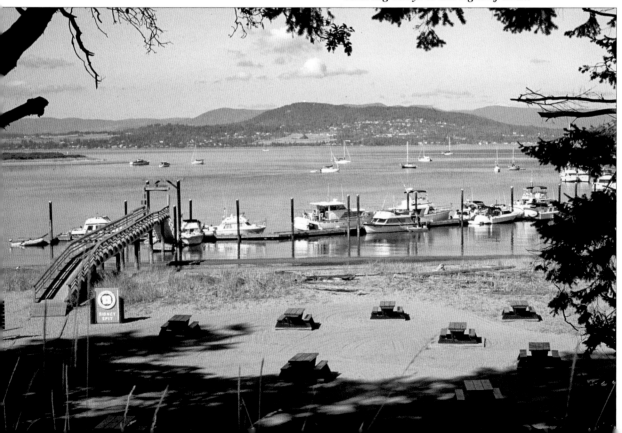

ly can be an unpleasantly noisy anchorage with speed boats roaring up to the beach for an evening beach party. One option for overnight visits is to anchor or moor in the buoy area of the park and visit this beach by dinghy.

Unlike most of the Gulf Islands, which are formed from hard rock outcropping, Sidney Island is made of glacial till. Back in the 1970s, in an effort to prevent erosion of its sandy spit, B.C. Parks workers drove log pilings into the spit to act as anchors for logs. These efforts have had no effect on stabilizing the spit, but the good news is the spit hasn't eroded from winter storms as quickly as first feared. The spit seems to be holding well. However, the main anchorage area where the mooring buoys are located, will likely fill in over the next 50 to 100 years.

Entering the anchorage at Sidney Spit can be confusing, for it is shallow in the middle and filled with eel grass. The two anchoring areas should be approached separately. The northern approach is along the one-fathom line, which runs almost parallel with the spit starting near the beacon light and terminating at the buoy area where the depths open up. The other approach is just off the south beach staying within the one-and-a-half fathom line (see map). In both spots, the holding ground is generally quite good with a mix of mud and sand that's agreeable to all anchors.

A dinghy dock is located beside the park floats and provides access to the park's network of trails. A passenger ferry offers summertime service between Sidney and Sidney Spit, docking at the park's floats. (which are removed in winter). This is a pleasant way to make a quick trip to the town of Sidney.

Park trails lead from Sidney Spit, through forest and meadows, to the shallow lagoon at the head of the anchorage. This is a productive feeding ground for waterbirds, especially during the spring and fall migration seasons. Mandarte Island, which lies off the NE side of Sidney Island, is the largest breeding colony in B.C. for double-crested and pelagic cormorants, glaucous-winged gulls and pigeon guillemots. Known locally as Bare Island, this private island is also a major nesting site for seabirds such as rhinoceros auklets and tufted puffins.

The natural attractions of Sidney Island were not always highly valued. Back in 1860, when the Hudson's Bay Company tried selling lots on the island at 6 shillings an acre, there were few takers. The island was called Sallas by the early settlers, possibly for the thick salal that covered the forest floor, but was renamed 'Sidney' by Captain Richards for the son of his friend Captain William Franklyn. Arriving in Nanaimo from England with his family in 1851, eight-year-old Sidney was brought up to the sea service and was the pilot aboard the *Grappler* when, on the night of April 29, 1883, the northbound steamer lost control after catching fire near Seymour Narrows. Seventy two people – including Sidney Franklyn – lost their lives.

Sidney Spit Marine Park. Below, beach at southwest side of park.

SIDNEY SPIT AT A GLANCE

CHARTS: 3479, 3313, 3441 3462
LAT, LONG: 48°39.00'N 123°21.00'W
PROS: Marine park, good trails, fine sand beaches, swimming, long sunsets, good holding ground, lots of room. Town with marinas nearby.
CONS: Often busy in summer. Comings and goings of small power craft and attendant wake. Anchorage open to NW and SW winds. Mooring buoys have a mixed reputation – check holding if tied up to one.
MUST DO: Swim off beautiful sands of south beach. Walk the trails. Enjoy the sunsets.

In 1902, George Courtney, a freight and passenger agent for the Canadian Pacific Railway in Victoria, bought Sidney Island for $25,000. He imported pheasants from China and held shooting parties on his island until he discovered a large clay deposit at the island's north end. This prompted him to establish the Sidney Island Brick and Tile Company, its bricks used in the building of Victoria's Empress Hotel and the Hotel Vancouver.

The brickyard, which operated for several years and employed about 70 men, ultimately foundered and the island was sold to a syndicate of Victoria businessmen in 1909 for $150,000, with Courtney retaining 200 acres, including his brickyard. In 1921, Courtney's property was acquired by the provincial government and it became, 40 years later, Sidney Spit Marine Park. Remains of the brickyard can be seen along the park's 1.2-mile (2 km) loop trail which leads past a portion of beach strewn with broken red bricks.

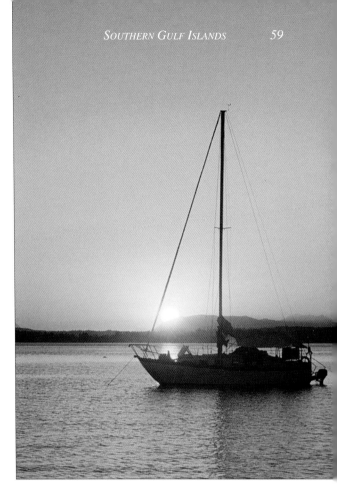

Above, beautiful sunsets are enjoyed at Sidney Spit, where low hills lend a tropical backdrop. Below, a fine beach lies on the bay's SW side.

Top, Sidney Spit Marine Park has good hiking trails. Below, an eight metre sloop beats into a southwesterly near Dock Island, which is part of the Gulf Islands National Park Reserve.

Other Nearby Anchorages

Sidney Spit is near other interesting anchorages which are worth a visit if conditions are agreeable.

D'Arcy Island, once the location of a leper colony, is now a marine park and offers temporary daytime anchorages in settled weather. The most commonly used anchorage is at the north side of D'Arcy near the one fathom (2 m) line but is open to north winds and to chop from Hughes Passage. There are trails on the island and some fine shell-and-sand beaches on the east side of the island. The east side is excellent for exploring by dinghy but watch for afternoon southwesterlies building in Haro Strait.

Rum Island, which obtained its name from its proximity to the United States during prohibition days, is the location of Isle-de-Lis Marine Park. Just 3 miles from Sidney Spit, the island makes for an interesting afternoon stop with fair protection from south winds behind the shell isthmus connecting Rum with Gooch Island, and affords a fine view to Haro Strait. The anchorage is open to swell from the strait and north winds. There is a loop trail around the island. Nearby, just SE of Comet Island and marked by white buoys, is the diving wreck of HMCS *Mackenzie*.

James Island, lying off the west side of Sidney Island, was purchased in 1994 by billionaire telecommunications pioneer Craig McCaw, who transformed the island into an eco-sanctuary. Subdivided into 80 lots, the island has two docks, an airstrip and a Jack Nicklaus-designed golf course. McCaw envisaged his island as a retreat for wealthy conservationists like himself, who would use only electric cars and pursue organic gardening, with part of the island – the saltwater marsh and spit at the north end – protected as a nature conservancy. However, the island was listed for sale in 2012 for $75 million.

SIDNEY

Sidney is the boating hub of the southern Gulf Islands. It has numerous marinas, charter operators, sailing schools, chandleries and boatyards, many of these situated in Tsehum Harbour (also called Shoal Harbour). Van Isle Marina is the harbour's largest facility for transient moorage and can accommodate vessels from 20 to 300 feet in length (call 250-656-1138 or VHF 66A to arrange for moorage). From Van Isle Marina, you can stroll along Harbour Road toward Armstrong Point to the Latch Country Inn, built of timber and stone in 1920 as a summer retreat for B.C.'s lieutenant governor and now a restaurant. You can also walk in the other direction to Resthaven Drive and from there catch a bus to the main part of town or into Victoria.

Across the water, marking the N entrance to Tsehum Harbour, is Curteis Point where Muriel Wylie Blanchet (1891-1961), author of *The Curve of Time*, lived with her five children and set off on upcoast adventures each summer in a 25-foot cabin cruiser. North of Curteis Point is Canoe Cove, where visitor moorage is limited but repair facilities for vessels are excellent. Just up the hill is the cozy Stonehouse Pub.

The Port Sidney Marina is just a short walk from the town. This modern marina and nearby waterfront restaurants are joined by a seaside promenade that leads to the public pier, used by commercial fishing boats and the summer passenger ferry to Sidney Spit Marine Park. Beacon Avenue leads from the public pier into the centre of town where a variety of shops, including supermarkets and a liquor store, are located.

Sidney is a convenient place to rent a car or take a bus to Victoria which is a 30-minute drive away. The Washington State ferry from Anacortes docks in Sidney, and a BC Ferries' terminal is close by in Swartz Bay.

Above, aerial view of Sidney looking north to Saltspring Island. Below, Port Sidney Marina.

VICTORIA

For visitors arriving in Victoria by boat, moorage is available in the heart of the city in its famous Inner Harbour. The city floats are located right in front of the Empress Hotel. Other marinas for visitors include the Coast Harbourside Hotel and Marina, which offers its hotel facilities to marina guests.

Victoria, the capital of B.C., began as a fur trading post when the Hudson's Bay Company built a fort here in 1843. British immigrants soon arrived by sailing ship, having rounded Cape Horn with their fine English china and Victorian ideals, ready to carve a new home in the rugged wilderness. No other Canadian city more openly displays a British colonial heritage, with its double-decker buses, English-style pubs and hundreds of flower baskets hanging from ornate street lamps.

The city was named in honour of Queen Victoria, Empress of India, whose statue graces the lawns leading to the Legislative Buildings. These were designed by British architect Francis Rattenbury and completed in 1898. Rattenbury also designed The Empress, a grand hotel built by the Canadian Pacific Railway. Restored to its Edwardian opulence, The Empress offers afternoon tea daily in the elegant Tea Lobby or expansive front veranda.

A **Visitor InfoCentre** is located north of the city floats. From here it's a short stroll north along Wharf Street, past the original Customs House (1876) at the

Above, B.C.'s provincial legislative buildings, designed by Rattenbury, overlook Victoria's Inner Harbour, as does the regal Empress Hotel (below).

foot of Broughton, to historic Bastion Square. Site of the original fur trading fort, Bastion Square's narrow streets and restored brick buildings include the original courthouse, which now houses the **B.C. Maritime Museum**, its ornate elevator built in 1900 for an elderly judge. Exhibits include Captain Voss's dugout canoe *Tilikum* which he sailed from Victoria to England in 1901. Across the street is the Garrick's Head Pub, which opened for business in 1867. Government Street, between Bastion Square and the harbour, is lined with restored heritage buildings now housing bookstores, chocolate shops and specialty stores selling, among other items, native art and crafts.

South of the harbour, Government Street leads past the Royal British Columbia Museum, rated one of the best museums in North America with its outstanding natural and native history exhibits. Next door is Helmcken House, the oldest house in B.C., built in 1852 by Dr. John Helmcken for his bride, a daughter of Governor Douglas. An island in Johnstone Strait is named for Helmcken, who came from England as a shipboard medical officer.

A few blocks south of Helmcken House, on Government Street, is Carr House – the birthplace of Emily Carr, one of Canada's most acclaimed artists, who was born here in 1871. One block east of Carr House is Beacon Hill Park, the city's oldest municipal park which is named for the navigational range markers that once sat atop its hill overlooking Juan

de Fuca Strait. Today's visitors can enjoy the park's classic English landscape garden while in the strait below a modern beacon (flashing green light) marks the position of Brotchie Ledge which lies on the approach to Victoria Harbour.

Victoria has numerous British-style pubs offering a good selection of local brews.

Princess Margaret Marine Park (Portland Island) 2

By the time Portland Island became a marine park in the 1960s, it had been sold, swapped, bought and bestowed several times over. Its owners have included the Hudson's Bay Company, a group of Hawaiians, an eccentric Englishman and a British princess. The island's most lasting legacy, however, was left by its original inhabitants – the Coast Salish natives. Their kitchen middens, created over time from heaps of crushed clamshells, remain as brilliant white beaches which once guided canoe-paddling natives safely back to shore after dark.

Designated Princess Margaret Marine Park in 1967 and now part of the Gulf Islands National Park Reserve, Portland Island is one of the few marine parks where a boater can check out all its anchorages on foot, for an extensive trail system allows visitors to hike from one anchorage to the next.

The most popular cove, **Princess Bay**, is at the island's SE end, behind the Tortoise Islets. A fair-weather anchorage open to south winds, this spot is popular in summer during settled conditions. Princess Bay is shallow and the holding is only fair in eel grass, soft mud and shell. If south winds come

Aerial view of Princess Bay looking north. South winds can bring uncomfortable swell into the bay.

up in the night, the anchorage will also be lumpy. However, in sunny, calm conditions it's a great anchorage and will probably be busy, so plan to arrive by noon to find a good spot.

The better overnight anchorage lies at the north end of the island in **Royal Cove**, located behind Chads Island. In this pretty cove, it's best to tie a stern line to shore and try to keep your bow pointed into the remnant ferry swells that roll in during the latter stages of a high tide. Holding here is good and the cove is fairly well protected from almost all wind. Although depths close to shore vary, up to a dozen boats can anchor here quite comfortably along the E and W shores. Use of outboards is eschewed in this small cove and most people row the short distance to the dinghy dock to access the park trails.

Royal Cove anchorage can accommodate plenty of boats moored with a stern line to shore.

There are several temporary anchorages at Portland Island. These include the anchoring areas north and south of Pellow Islets, which are frequented by dive vessels exploring B.C.'s first artificial reef, the wreck of the sunken freighter *G.B. Church*. Entering the narrow anchorage north of the islets requires careful pilotage to avoid numerous rocks and reefs. This is an excellent area to explore by dinghy or on foot along the shore. Other day stops can be found along the island's west shore, either in a nook SW of Royal Cove or in a bight south of Kanaka Bluff where a lovely shell beach stretches along the SW shore opposite Brackman Island, an off-limits ecological reserve. While anchored here, our boat bobbing in the ferry swells off Satellite Channel, we have enjoyed many a pleasant afternoon hiking the numerous trails of the island. Tree species include some beautiful stands of arbutus and Garry oak on the NW side of the island. In early spring there is plenty of birdlife, especially along the south and east sides of the island, including bufflehead, mergansers, surf scoters and other sea ducks. River otters and seals also frequent this side of the island.

The shoreside trail encircles most of the island while others cut across the middle, past the old fruit orchard planted in the 1920s by Frank 'One Arm' Sutton, who lost an arm while fighting in the Gallipoli campaign of World War I. Sutton, who bought the island with funds he won betting on horse races while living in China, planned to raise and train thoroughbred race horses on Portland Island. However, the stock market crash of 1929 wiped out his fortune and brought an end to his aspirations.

The island's next owner was Saltspring entrepreneur Gavin Mouat, who later traded Portland Island to the provincial government in exchange for timber rights elsewhere. When Queen Elizabeth's younger sister Margaret paid the province a visit during its centennial year, 1958, the government decided the island was fit for a princess and presented it to her as a gift. Princess Margaret returned the island when the province decided to designate it a marine park, naming it in her honour.

The island itself was named, in 1858, for the *HMS Portland*, commanded by Captain Henry Chads. The following year, the Hudson's Bay Company gave the island to a group of Hawaiians, known as Kanakas, who had been employed to act as interpreters between the coastal natives and the English-speaking fur traders. Sheep once roamed Portland, but were herded up in 1989 to prevent damage to the island's grassland and wild flowers. Park visitors are now more likely to encounter indigenous species, such as a river otter swimming near shore or, seen from the whiteshell beaches overlooking Satellite Channel, a pod of killer whales.

Top, a boardwalk trail leads across the swampy central part of Portland Island. Middle, a fine midden beach lies along the southwest shoreline. Bottom, a shoreside view of Princess Bay.

Russell Island [3]

Russell Island, lying at the entrance to Fulford Harbour on Saltspring Island, became protected park land under the Pacific Marine Heritage Legacy and is now part of the Gulf Islands National Park Reserve. Boats anchor in the lee of Russell Island, where the vista is one of mountains rising above Fulford Harbour. The anchorage is protected from most winds, with Saltspring Island providing good shelter from northwesterlies and Russell Island providing good protection from south winds which deflect away from the anchorage. Other than occasional ferry wake from Fulford Harbour, the anchorage is very quiet. Local boaters often tie a line ashore, pulling themselves out of the way of most current and the worst of errant chop.

Settled by Hawaiians (known as Kanakas) in the late 1800s, Russell Island is easy to explore. A trail leads round the west end of the island, past the original homestead, to a charming small shell

The anchorage at Russell Island is scenic and sheltered, with a shell beach and trails to explore.

beach at its western end. There, set among the arbutus and Garry oak which grow on the island, along with Douglas fir and lodgepole pine, are several picnic tables and wooden benches. The Hawaiian children who once lived on Russell Island would attend, by boat, the one-room schoolhouse at Beaver Point on Saltspring Island. Their ancestors had come to the region as employees of the Hudson's Bay Company, many of them eventually settling on nearby Portland Island and southern Saltspring Island.

RUSSELL ISLAND AT A GLANCE

CHARTS: 3313, 3478, 3441, 3462
LAT LONG: 48°45.00N 123°24.75W
PROS: Large anchoring area. Usually uncrowded. Pretty trail around west end of island, beautiful small shell beach good for swimming. Very good holding ground. Good protection from S winds.
CONS: Somewhat exposed to NW and E winds. Open to some ferry wake and current.
MUST DO: Visit clean shell beach and go for a swim. Take 30-minute hike around island.

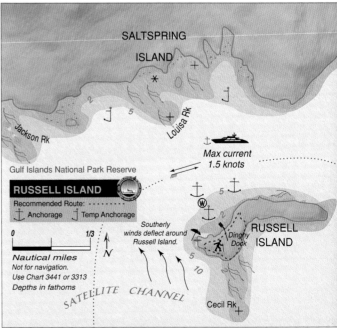

Tod Inlet   4

Boaters visiting fjord-like Saanich Inlet have the opportunity to visit one of B.C.'s most popular tourist attractions – the **Butchart Gardens**. Anchorage can be gained in adjacent **Butchart Cove** at the entrance to Tod Inlet, where a dinghy dock provides summer access to the gardens' back entrance. The cove also has 4 mooring buoys and stern-tie rings for

visitor use. Anchoring near the mooring buoys is not allowed because of submerged cables.

Butchart Cove can be crowded in summer, but Tod Inlet provides good alternative anchorage and is surrounded by parkland. The main anchorage near the head of **Tod Inlet** is reached via a narrow, cliff-sided entrance. A sheltered anchorage with good holding in mud, it is bounded by steep slopes on one side and gentle hillsides on the other, where wildflowers flourish in summer. A dinghy dock on the north side of the inlet provides access to shore, where a good hike can be taken up the trail that parallels Tod Creek to Wallace Drive. Another trail leads from the dinghy dock to the Butchart Gardens. Keep to the left at any forks as you head north out of the park for the five-minute walk to the main gates.

Jennie Butchart began cultivating her idyllic gardens in 1904, shortly after a summer home was built adjacent to her husband's cement factory near Tod Inlet. An inexperienced gardener at the outset, she quickly developed an eye for colour and form,

Above left, Butchart Cove with mooring buoys and dinghy dock. Left, The Butchart's Sunken Garden. Below, Tod Inlet is well sheltered and peaceful.

TOD INLET AT A GLANCE

CHARTS: 3313, 3441
LAT LONG: 48°34.43'N 123°28.3W
PROS: Quiet and pretty anchorage. Access to famous Butchart Gardens. Good holding, sheltered from all winds.
CONS: Occasionally busy. Long detour from main channels.
MUST DO: Well, visit Butchart Gardens of course! Also, hike the trail along Tod Creek.

and flower gardens soon surrounded the family residence. Assisted by a Japanese landscape artist, a Scottish gardener and workers from the cement plant, Mrs. Butchart next oversaw the completion of the Japanese Garden, the property's first formal garden, which sloped from the house's lawn to Butchart Cove where Mr. Butchart kept a boat moored.

The Japanese Garden was soon joined by the Sunken Garden – a challenge Mrs. Butchart couldn't resist after her husband's cement company had exhausted the site's limestone quarry. Hanging over the sides of the quarry in a bosun's chair, Mrs. Butchart spent hours tucking ivy into the rock walls' pockets and crevices. Water from a natural spring was allowed to fill the deepest part of the quarry, transforming it into a shimmering lake, with stone stairs leading up to a viewpoint.

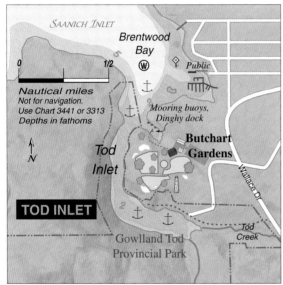

In winter, the Butcharts would embark on foreign voyages, collecting exotic flowers and Italian sculptures for their gardens. They named their home 'Benvenuto', Italian for 'Welcome', and warmly welcomed all visitors to their estate. Summer houses were scattered about the property where afternoon tea was served to all who came to view the gardens. This tradition continued until the sheer number of visitors made it impossible, although the gardens remained open to all.

Today more than a million visitors annually view the Butchart Gardens, which feature a Saturday night fireworks display in July and August. The summer season is the Gardens' busiest and boaters with flexible schedules are well advised to visit the grounds in late afternoon or early evening to avoid the crowds. At night the gardens are transformed with hundreds of tiny lights.

Sansum Narrows

The most direct route north from Saanich Inlet is via scenic, steep-sided Sansum Narrows, where the wind – fed by mountain valleys – often funnels its length. Currents flow N on a flood tide, south on an ebb, and rarely exceed 3 knots, although whirlpools and tide-rips can occur around Burial Islet, and between Sansum and Bold Bluff Points. The famous sailing couple Miles and Beryl Smeeton once owned a farmhouse at Musgrave Landing on a bluff overlooking the narrows. Cowichan Bay, Genoa Bay and Maple Bay offer nearby sheltered anchorage and marina facilities for boaters transiting the narrows.

The panoramic view from Mount Maxwell on Saltspring Island looking to Sansum Narrows.

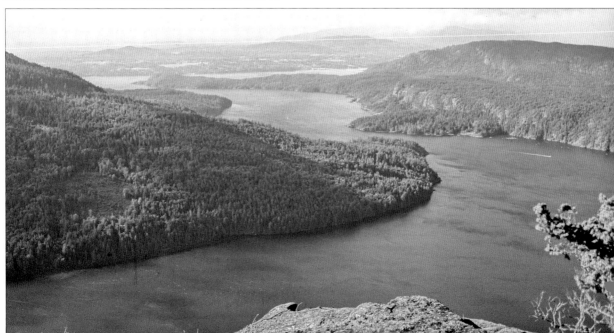

Bedwell Harbour, [5]
South Pender Island

Bedwell Harbour has long been a popular summer-time port of entry for boaters entering Canadian waters from the American San Juans. After clearing Canada Customs, boaters often stay at the adjacent resort facilities or head over to the mooring buoys at **Beaumont Marine Park**, which is part of the Gulf Islands National Park Reserve. There is also room to anchor in this wide bight, in good holding of mud

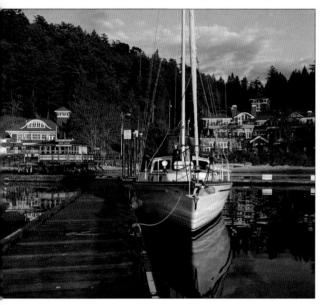

and sand, where some shelter is provided from the SE winds to which Bedwell Harbour is exposed.

Boaters entering (or re-entering) Canadian waters can clear **customs** by telephone in Bedwell Harbour from May through September. The **Poets Cove Resort, Spa and Marina** is located beside the customs dock. Its facilities include a fuel dock, swimming pool and restaurant. The resort sits on a site once occupied by a tiny shack of a post office built in 1902. Back then, the coal-fired *SS Otter* would dock twice a week in Bedwell Harbour, bringing mail and supplies to local residents.

An important archaeological site is located along the shores of the canal that joins Bedwell Harbour with Port Browning. Excavated in the mid-1980s, the Helisen site contained artifacts dating back 3,500 years. It's located on the North Pender Island side of the bridge joining the two islands.

South Pender Island is the more rugged and sparsely populated of the two Penders, and Beaumont Marine Park was established here back in 1962 on land donated by the philanthropist Ernest Godfrey Beaumont. He had purchased this property in 1918 from Gilbert Ainslie, an Englishman who had his log cabin on Saturna Island dismantled and moved to Bedwell Harbour in 1905 with the aid of the crew of *HMS Egeria* who were doing survey work in the area.

Poets Cove Marina is right beside the Canada Customs dock in Bedwell Harbour.

The boundary between Canadian and American waters was established in 1872, but the islanders who lived on either side of Boundary Pass treated this international border as an opportunity to pursue a profitable form of free trade, also known as smuggling. Pender Island residents would sail or row across Boundary Pass to Friday Harbor to buy cheaper groceries, and residents of the San Juans would buy wool from sheep farmers on Pender, then sell this commodity at twice the price back home. During prohibition, rum-runners would pay local farmers to hide sacks of bottled booze in their sheds, but the islanders opted out of this illicit and increasingly dangerous activity as hardened criminals became attracted to its high stakes.

Logging was another early industry on South Pender, and in the 1890s large schooners would arrive to take on their cargoes of small logs, called props, that were destined for Mexico and South America for shoring up mine tunnels. Decades later, when the provincial government was establishing Beaumont Marine Park, additional acreage was donated by the Crown Zellerbach forestry company.

The park's shoreside path, dotted with benches, provides splendid views overlooking the harbour. This trail, set atop a bluff, is accessed by a set of wooden stairs located near the park's westernmost mooring buoys, which lie east of Skull Islet.

Reefs extend westward from Skull Islet toward an islet connected to shore by an isthmus. This shallow, beach-lined cove is suitable for exploration by dinghy and offers good spots for picnicking. For hiking enthusiasts, the shoreside trail continues inland where it eventually leads into adjoining Mount Norman Regional Park. An hour-long climb to a viewing platform at the top of Mount Norman rewards hikers with a panoramic look at neighbouring islands and surrounding channels, where international boundaries dissolve into the seascape.

Above, the beach at Beaumont Marine Park.
Below, looking south across the anchorage.

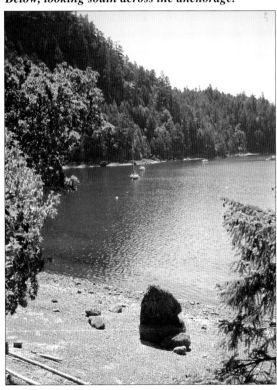

BEDWELL HARBOUR AT A GLANCE

CHARTS: 3477, 3313, 3441, 3462
LAT LONG: 48°45'N 123°14.04'W
PROS: Marine park, trails, beach. Large anchorage with very good holding. Pubs, resorts and marinas nearby. Good dinghy exploring. Handy spot after clearing customs for U.S. boaters.
CONS: Open to S wind, sometimes busy.
MUST DO: Hike trails of Beaumont Marine Park and Mount Norman Regional Park. Explore the pass to Shark Cove by dinghy.

Boat Passage, lying between Saturna and Samuel Islands, is a tight fit for most vessels.

Saturna Island

Saturna Island promises peace and solitude for residents and boaters alike. Sparsely populated and not directly linked by ferry to Vancouver, this scenic island has retained its rural atmosphere and small-town friendliness. Passing motorists wave to you when you're hiking the quiet roads of Saturna, and most of the island's summer visitors are boaters because there is no overnight campground on the island and only a handful of bed-and-breakfast inns.

We have enjoyed Saturna in every season and celebrated many a holiday in the embrace of her shoreline, including a peaceful Christmas in Winter Cove. We have hiked her quiet roads under a warm September sun and been blown out of Boot Cove during an Easter gale. Year after year we enjoy returning to Saturna where change comes slowly and our favourite anchorages are like familiar faces.

Nearly half of the Gulf Islands National Park Reserve is situated on Saturna Island, where BC Crown Lands, ecological reserves and recent land acquisitions interconnect to form a tract of mountainous parkland dominating the island's interior and stretching eastward to the shores of Narvaez Bay. Boaters can cycle or hike to Saturna's interior parkland from either Winter Cove or Lyall Harbour (the latter is closer) by taking East Point Road to the head of Lyall Harbour where the Saturna General Store is situated at the crossroads.

From here take Harris Road into the park area, turning left onto Staples Road. This gravel road loops through forest toward the summit of Mount Warburton Pike, Saturna's highest mountain at 1,425 feet (430 m). The distance from Saturna General Store to Mount Warburton Pike is about 1 1/2 miles (2.5 km). Nearby is the Brown Ridge Nature Trail, overlooking Plumper Sound and Boundary Pass. Mount Warburton Pike was named in honour of an settler who arrived in 1884 to pursue sheep farming. Not only was Pike widely travelled and Oxford educated, he was an astute businessman who soon owned much of Saturna Island. On the other side of

Left, the sweeping views from atop Mt. Warburton Pike. Opposite, the popular Winter Cove anchorage with the park's dinghy dock in foreground.

the island, a long, straight section of East Point Road runs from Winter Cove Marine Park to East Point Lighthouse, affording splendid views of the Strait of Georgia with some flat foreshore areas that are ideal for a picnic lunch. To make it to East Point and back in a few hours, a bicycle is recommended.

Saturna Island anchorages (and Samuel Island) are open to NW winds, although it does have to be blowing fairly strong before it is a problem in Winter Cove. If a really bad NW wind is forecast, consider Horton Bay or Port Browning.

Winter Cove 6

A circular-shaped cove lying between Saturna and Samuel Islands, this marine park anchorage provides good holding ground and shelter from all but strong northwesterlies. One October weekend we comfortably rode out a 38-knot southerly in this cove, which we had all to ourselves, in contrast to summer weekends when the anchorage fills up with boats. Winter Cove is especially busy when the popular Lamb Barbecue is held here on Canada Day, July 1st. The annual Dogs & Dog Show is held on the Sunday of the Labour Day Weekend.

A good spot to anchor is west of the marine park's launch ramp, between shore and a shallow spot in the middle of the cove. On shore, a dinghy dock is situated beside the boat launch, adjacent to a grassy picnic area with wooden tables and a small parking lot. From here a trail loops through the woods and along the Strait of Georgia shoreline to Winter Point where you can watch the tide rushing through Boat Passage.

During prohibition, rumrunners used this narrow, reef-strewn pass to dodge government revenue boats patrolling the Strait of Georgia. Today the pass is used as a shortcut by small boats heading to Cabbage Island and can be transited at HW slack. Currents in Boat Passage can reach 6 knots or more, with dangerous whirlpools during spring tides, and there is a set onto the rocks extending from Ralph Grey Point on Samuel Island. Should you decide to attempt it, do so at HW slack (when the pass will have about 15 feet of depth) and, if eastbound, proceed slowly in the centre of the channel. Remain parallel with the stream (and the Saturna shoreline) until you are about 100 yards (90 m) E of the entrance, then turn to port to clear the S end of Anniversary Island. Chart 3313, page 12, gives good detail of Winter Cove and this pass.

Should valour give way to caution, another shortcut is through Georgeson Passage, between Curlew

WINTER COVE AT A GLANCE
CHARTS: 3477, 3313, 3442
LAT LONG: Entrance: 48°48.93'N 123°12.61'W
PROS: Beautiful setting, large area for anchoring. Good holding ground in mud. Marine park with excellent trails. Store and fuel nearby. Good dinghy exploring nearby. Views out to Georgia Strait.
CONS: Occasionally busy. Somewhat open to NW wind. Shallow in parts, with several drying reefs and submerged rocks.
MUST DO: Walk the trail to Boat Pass when current is running at full flood. Explore the Belle Chain Islets by dinghy.

use this pass at HW slack

Georgeson I

Bennett
Bay

Georgeson Passage

5

Curlew
Island

10

HORTON
BAY

Robson
Channel

Public

Max current
5 knots

MAYNE
ISLAND

5

Lizard I

SAMUEL
ISLAND

IRISH
BAY

St. John Pt

0   1/2

Nautical miles

Not for navigation:
Use Chart 3477 or 3313
Depths in fathoms

N

SATURNA ISLAND & AREA

CRUISE ROUTES

Recommended Route: ·········
⚓ Anchorage   ⚓ Temp Anchorage
Ⓦ Waypoint 50°36.89'N 126°38.25'W

PLUMPER
SOUND

An aerial view of Winter Cove

S T R A I T   O F   G E O R G I A

Belle Chain Islets

Anniversary I

Northerly
winds can come
thru low point here

Ralph Grey Pt

BOAT PASSAGE
Max current
8 knots

Russell Reef

Ⓦ

2

Minx
Reef

5

Veruna
Bay

King
Islets

WINTER
COVE

Dinghy
Dock

WINTER COVE
MARINE PARK

Gulf Islands National Park Reserve

Winter Cove Rd

East Pt. Rd

East Point Rd

SATURNA
ISLAND

MT. D

Crispin
Rk

Fl(2+1)R

LYALL
HARBOUR

2

B.C. Ferries

U58

Fuel /
public

Store/
Pub

East Pt. Rd

Payne Pt

Boot
Cove

Saturna
General Store / LCB

Narvaez Bay Rd

Schoo
(tennis cou

Payne Rd.

To Mt Warburton Pike

Elliot
Bluff

Harris Rd.

Staples Road

A boardwalk trail in Winter Cove Marine Park

and Samuel Islands. Upon clearing Samuel Island, turn to starboard and navigate between the islands (see map) south of the Belle Chain Islets and continue past Russell Reef to Cabbage Island. Vessels proceeding north into Georgia Strait can take the small pass between Georgeson Island and the reef extending from Mayne Island, being careful to transit at HW when there is ample depth to maneuver (depth at LW is about 8 feet). Currents in this little pass can be significant, in the 5-knot range, and because of the adjacent reef should be navigated with care. At LW in calm conditions there is room to go between Georgeson Island and the S reef or go around the last island in the Belle Chain group. Currents in Georgeson Passage between Curlew and Samuel Islands can also reach 5 knots.

Lyall Harbour 7

When other Gulf Island anchorages are chock-a-block with boats at the height of summer, Lyall Harbour can be surprisingly quiet. The inter-island car ferry docks at the mouth of this harbour and pleasure craft can tie to an adjacent public float, but the anchorage itself is often ignored. We avoid the

Right, a trailside view of the Strait of Georgia and Mount Baker from Winter Cove Marine Park.

Below, a summer sunset in Lyall Harbour.

area just to the east of the public dock where we once snagged our anchor on some debris and prefer instead to anchor near the head in about 30' of water. The anchorage is exposed to NW winds but the holding ground is very good in thick mud and there is plenty of room to let out scope.

Lyall Harbour's steep slopes are thickly treed and dotted with hillside homes. A private marina lies along the south side. You can disembark by dinghy at this marina and hike up to East Point Road which, if taken in a westerly direction, leads to Saturna's main general store (at Narvaez Bay Road junction) where you can purchase groceries, locally baked bread and cookies, fresh produce and liquor (including wines produced locally by the Saturna Island Family Estate Winery). A smaller general store is located beside the government float, where the Lighthouse Pub is open year-round. Fuel is available from the government dock.

At the head of Lyall Harbour, where rubber boots are recommended for hauling your dinghy across the muddy foreshore, a waterfront village lies on the floor of a small valley. Sunset Boulevard leads through the centre of this hamlet, past the school-

house, playground and adjacent tennis courts. We have often headed ashore for a leisurely game of tennis, enjoying the early morning coolness on a hot summer's day or, better yet, the bright afternoons of autumn when the falling leaves of surrounding maple trees drift lazily onto the courts.

Nearby **Boot Cove** is not attractive as an anchorage. It has numerous small buoys and an aquaculture operation is located along the west side. The cove can also be surprisingly gusty in SE winds.

Irish Bay, Samuel Island 8

Situated on the S side of Samuel Island is the excellent anchorage of Irish Bay. We tend to anchor here in bad weather, when shelter from the wind is more critical than shoreside activities, for privately owned Samuel Island offers no opportunities for exploration above the HW mark. However, the anchorage is lovely in fair weather, when sunlight sparkles on the water and the shoreside trails of Winter Cove Marine Park are a short dinghy ride away. When seeking shelter from northerlies, we anchor beneath the treed cliffs at the NW end of the bay. The S part of the bay is sheltered from southeasterlies.

Samuel Island has been owned by various prominent people, including a relative of Earl Grey, who was Governor General of Canada from 1904 to 1911, and A.J.P. Taylor, the Vancouver engineer who developed British Properties and the Lions Gate Bridge. Taylor had a lodge built overlooking Winter Cove where he would entertain whenever he and guests visited the island, their luxury yachts anchored in Irish Bay. He eventually sold Samuel Island to food-store magnate Garfield Weston.

During World War II, the Belle Chain Islets were used for target practice by fighters and bombers, much to the dismay of the resident caretaker on Samuel Island. Not only did he and his family have to endure the incessant drone of aircraft and their dropping of cartridge cases, in one instance the lodge overlooking Winter Cove was mistakenly fired at, with a bullet narrowly missing one of the caretaker's daughters. A complaint was filed and the training pilots were told to be more careful about hitting their target.

Nearby **Horton Bay** on Mayne Island offers good shelter in NW winds. The anchorage does, however, experience tidal current, which should be taken into account when anchoring.

Samuel Island's Irish Bay is wide, deep and a good alternative anchorage to Winter Cove.

Cabbage Island
Marine Park 9

There's an exotic, isolated feel to Cabbage Island, lying as it does on the outer edge of the Gulf Islands with the Strait of Georgia stretching into the distance. When approaching the anchorage of Reef Harbour, the island appears almost tropical with its green foliage and fringe of white sand. The park's mooring buoys are located in Reef Harbour (not really a harbour) where the reef regularly disappears at HW. The buoys are well utilized in summer, and you'll be lucky to find one empty if you arrive late in the day. However, the holding ground is good in mud and broken shell and, in settled conditions, the anchorage is more than adequate.

In addition to the beautiful beach overlooking the anchorage, there are also camping and picnicking facilities on shore. At LW, you can take an interesting half-hour hike around Cabbage Island, where conglomerate rock extends from its eastern shore toward Tumbo Island. Only 11 acres in size, tiny Cabbage Island reportedly sold for a dollar an acre in 1888. A coal mine briefly operated on adjacent Tumbo Island in the 1890s, and in the early 1900s a

Above, aerial view (looking north) of Cabbage Island and Reef Harbour with mooring buoys. Below, the beach makes for good swimming.

hermit lived on the island's west side until he was shot dead one night while exchanging gunfire with an unwelcome visitor.

Tumbo Island was purchased by the Pacific Marine Heritage Legacy program in 1997, and is now part of the Gulf Islands National Park. The island's natural vegetation includes groves of Garry oak, arbutus and old-growth Douglas fir, and its freshwater marsh is a habitat for waterfowl.

CABBAGE ISLAND AT A GLANCE
CHARTS: 3313, 3441, 3462
LAT LONG: 48°47.92'N 123°05.86'W
PROS: Marine park with good trails and swimming beaches. Fairly large area for anchoring with good holding ground.
CONS: A fair-weather anchorage, shallow in places. Open to winds coming off Georgia Strait. Attracts revellers on summer long weekends.
MUST DO: Walk Cabbage Island, relax on the beach, explore the tidal pools.

Otter Bay, North Pender Island 10

Otter Bay is best known for its marina (located in Hyashi Cove), which is an ideal family destination with facilities that include a heated swimming pool, playground, general store, showers, laundry and washrooms. Bicycles can be hired at the marina for a tour of North Pender, its hilly and winding roads leading past leafy lanes and country craft shops. Nearby attractions include the island's nine-hole golf course, which is a 15-minute walk or a quick shuttle ride from Otter Bay Marina.

A breakwater protects the floats from most of the wash generated by the car ferry that docks at the small terminal around the corner from Otter Bay.

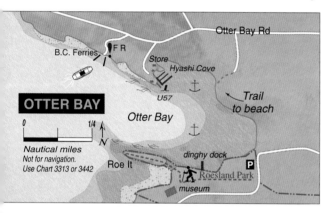

Keep the green spar buoy to port when approaching the marina. If the marina is full, you can anchor in Hyashi Cove east of the marina, riding parallel with the outside dock. With a stern anchor or a line ashore, the rolling action from the ground swell of the ferry traffic will be reduced.

The anchorage at the head of Otter Bay provides shelter from SE weather and the mud bottom is very good. Setting a stern anchor will keep your bow pointed into the occasional ferry wave coming into the bay. The south shore of Otter Bay, where the Roesland resort operated for 70 years, is now parkland. Part of the Gulf Islands National Park Reserve, this parcel of second-growth forest contains numerous trails and can be accessed by a Parks Canada dinghy dock. Roesland was the homestead of Scottish pioneers Robert and Margaret Roe before it became a rustic cottage resort in the 1920s. The original farmhouse became the resort's main lodge and is now a museum operated by volunteers and open to visitors on summer weekends. The park trails lead to a viewpoint on Roe Islet, accessed by a footbridge, and inland to a small lake.

Prevost Island 11

One of our perennial favourite destinations of the entire coast is Prevost Island. Situated in the hub of the southern Gulf Islands, surrounded by ferry routes and marine traffic heading to and from Active Pass, this island has miraculously maintained an aura of

Otter Bay Marina

isolation. Accessible only by private craft, pastoral Prevost Island remains relatively unchanged by the waves of development that have washed over many of the Gulf Islands.

Prevost Island was named by Captain Richards in 1859 for Captain James Charles Prevost, commander of the *HMS Satellite* and the commissioner appointed to settle the San Juan boundary dispute between B.C. and the United States. However, it was Digby de Burgh, an Irish nobleman from County Limerick, who determined the fate of Prevost when he bought the island in the 1920s for raising sheep, goats and cattle. De Burgh's son Hubert and daughter-in-law Jean eventually took over the island farm, where they raised four daughters – one of whom became a concert pianist.

Much of the island remains in the family's hands, although waterfront houses began appearing in the 1980s along the northwest side. When one was built at our favourite nook in Selby Cove, we gloomily speculated that Prevost's days as a destination providing pristine anchorages were numbered. Then, in 1996, the Pacific Marine Heritage Legacy came to the rescue. This federal/provincial program, established to protect a network of marine areas along the B.C. coast, bought portions of waterfront in James Bay and Selby Cove. Private property became park-

Looking north over Prevost Island to Glenthorne Passage and Annette Inlet. (See map page 82.)

land and sheep trails became public footpaths. This parkland has since become part of the Gulf Islands National Park (see map page 82).

The channels and currents around Prevost provide interesting cruising and a few challenges. Although currents rarely exceed 2 or 3 knots in Captain Passage, it would be easy, with a lapse of concentration, to be swept toward Horda Reef (named after the Norwegian steamer that ran aground here in 1901) off the west side of Prevost. This is especially hazardous if you are southbound with an ebb current, as the set to the reef is quite pronounced. Otherwise, the currents follow the channel. The only cross eddy we've noticed is in the narrowest part of the passage near Nose Point, where some of the current splits off into Long Harbour with a set to Nose Point.

Prevost is deeply indented with an abundance of anchorages, and it seems everyone has a favourite among the four facing Captain Passage. **Glenthorne Passage** provides good shelter in most winds but is the most developed, with private docks lining the anchorage's SW side along Secret Island. The next anchorage over is **Annette Inlet**, a long narrow inlet which provides good shelter, but is shallow in parts and has limited swinging room, so is suited for tying a stern line ashore. The entrance should be approached with caution for there is a drying rock lying off its mouth and shoal depths on the north side. Hiking in Annette Inlet is limited to the fore-

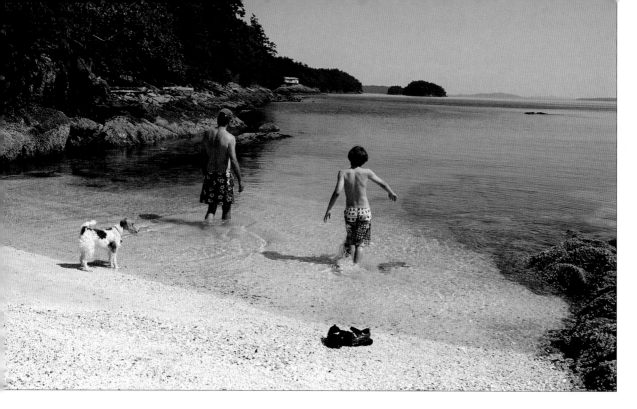

Above, a shell beach lies between Owl Island (privately owned) and an adjacent islet on the southwest side of Prevost Island. Below, Selby Cove on Prevost Island provides a tranquil retreat from the busier parks.

shore and, with an extensive mud flat at the head, heading ashore at LW means wearing a pair of rubber boots. At HW it's possible to see right across the lowland at the head of Annette Inlet to Ellen Bay on the other side of the island.

Selby Cove, on the island's NW side, is our favourite for its peaceful setting, with sheep often seen grazing in the pasture at its head. River otters frequent the foreshore, and surf scoters, mergansers and other sea ducks gather here in winter. Selby Cove is fairly well sheltered and most westerlies die out about halfway into the cove. The worst winds seem to come from the south. There is an intriguing

blind spot in strong S winds, about 150 yards S of the islet that is joined to shore by a drying tombolo near Annette Point. We once noticed that a boat anchored in this spot didn't receive a breath of wind even with 25 knots gusting through the cove.

What appears to be a derelict float lies about two-thirds of the way into the cove with a sign telling boaters to keep off. Fortunately, the main anchoring area remains unencumbered, and the holding ground is good in mud and shell in about 20 feet. We normally anchor between the derelict float and a private dock extending from the west shore which serves a solitary house perched dramatically atop the cliff.

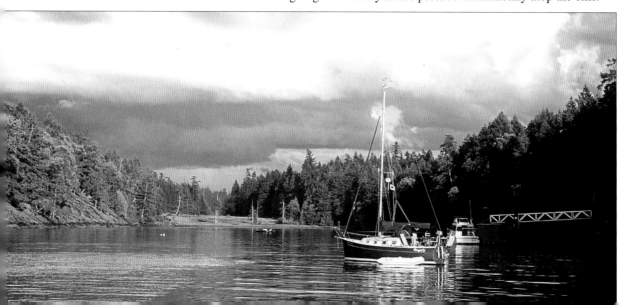

The opposite shoreline is only slightly less rugged, with a hillside house situated in a bight near the entrance. Further into the cove is another, broader bight where we have anchored with a stern line ashore. Its small beach is backed by a grass clearing bordered by young spruce trees that provides a good picnic spot with views overlooking the anchorage and passing boat traffic in Captain Passage. This property is part of the island's parkland, and a trail can be followed from here to James Bay.

Although exposed to northwesterlies, **James Bay** has good holding ground and the water is fairly deep, making it a safe anchorage in most conditions. We once rode out a winter gale here with SE winds of 49 knots reported at East Point on Saturna Island. Although a few strong gusts did find us in James Bay, the thickly treed shoreline acted as a buffer and our anchor easily held in 50 feet of water near the head of the bay.

James Bay is now almost completely surrounded by park property, from its NE entrance point to the head and halfway along its SW shoreline, where a small orchard has always been an attraction with its springtime apple blossoms and fall fruit. The reef extending from the W shore makes for interesting exploring at low tide. Boaters can head ashore to the broad gravel beach at the bay's head (called O'Reilly Beach) where a valley leads inland and a sheep trail can be hiked to Peile Point. The entire Peile Point peninsula, with views overlooking Trincomali Channel, is part of the park.

Exposed to southeasterlies and ferry wash off Swanson Channel, **Ellen Bay** is nonetheless an adequate anchorage with its deep water and mud holding ground. Depths here reach 90 feet (27 m) in the middle of the bay and are 55 feet (17 m) near the head, so the ferry swells are long and gentle. Where the foreshore of Ellen Bay ends, private farmland begins. When a friend of ours anchored in Ellen Bay one spring to avoid a northwesterly forecast for overnight, he said he hardly noticed the ferry swells but he could hear the sound of a tractor on shore.

Above, the James Bay shoreline includes an old orchard. Below, vessels can tuck well into the bay.

PREVOST ISLAND AT A GLANCE

CHARTS: 3478 or 3313 (See map page 82.)
PROS: The four anchorages facing NW all have their charms with, generally, good holding ground. Good dinghy exploring. Annette Inlet is safest in a NW wind. James Bay is best in S winds.
CONS: James Bay and Selby Cove are open to NW winds, Annette Inlet has a tricky entrance and Glenthorne Passage anchorage is usually busy in the summer.
MUST DO: Walk trails from James Bay. Visit shell beaches on Hawkins Island or nearby islets.

Hawkins Island 12

These tiny islands tucked along the east shore of Prevost Island have long been one of our secret get-away spots in the Gulf Islands. Now that they are part of the Gulf Islands National Park Reserve, access is restricted due to their being a habitat for several species of birds, including oystercatchers and migrating surf scoters. However, the foreshore is still a good place to picnic or spend a summer afternoon lounging in the sun.

The midden beach at Hawkins Island.

After anchoring in the channel between Prevost and Hawkins Islands, we like to row ashore to the clamshell midden at the NW end of the largest of the three islets. An aquaculture operation for scallops currently occupies part of the channel between Hawkins and Prevost, but the little beach has retained its appeal and on a sunny summer afternoon it provides a splendid view of boats lazily sailing up

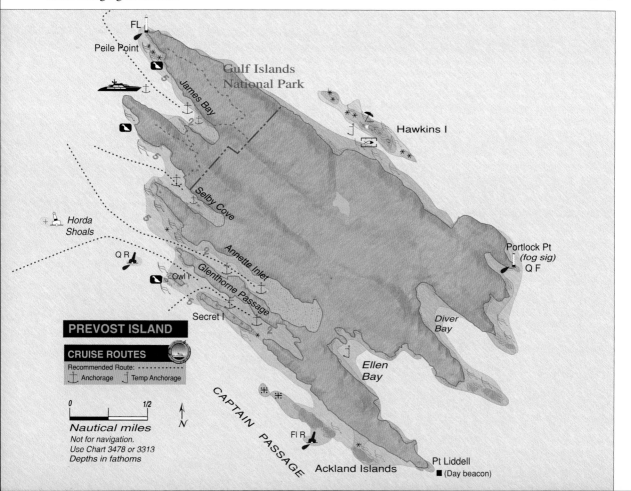

FL
Peile Point
Gulf Islands
National Park
James Bay
Hawkins I
Selby Cove
Horda Shoals
Portlock Pt
(fog sig)
Q F
Q R
Annette Inlet
Owl 'r
Glenthorne Passage
Secret I
Diver Bay

PREVOST ISLAND

CRUISE ROUTES
Recommended Route: ·········
⚓ Anchorage   ⚓ Temp Anchorage

Ellen Bay

0   1/2
Nautical miles
Not for navigation.
Use Chart 3478 or 3313
Depths in fathoms

N

CAPTAIN PASSAGE

Fl R
Ackland Islands
Pt Liddell
■ (Day beacon)

and down Trincomali Channel. We like to linger here, leaving only when forced to do so by a rising tide, when all that remains of the beach is a strip of crushed clamshells.

There can be impressive current (over 2 knots) between Hawkins Island and Prevost Island, which can make anchoring a challenge. The best place to drop the hook is in the area between the islands and the shellfish farm. Holding is good but the anchorage gets regular ferry swell and is not suitable for an overnight stay.

Ganges Harbour 13

Ganges Harbour on Saltspring Island is a fine if sometimes busy anchorage with excellent holding ground. Summer winds often funnel up the harbour from Captain Passage, providing sailing yachts with a downwind sail into Ganges and a tacking duel with other sailboats upon departure (dodging the numerous crab pots that line the entrance to the harbour). The wind, in summer, usually dies down by early evening.

Moorage is available at the government floats or at two full-service marinas, where scooters and bikes can be rented. Local services include two banks and a credit union (all with bank machines), a post office, supermarket and liquor store.

With a population of about 10,000, Saltspring is the largest and most populated of the Gulf Islands, and the seaside village of Ganges is the island's commercial hub. Pedestrian-oriented Ganges is perfect for boaters setting off on foot along boardwalks leading past restaurants, shops and a waterfront park.

For provisions, Thrifty Foods is located right on the waterfront. For chocolate delicacies, Harlan's on Lower Ganges Road is highly recommended. And boaters seeking a gourmet meal can make dinner reservations at Hastings House, located a short walk east of Salt Spring Marina along Upper Ganges Road. A *Relais et Chateaux* property, this luxury inn, set on manicured grounds atop a bluff, was the former home of Warren Hastings, an English naval architect who moved to Saltspring in 1937 and modelled his new manor on his 11th- century country estate back in Sussex. For a more casual meal, the restaurant at the Saltspring Inn, located in the centre of town across the street from the Visitor Information Centre, is recommended.

From April to October, a Saturday food-and-crafts market is held at Centennial Park, and throughout the summer ArtCraft is held at Mahon Hall where locally hand-crafted jewellery, clothing and folk art are sold. Saltspring has long been an artists' haven and the island's art galleries are concentrated in Ganges, including the well-known Pegasus Gallery, located in Mouat's Mall which was built in 1912 by the Mouat brothers.

Thomas Mouat was the first to arrive from the Shetlands in 1895, but this entrepreneurial family's most successful businessman was Gavin Mouat, who once owned Portland Island before trading it to the provincial government in exchange for timber rights elsewhere. The Embe Bakery is housed in the island's first creamery, built by the Mouats in 1903 and a thriving business until 1957, when farmers throughout the Gulf Islands shipped their fresh milk

Ganges is a good place to reprovision, fuel up and enjoy a meal ashore.

did not always prevail, however, and the first farmers faced numerous hardships, including long winters without mail service, wolf attacks on their farm animals, and raids by local Cowichans, not all of whom took kindly to the newcomers.

The Cowichans also had a long-simmering dispute with the northern tribe of Bella Bella natives, and in the summer of 1860 they massacred a number of them at Ganges Harbour. The Deadman Islands were used as a mass burial site and they form part of the Chain Islands, which run the length of Ganges Harbour. We have threaded our way past these islands and dropped anchor in the NE arm of the harbour, away from the hustle and bustle of Ganges. Although exposed to southeasterlies, the holding ground here is good in mud and clay, and the numerous islets and islands dispel some of the wave action coming off Captain Passage. This is, however, a fair-weather anchorage.

The two main marinas, Salt Spring Marina and Ganges Marina, can be contacted on VHF channel 66A. Both have good dock facilities, showers and laundry.

Long Harbour 14

Long Harbour on Saltspring Island is protected from most winds, although strong northwesterlies can gust through the central area of the anchorage. Southeasterlies can be felt near the entrance but you can dodge these if you pull in close to the N shore behind a number of bights or in the lee of a cluster of islands near the entrance. South winds tend to weaken as they travel the length of the inlet, which is over 2 miles long. There are several nooks in which to anchor along the harbour's NE shore but we invariably pick one of the bights near the southeast end.

The fair weather anchorage closest to Nose Point lies between a reef on the N side of a small cove and the rock outcropping to the south. This spot is fairly shallow and requires a line ashore to keep your boat away from the dangerous N reef – we saw a raft of boats land on this in strong January S winds and it was not a pretty sight. The anchorage north of the small group of islands (the largest of which is known locally as Fisherman Island) provides superb holding and lots of swinging room between the red buoy and Athol Peninsula. A small house and private dock occupy Fisherman Island owned, naturally, by a local fisherman. The nearby islets and rocky shoreline are ideal for exploring by dinghy or kayak, and the bight's two beaches are lovely for picnics. Walks ashore are

here for processing. The Salt Spring Island Chamber of Commerce and Tourist Information Centre, located beside the Fire Hall, provides walking maps of the town and its heritage buildings.

Saltspring Island was named for the springs of brine discovered there by some Hudson's Bay Company officers, and Ganges was named for *HMS Ganges,* the flagship of Rear Admiral Baynes who served in local waters from 1857 to 1860. Saltspring's early pioneers were a hardy lot and included Australians who had failed to strike it rich in the Fraser River gold rush. The island's first house was built in 1859 by a handful of settlers at Ganges Harbour, near the site of the present Harbour House Hotel. The local Cowichans, who had for centuries picked berries and hunted on the island, continued to gather clams in the harbour, and intermarriage took place among the natives and settlers, who were of various races and nationalities, including Hawaiian, Scottish and African American. Peace and harmony

Left, midden beaches dot the north side of Long Harbour. Opposite, a quiet nook in Long Harbour.

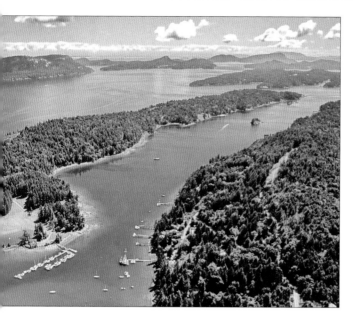

Long Harbour, looking southeast.

LONG HARBOUR AT A GLANCE

CHARTS: 3478, 3313, 3442, 3462
LAT LONG: Entrance, 48°50.50'N 123°25.34'W
PROS: Interesting harbour with numerous spots to anchor. Good to excellent holding ground in soft or sticky mud. Generally provides good shelter.
CONS: Some wake from the ferry which usually comes twice a day. No access to north shore.
MUST DO: Explore by dinghy the lagoon at head of harbour. Go swimming.

limited, however, for the adjacent land is privately owned by a consortium of home owners. Fortunately this has not diminished the privacy of the anchorage, for the development's waterfrontage has been set aside as a communal park for its residents and the foreshore is usually very quiet.

As noted, there are several bights along the NE shore to drop the hook, several with midden shell beaches. Be sure to stay well away from Clamshell Island for the BC Ferry turns around the N side of this island when departing Long Harbour. At the very head of Long Harbour is a fairly sheltered spot to anchor in about 10 feet (3 m) opposite a private marina. Although there are many boats moored here on buoys, there is usually space for visiting yachts to anchor. Holding, in soft mud, is good and this end of the bay is usually well sheltered from wind. Be sure to take a dinghy ride to the head of the slough at HW. This half-mile sojourn takes you past low banks, small wooden docks and pretty waterfront cottages.

Montague Harbour & Marine
Park, Galiano Island 15

It's only fitting that this beautiful anchorage contains the first marine park established in B.C. in 1959. A favourite destination with just about everybody, the park's mooring buoys and small boat dock are busy throughout the summer, as is the tent-filled campground, but there's always

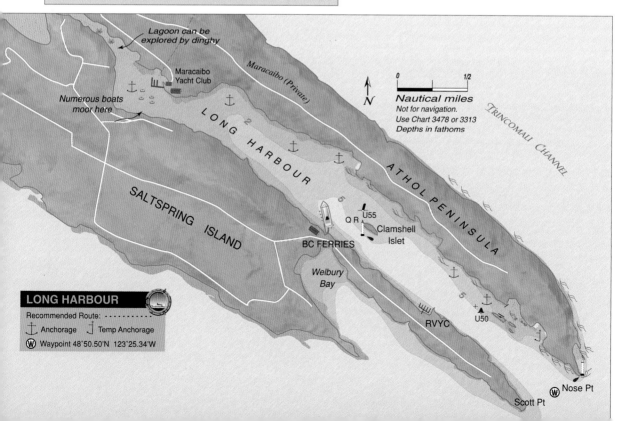

room to anchor in this large harbour which can easily handle dozens of vessels. The marine park occupies the NW end of the harbour and is the busier side of the bay, but there are excellent anchoring possibilities at the SE side of the harbour, a good spot to be if south winds pipe up in the night. Northwesterlies can also blast over the gut of the lagoon into the anchorage, and the holding ground SE of the lagoon is only fair with a layer of ooze over mud and sand. The holding east of the dinghy dock is better, as is the bottom in the south part of the harbour.

The park's shoreside trails can be enjoyed year-round and in summer the adjacent white shell beaches are dotted with sunbathers. These extensive middens of crushed clamshell are evidence of a large settlement of Coast Salish natives which thrived at Montague Harbour for thousands of years. Various archaeological digs have unearthed artifacts (stone and bone implements) from three distinct cultures, the oldest dating back 6,000 years.

A store and marina, located beside the public dock and old ferry wharf, are open during summer months. The Montague Harbour Marina operates a restaurant, fuel dock and moped rentals. A half mile walk away, at the junction of Montague Park Road and Montague Harbour Road, is a popular French country restaurant and cafe called La Berengerie. The Hummingbird Pub, located across the island near Whaler Bay,

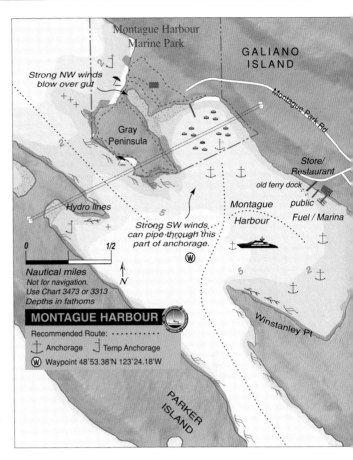

B.C.'s first marine park, Montague Harbour is a very popular destination for boaters.

MONTAGUE HARBOUR AT A GLANCE

CHARTS: 3473, 3313, 3442
LAT LONG: 48°53.38'N 123°24.18'W
PROS: Popular marine park with lots of mooring buoys and plenty of room to anchor. Store and restaurants nearby. Fair to good holding.
CONS: Be careful where to anchor if winds are forecast. Some parts are less protected than others and holding is poor south of lagoon.
MUST DO: Walk around Gray Peninsula and enjoy the beautiful beaches.

Below, the beaches at Montague Harbour Marine Park are good for swimming in summer. Bottom, an aerial view of north bay and main anchorage.

can be reached by the Hummingbird Pub Bus, which runs daily from mid-June to the end of September, from 5:00 pm to 11:00 pm, stopping near the Montague Harbour Marina and at the entrance to Montague Park.

A recommended hike from the public floats is the 4-mile (6.5 km) walk to Bluffs Park overlooking Active Pass. Starting at the public docks, follow Montague Harbour Road to Georgeson Bay Road, then turn right onto Georgeson and take it to Bluff Drive which leads to the park entrance. The distance is about 4 miles (6.5 km) over hilly terrain. Montague Harbour Road can sometimes be busy with ferry traffic from Sturdies Bay, but once you turn onto Georgeson Bay Road the pastoral scenery will draw you toward wooded Bluffs Park. A short distance within the park entrance is a path that leads to the edge of a bluff overlooking the western entrance to Active Pass, and this eagle's eye view is well worth the effort of getting here. A lofty picnic can be enjoyed while watching vessel traffic below and eagles soaring above the pass.

In winter, Montague Harbour is reclaimed by shorebirds and the park trails are all but deserted. One year, over the Christmas holidays, we tied to a mooring buoy and awoke the next morning to a strong southeasterly and blowing snow. At midday we moved our sailboat to the empty dock and that night we all slept in the saloon to be close to the diesel stove. The snow stopped sometime in the night and by morning the wind had shifted to a northeasterly with gusts to 35 knots at East Point. When the winds finally subsided and the sun made a brief appearance, we ventured ashore in the knee-deep snow. The marine park we knew so well had been transformed into a winter wonderland and we happily trudged through the deserted campground in our rubber boots.

Nearby Anchorages: If Montague Harbour is packed out or you want to try something different, the bay north of Gray Peninsula is a possibility in settled weather. Swimming is good here, with a long midden beach offering some protection from the south. A chop comes into the anchorage in any sort of a north wind. The two bays on either side of the isthmus at Parker Island also can be viewed as possible anchorages.

Walker Hook 16

This summertime lunch stop is situated on the west side of Trincomali Channel, about three and a half miles west of Montague Harbour. Anchor on the SE side of the isthmus connecting Walker Hook – a narrow, wooded peninsula – with Saltspring Island. The beach of sand and crushed shell lying along this isthmus is popular with island residents and used to attract nude sunbathers to its remote location.

The anchorage's sand-and-mud bottom provides good holding but because of its exposure to both northwesterlies and southeasterlies, is not always a comfortable place to spend the night at anchor. Northwesterlies can send a bad swell around the corner of the hook, making for a rolly and sleepless night. If you have decided to chance it, go as far into the crux of the anchorage as possible where the swell is moderate. Tying a line to shore is not viable because of the constant current which flows parallel with the foreshore. Entry can be made through a narrow gap between the two rocks lying off the SE point of Walker Hook and Atkins Reef, which parallels the shoreline. For afternoon stops, we usually anchor close to the beach to avoid any wash from traffic in Trincomali Channel. The bottom shelves gradually to about 3 fathoms (6 m), then rises more steeply. The swimming here is good, with warm water and a fairly clean beach. Views to the south, toward Active Pass, are spectacular.

Below, Walker Hook's sandy beach is ideal for children. Bottom, an aerial view of Walker Hook.

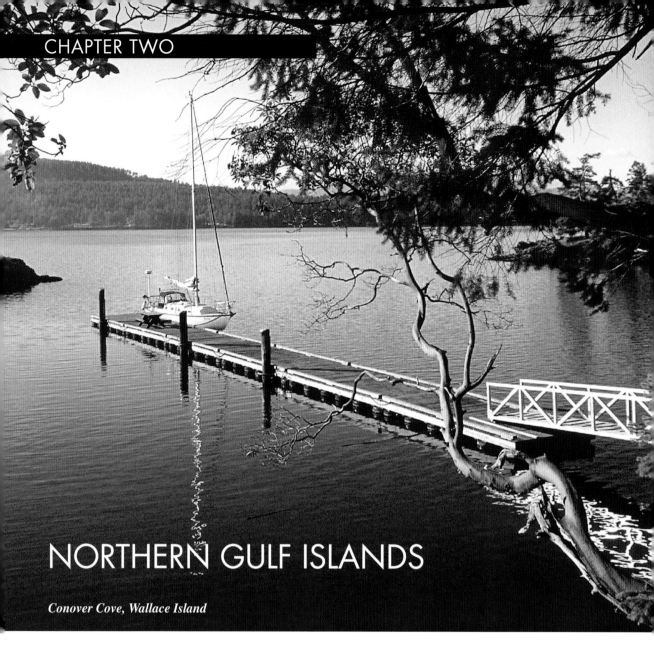

CHAPTER TWO

NORTHERN GULF ISLANDS

Conover Cove, Wallace Island

For an overview of the Gulf Islands, please see pages 50 to 53.

Trincomali Channel, stretching from Active Pass to Pylades Channel, is the main channel connecting the southern Gulf Islands to their northern neighbours. Tidal streams are generally weak (up to 1.5 knots) except in the vicinity of Porlier Pass where rates in Trincomali can reach 3 knots. Tidal reference for most anchorages within Trincomali will be on Fulford Harbour and for locations on the Strait of Georgia side are on Point Atkinson. A handful of anchorages lie near the junction of Trincomali Channel and Porlier Pass, and boaters seeking solitude can still find a few surprises in this area. Stuart Channel is not as direct a route for northbound boats and can be brutal in NW winds.

TIDES AND CURRENTS
Porlier Pass

The largest gate pass south of Campbell River, with currents reaching 10 knots, Porlier Pass can generate impressive whirlpools and overfalls from Race Point to the reef opposite Dionisio Point. This is especially dangerous if the current is flowing against strong easterly winds. The flood current, which piles up on the Trincomali Channel side of the pass, can be seen spilling into the Strait on large tides and is especially impressive along the rocky west shore of Race Point. In addition to fast currents, it is the degree of turbulence due to numerous shoals and reefs that makes Porlier Pass potentially the most dangerous of all the Gulf Islands passes.

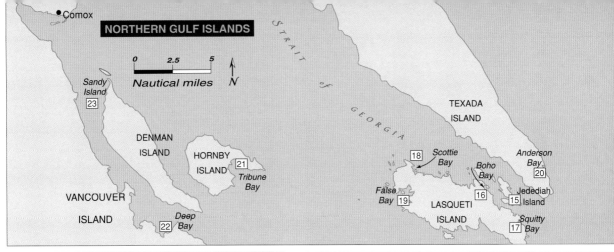

NORTHERN GULF ISLANDS

0 2.5 5
Nautical miles N

Comox

Sandy Island 23

Strait of Georgia

Texada Island

Denman Island

Hornby Island 21
Tribune Bay

Vancouver Island

Deep Bay 22

Scottie Bay 18
Boho Bay

Anderson Bay 20

False Bay 19

Lasqueti Island

16
Jedediah Island 15

Squitty Bay 17

CHARTS AND PUBLICATIONS:

Use: CHS Charts 3442, 3443, 3458, 3473, 3475, 3477, 3512 and 3527. Also, the book of charts 3313, which covers the Gulf Islands in detail up to Nanaimo; Sailing Directions for the BC Coast, South Portion; and the Canadian Tide and Current Tables, Volume 5.
Contact marinas on VHF ch. 66 or by phone.

Because of strong currents in this pass, try to arrive at or near slack. If slack water has been missed, and the tide is not too large, you can usually work your way through Porlier by staying parallel with the current, clear of the heavy water, while steering as close to the centre of the pass as possible. The stream is a fairly straight and short run through the restrictions presented by Galiano and Valdes Islands, with two major deflections, a result of the island topography and numerous reefs. The main danger when transiting Porlier is being swept onto reefs at the E and W ends of the pass. Boaters sometimes steer a little too close to Galiano Island and find they are being set onto the reef extending from Dionisio Bay where depths at LW can be just a few feet. The area NE of this shoal water can be very dangerous in gale conditions and is where some of Georgia Strait's roughest and largest seas can occur.

Over the years a number of vessels have gone down in and around this pass, including the 190-foot sidewheel steamer *Del Norte* which sank after striking the reefs south of Canoe Islets after trying to back out of the pass in 1868. This wreck is still noted near these reefs in the current edition (2004) of the CHS Sailing Directions. The tug *Peggy McNeil* sank in the pass in 1923 and only one of her crew of 6 survived. Of note for tidal pool explorers, Canoe Islets are an Ecological Reserve and landing is not permitted without a permit.

In our westbound transits of Porlier, we pass within a quarter-to-a-half mile off the green flashing buoy at the N entrance. Lining up this buoy with the

Hammond Bay 14

Strait of Georgia

Departure Bay
Newcastle Island 13
Nanaimo

Snake Island

Entrance Island

Jack Pt.

Duke Pt.

Northumberland Channel

Gabriola Island

Dodd Narrows

Maude Island

Degnen Bay

Silva Bay 11

8

Vancouver Island

Boat Harbour

Decourcy Island 12

9
Gabriola Pass

Wakes Cove 10 Kendrick Island

Pirates Cove

7

Ruxton Island

Whaleboat Passage Marine Park

0 2.5 5
Nautical miles N

Kulleet Bay

6 Bute I
Ladysmith

North Cove 5

Trincomali Channel

Valdes Island

Thetis Island

Reid Island

Porlier Pass

Clam Bay 3

4

Telegraph Cove

Mowgli Island 2

Galiano Island

Kuper Island

Secretary Islands

Chemainus

Tent Is.

Wallace Island 1

Saltspring

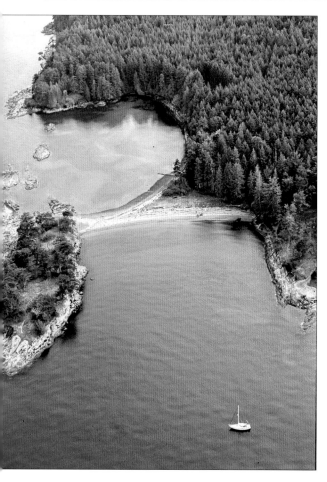

Above, Dionisio Bay, on the SE side of Porlier Pass, is a good spot to wait for slack tide. Below, anchorage in pretty Dionisio Bay, at the east end of Porlier Pass. Race Point is in background.

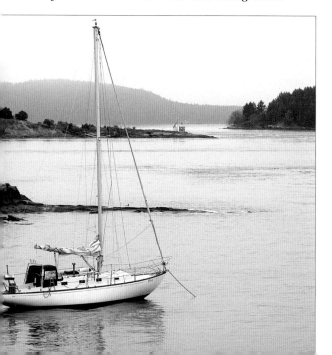

Pass tip sheet – Porlier Pass

Location: 49°00.94'N 123°35.27'W Between Galiano and Valdes Islands. Pass is less than a quarter mile wide.
Maximum Flow: Flood, 10 knots, Ebb, 7 knots.
Slack: 15 minutes on large tides.
Nearby Anchorages: In calm, Dionisio Bay if westbound. Eastbound Clam Bay, Reid Island.
Direction of Flood: North
Key to safe transits: Arrive at or close to slack. Give reef N of Dionisio Point a wide berth and be aware of the set near Virago Rock and Black Rock. Set your course using U41 buoy.

light at Race Point allows us a course through the deep water of the pass and out of danger of the rocks off Valdes Island. Once we are a half mile from Race Point, we turn to a middle route through the pass between Virago Rock and Virago Point. There is a Q RW sector light on Virago Rock for night transits. Sometimes there can be strong turbulence off Romulus Reef and a N set towards the reef extending from Black Rock. It is essential to maintain your bearings, especially at night, to ensure you are clearing these dangers.

The only times we've had engine problems in a pass have been in Porlier. Both times, fortunately, we were east of Race Point, travelling with the current along the axis of the pass, and our boat easily drifted to the inside waters. The ebb is, generally, a smoother and less-turbulent flow because the seaward side contains fewer obstructions.

One of the main drawbacks of Porlier Pass is, during strong N winds, the lack of shelter on the Strait of Georgia side for vessels waiting for slack. **Dionisio Bay**, a marine park at the N end of Galiano Island, provides some shelter in S winds but is quite open to the north. This bay makes for a good temporary stop in settled weather with good holding in sand and mud. The marine park has a rich history as evidenced in the shell middens which make up the beach and date back more than 3,000 years. Archaeologists conclude this beach has been used extensively by the Penelakut First Nation.

Tugs and barges often use Porlier Pass and you can obtain information on their movements by listening to Channel 11, Victoria Traffic. Tug operators can usually be contacted directly on Channel 16.

Gabriola Passage

Few passes along the entire B.C. coast are as straightforward as Gabriola Passage. This pass is a yes/no situation and either your boat has the guts to buck the current or it doesn't because, in a slower moving sailboat at least, there is no chance to wiggle through if arriving too late.

In the 1950s, CHS field workers were using baby bottles with flashlights inside to measure nighttime currents at Gabriola Passage. The bottles were cast out by fishing rods from shore and as they gained speed and were swept through the pass, the workers would take transits on the lights and reel the bottles back to shore. By the 1970s, field workers were experimenting with fixed pods on boats to measure current. As a result of study and analysis done in 1979, daily tables were introduced for Gabriola

COWICHAN GAP:

Cowichan Gap is what the local natives called Porlier Pass long before the Spanish explorer Jose Narvaez named it in 1791 for an official in Madrid. The following summer two more Spanish explorers, Galiano and Valdes, decided to transit Porlier Pass in search of sheltered anchorage. A fresh easterly was blowing in the Strait of Georgia as they sailed their schooners into the pass. They soon regretted this decision, for a current was running and they "saw at once how risky it was to entangle ourselves among these islands." So they spent two hours rowing their ships back through the pass, dodging reefs and taking soundings as they struggled "in constant labour and danger."

Above, Porlier Pass, looking toward the Strait of Georgia. Below, east end of Gabriola Passage.

Passage starting with the 1987 edition of the Tide and Current Tables. (Prior to this, predictions for Gabriola were based on Active Pass.)

Gabriola Passage is basically a straight-line stream with the main turbulence occurring with the flood, beginning at the pass and extending to Rogers Reef. Turbulence and whirlpools can also be expected near the reefs off Dibuxante Point and those south of Degnen Bay. Current in this pass can attain over 8 knots on both flood and ebb. The danger at the W end is near the light beacon off Dibuxante Point, where a vessel can get swept onto this reef in either tide direction. You can wait out the tide behind Kendrick Island if bucking a flood or in Wakes Cove if fighting an ebb. (See map, page 105.)

Dodd Narrows

This short pass, with no submerged hazards and a straight-line stream, presents few problems except those created by other boaters. Because this pass is very narrow, often with fast streams (9.5 knots on flood) and no room to work back eddies, it is susceptible to wash from fast-moving power boats which, when bucking the current, can trigger large standing waves capable of swamping smaller craft. When the pass is busy, as it often is in summer, slower vessels may want to stand-off a short distance to check for oncoming powerboat traffic.

A flood current pushing into Northumberland Channel against a strong summer northwester can result in a significant chop for a few miles beyond the pass. Also, there can be strong turbulence on ebbs just east of Joan Point.

Nearby lies one of the great temptations in passes – **False Narrows**. This is a pretty pass to explore – in a dinghy. We haven't mustered the courage to go through in our sailboat. With currents up to four knots, shoal water, kelp and numerous reefs, this is obviously not a safe pass for deeper draft boats and best left to the locals who know it well.

THE ANCHORAGES

Wallace Island [1]
Marine Park

Every island has a story, and Wallace Island is no exception. Over the last century this island has been a hermit's haven, a youth camp, a summer resort, a potential subdivision and, since 1990, a provincial marine park. In some ways, the island has come full circle, its park status preserving the natural beauty and peacefulness that so appealed to its first full-

Looking south, Dodd Narrows at full flood.

time resident, a Scotsman named Jeremiah Chivers who lived alone on the island from 1889 until his death at the age of 92 in 1927. A long, low-lying island, it was called Narrow Island until renamed in 1905 by Captain Perry of the Royal Navy to honour Captain Wallace Houston, HMS *Trincomali*, who served in local waters in the 1850s.

Following the death of Chivers, Wallace Island became a summer camp for boys. One of the respondents to an American newspaper ad seeking youth counselors for an island retreat in the Canadian wilderness was a young man named David Conover, who was then living in Los Angeles. After two summers spent working at the camp on Wallace Island, Conover returned with his wife Jeanne and, although having little experience living in the bush, they bought the island and moved there in 1946.

The next summer they opened a resort at Conover Cove, which they operated until the mid-60s. Summers were idyllic days for young Davey, the Conovers' only child, who grew up on Wallace Island. On his website (www.dconover.com), David Conover Jr. recalls that his summers were a boyhood dream of outdoor activities centred around the holiday resort where he played with the children of families staying in the rental cabins. Winters were decidedly different, however. An only child living on a private island, Davey saw other children only when he commuted by boat to school on Saltspring Island, and "those long, cold, isolated winters seemed to stretch into eternity."

When the Conovers sold their resort in the 1960s, Jeanne moved to Victoria where Davey attended high school. David Sr. moved to a new home he had built on an unsold waterfront acreage overlooking Princess Cove, which remains in private hands. Jeanne didn't move back to Wallace Island but David Sr. lived there until his death in 1983 at the age of 63, writing two books about his life there, namely *Once Upon an Island* and *One Man's Island*.

In the latter Conover states, "For weeks now I have had no inclination to leave the island. If I don't watch out, I'll soon take root like a fir. The prospect, I admit, I find not unpleasant." This is a sentiment easily understood by anyone who has visited Wallace Island for any period of time.

For boaters seeking a bit of peace and solitude, the off-season is the best time to visit Wallace Island and relive its storied past, when the sounds of summer have fallen quiet, the calls of children and dogs now replaced with the twittering of eagles. Apart from two private properties at the mouth of Princess Cove, the entire island is a marine park. Trails run the length of the island, joining the two main anchorages, and these are

Above, Conover Cove is protected but shallow.

Right, Princess Cove is sheltered from southerlies.

often deserted, as are the anchorages themselves, in contrast to the bright bustle of summer when anchored boats line up Mediterranean-style with stern lines to shore.

'Chivers Pass'

From Porlier Pass there are several routes to get to the anchorages of Wallace Island but our favourite is through the small pass just N of Chivers Point between Wallace and Secretary Islands and known

GOVERNOR ROCK

Governor Rock in Trincomali Channel south of Wallace Island was named by Captain Richards after an incident in 1859. His ship had been lying at anchor in Nanaimo Harbour when he received an urgent order from Governor Douglas to return to Victoria. While steaming south down Trincomali Channel, HMS Plumper ran full speed into an unknown rock and Richards promptly named it Governor Rock.

James Douglas, who became governor of British Columbia in 1858, came to British North America as a fur trader and was an agent of the Hudson's Bay Company when he oversaw the construction of Fort Victoria in 1843. Douglas married Amelia Connolly, the 16-year-old daughter of a native woman and a white man. She and Douglas had 13 children and although she became Lady Douglas when her husband was knighted, she was never fully accepted by the ladies of Victoria society.

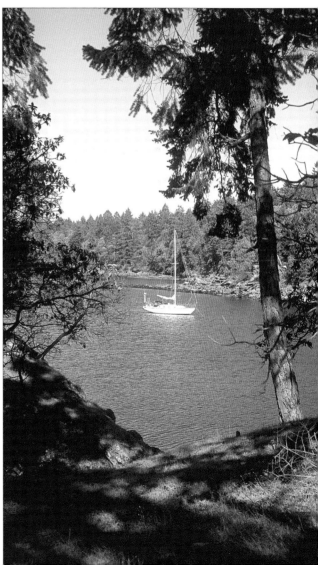

WALLACE ISLAND AT A GLANCE

CHARTS: 3313, 3442, 3463
LAT LONG: Princess C, 48°56.66'N 123°33.57'W
PROS: An excellent marine park with hiking trails, summertime swimming, fair-to-good shelter, good holding and stern tie rings allowing for plenty of boats. Good dinghy exploring along its shoreline.
CONS: Often busy in summer. Anchorages vulnerable to strong NW and SW wind.
MUST DO: Hike the entire island, visit Chivers Point at low tide and explore the tidal pools.

locally as Chivers Pass. This pass has a minimum of about 6 feet of water at LW, but it must be navigated very carefully because of currents and nearby reefs.

The approach to the pass is made by first locating the large drying reef situated in the middle of the channel. If southbound, approach the pass at right angles to Wallace Island on a course of about 220°. We aim for the reef until about 150 feet away, then turn right about 45° toward the small E point on Secretary Island until we're between the reef and the island. We then turn S in an arc to exit. If the reef cannot be seen, aim for the midway point between Chivers Point and the point on Secretary Island and, proceeding slowly, begin turning toward Secretary Island when you are abeam of Chivers Point. When

about 60 feet off the point of Secretary Island, turn S and exit. The pass appears to receive about 2 to 3 knots of current, which would make a transit a little challenging during a strong N wind and ebb tide because of the set to the reef.

Princess Cove

Although the approach to Princess Cove is guarded by an ominous line of reefs, there is plenty of water on either side for pleasure craft. At LW, this reef is a popular haul-out for seals, while oystercatchers and other shore birds can also be spotted here. If entering the cove from the SW, the channel between the outer reef and the point at the entrance to the cove provides an easy route.

The cove has limited swinging room and a line to shore is de rigueur in summer when the anchorage gets busy and boats line up Mediterranean-style along the cove's west side, where stern tie rings are available. Rock ledges lie along the W side of the cove and it's a good idea to check your depth as the tide drops to ensure your vessel doesn't drift back onto one of these. A dinghy float is located on the W side, opposite a private dock.

Princess Cove affords excellent shelter from southeasterlies but is quite open to strong N winds. In a SE wind, Princess Cove is an absolute hurricane

Princess Cove often requires stern-ties in summer.

hole. During a SE gale you can hear the wind howling overhead and barely receive a gust in this snug anchorage. Winds from the SW, however, do come over the saddle from Conover Cove and vessels lying broadside to strong SW winds will be straining their ground tackle. The cove is also exposed to NW winds which often bring a low swell into the cove. Although the holding is very good, consider moving your boat if a NW gale is in the offing.

Conover Cove

This cove still bustles with life each summer, its small float holding 6 to 10 boats. There's little depth to play with in this tight anchorage and, because of limited swinging room, most boats anchor in the N part of the cove and tie a line to one of the rings anchored to the E or W shore. Minimum depth in this area can be less than a fathom, so it's crucial to consult the tide tables.

The greatest depth, and best spot for anchoring, is N of the dock on the E side of the cove with a stern line ashore. Be sure to bury your anchor well because strong winds can whistle through the anchorage and often vessels are broadside to the wind. If you're tying to the dock, the deeper water, by about a foot, is on the N side of the dock. Northerly winds can also whistle through the cove.

On shore, opposite the dock, is an original signpost pointing to the island's various trails and points of interest. Several heritage buildings, including one of the resort cabins and the main house where young Davey grew up, stand on the edge of a grass clearing that overlooks the anchorage and is bordered by purple pea-like flowers which flourish in summer. As children play along the sandstone foreshore and dogs leap into the water for sticks, a visitor stepping ashore can quite easily envision the island as it would have been a half century ago.

Exploring Wallace Island

Hiking the trails of Wallace Island is one of the great treats of cruising the Gulf Islands. There is a dinghy dock on the W side of Princess Cove, making it very easy to get ashore and begin the hike. The trail from the dinghy dock leads to the head of the bay where it connects with another trail leading to Conover Cove. Along this trail is a rusting 1950s-style jeep, a reminder of days past when roads were bulldozed and wells drilled in a failed attempt by the Wallace Island Holding Company to sub-divide the island after it was purchased from the Conovers. Today not even bicycles are allowed on the park trails, a measure aimed at protecting the island's sensitive flora and fauna. Black-tailed deer live on the island, amid thickets of salal and the springtime proliferation of lupine, Indian paintbrush and wild peas.

At Conover Cove there is a bomb shelter (built by David Conover), as well as a picnic shelter built when Wallace Island was a summer youth camp. The

Above, tidal pools are a major attraction on Wallace Island. Below, Mowgli Island at sunset.

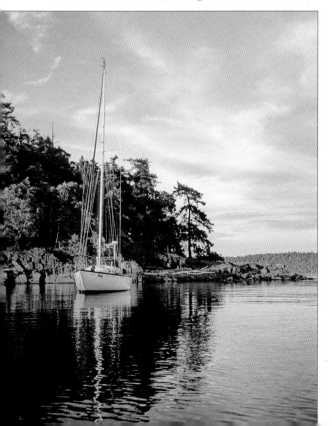

names of boys from those long-ago summers are carved into the open-air structure's supporting logs. Pieces of driftwood adorn the wall on either side of the stone fireplace with names of boats that have visited Wallace Island since it became a marine park in 1990. Nearby, on the edge of a grassy clearing, are several more heritage buildings, including resort cabins and the main house, built on the foundations of Chivers's cabin.

A trail runs the length of the island, terminating near Chivers Point at its N end where there are several campsites. Campfires are not permitted anywhere on the island, which becomes tinder dry in summer. Back in the 1920s a negligent camper started a fire on the island and burn marks remain on some large firs and cedars. There is a small cove beneath Chivers Point, where erosion has hollowed out puddingstone formations in the rock ledges.

Mowgli Island 2

This small anchorage, sometimes used by fishing boats, is often passed over by pleasure craft but is a pretty overnight stop in settled weather. Its NW shoreline is formed by Mowgli Island (known locally as Spike Island) and to the south are the Secretary Islands. A reef extends from Mowgli Island's SW shore and must be given a wide berth as you come into the anchorage. This same reef deflects much of the wave action created by passing vessels in Houston Passage. Oystercatchers and gulls frequent this reef, their medley of calls punctuated by the chattering of kingfishers.

A few houses have been built on Mowgli Island but the shoreline remains pleasing, its slopes covered with grass and a variety of trees. Along the foreshore, small patches of white shell beach appear as the tide recedes. The channel separating Mowgli Island from the Secretary Islands is shallow and not recommended as an entrance. Skiffs sometimes cut through the anchorage but most boats keep to the main channel and pass right by. Holding is good in mud and sand, and the anchorage is protected from NW winds but somewhat open to S winds.

Clam Bay / Telegraph Harbour, Thetis Island 3

Nestled on the north side of Kuper Island, Clam Bay is a convenient anchorage for boats entering or exiting the Gulf Islands through Porlier Pass. It also is a good spot for northbound boaters to pause and rest before heading into the Strait of Georgia.

Clam Bay is a big bay, allowing for dozens of vessels to find shelter for the night. Entrance is made between the SE end of Centre Reef (marked with a starboard hand buoy) and Penelakut Spit, comprised of a long strip of crushed clamshells. At night, you may have trouble spotting the entrance buoy, but Penelakut Spit can usually be seen and used to navigate into the anchorage.

Once inside Clam Bay, most boats anchor in its southern half, where Penelakut Spit provides shelter from SE seas and the thick mud bottom provides superb holding. In summer, we tend to anchor outside the 2-fathom (4-metre) line to avoid the crowds and allow ourselves plenty of swinging room. In strong N winds, the north half of the bay provides better shelter.

Penelakut Spit is named for the inhabitants of Kuper Island whose village is situated on the hillside overlooking the spit. Their ancestors, who were skilled at hunting sea lions entering the Gulf Islands through Cowichan Gap (Porlier Pass), would paddle their canoes across the Strait of Georgia in summer to fish for salmon in the lower reaches of the Fraser River near present day Sand Heads.

On the W side of Clam Bay is the entrance to a narrow, dredged channel called **The Cut** – suitable for dinghies – that leads to Telegraph Harbour, cutting between Thetis and Kuper Islands. A narrow strip of land once joined Thetis and Kuper Islands, until a canal was dug in 1905 to allow the passage of small craft between Clam Bay and Telegraph Harbour. A bridge was built to rejoin the two islands, but this was knocked down in 1945. This did not stop cattle owned by the residents of Kuper Island, which is an Indian Reserve, from crossing over to Thetis at LW and helping themselves to the farmers' crops.

Although we've taken a 35-foot sailboat through The Cut, that was many years ago and the channel has filled in somewhat since then. Taking a keel boat through The Cut should not be attempted during

---

CLAM BAY AT A GLANCE

CHARTS: 3477, 3313, 3442, 3463
LAT LONG: 48°59.00'N 123°38.52'W
PROS: Clam Bay is a large, wide anchorage and, although somewhat open to the north, provides good shelter in most winds. Holding in sticky mud is excellent.
CONS: Entrance encumbered with a marked reef. Anchorage somewhat open to strong N winds and even S winds will gust across Penelakut Spit.
MUST DO: Take your dinghy through The Cut to Telegraph Harbour. Explore Penelakut Spit.

---

anything less than tides of 12 feet, as the channel dries in two spots to about 6 feet at datum. Chart 3477 and the CHS chart book of the Gulf Islands – 3313 – provide good detail of the pass.

Below, exploring The Cut by dinghy at low tide.

Bottom, a quiet evening at anchor in Clam Bay.

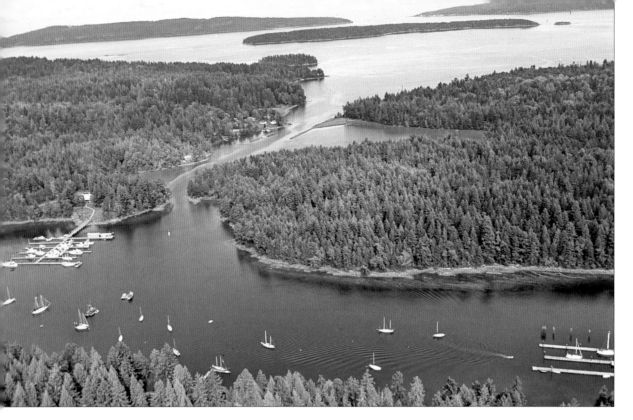

Looking east over Telegraph Harbour to Clam Bay and Reid Island. Porlier Pass in background.

Telegraph Harbour, a popular place in summer with its two marinas, provides snug, although sometimes crowded anchorage just north of Thetis Island Marina. Be careful of the depth as the entire anchorage is quite shallow. There is an inviting pub and restaurant at the Thetis Island Marina (phone 250-246-3464) and a licensed bistro and old-fashioned soda fountain at Telegraph Harbour Marina (phone 250-246-9511). Within walking distance of both marinas are several island crafts shops as well as the ferry terminal at Preedy Harbour. The ferry makes regular crossings of Stuart Channel to Chemainus on Vancouver Island – a pleasant day trip for boaters who travel as foot passengers to take a look at the colourful street murals and enjoy the sidewalk cafes of this former mill town. Temporary anchorage is possible in the north section of Preedy Harbour, N of the submarine cables and away from the ferry route, with the local public dock providing dinghy access.

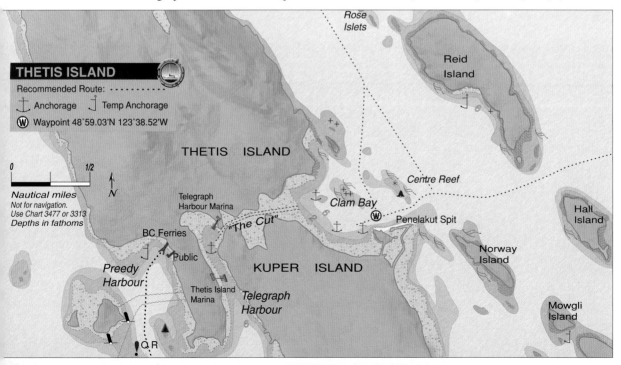

Reid Island 4

This wide bight on the SW side of the island is bordered by an attractive pebble beach. This is a quiet spot to anchor when Clam Bay and Telegraph Harbour are busy. Although open to the south, it provides fair shelter from NW winds and, in settled weather, is an excellent spot to watch the sun set while tending the barbecue. This anchorage is also easy to access in darkness if you're concerned about the more difficult entrance to Clam Bay. The holding ground is very good in sticky mud.

The gravel beach at Reid Island is ideal for children to explore and the view, past the decaying wooden pilings of a remaining Japanese saltery, is lovely. Many a sunny afternoon we have picnicked on the foreshore, enjoying this view across the sparkling water to Clam Bay.

Reid Island is privately owned, with cabins clustered along its NW shoreline where pocket beaches of crushed clamshell reveal themselves at low water.

Another small temporary anchorage lies at the south end of Reid Island, formed by an islet and some drying rocks. This spot provides some protection from the north but the anchorage's exposure to south winds and current from Porlier Pass, and the unpleasant proximity of reefs, make an overnight stay something to think about carefully.

When rounding the south end of Reid Island during a flood tide, be careful not to cut the curve too sharply as the strong current in this area can set a vessel onto the reef at this end of the island.

Beachcombing along the bight on Reid Island.

North Cove, Thetis Island 5

This lovely cove (more accurately a bay) at the north end of Thetis Island is a pleasant alternative to the often-busy anchorages of the northern Gulf Islands. Although open to northwesterlies, the bay is wide and deep, allowing for plenty of scope in excellent holding ground. The reefs in the area are well marked, making entry and exit easy. The passage between the Ragged Islets and Pilkey Point has ample depth, however, the reef from the point must be given a wide berth. One mile north of Pilkey Point are Miami Reefs, named after the steamer *Miami* which struck and sank on the reefs in 1900.

Development around North Cove is minimal, with hillside houses nestled unobtrusively among the evergreens and arbutus. We usually drop the hook in about 60 feet (18 m) near the west side of the bay, opposite the summer youth camp which has

Above, a large yacht anchors at the mouth of North Cove with the Ragged Islets in the background. Left, the anchorage south of Bute Island in Ladysmith Harbour.

Ladysmith Harbour / 6 🍽 🧺 ⛽ Kulleet Bay

There is a dearth of anchorages offering good protection from northwest winds in the upper Gulf Islands and many popular anchorages, such as Pirates Cove and Silva Bay, can be uncomfortable in strong winds from this direction. Discretion being the better part of valour, retreating to a marina for a night of peaceful sleep can be a welcome respite and there are several in the area to offer refuge.

In addition to the marinas in Telegraph Harbour there are guest moorage facilities in Ladysmith Harbour, including Ladysmith Maritime Society (250-245-1146); Ladysmith Marina (250-245-4521); and Page Point Marina, which also has a restaurant (250-245-2312).

If you're looking for an overnight anchorage, the spot between **Bute Island** and the Dunsmuir Islands is usually quiet (although there is a large booming ground to the west). Protection from most winds is good and holding in about 15 to 20 feet in mud is also good. **Sibell Bay,** a half mile to the east, offers better protection from NW winds, but it and **Evening Cove**, further east another mile, can sometimes be busy with local crabpots and buoys.

Kulleet Bay, three miles around the corner from Evening Cove, has good protection from NW winds and the two spots we've used are off the east side of Deer Point in about 30 feet as a lunch stop (a little bumpy from passing boats) or well into the SW part of the bay past a shallow arm jutting out at the mid-point. Holding is good in about 40 feet in sand and mud.

a small dock for its sailing dinghies. There are, however, numerous other locations to anchor in the bay with the eastern side of the cove in 30 to 40 feet of water being more popular for boaters.

There are several bible camps on Thetis Island, a tradition that began back in 1904 with the establishment of an Anglican retreat by a retired British major and his sister. The island had become known as an English colony through the efforts of Mr. and Mrs. Henry Burchell who settled at Preedy Harbour in 1892 where they built a new home, store, farm and orchard. At Christmas they held a children's party and each fall they threw a dance complete with oysters and sparkling white wine, which was attended by guests who would sail or row from the other Gulf Islands.

North Cove is wide open to the north and in summer, when northwesterlies prevail, mariners should keep an ear to the weather. If you do get caught here overnight, the good holding ground should keep you until the dawn. Alternatively, nearby Kulleet Bay provides shelter from N winds. In winter, North Cove offers excellent shelter from SE winds – we've been here during a gale and nary a puff of wind ran through the rigging. It is a good spot to unwind for a day or two and explore the long Cufra Inlet.

Nearby **Tent Island** has long been popular with locals for its fine sand-and-pebble beach and is a popular swimming stop with boaters and kayakers. The island is part of Penelakut Band reserve (which also includes Kuper Island). Although the island makes a good lunch stop in fair weather, it is quite exposed to the west and should only be considered for an overnight stay if conditions are settled. An escape plan should be thought out in advance.

Pirates Cove Marine Park, De Courcy Island 7

Although this picturesque marine park at the SE tip of De Courcy Island is protected in moderate conditions, strong NW winds penetrate the entire cove and can make for an uncomfortable night. Pirates Cove is popular with many boaters for its unique location at the north end of the Gulf Islands and for the excellent trails lacing the park. The park's shoreside also includes two dinghy docks and a decent beach area looking out to Ruxton Passage.

The challenges of Pirates Cove begin with an entrance guarded by a long narrow reef extending 100 yards NW beyond the beacon. There is also a rock that juts out due N of the end of this reef (shown as 03 on Chart 3313) and it is this rock that many boats have grazed when approaching the cove. The other rock that catches vessels is just inside the entrance and is marked by a red buoy (keep to starboard entering). Favour the E side of the entrance passage to avoid this rock. The holding ground (oozy mud) is mediocre and when a big northwesterly blows through the anchorage, it's not unusual to see large boats dragging anchor. At LW they have no choice but to stay because there's not enough depth

PIRATES COVE AT A GLANCE
CHARTS: 3475, 3313, 3443
LAT LONG: 49˚6.04'N 123˚43.95'W
PROS: Marine park, good trails, and generally good shelter from moderate winds and wash from boats in Trincomali Channel.
CONS: Often busy in summer. Holding only fair.
MUST DO: Walk the trails and contemplate the colourful character of Brother Twelve.

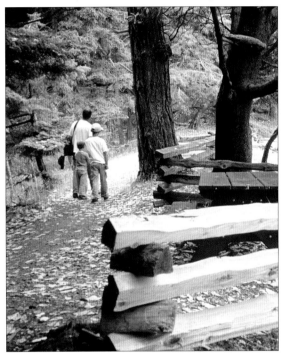

Below, the pleasant trails at Pirates Cove Marine Park. Bottom, entrance to the anchorage is tricky.

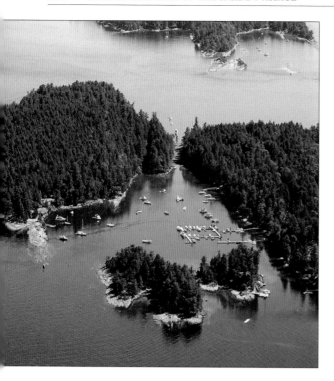

Aerial view of Pirates Cove and Ruxton Passage.

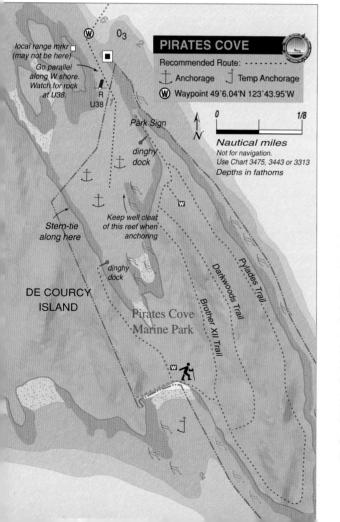

at the entrance to get out. Regulars to Pirates Cove are usually seen tying a stern line to shore, but in strong winds they'll anchor in the centre of the cove to point into the wind. The anchorage performs far better as a refuge from south winds.

Most boaters are willing to put up with Pirate Cove's deficiencies, for it is a beautiful anchorage. It also has a colourful past. Brother XII – one of Canada's most infamous false prophets – established a communal settlement here in the early 1930s. An itinerant sea captain cum charlatan, Edward Arthur Wilson was a charismatic occult leader who called himself Brother XII and whose Aquarian Foundation headquarters were located at Cedar-by-the-Sea, south of Nanaimo. Using funds donated by followers willing to denounce all of their worldly possessions, Brother XII was able to acquire property at Pirates Cove on DeCourcy Island. He didn't like outsiders and would curse – and occasionally shoot – from shore anyone who ventured by boat into his harbour. He eventually disappeared with a stash of gold he had collected from members of his cult, and died some years later in Switzerland, but his legend lives on. (See Wakes Cove for more on Brother XII.)

Alternative Anchorages: If Pirates Cove is full, an alternative anchorage in settled weather is the marine park's outer bay facing Ruxton Passage. This bay has decent protection from W wind and the holding is good. It does, however, get some swell from boats taking the passage and is open to the SE. Another option is **Herring Bay** at the north end of Ruxton Island where the holding ground is better than Pirates Cove and the bay affords a good view over to Vancouver Island. It is, however, a tight anchorage with some shallow patches, including an uncharted rocky ledge that dries one foot (0.3 m) in the middle of the west entrance to the bay. Another good spot, in settled conditions, is **Boat Harbour** on Vancouver Island (see page 108).

We sometimes stop at **Whaleboat Passage Marine Park** at the SE end of Ruxton island, for it is usually quiet. Lying at the eastern entrance to Whaleboat Passage, the anchorage itself can accommodate only a few boats due to a drying rock that limits swinging room. Most boats anchor N of the drying rock. Some caution is required when approaching the anchorage from Pylades Channel, for a reef extends from the NE end of Pylades Island, forcing a northbound vessel to swing wide when entering the anchorage. Whaleboat Passage is navigable only by small craft. The park's islet was known locally as Eagle Island before it was renamed Whaleboat Island in 1981 when the marine park was established. It is completely treed and has a steep sandstone foreshore.

Degnen Bay, Gabriola Island 8

A pretty anchorage and a good hurricane hole, this bay is well protected from wind but often clogged with local boats on permanent mooring buoys. Although the holding ground is good, there is some mooring debris on the bottom which could foul your anchor.

Despite its drawbacks as an anchorage for visiting boaters, the natural and historical attractions of Degnen Bay endure. A single petroglyph of a killer whale can be found on a foreshore rock near the head of the bay, while a walk ashore heading west on South Road leads to the site of more petroglyphs, located behind the United Church. The land around Degnen Bay was settled in the 1860s by an Irish immigrant named Robert Degnen. He had married the daughter of a local chief and together they farmed the land and raised nine children.

Wakes Cove, Valdes Island 9

Wakes Cove, a provincial marine park, provides good shelter from SE winds. The cove is a little exposed to the NW, but the fetch is limited. Although the cove is out of the current stream of Gabriola Passage, which can reach 8 knots, it does receive some wake from vessels transiting the pass. The holding in mud here is good, but there are usually large patches of kelp and reports of bottom debris from its years of logging operations.

Created in 2002, the park encompasses the Valdes shoreline from Coal Mine Bay on its Pylades Channel side to a point SE of Kendrick Island on its Georgia Strait side. Several waterfront parcels are excepted from the park, including Kendrick Island and Dibuxante Point, as well as most of the E shoreline of Wakes Cove. Some private floats are situated here and the point of land opposite Cordero Point is also private. The head of the cove is parkland, however, and provides access to a forest of arbutus, Garry oak and old-growth Douglas fir trees. There are numerous well-maintained trails through the park; one leads past an old logging winch just west of the dinghy dock and two old cars from the 1920s are along the trail leading south. There is also a trail leading east to the neighbouring anchorage.

The park's southern boundary lies next to reserve land owned by the Lyackson First Nation, their traditional village located south of Coal Mine Bay, where a nook in the rock bluff provided a safe landing place for canoes. The property around Wakes Cove was acquired in 1876 by a retired British naval officer, Captain Baldwin Wake, who regularly rowed across Gabriola Passage to teach at the local school. Wake died mysteriously while sailing his sloop home from Nanaimo.

His widow moved to Esquimalt with their daughters but their son Baldwin stayed at Wakes Cove. His widow, Amelia, was still living there in the late 1920s when much of the surrounding land was purchased by Edward Arthur Wilson, better known as Brother XII, the occult leader whose followers donated money to his foundation headquartered at Cedar-By-The-Sea. Brother XII's plan for Valdes was to establish a retreat where he would train selected disciples, but the communal settlement was never completed. Brother XII eventually fled to Switzerland with a fortune in gold, leaving only scandal in his wake.

Wakes Cove

Kendrick Island Anchorage

If Silva Bay is too crowded or you are waiting for slack at Gabriola Pass, this anchorage on the west side of Kendrick Island is a great choice. Charts 3475 and 3313 give good detail of this area. Kendrick Island, owned by the West Vancouver Yacht Club, forms one side of this long narrow cove, which is a better overnight stop than nearby Wakes Cove, receiving less wave action from vessels transiting Gabriola Passage.

Although strong south and north winds will gust through the cove, the holding in thick mud and sand is excellent, making the anchorage safe for most summer conditions. There is a constant (about a knot or so) current flowing through the anchorage and, strangely, almost always in a northerly direction. The best area to anchor is north of the docks and buoys belonging to the West Vancouver Yacht Club in about 25 to 35 feet. South of these facilities, the water shoals quickly to a rocky kelp-strewn bottom.

At low tide there is a pretty midden beach along the anchorage's east shore. The islets lying southeast of Kendrick Island are part of Wakes Cove Marine Park – great for sunning and swimming. The sandstone formations along the shoreline here have been created over time by the evaporation of water in this porous rock. These beautiful caverns and honeycomb patterns are interesting to explore by dinghy.

The Kendrick Island anchorage is adjacent to Wakes Cove Marine Park, where hiking trails can be

Left, a pocket beach and sandstone formations along the shoreline at Kendrick Island anchorage. Below, aerial view of the Kendrick Island anchorage, Gabriola Passage and Wakes Cove.

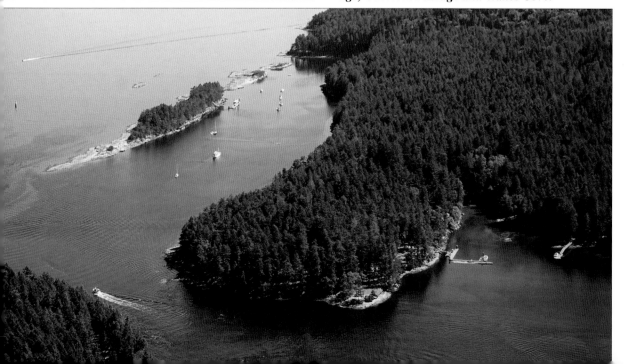

accessed either by motoring through Gabriola Passage to the dinghy dock in neighbouring Wakes Cove or by landing on the anchorage's west shore opposite Kendrick Island. Here a shoreside trail eventually leads inland to connect with the park's other trails.

Drumbeg Park's swimming beaches are a short dinghy ride across Gabriola Passage.

Silva Bay, 11
Gabriola Island

Silva Bay lies outside of the tidal passes, so it's a popular resting stop for boats approaching the Gulf Islands from the Strait of Georgia. A large bay with room for "one more," its proximity to Vancouver makes it a favorite for charter vessels. But, with two marinas, its popularity is justified – especially as a departure point for northbound vessels.

There are, however, a few problems with Silva Bay as a destination. The approach to Silva Bay from Vancouver requires close attention to the chart. Starting with Thrasher Rock, there are numerous reefs, especially around Acorn Island. Many boaters use Thrasher Rock as a waypoint and line up with the light SE of Tugboat Island before turning north into Commodore Passage. The final challenge is wending your way between the reefs of Tugboat and Vance Islands on the final turn into Silva Bay. Some vessels, turning too soon, have ended up on Shipyard Rock SW of the beacon, but going slow, keeping an eye on the depth and favouring Vance Island will get you through. Be sure also to keep U39 on your port side.

The narrow channel S of Sear Island, with a minimum depth of about 4 feet, can be used for entering and exiting Silva Bay, depending on the stage and size of the tide, but be careful if your boat draws more than 6 feet. In strong southeasterlies, large swells will be breaking at the E end of this channel, which can be dangerous for sailboats equipped only with an outboard.

Although we've never had a problem with our CQR holding in Silva Bay, we've seen other boats drag anchor. The holding is only fair, with a layer of mud over rock (or something equally hard) that doesn't provide great holding. Although the anchorage is well sheltered from seas off the Strait of Georgia, winds blow strongly through the islands ringing the bay. We like to anchor north of Sear Island, which keeps us out of south winds while giving ourselves room to let out line should a north wind come up. Recently, Transport Canada has been clearing out some of the derelict buoys and vessels from the bay.

For boaters who would prefer to tie to a dock for the night, your choices are Silva Bay Resort & Marina (tennis courts and a playground are located a short walk up the road from the marina) and Pages Resort & Marina (where scooters and mountain bikes can be rented). A Royal Vancouver Yacht Club outstation is located on Tugboat Island.

Although Spanish place names dominate Gabriola Island, Silva Bay is named for the large Portuguese family that settled here. The family patriarch, Joseph Silvey, arrived in B.C. in 1852 aboard a whaling ship. When anchored in Silva Bay, we like to explore by dinghy the nearby shoreline which includes **Drumbeg Park,** located about a mile south of Silva Bay near the entrance to Gabriola Passage.

The main entrance to Silva Bay is at top centre, between Vance Island and Tugboat Island.

Above, Boat Harbour and marina at Kenary Cove.
Right, Hemer Park trails lead to Holden Lake.

Boat Harbour (Kenary Cove) 12 🏃

An uncrowded anchorage, this bay does get some swell and chop from passing boats and is open to the south but is relatively sheltered from northwesterlies. We have spent the night here in settled weather, and we usually anchor opposite or north of Flewett Point in about 50 feet over a mud bottom although you can anchor closer to the private marina in Kenary Cove to get out of a S swell.

Other than the private marina in Kenary Cove and a few homes on the harbour's northern shoreline, Boat Harbour is usually quiet, with a pastoral setting of treed and grassy slopes. The area between the marina and the small peninsula offers limited anchoring but it is shallow and buoys dot the waterline. The peninsula, which is joined to shore by a neck of land, was formerly a railway embankment used when coal was shipped out by steamer in the 1870s and is now owned by an offshore consortium. You can row ashore and quickly find the path used by locals that leads to the edge of Hemer Provincial Park – a gift from John and Violet Hemer. The park itself provides groomed trails that can be hiked for about a mile and a half to Holden Lake where wood benches overlook the lake.

Back at Boat Harbour, a good picnic site is atop the peninsula on a gentle bluff overlooking the anchorage, its low banks of sandstone eroded into smooth and unusual shapes. The marina in Kenary Cove is known for its woodworking shop where master shipwright Bruce Martyn and his apprentices have worked on restorations of classic boats.

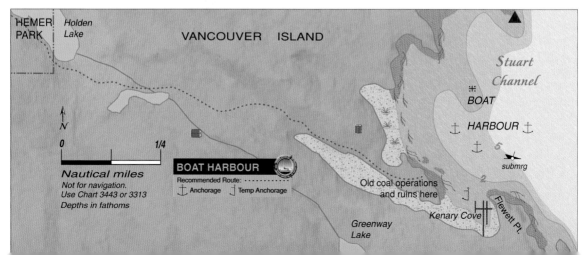

HEMER PARK · Holden Lake · VANCOUVER ISLAND · Stuart Channel · BOAT HARBOUR · submrg · N · 0 · 1/4 · **Nautical miles** · Not for navigation. · Use Chart 3443 or 3313 · Depths in fathoms · **BOAT HARBOUR** · Recommended Route: ·········· · ⚓ Anchorage ⚓ Temp Anchorage · Old coal operations and ruins here · Kenary Cove · Flewett Pt. · Greenway Lake

Newcastle Island Marine Park 13

Newcastle Island is Nanaimo's version of Vancouver's Stanley Park but with no vehicle access, so it's perfectly suited to boaters who can tie at the park floats or to one of the park's 43 mooring buoys. Because of the shallow depths in **Mark Bay**, the size of vessels tying to them is limited to a maximum length of either 30 or 40 feet (this is noted on each buoy). Anchoring is not permitted among the mooring buoys but there's room to anchor just beyond them. The holding ground is excellent and protection is good from most winds although strong S winds will make it around Protection Island into the bay.

If you're approaching Mark Bay from McKay Channel, the only hazard is Satellite Reef which extends close to the 2-fathom (4 m) line around Protection Island. Tugs often moor barges to the buoys east of Satellite Reef. For these reasons, we normally keep the reef to starboard when approaching Mark Bay.

A dinghy dock is located at the park floats, located next to the ferry wharf where foot passengers from Nanaimo disembark. The visitors pavilion, open during the summer, is located nearby.

Named after the famous coal town in Northern England, Newcastle Island was the site of a coal mine, sandstone quarry, saltery and shipyard before it was bought by the Canadian Pacific Steamship Company in 1931 and transformed into a holiday resort. On summer weekends as many as 1,500 steamship passengers would arrive for the day from Vancouver. They came to enjoy such facilities as a dance pavilion, tea house, picnic areas, change houses, soccer field and wading pool. World War II brought an end to these excursions as ships were diverted by the war effort, and Japanese residents operating a saltery and shipyard here were interned. After the war, in 1955, the City of Nanaimo acquired the island, turning it over to the Province in 1961 as a marine park. The restored dance pavilion now houses the Visitor Centre, open throughout the summer, where a map of the island's extensive trail system is available.

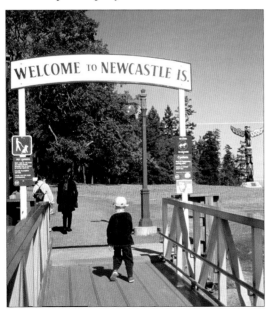

Boaters docked in Nanaimo have the option of taking the passenger ferry to Newcastle Island.

The trails, covering more than 12.5 miles (20 km) in total, encircle and crisscross the entire island, providing access to many natural attractions such as Mallard Lake. Ringed by steep sandstone cliffs and sandy gravel beaches, the island's interior is gently hilly and forested with Douglas fir, arbutus, Garry Oak and dogwood trees. One of the highlights of a hike on Newcastle is Nares Point at the island's NW tip where Giovando Lookout provides a sweeping view of the Strait of Georgia. The wooded trails give way to open grassy areas at the south end of the island where picnic sites, a playground and the old sandstone quarry are located near the floats.

The animals living on Newcastle include raccoons, blacktail deer, beavers, river otters and rabbits while Mark Bay is a popular gathering place for Canada geese who like to cruise through the anchorage. A short dinghy ride away is neighbouring Protection Island where a floating pub and shoreside store are located.

Top, Newcastle Island's visitor pavilion. Left, trails criss-cross the entire island. Below, aerial of Newcastle Island and Mark Bay anchorage – a popular place in the summer.

NEWCASTLE ISLAND AT A GLANCE

CHARTS: 3457, 3313, 3458, 3463
LAT LONG: Mark Bay 49°10.60'N 123°55.84'W
PROS: One of the best marine parks in the province, excellent trails through a variety of scenery. Good jumping-off location for points north or as a terminus for southbound vessels. Good shelter and holding is very good.
CONS: Often busy in summer and anchorage somewhat open to the south.
MUST DO: Walk the circumference of the island. Check out the pulp stones and beach.

NANAIMO

Nanaimo is a great place to reprovision and enjoy some shoreside attractions with the city's public floats conveniently located in the Boat Basin adjacent to downtown. Small to medium-sized boats tie up in the inner boat basin and larger vessels are directed to the W.E. Mills Marina (formerly Cameron Island Marina). A short walk away is the Port Place Shopping Centre (formerly the Harbour Park Mall) which contains a Thrifty Foods grocery store, pharmacy, liquor store and specialty shops. Across the street from the Boat Basin is the Coast Bastion Hotel where a dinner ashore can be enjoyed at the Minnoz Restaurant. A pedestrian-only waterfront promenade winds from the Boat Basin to Maffeo Sutton Park, location of an excellent children's playground and a man-made tidal pool called Swy-A-Lana Lagoon, beyond which are the marinas and chandleries lining Newcastle Island Channel.

The harbour is the hub of Nanaimo, with floatplanes landing and taking off, and small passenger ferries bobbing across the water to nearby Protection Island and Newcastle Island. In summer, on the fourth Sunday of July, about a hundred vessels gather here for the start of the World Championship Bathtub Race, first launched in 1967. To qualify for this unusual race, which ends on the other side of the Strait of Georgia in Vancouver's English Bay, an entry "must contain a component which conforms to the general shape and design of an old-style roll edge bathtub," be propelled by a 7.5 horsepower motor and have an escort boat.

Standing guard over Nanaimo Harbour is a wooden military bastion, built by the Hudson's Bay Company in 1853 to protect the white settlers who came from England and Scotland to work in the local coal mines. They called their new home Colville Town, but the native name of Nanaimo, which means 'big strong tribe' in reference to the five villages located in the area, has endured.

In summer, The Bastion serves as a Tourism Infocentre. The nearby museum, at the Vancouver Island Conference Centre, displays a replica coal mine and an exhibit showcasing the history of Nanaimo's harbour. Heritage buildings, many now housing shops and restaurants, can be found on Front Street and along winding Church Street, while a walk up Bastion Street leads to the Old City Quarter of restored brick-and-stone buildings where more shops and eateries await. The adjacent Arts District contains a selection of art galleries.

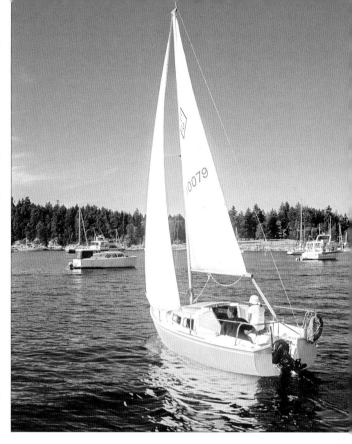

Above, Mark Bay, Newcastle Island. Below, Nanaimo's harbourfront looking toward Mark Bay.

Hammond Bay [14]

Hammond Bay, six miles north of Nanaimo, provides shelter from northwesterlies but is exposed to easterlies. It's a good spot to wait out a strong headwind when proceeding up or down the west side of Georgia Strait. During northerlies, gusts and swells will snake around Neck Point into the bay, but the sand-and-mud bottom provides good holding ground. Anchorage can be gained at the head of the bay, opposite a Crown islet known locally as Shack Island.

During the Depression of the 1920s, as many as two dozen families squatted on this 4-acre islet, living in makeshift shacks. The men worked in the Nanaimo coal mines and augmented their income by rowboat fishing in local waters. They trolled for salmon with a hand line and for ground fish with a leg line – the latter tied around one of their legs.

Among the rowboat fishers living on Shack Island was the Luoma family from Finland. The father, Matt, and his two sons, Ed and Pat, established a boatyard on Shack Island, building their

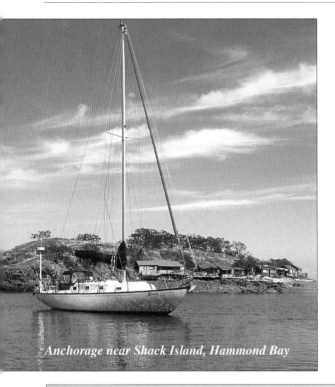

Anchorage near Shack Island, Hammond Bay

Sunset over Whiskey Golf

WHISKEY GOLF

Exercise Area WG is an underwater test range operated off Nanoose Bay by the Canadian Navy. Whenever Whiskey Golf is being used for testing non-explosive t o r p e d o e s , sonobuoys or sonars, vessels are not

TEXADA ISLAND	THORMANBY ISLANDS	A 49°21.35'N 124°07.70'W
LASQUETI ISLAND		B 49°21.00'N 123°48.40'W
		C 49°14.83'N 123°48.40'W
		D 49°16.75N 124°00.90'W
		E 49°19.35'N 124°07.70'W

allowed to pass through the "active" portion of this restricted area, but can pass N of Winchelsea Island and E of South Ballenas Island in the safe transit lane, its location marked on CHS charts 3512 and 3459. The no-trespassing policy is for the public's safety, and even a killer whale passing through will result in a test being cancelled. Tests take place four days per week, usually Tuesday through Friday from 0800 to 1730, and active times are broadcast on VHF 21B and Weather 3.

The test site, established in 1967, is owned and operated by the Canadian government. It was chosen because its bottom topography is perfectly suited for technical acoustic testings. Most of the tests are conducted by Canadian and American surface ships and submarines. The range is linked to the U.S. Naval Underwater Warfare Centre at Keyport, Washington, and although the U.S. Government has invested heavily in the site, it is owned and operated by the Canadian government on land leased from British Columbia. Two other testing ranges are situated in quiet deepwater areas off Jervis Inlet.

Radio contact with Winchelsea Island Control can be made on VHF CH 10 or 16 for permission to transit WG.

classic double-ended rowing skiffs with hand- or treadle-powered tools because there was no electricity. Driftwood logs of yellow cedar were their source of softwood lumber, and the hardwood needed for structural pieces came from an oak bar they salvaged from a hotel. With painstaking craftsmanship the Luomas produced lightweight but strong skiffs prized by local fishermen for their speed, handling and seaworthiness.

Many of the original dwellings still stand on Shack Island and descendants of these fishing families can claim inherited squatters' rights. Some of the shacks are used by summer campers who walk out to the islet at LW and set up temporary house in one of them. The nearby tidal lagoon is a protected reserve, and Hammond Bay's laid-back atmosphere is reminiscent of the 1970s, when a back-to-the-land movement saw the B.C. coast dotted with squatters.

Sailing North: The last set of Gulf Islands begins with Lasqueti and Jedediah Islands, which are well worth including in any sail plan. The two islands are split by **Bull Passage**, which usually has one or 2 knots of current flowing either north or south, depending on the tide. A thoroughfare for recreational boats, this pass is sometimes used by commercial fishboats and tugs with stick booms.

Bull Passage is a good haven if a SE gale is blowing in the Strait of Georgia, providing welcome shelter from the rough seas south of Lasqueti. During a northwesterly however, Bull Passage receives its share of wind but Jervis Island acts as a breakwater and reduces much of the swell coming into the pass. The best place to be in NW conditions is either in Deep Bay or tucked well into Boho Bay.

Jedediah Island [15]

Long before Jedediah Island became a marine park in 1995, the anchorage at its north end was used by tugboats and fishing vessels working in local waters. Known locally as **Deep Bay** and protected from NW winds by Paul Island, it is one of the safest anchorages in the area although it can be crowded and, once the sun goes down, gloomy. Swinging room is limited and most boaters tie a stern line to shore, allowing a dozen or so boats to anchor in this sheltered cove. Be sure to set your bow anchor as close to the opposite shore as you can to get a good set and to be able to pull yourself away from your stern shore once the tide drops. We have seen numerous vessels get hung up by the stern and we have come close ourselves. A trail leads from Deep Bay, through an old-growth forest of fir, hemlock, arbutus and pine, to a hilltop meadow and the old homestead overlooking **Home Bay** on the east side of the island.

There are several other anchorages around Jedediah Island, none of which provide the same landlocked security as Deep Bay, but which are worth investigating if you are spending a few days around the island. Our two favourite coves are on opposite sides of the island – one is **Sunset Cove** on the west side opposite Boho Bay; the other is at the SE end and is known as **Codfish Bay.**

Sunset Cove has a reef at its entrance which knocks down wake from other boats and keeps westerly swell from coming into the cove but presents a hazard if trying to enter the cove at night. We keep the reef to starboard coming into the cove and favour the north shore where there is plenty of water (minimum of 12 feet). We set the bow anchor in the middle of the cove and either use a stern anchor or tie off to one of the trees on shore to lie parallel with the north shore. Holding is good in soft mud and shell, and minimum depth in the centre of the cove is about 12 feet (4 m). This little cove will fit two or three boats, with vessels using shorelines.

The next cove over, known as **Otter Cove**, also fits one or two boats with stern lines. This spot provides similar protection to Sunset Cove with the same steep-sided features. This cove gets a bit more wake and swell however.

Long Bay and **Boom Bay** back onto mud flats which at LW can have that familiar decaying smell. However, we have seen lots of vessels contentedly anchored here when Deep Bay fills up. Part of the problem with these bays is that the bottom shelves steeply and many boaters are reluctant to drop the

Numerous small anchorages indent the rugged shoreline of Jedediah Island.

A marine park, Jedediah Island receives lots of visiting boats in summer. From left is Deep Bay, White Rock Bay, Boom Bay, Long Bay and finally Otter Cove. All offer good protection from south winds but will get some breeze in northerlies.

hook in a hundred feet of water and so they come too close to the shore when heaving the stern line. There is a nasty reef at the north entrance to Boom Bay which seems to regularly catch the unwary, so give your keel lots of room if anchoring in this small bay. **White Rock Bay**, the next over, is another popular spot and gets less swell and chop. This bay also gets the best sunsets. There is a rock reported just off the north outcropping. If all of these anchorages are full and you need to get out of a south wind, there is a sheltered spot in Tucker Bay W of Potter Point. South winds can really funnel through the two "Bull" passes so anchor near them as a last resort.

Codfish Bay, entered from Sabine Channel, is sheltered from all NW winds and from moderate SE winds and swells off the Strait of Georgia by a cluster of small islands near its entrance. Inside this narrow cove, the setting is starkly beautiful with a cliff-sided islet forming part of the northeast shoreline and grassy bluffs on the opposite shore. A broad beach lies at the head of this narrow cove where a path leads inland and connects with other trails, one leading to the old homestead and fruit orchard at **Home Bay**. This is the

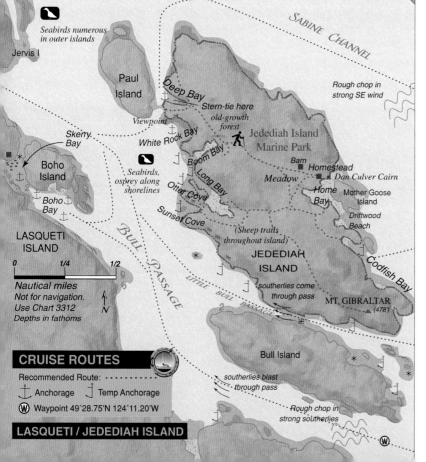

former home of Al and Mary Palmer, the last private owners of Jedediah, who were known for their friendliness and hospitality toward visitors. A previous owner, a gentleman farmer from Ireland named Henry Hughes who owned Jedediah Island in the 1920s and '30s, was not so receptive to uninvited guests. Suspecting trespassers of poaching his sheep, the reclusive Hughes once greeted a tugboat captain named Jim Anderson with the pointed barrel of a gun and an order to get off his land. Anderson, who regularly anchored his tug in Deep Bay, was determined to befriend the bearded, bookish Hughes whose eccentricities were widely known and included setting a place at the table for his dog. So the next time he ventured ashore he brought a peace offering – some back issues of Vancouver and London newspapers. Anderson later wrote that "folks had told me if he'd spend more time working his place and less time reading he would be better off, so I knew I had the right ammunition." Over time, Anderson befriended both Hughes and his black dog Caesar, inviting them back to his vessel one day for supper where the dog enjoyed dining at the special place set for him next to his master.

Well educated and wealthy enough to bring with him from Ireland a manservant, cook, gardener and shepherd to tend the sheep he planned on raising, Hughes was apparently more suited to the academic world than the farming life. After depleting his financial resources and losing all of his hired help, Hughes lived alone on the island with his faithful dog until meeting his future wife, an English nurse named Jenny, when she arrived one summer by boat with some sailing friends. Her party had ventured ashore to walk the trails when they bumped into Hughes who invited them to his house at the head of Home Bay. When sheep farming didn't pan out for Henry Hughes, he hoped to sell Jedediah Island to the Canadian Pacific Steamship Company for development as a summer resort, one that would compete with the Union Steamship Company's resort on Bowen Island, but the CPR instead purchased Newcastle Island near Nanaimo.

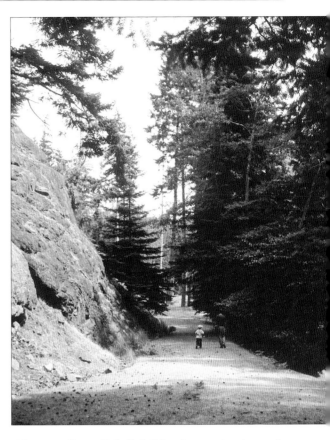

Above, trails on Jedediah Island are extensive and offer scenic views. Below, unique Codfish Bay has a wall of granite surrounding much of it.

JEDEDIAH ISLAND AT A GLANCE

CHARTS: 3312, 3512
LAT LONG: Bull Passage, 49°28.70'N 124°11.20'W
PROS: Variety of anchorages, lots of room. Great island for walks with several good trails. Fair to good protection offered from most winds. Holding ground generally very good.
CONS: Some anchorages can be crowded. Limited protection from NW winds. Can get busy.
MUST DO: Explore the island, walk the trails. Try more than one anchorage.

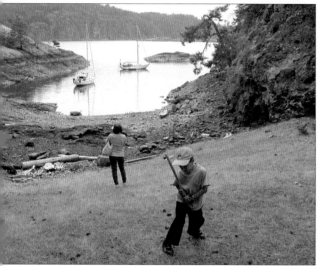

Top, sheltered from all winds, Deep Bay attracts the most boats. Above, two or three boats can fit into Sunset Cove. Below, the dock at Squitty Bay.

Jedediah Island was eventually bought, in 1949, by Mary Palmer and her first husband. The island, 640 acres in size, has never been subdivided and contains a network of sheep trails that pass through old-growth forest, open fields and a hilltop meadow. Human hikers share the trails with the island's four-footed residents which include deer, sheep and goats whose ancestors were left to graze on Jedediah by 18th-century Spanish explorers. The island's highest point, dubbed Gibraltar, stands at the south end of the island and is reached by a trail that ascends 500 feet above sea level, winding past ferns, salal and dwarf conifers. The summit provides views of nearby islands and Jedediah's rugged shoreline.

Overlooking the water at Home Bay is a plaque dedicated to the memory of Dan Culver – an outdoorsman, yachtsman and mountain climber who fell to his death in 1993 at the age of 41 after ascending K2. His will stipulated that a piece of coastal wilderness be saved, so his brother donated $1.1 million to a highly publicized fund-raising campaign to purchase Jedediah Island from the Palmers for preservation as a provincial marine park. The funds, as visiting boaters will attest, were well spent.

LASQUETI ISLAND
Boho Bay / Skerry Bay 16

When making tracks up or down the Strait of Georgia, we often pull into Boho Bay for the night. With its straightforward entrance off Bull Passage, the anchorage is easy to slip into during fading light or darkness. We usually anchor in the main part of the bay, south of Boho Island, although we have proceeded into the small inner cove, known locally as Skerry Bay, which provides better protection from southeasterlies within its rugged, cliff-edged shoreline. Both anchorages offer good shelter from northwesterlies with very good holding.

Squitty Bay Marine Park 17

This marine park at the southeast tip of Lasqueti provides shelter and limited dock space, but the anchorage is shallow and its entrance is a bit tricky – a small channel with about 5 feet (1.7 m) of depth at LW. Favour the channel's port side when entering the bay, leaving the mid-channel drying rocks to starboard. The anchorage is picturesque, with picnic tables overlooking the water. A park trail leads to a beautiful juniper reserve on the adjacent peninsula that was bought by the Nature Trust of B.C. – an organization that purchases park land, then hands it over to B.C. Parks for their care.

A quiet road leads out of the park and winds the length of Lasqueti Island to False Bay, the island's

Above, Boho Bay is a good anchorage during a westerly. Below, Squitty Bay Marine Park.

main harbour where the foot passenger ferry from French Creek docks. No car ferry docks on Lasqueti, so there is only local traffic on the roads, which makes them pleasant for walking.

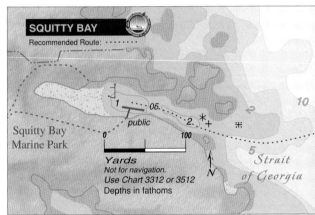

SQUITTY BAY
Recommended Route: ·······
Squitty Bay Marine Park
public
Yards
Not for navigation.
Use Chart 3312 or 3512
Depths in fathoms
Strait of Georgia

Scottie Bay [18]

Scottie Bay is an excellent anchorage on the north-west end of Lasqueti. The cove in the SW corner of this bay, south of Lindbergh Island, is sheltered from all winds and although tight, provides excellent anchorage for half a dozen visiting craft. Some small resident vessels are moored further inside at the west end of the bay. Entry is made through a narrow channel, staying close to the Lasqueti Island shore to avoid the reef extending halfway across the channel from Lindbergh Island.

There is a wharf and some buildings for a small fishing operation along the south part of the bay, and fish boats will arrive at almost any time of day and

The inner cove of Scottie Bay provides excellent shelter in all winds.

night. The road that connects to other parts of the island can be accessed here.

If the inside bay is busy, north of Lindbergh Island there is another, more-open bay where we have anchored many times in settled weather. The holding is good and the bay provides adequate protection from NW winds and a perfect venue for viewing summer sunsets. We usually anchor S of the islet marked '66' on Chart 3312. Other good anchorages on the N side of Lasqueti include two locations in **Tucker Bay** – one just west of Potter Pointer and the other, to the east, in front of a wide creek bed.

LASQUETI ISLAND AT A GLANCE

CHARTS: 3312, 3512
LAT LONG: Scottie Bay 49°30.98'N 124°20.22'W
PROS: A large island with a variety of lunch stops and overnight anchorages, Lasqueti makes a good destination to spend a few days. Interesting vegetation ranges from juniper in Squitty Bay to arbutus and spruce on N side.
CONS: West side of island has limited anchorages; False Bay is very dicey during summer Qualicum's – fierce southwesterly winds.
MUST DO: Anchor in Boho Bay and explore the nearby reefs by dinghy. In Scottie Bay – visit the nearby pebble beach and Fegan Islands.

Both provide good shelter in most winds. Another spot, sheltered from S winds, is north of **Jelina Island** and, although sheltered from light north winds, it is subject to an uncomfortable swell during northwesterlies.

False Bay 19

When anchoring in False Bay, stay close to the bay's northern shore to avoid a local southwesterly that can send erratic swells into the anchorage. Called the Qualicum, this strong wind blows in from the Pacific Ocean, funnels down the Alberni Canal on Vancouver Island, then sweeps across Qualicum Beach and over the open water into False Bay. The public dock provides access to a store, pub and post office which is just up the road.

Several drying lagoons border the main anchorage which are pleasant to explore by dinghy. One of these secluded lagoons was once home to China Cloud, hand built and launched on Lasqueti Island by the late Alan and Sharie Farrell, legendary west coast sailors. This beautiful wooden vessel was engineless and, with two bilge keels drawing only 2 1/2 feet, the Farrells would pole her into shallow inlets where she sat comfortably on the mud at LW.

China Cloud, built by the Farrells, is shown here at anchor in a lagoon of False Bay.

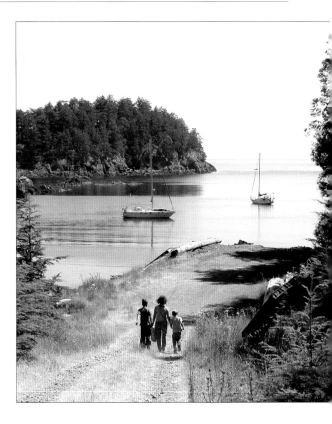

A beautiful trail lies at the head of Anderson Bay.

Anderson Bay 20

At the SE end of Texada Island is an excellent haven, especially if you're slogging up the Strait of Georgia in a northwesterly. Much of Anderson Bay is a provincial park which encompasses the small island and peninsula, for a total of some 78 acres (35 hectares.) This anchorage can be approached easily from the south or from the east through the small pass between Texada Island and the small island protruding from the point. Minimum depth in the pass is about about 15 feet (4 m). Be sure to stay in the middle of the pass and be careful rounding the peninsula as the reef shown on the chart extends further south than you might guess. Holding is very good in thick mud, but stay well south of the log dump area where debris can be expected. The bay is open to south and SE winds.

A hike can be enjoyed on the old logging road that starts at the dumpsite on the west side of the bay and connects with the Pipeline Trail, which travels the length of the island. This is a fairly easy hike along the natural gas pipeline right-of-way and is a very pleasant way to spend a sunny afternoon beneath the forest canopy. Blacktail deer, birds and intertidal life can all be found in the park.

Tribune Bay Marine Park, Hornby Island 21

In settled weather, this is a splendid summertime anchorage. Its wide and sandy beach is considered one of the best in the Gulf Islands and is ideal for small children, sloping gradually into the water and allowing swimmers to wade a considerable distance from shore. This same shelving bottom forces boats to anchor a fair distance from the head of the bay.

The bay provides good shelter from the prevailing summer northwesterlies but is completely open to the south. The holding ground, however, is good (sand and mud) and most anchors should be able to handle summer breezes from the south. If stronger S winds (over 15 knots) are predicted, think about moving to Ford Cove on the west side of Hornby Island, or Deep Cove on Vancouver Island or, in very strong SE winds, Comox Harbour. CHS chart 3527 gives good detail of this entire area.

Overlooking the entrance to Tribune Bay is beautiful Helliwell Park, a gift from an accountant named John Helliwell who donated this land to the province in 1964 because he felt "it was too beautiful to not share." We have walked to this park after landing our dinghy along the bay's eastern shoreline where the sandstone bedrock has been eroded into mushroom-shaped outcroppings and honeycomb hollows. Park land lies at the head of Tribune Bay, where a footpath leads up a grassy slope past windswept clumps of trees which give way to forest as the trail winds through a picnic area to the road. Follow this road for about a mile and a half to Helliwell Provincial Park, where a sign-posted trail at the entrance takes you through thick stands of Douglas fir as well as arbutus and oak. At the edge of the forest is a sweeping meadow of golden grass which shimmers in the sea breeze. The panoramic view from this bluff is of the Strait of Georgia with the mountains of Vancouver Island stretching across the horizon. The park's 3-mile circle walk goes right to St. John Point before looping back to the entrance. The sea cliffs below consist of sandstone and conglomerate rock, which attracts great numbers of nesting cormorants and gulls.

In 1997, Flora Islet, which lies within Tribune Bay Marine Park, was added to Hornby Island's park land and is popular with scuba divers for its sheer wall dropping off in steps and marine life that includes six-gill sharks. In spring this treeless islet is carpeted with wildflowers, as are the meadows of Helliwell Park.

Deep Bay, Vancouver Island 22

Of all places to run aground at anchor, Deep Bay seemed an unlikely spot. Maybe it was the name that lulled us into complacency. Or perhaps it was the scenic setting of this anchorage with its mountainous backdrop and sandy, grass-covered spit extending from the end of Mapleguard Point and once covered with maple trees before some houses were built there. During the 1946 earthquake, a huge wave momentarily engulfed this spit.

Shoal water extends northward from the spit, jutting into Baynes Sound. After making the wide turn

Top left, skim boarding at Tribune Bay, its beautiful broad beach shown opposite. Left, not-so-deep Deep Bay snares another skipper .

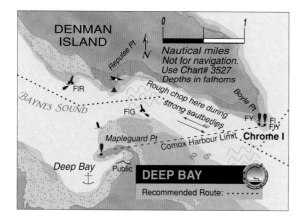

The passage leading to Baynes Sound from Chrome Island can be dangerous if a large tide is ebbing against a SE gale; such conditions can produce waves in the 10- to 15-foot range.

Sandy Island Marine Park / 23
Comox Harbour

Sandy Island, known locally as Tent Island, is located on White Spit at the N tip of Denman Island and is a great beach stop. At spring LW, this drying spit of sand and mud connects Sandy Island and the adjacent Seal Islets to Longbeak Point on Denman Island, with over 2 miles of beach to stroll along. The area abounds in tidal pools thriving with crabs and other shell fish. When herring are spawning in the spring, the beach at LW is often lined with bald eagles enjoying the feast. Good temporary anchorage lies off the W end of Sandy Island, in about 50 feet (16 m), where the sand spit drops off sharply and provides protection from SE seas (but not SE winds). If a fresh NW is blowing, anchor in nearby **Henry Bay** in 50 feet (16 m), which is close enough to visit Sandy Island by dinghy.

Boaters heading up or down the west side of Georgia Strait can pull into **Comox Harbour** for fuel, provisions and some shoreside activity. The Beaufort Mountains and Comox Glacier provide a beautiful backdrop to this harbour, while the extensive breakwater provides shelter for visiting vessels. Crossing the bar into the harbour can be tricky in strong SE conditions during an ebb, when swells will develop at the entrance area and along the bar. Be sure to locate the red entrance buoy (FlR and marked P54) and come within a quarter mile to the south of it, then aim for the last red conical buoy to the west (P50, lighted). The shallowest area of the bar is immediately east of the cone buoy. Range markers on the Vancouver Island shore are also of assistance in poor visibility. The area south and east of Cape Lazo must be given a wide berth during strong SE winds, when steep falling seas are common near the cardinal buoys. See Chart 3527 for detail.

into Deep Bay, we dropped anchor in 24 feet (8 m) over a mud bottom and tucked ourselves close to the SW shore to gain some protection from the S winds that blow with force through this anchorage. It turned out we tucked in a little too close. Early next morning we were aground. Our first clue was the chatter of clam diggers on shore. They sounded uncomfortably close. Bill got up and noticed we were listing slightly to starboard. A glance out the porthole as he turned on the depth sounder confirmed that we had just touched bottom. On a falling tide, our Spencer 35 had swung towards shore and planted her keel in the mud. We rowed out the spare anchor and tried to kedge off, but this didn't work because the tide was still dropping. Fortunately the ebb finished before *Sway* heeled right over, and by noon we were afloat on a rising tide.

Protection from strong SE winds is generally poor in Deep Bay and reports about the holding are mixed, with some people saying they have dragged in this anchorage. The problem may be that since the anchorage is so deep – anchoring depths start at over 85 feet (26 m) and shelve quickly from there – some boaters may not be putting out enough scope. Still, Deep Bay has the advantage of being near two great beach locations at Tribune Bay and Sandy Island Marine Park.

Enjoying the beach at the west end of Sandy Island

The Comox Valley Harbour Authority welcomes visiting pleasure craft and monitors VHF Channel 66A. The guest moorage for recreational boats is on the E side of the main breakwater. Services include fuel, fresh water, 20-amp plug-ins and a marine pump-out. Nearby are washrooms, showers, laundry facilities and a hydro-hoist, while within easy walking distance are shops, pubs and restaurants. Anchorage is available between the permanent buoys and the DND wharf area, where the holding is good.

Local attractions include Filberg Heritage Lodge & Park, located a short walk east along the harbourfront. The park grounds feature flower gardens and paths that lead to the stone-and-timber home of the Swedish-born lumber baron and philanthropist Robert Filberg, who arrived as a young man in 1909 and soon became chief engineer of Comox Logging Company. Near the water stands a totem pole depicting the four main family crests of the Comox First Nations – thunderbird, sun man, white whale and bear.

Comox was chosen in the 1850s as a training site by Britain's Royal Navy. Settlers soon moved into the area to farm the fertile valley, and Comox became a service centre for steamer traffic. In 1942, a Canadian Forces Base was opened, its personnel specializing in air-sea rescue. The Comox Air Force Museum is beside the airport, and visitors can wander freely among the vintage aircraft on public display at the Heritage Airport.

Above, the Henry Bay anchorage at Denman Island. Right, a Hobie Cat in Comox Harbour.

CHAPTER THREE

THE SUNSHINE COAST

Hardy Island Marine Park

The mainland side of the Strait of Georgia encompasses one of B.C.'s busiest boating areas, its waters stretching over 100 miles from Boundary Bay in the south to Desolation Sound in the north. In between are the Fraser River estuary, the port city of Vancouver, the glacier-carved fjords and inlets of the Sunshine Coast, and some of the best beaches this coast has to offer.

Strait of Georgia

This major body of water is busy with commercial traffic, including car ferries, freighters, tugs with barges and, from May through September, cruise ships. A vigilant lookout is a must when crossing the ship traffic lanes, which are about 5 miles wide near Sand Heads. In clear weather, freighters can be spotted heading to or from Boundary Pass and Vancouver and we limit our time in these traffic lanes by cutting straight across them. Recreational vessels should always defer to large ships in the strait and in a close situation we make our intentions obvious by making course changes that cannot be misunderstood. Freighters don't always respond to calls on Channel 16 (tugs and cruise ships are better on that score); if you don't get a response, try Victoria Traffic on Channel 11 or Vancouver Traffic on Channel 12 to get details on the movements of freighters and alert them to your sailing plan.

The southern Strait of Georgia is dominated by the Fraser River's outflow, especially from May to early August, when the freshet is running. This freshwater run-off from mainland mountains pushes huge volumes of green, silt-laden freshwater over 12 miles across Georgia Strait to Active Pass and south to Boundary Pass. So, unless you're planning a visit to the village of Steveston on the Fraser River, you should keep to the west side of the strait when northbound. This is especially important if you're bucking an ebb which can reach 5 knots near the river banks stretching from Point Grey to Point Roberts.

THE SUNSHINE COAST

CHARTS AND PUBLICATIONS
Chart 3490 for Fraser River, 3481 for Burrard Inlet and 3493 for Vancouver Harbour. Smaller scale charts for the Strait of Georgia: 3463, 3512, 3513 and 3538. Chart 3514 covers Jervis Inlet and Princess Louisa Inlet. Chart book 3312 shows good detail of Jervis Inlet and strip charts 3311 show almost the entire area in detail. CHS Tide Tables Volume 5 and Volume One of the SD. Call marinas on channel 66A or phone.

Timing your passage with a flood tide is a good idea, but be aware that during a large flood there is a set onto these banks on the east side of the strait with flood currents often in the range of 2-3 knots. Currents in the middle of the strait are usually about 1-2 knots. The Sailing Directions also notes 'residual currents' can cause water circulation to differ significantly from that expected from the combined action of wind, tides and river runoff, meaning the current you expect to help, can be contrary.

The prevailing summer winds in the Strait of Georgia generally blow NW or SE, with variants to the south and southwest. A northwest breeze will usually start mid-morning and often build to 12-to-16 knots by early afternoon, with a resulting chop of 2 to 3 feet. A SE wind will be foretold by high cirrus clouds and mare's tails. Southwest winds can be transition breezes, indicating a clearing trend, and are otherwise common near the south end of Saturna Island and off Qualicum Beach where they can blow strongly. Winds from this latter location often send a tedious ground swell into False Bay on Lasqueti Island making the anchorage uncomfortable. Mainland inlets such as Howe Sound often have onshore winds in the day (up the sound) and offshore winds at night (down the sound).

Coast Guard continuous marine weather broadcasts should be monitored throughout the day, as revisions for the Strait of Georgia are common. Luckily, safe havens are never too far away. Boaters arriving from U.S. waters can pull into Point Roberts, where an excellent marina provides transient moorage, before heading north into Canada.

The seas in the Strait of Georgia can quickly develop into a steep, uncomfortable chop in moderate winds. Especially nasty seas can develop within 3 or 4 miles of Roberts and Sturgeon Banks, and also at Halibut Bank and off the major passes when a northwest wind is blowing. The most dangerous seas, however, are those off Sand Heads at the mouth of the Fraser River's south arm.

The Fraser River

All arms of the Fraser River influence the Strait of Georgia but none more so than the main (south) arm, its entrance marked by the imposing structure at Sand Heads. This tower was rebuilt in 2002, when the old white-and-orange building was removed and a new white structure erected 100 feet further west. The light has changed to a flashing green every 6 seconds, visible for 10 miles. Between strong currents, shoal banks and freighters entering the river, the mouth of this arm is one of the most hazardous bodies of water on the B.C. coast. Add NW winds to an ebb current and the ensuing steep chop makes conditions challenging for all small vessels.

A trip up the main arm of the Fraser River is worthwhile, however, and is an opportunity to visit the ports of Steveston and Ladner (5 and 10 miles upstream respectively). Low-powered vessels navigating up the river should arrive well after the flood has started (reference **Point Atkinson**) and this is especially important during the months of freshet from June to early August when the river is discharging large volumes of water from mountain snowpack. During these months we usually arrive at Sand Heads with two or three hours left in the flood. Currents can be unpredictable around Sand Heads and the buoys should be given lots of room when entering the river mouth. Using chart 3490, small craft often proceed upstream keeping the red buoys to port by one or two boat lengths where the stream is weaker and where they will be out of the way of commercial traffic. This route can be taken right up to buoy S16 near Garry Point (see map on page 128 for route).

A sailboat under spinnaker heads north in the Strait of Georgia.

There's a good chance you will encounter freighters or tugs with barges at some point on the river and, as always in tight channels, these vessels have the right of way because of their limited ability to maneuver. The waters around Sand Heads can be nerve-racking when commercial traffic is entering or leaving the river. As mentioned, you can report your vessel's position to Victoria Traffic on Channel 11 if you want clarification or direction entering the river. If you want to speak to a ship entering the river, which we have done, pilots can usually be reached on Channels 16 or 17.

A common sight on the Fraser is the bright-red pilot vessel heading up and down the river. The crew are members of the Fraser River Pilots Association and they guide the comings and goings of large freighters. They also have to know the river like the back or their hand and they receive regular updates of channel depth from the Coast Guard. Silting of the main channels during freshet can be dramatic and depths can change overnight. A chairman of the association says he remembers having to send freighters on the wrong side of the red buoys (between S4 and S6) during a time of severe silting in 1999. "That really confused the yachts coming up the river," he recalls.

The job of keeping the river clear of sediment falls to the Fraser River Port Authority (a federally mandated port authority) which keeps a dredger stationed near Steveston for most of the winter and early spring months. Patiently dredging away at areas of infill (typically between Steveston and the bend to the west and south to S4), the dredge draws silt into its belly and hauls it away to a storage site to be sold for construction purposes. In late spring, when dredging might damage fish stocks during salmon fry migration, the Port Authority relies on the strong current (up to five knots on large tides) during freshet to take most of the silt out into the strait.

Dredging is crucial not only to ensure there is enough depth for freighters, but to keep the river deep enough to handle the additional water volume during freshet. Without dredging, large parts of the river delta could flood during spring freshet.

In late July and August, gillnetters are often fishing the river between Sand Heads and Steveston. Although the openings are fewer and shorter than in the past, boaters cruising the river in this period should monitor weather channels or call the Department of Fisheries at (604) 666-2828 for a 24-hour recording on opening information. Recreational vessels must keep clear of the nets laid across the river by gillnetters.

Top, Sand Heads light station at mouth of Fraser River. Below, tugs, barges and freighters are part of the traffic encountered on the river. Bottom, Steveston Lifeboat, Artist's Life, rescues a jet skier who hit a breakwater in the Fraser River.

Above, Steveston Harbour on the Fraser River.
Below, Captain's Cove Marina near Ladner.

FRASER RIVER HISTORY

The Fraser River is B.C's most important watershed. It originates in the Rocky Mountains, at Yellowhead Pass, and meanders for 850 miles before emptying into the Strait of Georgia. Along the way, its tributaries drain a watershed of nearly one-third of the province and its basin supports half of the province's agricultural land. Thousands of waterfowl nest annually on the river's delta and migrating salmon return regularly to the mouth of the Fraser at Sand Heads, which contains North America's chief spawning grounds for the Pacific salmon. In the 19th century, salmon canning became a thriving industry and by the 1890s there were 45 canneries on the river, concentrated in Steveston and Ladner, the latter founded in 1868 by William and Thomas Ladner, farmers from Cornwall, England.

Steveston 1

Enter Steveston between Garry Point and the QR beacon on Steveston Island, favouring the W side of the entrance where depths are greater. Transient moorage is available on the E side of the main wharf; you can call Steveston Harbour Authority at 604-272-5539 to reserve a berth. The office is at the top of the main wharf. Although anchoring is prohibited in summer in the W end of Cannery Channel, you can anchor east of the old Esso dock, with the better overnight anchorage lying at the far east end of Cannery Channel in about 12 feet (3.5 m). This is near the last marina basin. Holding in sand and mud is good but you will experience some current and boat traffic in the channel. The channel's east end is closed by a rock finger.

Steveston's townsite was established in 1878 by a dairy farmer named Manoah Steves. The village quickly grew into a bustling harbour, busy with large numbers of fishboats arriving to unload their catches. Local canneries employed hundreds of workers, and sailing ships from around the world pulled into port to take on cargoes of canned salmon. The Gulf of Georgia Cannery, built in 1894, is now a national historic site and since 1994 has operated as a museum, open to visitors throughout the summer.

Steveston is known for its excellent seafood restaurants which overlook the fishboat docks, where fresh fish is sold off the boats. Other nearby attractions include marine stores, gift shops, and a waterfront park with cycling trails.

Ladner 2

Located upriver from Steveston, the town of Ladner can be reached via Sea Reach or by proceeding along the river's main arm to Deas Slough where visitor moorage is available at **Captain's Cove Marina** (phone 604-946-1244) a full-service facility with a fuel dock, 60-ton travel lift, pub/restaurant and adjacent walking/cycling paths and a golf course. The entrance to Deas Slough, less than 3 feet at zero tides, is scheduled to be dredged in 2014. Vessels can anchor in the slough in about 8 to 10 feet in mud.

The town of Ladner is a half-hour walk (or a 5-minute taxi ride) west of Captain's Cove Marina. The town, centred around the historic village, has shopping centres, several good restaurants and hardware stores.

Aerial view of the Fraser River and Steveston,
with the tall ship Nippon Maru in foreground.

Outbound on the Fraser

When heading downriver, stay on the starboard side of the river to give way for commercial craft. We sometimes draw close to the jetty if we spot sea lions or seals on the rocks. This must be done carefully as the jetty has several gaps through which a strong cross-current flows, creating turbulent water on spring ebbs. Currents during freshet on strong ebbs can be up to 10 knots.

In summer months, NW winds will create very steep seas off Sand Heads for a distance of 2 to 3 miles into the Strait. These seas can be dangerous to small craft if winds reported at Sand Heads are above 16 knots, so be sure to listen to the weather before heading down river. If strong winds are predicted, try to leave early in the morning.

Once your vessel is clear of the last buoys off Sand Heads, a crossing to Active Pass, Porlier Pass or Silva Bay is straightforward. Porlier Pass is 12 miles from Sand Heads, while Active Pass and Thrasher Rock (the entrance to Silva Bay) are just over 13 miles away. Further up the Strait, Lasqueti Island, Smuggler Cove and Bargain Bay (near Pender Harbour) are all about 40 miles distant.

VANCOUVER 3

Set on the scenic shores of English Bay, the city of Vancouver is an exciting destination to approach by boat. Its famous skyline seemingly rises from the waters of English Bay and floats on the horizon. Gradually the shoreside parks appear as a green ruffle on the watery edge of a city flanked to the north by mainland mountains and to the south by sand banks and beaches. If approaching from the south, be very cautious of the drying and shifting shoals off Spanish Banks, and stay well west of all markers, with your depth sounder on at all times.

Upon entering False Creek or Coal Harbour, boaters can obtain moorage at several marinas located right on the downtown's doorstep, within walking distance of the city's major attractions. Visiting boaters can obtain city information and assistance with making slip reservations at the **Boater Welcome Centre**, which is located in a restored boat moored at the False Creek Yacht Club on the north shore of False Creek under the Granville Street Bridge. This centre can be reached by phone at 604-648-2628 or (toll-free) 866-677-2628. The fuel dock at the entrance to False Creek and the fuel barges in Coal Harbour are also sources for temporary moorage information.

False Creek

False Creek is easy to enter by boat and the marinas lying along its south shore offer transient moorage when slips are available. The docks at Granville Island Public Market provide a few hours of free moorage for boaters who want to shop for provisions

or enjoy the restaurants or walk to one of several nearby marine stores.

Anchorage for small craft is available in False Creek along its south side, between Spruce Harbour Marina and Heather Civic Marina, provided you are not in the way of commercial craft heading to and from the head of False Creek. When the proliferation of boats permanently moored in this area generated a plethora of complaints by local residents, new regulations were made to allow visiting boaters to anchor here for a maximum of two weeks in summer and three weeks in winter. Permits to do so, which are free, can be obtained at the **Boater Welcome Centre** (phone 604-648-2628 or call on VHF 66A) which is located under the north side of Granville Street Bridge beside the False Creek Yacht Club.

Once you're anchored, dinghy access can be made at **Charleson Park**, which is a 5-minute walk to Granville Island, and at **Quayside Marina** (call VHF 66A to reserve a dinghy spot). Passenger ferries servicing Granville Island will sometimes pick up passengers from anchored vessels.

False Creek's remarkable transformation from industrial waterway to livable neighbourhood began in the early 1980s when its former railyards on the north side became the site of Expo 86, Vancouver's world's fair. Granville Island, on the south shore of False Creek, had already opened in the late '70s, and was soon attracting visitors year-round to its public market, crafts boutiques, restaurants and live theatres. The visitor information centre, which provides maps, is opposite the Public Market.

Vanier Park can be reached on foot from Granville Island via the False Creek seawall or by False Creek Ferries. Several museums are located within this park, including the Vancouver Maritime Museum which houses the historic St. Roch, the first vessel to navigate the Northwest Passage. Floating vessels are displayed at the adjacent Heritage Harbour dock.

English Bay's waterfront is the West End's favourite gathering spot and can be reached by taking a ferry to the north side of the creek and walking along

Above, an aerial view of False Creek with Vanier Park in the foreground and the anchorage in the upper right hand corner. Below, Stanley Park's Brockton Point at the entrance to Coal Harbour.

the seawall which runs past Sunset Beach at the entrance to False Creek. The blue-coloured False Creek Ferries, which make regular summertime runs to the Maritime Museum at Vanier Park, depart from the west end of Granville Island while the multi-coloured Aquabus ferries use the east float of the visitors dock fronting the Public Market. You can access other creekside attractions, including Science World at the head of False Creek, with these ferries.

Above, an aerial view of Point Grey and downtown Vancouver, with freighters anchored in English Bay. Below, a powerboat passes Point Atkinson lighthouse at the entrance to Burrard Inlet.

Vancouver Shoreside Attractions

Coal Harbour, inside Burrard Inlet, is reached via the First Narrows, which is spanned by the Lions Gate Bridge. Sailing vessels must be under motor power when transiting the narrows, where tidal currents can be strong and commercial traffic heavy. Once inside this scenic harbour, boaters can choose from two large marinas offering guest moorage and immediate access to Stanley Park and the West End. A reservation at any of the city marinas is recommended when planning a visit to Vancouver. Anchoring is strictly prohibited in Coal Harbour.

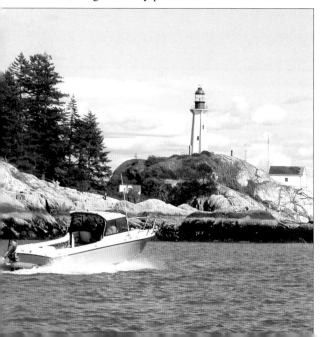

A few blocks east of Coal Harbour is the downtown core, where a Travel Info Centre is located at the Waterfront Centre, right across the street from Canada Place Cruise Terminal – a city landmark with huge white sails crowning the waterfront complex which contains a luxury hotel, restaurants, shops and a CN IMAX Theatre. Built for Expo 86, a world's fair celebrating Vancouver's 100th birthday, the terminal is busy throughout the summer with passengers boarding cruise ships bound for Alaska while sightseers stroll the outdoor promenades.

For a bird's eye view of the city, visit The Lookout!, downtown Vancouver's highest viewpoint at the top of the Harbour Centre Tower, located a few blocks east of Canada Place. Nearby is Gastown, Vancouver's original townsite, where visitors can stroll along cobblestoned Water Street and enjoy upscale shops and restaurants housed in refurbished brick buildings. Beyond are the streets of Chinatown, the second largest in North America.

Directly west of Coal Harbour is Stanley Park, the largest urban park in Canada, which originated as a 1,000-acre military reserve in the mid-1800s. A 12-pound muzzle-loader was eventually installed near Brockton Point, but its use became one of a time check for local fishermen when it would fire each Sunday at 6 p.m. Today, it booms across the water each evening at 9 o'clock and be easily heard throughout the city. A pedestrian seawall encircles Stanley Park, which can also be toured by horse-drawn tram or on a free shuttle bus, both departing from the lower parking lot throughout the summer. Bicycles and rollerblade skates can be rented near the entrance to the park. Among the park's many attractions are a rose garden, a totem pole display and the Vancouver Aquarium.

HOWE SOUND

A popular weekend destination for Vancouver-area boaters, Howe Sound is one of the most developed fjords on the B.C. coast. Its shorelines and islands are edged with waterfront homes and its waters are busy with car ferries transporting passengers between West Vancouver's Horseshoe Bay and the bedroom community of Bowen Island or Langdale at the bottom of the Sunshine Coast. The busy Sea-to-Sky Highway (leading to Whistler) traces Howe Sound's eastern mainland shore.

Several villages and fish camps of the Squamish First Nation dotted the shores of Howe Sound when Spanish explorers arrived in 1791. The following year Captain Vancouver's expedition surveyed the sound and named it after Admiral Earl Howe, a British naval hero.

Bowen Island was transformed from a logging and farming community into a holiday resort in 1920 when the Union Steamship Company bought property at Snug Cove, including the local hotel. In summer, day-trippers came by the thousands from Vancouver to enjoy company picnics and dances in the pavilion. Snug Cove remains a popular destination for Vancouver-area boaters, while the upper reaches of Howe Sound attract those seeking a bit of off-season seclusion among its steep-sided channels.

In summer, Howe Sound's wind pattern is dominated during sunny weather by daytime sea breezes (southerlies or southwesterlies) and nighttime land breezes (northerlies). This pattern is frequently interrupted by a passing weak front or the prevailing westerly flow of air from the Pacific onto the coast.

In winter, Howe Sound is dominated by inflow and outflow winds. If a southeasterly is blowing, it funnels into strong up-channel winds. If a Squamish is blowing from the north, fed by cold air masses inland, it will cause strong down-channel winds.

Above, regatta sailing in Queen Charlotte Channel in Howe Sound. Below, aerial of Howe Sound showing Gibsons and Keats Island.

Gambier Island 4

The southern bays of this large and mountainous island were once used extensively for storing log booms, to which boaters would moor their vessels with the aid of metal eye hooks (called 'dogs') which they would hammer into an outside log when docking, then remove when leaving. Now that most logs are sorted and stored on dry land, visiting boaters should be prepared to anchor. Because there is some leftover logging debris lying on the bottom of these bays, a trip line is recommended.

Halkett Bay Marine Park

This bay offers sheltered anchorage during summer winds, but is open to southerly winds and wash from passing ferries. A cluster of rocks lies in the NW part of the bay, and a detached rock with less than 6 feet (2 m) over it sits in the middle of the fairway near the head. Log booming continues in Halkett Bay, along its east shore.

The marine park provides one mooring buoy and a dinghy float. On shore are wilderness walk-in campsites and trails leading in several directions. One connects with Centre Bay; another winds through forested uplands to Mt. Artaban, which has a lookout tower at its summit. The last third of this trail is rough and steep, and the 6-mile (10 km) round trip takes about 5 hours. Another trail leads to Brigade Bay on the east side of Gambier Island.

Port Graves has a wide open entrance with room for lots of boats in good holding.

GAMBIER ISLAND AT A GLANCE
CHARTS: 3311, 3526, 3512
LAT LONG: Port Graves, 49°26.95'N 123°22.42'W
PROS: Gambier Island, with numerous good anchorages, remains very popular throughout the year especially with Vancouver boaters. A convenient destination for northbound vessels after visiting the city. Walks beginning from the government dock at Camp Artaban are excellent. Holding ground is generally very good.
CONS: Busy in summer. The south-facing anchorages are somewhat exposed to winds from this direction. Old logging debris in south bays.
MUST DO: Walk the trails from Port Graves.

Port Graves

Also known as 'East Bay' or 'Long Bay,' this is the principal anchorage in Howe Sound, providing shelter in all winds except for southerly gales. Many boaters anchor near the head of the bay near the red public dock in depths ranging from 15 to 45 feet (5 to 15 m) in sticky mud. In summer, moderate afternoon southerlies usually die down by early evening. Occasionally, strong outflow winds blow over the saddle from Bridgade Bay making Centre Bay a better bet in such conditions for overnight.

Leading from the dock is a system of trails, maintained by hikers and members of local yacht clubs, which provide excellent walks on the southest side of Gambier Island. Follow the trail markers that lead visitors around the property belonging to Camp Artaban, which is located above the public dock. Beyond the camp are trails leading to Centre Bay, Lost Lake, Mt. Artaban and Brigade Bay.

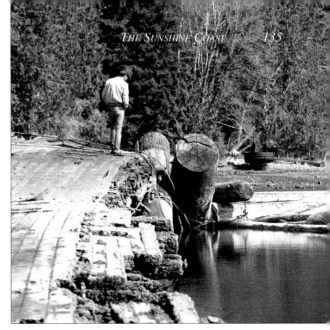

Centre Bay

Although recent residential development has lessened its appeal, Centre Bay remains attractive for local boaters with numerous spots along the shoreline to drop anchor. The holding ground is very good but boaters have lost ground tackle that snagged on discarded logging gear, such as cables, near the head of the bay or close along the shoreline. An anchor trip line is a wise precaution here .

The busiest area is on the west side of the bay behind a small point known locally as 'The Hook' with anchorage in 18 to 24 feet (6 to 8 m). This spot provides good shelter in prevailing summer conditions, although its anchoring room was diminished after local landowners built a dock in this cove, Royal Vancouver Yacht Club has an outstation on the west side of Alexandra Island.

West Bay

Wide and deep, West Bay is often quieter than Gambier's other bays, with a good view out to the Strait of Georgia. However, recent residential developments along the shore of this bay have limited shore access and diminished the bay's feeling of remoteness. On entering West Bay, beware of extensive shoal water on the east side of the entrance; the safest route is along the bay's western shore. Near the head of the bay, rotting remains of the wreck of the ship *Sir Thomas Lipton* can still be seen at LW.

Brigade Bay

Located in the middle reaches of Howe Sound, on the east side of Gambier Island, this bay is fairly well sheltered from S winds and is recommended during summer calms. A treed bluff forms the bay's northern entrance, and it's just inside this point that we have anchored, setting the stern anchor off the broad mud beach at the head of the bay, then powering forward to drop the bow anchor in the steeply shelving bottom.

The anchorage provides sublime views of mainland mountains, including The Lions. On shore, trails lead through the thin forest behind the bay where recent logging has taken place. At the turn of the last century, this land was the site of a homesteader's cabin and fruit orchard. Trails lead from Brigade Bay to the head of Port Graves, and an old logging road leads up the north face of Mt. Artaban.

Top, remains of wreckage of Sir Thomas Lipton in West Bay as seen in late 1980s. Bottom, Brigade Bay provides a view of The Lions.

Above, Ekins Point nook provides good anchorage in most conditions. Below, aerial of Gibsons and Plumper Cove on Keats Island.

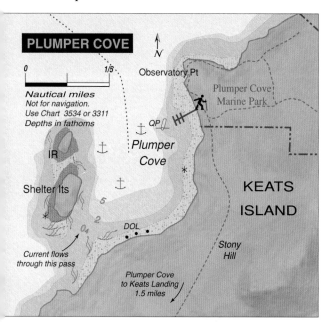

Ekins Point

On the 'back side' of Gambier Island, this nook lies west of Ekins Point, between a thumb of land and a private marina. We have anchored here in 30 feet (10 m) at LW with a stern line to shore. The down-channel view of the Port Mellon pulp mill is not the prettiest, but the view in the other direction is of snow-capped mountains. A swath of grass graces the water's edge just inside the eastern point of this nook, while the rest of this pristine section of shoreline is treed and hilly, part of a recreation reserve that extends for a half-mile on either side of Ekins Point. Moderate winds dissipate in the vicinity of Ekins Point, allowing for sheltered anchorage inside this small nook. Strong outflow winds will gust through the anchorage and this spot will experience swell from the channels outside.

Plumper Cove Marine Park, Keats Island 5

Located just 3 miles (5 km) east of the town of Gibsons, this popular cove offers good shelter from the Strait of Georgia with marine park facilities including a wharf for boats and dinghies, and eight mooring buoys. SW of the park is a roomy anchorage with depths of 40 to 50 feet (12 to 15 m). The holding is generally good in soft mud and shell, but due to current running between Keats Island and the Shelter Islets, there are kelp patches which frustrate some anchors. We generally anchor just to the NE of the larger islet to stay out of afternoon westerlies which snake around both sides of this islet.

On shore is a pebble swimming beach and a grassy picnic area which provides access to the park's 165 acres (66 hectares) of well-maintained hiking trails. The loop trail of about 1.5 miles (2 km) takes about one hour to hike, while a longer trail leads to Stony Hill (710 ft) and Lookout Mountain, the highest point on Keats Island at 795 feet.

The shallow gap between Keats Island and the mainland's Steep Bluff near Gibsons can present a hazard at LW when a strong W or S wind is blowing. Often a bad chop develops from the bar out to Gower Point. During such conditions, exiting Howe Sound via Barfleur Passage may be a better tactic. In light winds during mid- to HW, the bar is safe for most vessels. Use charts 3534 or 3311 for good detail.

THE SUNSHINE COAST

The Sunshine Coast, which stretches from Howe Sound to Desolation Sound, has been attracting visitors since the late 1800s when steamships began running excursions to summer resorts along this scenic coastline. The name 'Sunshine Coast' was coined by Harry Roberts, whose grandparents founded Roberts Creek in 1889. The Union Steamship Company adopted the term for its 1925 brochure, touting the region's 'Sunshine and Sea-charm along Holiday Shores on the Gulf Coast.' The Sunshine Coast does receive more sunshine than Vancouver, but less than Victoria. Its appeal for boaters lies more in its variety of anchorages – from beach-lined bays and craggy coves to glacier-carved fjords.

MALASPINA STRAIT / WELCOME PASSAGE

Malaspina Strait, like the Strait of Georgia, is a wonderful place if the wind is with you. For northbound cruisers, however, summer northwesterlies often start blowing in mid-morning and usually increase to 15 to 20 knots. As in the Strait of Georgia, a short steep chop quickly develops and will often be in the 2- to 4-foot (.8 to 1.2 m) range which can make the journey a real slog. Fortunately, there are good anchorages along the southern half of the 30-mile strait in which to pull out if the going becomes too tedious.

The first hurdle to enjoying the delights along Malaspina Strait is getting beyond Merry Island and Welcome Passage, where currents can be 3 or more knots. During spring tides, the current will be felt at the S end of Merry Island and, if you happen to be bucking an ebb, it can make the trek up to Smuggler Cove a long day. If setting out from the W side of Georgia Strait (the Nanaimo area or Silva Bay, for example), following a course to the west of the Thormanby Islands is a good way to approach Smuggler Cove, Bargain Bay or Pender Harbour. You will be free of obstacles and most of the current and tug traffic. Also, if a northwesterly is blowing, Lasqueti and Texada will provide a decent lee right up to Pender Harbour.

There are also plenty of marinas along the Sunshine Coast, where much of the shoreline is lined with recreational and retirement homes, and where several major towns are located. Gibsons marks the S end of the Sechelt Peninsula and is the former setting of the long-running *Beachcombers* television series. The show's fictitious coffee shop, called Molly's Reach, is now a seafood restaurant located at the head of the wharf in Gibsons. Sechelt is the cultural centre of the Lower Sunshine Coast. The Sechelt natives' House of Hewhiwus (Chiefs) is located here and contains an art gallery, theatre and museum. Each August, the town hosts the Sunshine Coast Festival of the Written Arts, which is held at the heritage Rockwood Centre.

Farther up the coast is **Secret Cove**, another former steamship landing and today the site of several marinas. Farther north still, **Pender Harbour**'s numerous bays contain several marinas and coastal communities, the main one being Madeira Park where a marina, public wharf and shopping mall are located. Madeira Park is also home to Harbour Publishing, founded by Howard and Mary White in 1974 and featuring regional titles by B.C. authors about living and working along the coast.

Powell River, on the Upper Sunshine Coast, is a classic company town (declared an official heritage district in 1995 by the federal government) which grew up around the pulp-and-paper mill that was constructed between 1910 and 1912. A large marina is located south of the city in Westview, a seaside suburb of Powell River, and provides moorage for transient vessels in its north and south harbours. The

A sailboat northbound in Malaspina Strait passes the water tower located near Stillwater Bay.

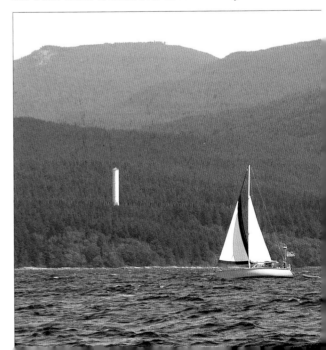

wharfinger's office is located on a boardwalk between the two harbours, where you'll find showers, washrooms and laundry facilities. A chandler is located at the marina and fuel is available. Groceries and other supplies are a walk up a steep hill and a shuttle is available in July and August.

South of Grief Point, the **Beach Gardens Resort & Marina** welcomes visitors to its 45-berth marina. Showers, fuel in summer and a beer-and-wine store are on site. In July and August, a shuttle service is provided to Town Centre Mall for provisioning. This marina is a good pull-out in strong winds.

Near the north end of the Sunshine Coast, at the end of the Sunshine Coast Highway, is the coastal hamlet of **Lund** – founded in 1889 by Charles and Frederick Thulin, brothers who had recently arrived from Sweden. They named the townsite Lund, which means 'forest grove' in Swedish, and built the historic Lund Hotel. Lund is the termination of Highway 101 which connects, via ferry, with Vancouver. For boaters, Lund operates a public wharf and there is a haulout here also.

Another small settlement was established at **Bliss Landing** during World War I, and today this former steamship stop is home to a private marina.

Anchorage at peaceful and protected Surrey Islands in Buccaneer Bay.

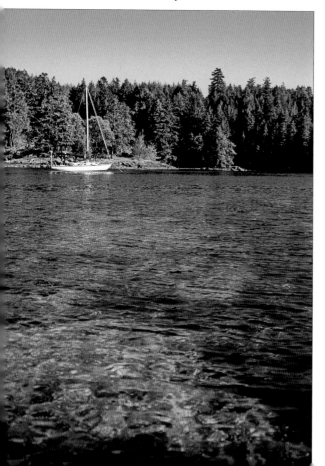

The Sunshine Coast has several sandy beaches, thanks to the glaciers that left behind drift deposits of pulverized sand, gravel and clay when they retreated from the Strait of Georgia some 10,000 years ago. Remnants of these glacial outwash plains are found at Harwood, Savary and Hernando islands, but the area's most extensive beach is at Buccaneer Bay in the Thormanby Islands.

Buccaneer Bay, Thormanby Islands 6

The unconsolidated sands and gravels on North Thormanby Island have been eroded, over time, from its steep cliffs and washed onto the shores of Buccaneer Bay, forming a sweep of sandy white beach that stretches down the west side of the bay to its head. Part of the beach is actually a drying flat that joins North Thormanby with South Thormanby; the passage between them dries at about 10 feet (3 m). A tiny marine park is located at Grassy Point, on the S tip of North Thormanby, but most boats anchor closer to the head of the bay off Gill Beach or in adjacent **Water Bay**, which offers better protection from northwesterlies.

Another option is to anchor behind the **Surrey Islands** on the east side of Buccaneer Bay, and dinghy over to the beach. This anchorage offers better protection from NW winds and is only exposed to southwesterlies. Using a stern line, we like to pull ourselves close to the South Thormanby Island shore. To minimize wake from the many small powerboats zipping around the bay, we anchor with the bow pointed west. Holding ground throughout the bay is very good in mud and sand.

Captain Richards and the officers of H.M.S. *Plumper* apparently had horse racing on their minds while surveying these waters in 1860. They had just received the 'welcome' news that the racehorse Thormanby, owned by Mr. J. C. Merry, had won the

---

BUCCANEER BAY AT A GLANCE

CHARTS: 3535, 3311, 3512
LAT LONG: 49°30.40'N 123°59.25'W
PROS: Great family destination with excellent swimming on the fine sand-and-shell beach. Holding is good in sand and mud. Large bay with many anchoring opportunities. Surrey Islands provide best-sheltered spot. Smuggler Cove is a short distance away for more secure anchoring or for exploring by dinghy.
CONS: Open to NW winds; head of bay also open to S winds. Swells from Malaspina Strait can make their way well into the bay.
MUST DO: Go swimming off this beautiful beach.

Above, aerial view (looking east) of Buccaneer Bay, Welcome Passage, Smuggler Cove and Secret Cove. Below, Vaucroft Beach at Buccaneer Bay.

Derby back in England and that Buccaneer had placed second. Other area names inspired by the horse races at Epsom include Oaks Point, named for 'The Oaks', an annual race for three-year-old fillies, and Tattenham Ledge, named for 'Tattenham corner', the race course's last turn.

For boaters approaching Buccaneer Bay's entrance, the thrill of the turf gives way to some navigational caution. Both Epsom and Oaks Points should be given a wide berth on rounding due to a continual shifting of the shallows, which could result in less depth than indicated on the chart. When entering Buccaneer Bay from Welcome Passage, between Tattenham Ledge and the drying reef off Derby Point, be aware of tidal streams that could push your vessel sideways onto the rocks. In December 1953, a tug seeking shelter from a SE gale hit a reef here, rolled over and sank, claiming 5 of the 7 crewmen's lives. The captain had been able to radio a Mayday, but two tugs tied up in nearby Secret Cove didn't respond to the distress call because their crews had switched to the broadcast band to listen to a hockey game. This tragedy prompted the Tugboat Owners Association to require all tugboats monitor the emergency channel and the Department of Transport ordered the broadcast band removed from all radio-telephones.

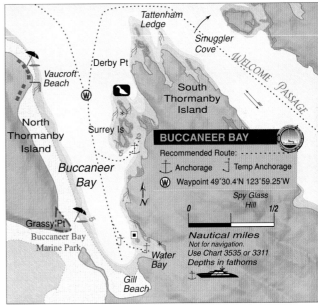

BUCCANEER BAY

Recommended Route: - - - - - - -

⚓ Anchorage   ⚓ Temp Anchorage

Ⓦ Waypoint 49°30.4'N 123°59.25'W

Spy Glass Hill

0   1/2

Nautical miles
Not for navigation.
Use Chart 3535 or 3311
Depths in fathoms

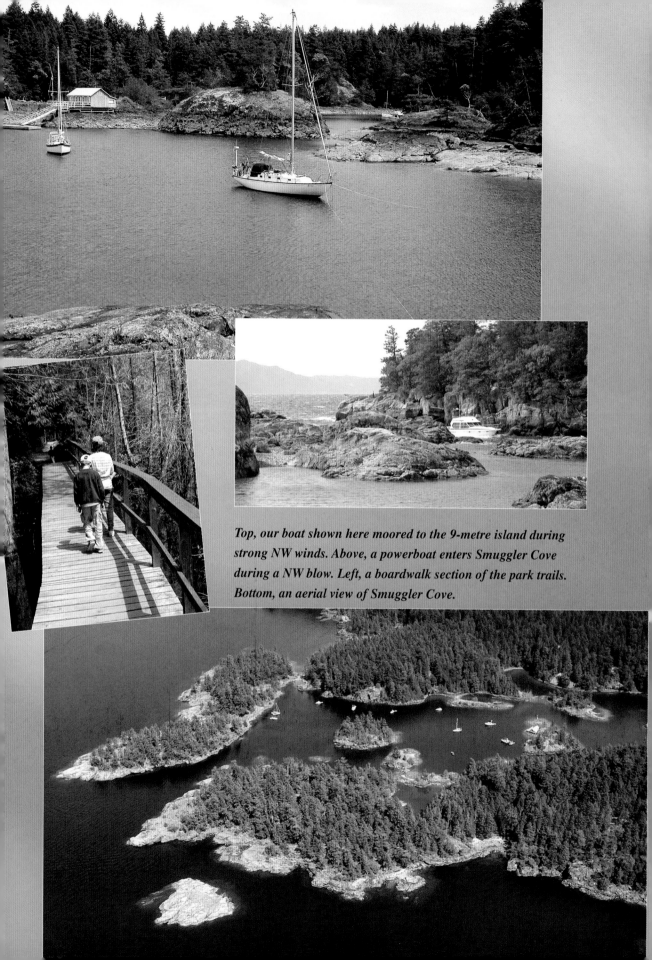

Top, our boat shown here moored to the 9-metre island during strong NW winds. Above, a powerboat enters Smuggler Cove during a NW blow. Left, a boardwalk section of the park trails. Bottom, an aerial view of Smuggler Cove.

Smuggler Cove 7

Some anchorages beg to be explored by dinghy or kayak, and Smuggler Cove is one of those. This provincial marine park's collection of islets and coves offers an idyllic setting for leisurely exploration, especially on clear summer evenings when a setting sun lingers above the treetops and casts its glow across the anchorage. One of the Sunshine Coast's most popular boating destinations, Smuggler Cove manages to retain the charm of a small-craft anchorage even on busy summer weekends when boats are tucked into its every nook and cranny.

Anchoring in Smuggler Cove usually requires vessels to tie a stern line ashore or set a stern anchor in order to make room for other boats. Strong NW winds can make their way through the small islands near the entrance, sending gusts to boats anchored behind the small islet marked '9' on strip chart 3311. There is a least depth of 6.5 feet (2 m) in the small easternmost cove and the channel leading to it. This cove has the best protection from all winds.

Near the entrance to Smuggler Cove, vessels tie to shore with bows pointed first south and then west, following the curve of the shoreline. Although this stretch is fairly protected from NW winds, southerly gusts make themselves keenly felt.

Eight islets lie within the cove and most are connected to shore by drying reefs. Private cottages occupy some of the islets, built before Smuggler Cove was transferred to the Parks Branch in 1971. The cove is completely surrounded by parkland and its trails wind through the surrounding woods to the outer shorelines and inland to a small parking lot used by visitors arriving by road.

Smuggler Cove was once the hideout of Larry 'Pig-Iron' Kelly, a 19th-century seaman of the Royal Navy who, in a career move, turned to smuggling immigrant workers by boat from Canada into the United States. During prohibition, the cove was said to be a storage area for bootleg whiskey that was distilled on Texada Island and smuggled by boat into American waters. Providing shelter from all winds and discouraging casual visitors with its narrow entrance, the cove was a natural choice for clandestine activities.

SMUGGLER COVE AT A GLANCE

CHARTS: 3535, 3311, 3512
PROS: A real haven, secure and usually roomy anchorage; good protection from most winds with good holding. Interesting to explore by dinghy, kayak or on foot.
CONS: Often busy, usually requires a stern line.
MUST DO: Hike trails, explore islets and reefs.

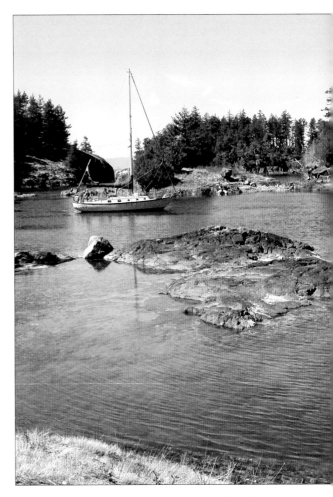

One of several inviting nooks in Smuggler Cove.
Most vessels stern-tie for secure overnight moorage.

Smuggler Cove's narrow entrance no longer keeps pleasure-seeking boaters away but it still demands careful pilotage and a close eye to Chart 3535 or 3311. When entering, boaters should favour the Isle Capri's shore (which has a provincial park sign). Although entering in strong winds can be intimidating, the wind and chop die quickly once you're just past the park sign.

Pender Harbour 8

Pender Harbour is a major service centre for pleasure craft cruising the Sunshine Coast, its collection of populated bays offering an array of good marinas, repair facilities, stores, restaurants and a nearby golf course. The most popular anchorage in Pender Harbour is **Garden Bay,** which also has a provincial marine park. This anchorage has good holding in 30 feet (10 m) over mud. Swinging room is limited and your anchor light should be on at night to alert boats heading to and from Madeira Park. NW winds can gust through the anchorage keenly.

The marine park has a dinghy dock connecting to a trail leading inland for a mile to the spectacular views from Mount Daniel, its summit a protected archaeological site in recognition of its importance to the local Sechelt natives. Before a smallpox epidemic in 1782 wiped out 90 percent of the native population in the Strait of Georgia, the shores of Pender Harbour were the location of a major settlement. Its main village, situated at Garden Bay, con-

The dinghy dock and anchorage at Garden Bay, with Madeira Park on the far shore.

sisted of seven huge longhouses – 800' long by 300' wide by 50' high. The native cemetery on the waterfront is now a protected archaeological site.

Other anchoring options for smaller craft in Pender Harbour include Hospital Bay and Gerrans Bay, just south of Dusenbury Island. Gunboat Bay at the head, is a pretty bay which provides good holding in soft mud but entry is along a narrow channel with a least depth of 2 feet (.7 m). Current and a drying rock that lies close to the N shore in the entrance dissuade many cruisers.

Several marinas line the shores of Pender Harbour, including the large public wharf at Madeira Park. With over 600 feet of visitor moorage available, this is a good location to reprovision at the nearby grocery stores and liquor store.

Bargain Bay 9

Entered off Malaspina Strait between Edgecombe Island and the east side of Francis Peninsula, this excellent harbour extends south of Pender Harbour

> ### Pender Harbour at a Glance
> **CHARTS:** 3535, 3311, 3512
> **LAT LONG:** Garden Bay, 49°37.85'N 124°03.66'W
> **PROS:** Pender Harbour and area has some good anchorages and is generally very well protected. Many good marinas. Fuel, groceries and marine supplies can be purchased here. Good dinghy exploring and hiking at Garden Bay Marine Park.
> **CONS:** Can be a little hectic on weekends with small powerboats and dinghies zooming about. Many rocks and reefs to watch for.
> **MUST DO:** Explore Canoe Pass by dinghy. Go for a walk at Garden Bay.

and is joined to it by a narrows. Vancouver-area boaters heading north like this spot – it is a short drive off the watery highway north and is usually quiet. Two rocks, each with less than 6 feet (2 m) of water over it, lie in the entrance fairway; the SW rock is large and locals have marked it with a makeshift white float. When entering, favour the starboard side of the channel, keeping the makeshift buoy to port for safe passage between the two rocks. If the buoy is not there, favour the east shore and follow the contour of this shoreline into the main anchorage.

The anchorage at the head is well sheltered from most winds (strong southerlies will send gusts into the west side of the bay) and the holding is good in depths of 40 feet (12 m) in sticky mud. Bargain Narrows, sometimes called Canoe Pass, connects this anchorage with Pender Harbour. It leads from Bargain Bay to Gerrans Bay, and is navigable at or near HW in a dinghy only, for it dries over 6 feet (2.1 m). Overhead, a road bridge connects the mainland with Francis Peninsula, formerly known as Beaver Island.

Bargain Bay has retained an atmosphere of bygone days, when the Pender Harbour area was

Anchorage at the head of Bargain Bay. The nearby narrows connects with Pender Harbour

SPILSBURY'S COAST

Coastal pioneer Jim Spilsbury (1905-2003) spent much of his long life living and working along the Sunshine Coast. When he was nine, his English-born parents moved from a farm in the Fraser Valley to Savary Island where they lived in a large tent for the next 10 years. The tent's platform was made of planks salvaged from the beach and the tent frame supported canvas walls. In 1924, his Cambridge-educated father received an inheritance and the family built themselves a comfortable home beside the wharf. Spilsbury's mother, who had enjoyed roughing it, didn't like being back in a real house and within a year had moved into the shed out back.

As a young man in the 1920s, Spilsbury began selling and servicing radio equipment in remote coastal communities up and down the south coast, travelling by boat and then, in 1944, by floatplane. This single aircraft was the beginning of what would become Queen Charlotte Airlines, a commercial carrier that Spilsbury sold in 1955 to return full-time to exporting radiotelephone equipment.

In his later years, Spilsbury and his second wife owned a cabin at Ballet Bay on Nelson Island, to which they traveled from Vancouver in their cabin cruiser *Blythe Spirit*. His entertaining anecdotes about life on the B.C. coast in the last century are contained in his bestselling books *Spilsbury's Coast* (co-written with Howard White) and *Spilsbury's Album*. His days in the airline industry are retold in *The Accidental Airline*. All three books are published by Harbour Publishing, located at Madeira Park, Pender Harbour.

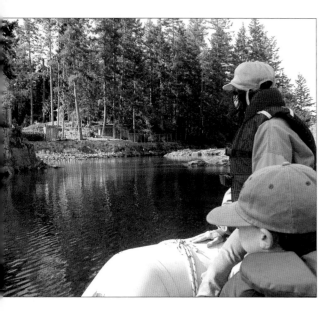

The narrows joining Pender Harbour and Bargain Bay can be traversed by dinghy at HW.

much less developed. The anchorage is quiet compared to Garden Bay, and loons still visit here in summer.

A temporary anchorage lies at the mouth of Bargain Bay. This scenic spot is north of Edgecombe Island and its reefs and rocks are all visible, allowing for straightforward pilotage and making it a good pull-out spot if you're arriving late at night. Although the holding is good, southerly winds can blast through the anchorage.

Ballet Bay, Nelson Island

Nestled along the southern shores of Blind Bay behind a cluster of islets, Ballet Bay is well sheltered with good holding ground. There are, however, several reefs and rocks encumbering the entrance into the anchorage, and the Sailing Directions advises mariners without local knowledge to enter at LW, when the reefs reveal themselves. Entry is best made from the west, proceeding with caution, for a rock lies well off the point on Nelson Island that juts into the anchorage. Submarine cables are another hazard to avoid in Ballet Bay, and the location of these is marked on Chart 3312, which has excellent detail.

Once the hook is set, the numerous islets beckon to anyone who enjoys poking around by dinghy or kayak. Waterfront homes surround the anchorage, precluding the possibility of hiking to Hidden Basin. (Hidden Basin is best visited by dinghy because of its treacherous entrance. We know of one boater who was trapped in Hidden Basin for several days waiting for a tug to arrive after his sailboat was wrecked in the shallow, bottleneck entrance.)

Ballet Bay, named for the ballerina Audree Thomas whose parents homesteaded here, is a bit of an anomaly in an area dominated by place names associated with famous officers and battles of the British navy. Horatio Nelson's victory at Copenhagen is recalled in the names of Blind Bay and Telescope Passage. It was at this battle that Nelson claimed not to see his commander-in-chief's signal of recall because he had put his telescope to his blind eye.

Telescope Passage is also a useable exit for small craft wanting to make their way further north into Jervis Inlet and the delights of Hotham Sound and Princess Louisa Inlet. The passage has a least depth of about 23 feet (7 m) but with rocks in mid-channel and on the west side, it must be transited carefully, favouring the Nelson Island shore.

Ballet Bay offers sheltered anchorage at the mouth of Jervis Inlet.

Above, Hardy Island anchorage. Right, adding the finishing touch to some rock art on Musket Island.

Hardy Island (Musket Island) Marine Park, 11

First impressions needn't be lasting impressions when it comes to an anchorage. The first time we sought shelter along the southern shores of Hardy Island, at the mouth of Jervis Inlet, the spring weather was wet and dreary, and the area looked uninspiring. We anchored in the 9-fathom cove and spent the night listening to rain pounding on our coachroof. Years later we visited Hardy Island again when the summer weather was hot and sunny and not a drop of rain had fallen for weeks. It was now the site of a marine park, initially called Musket Island, then changed in 2004 to Hardy Island because this was the name commonly used for the anchorage (the park encompasses Musket Island and the foreshore of Hardy Island, which is private).

The day we arrived at the Hardy Island anchorage, we had taken advantage of favourable winds and made a run from the Copeland Islands down to Jervis Inlet. By early afternoon the seas were building in Malaspina Strait as a northwesterly funneled between Texada Island and the mainland, and we were glad to pull into the lee of Hardy Island. Again we sought shelter along Hardy Island's southern shore, but this time we pulled into the anchorage formed by tiny Musket Island, which at LW is joined

HARDY ISLAND ANCHORAGE AT A GLANCE

CHARTS: 3312, 3311 and 3512
LAT LONG: 49°43.32'N 124°12.875'W
PROS: Marine park; undeveloped; excellent anchorage with room for lots of vessels, large and small. Good holding and well protected. Swimming can be enjoyed from the clean rock foreshores.
CONS: Can be busy at height of season; some exposure to southeasterly winds. Limited hiking.
MUST DO: Swim and explore tidal pools.

at its western end to Hardy Island by a drying tombolo. A few boats were anchored here with stern lines to the Hardy Island shore, but there was room enough for us to tuck well into this bight and tie off. This is a secure spot with good depths at LW (at least 10 feet). Anchoring depths are greater (50 feet or more) near shore along other parts of this pretty bay. Holding is very good throughout the anchorage.

This T-shaped anchorage is sheltered from most winds, especially northwesterlies. (If a strong SE wind is in the offing, Ballet Bay would be the safer anchorage.) Mediterranean-style mooring allows many vessels to tie along the shoreline thoroughout the anchorage. Large vessels often anchor in the middle of anchorage at the entrance where depths and room allow for two or three big boats.

Musket Island is a pleasant spot to picnic or explore the many tidal pools and there is a short trail around the perimeter of the island. Swimming is good, with wide flat rocks along the shore of Hardy and Musket Island, providing convenient and safe access into the water.

An old granite quarry on Hardy Island, adjacent to this anchorage, has resumed operations but its activities do not spoil the appeal of this marine park. The quarry first operated during World War II, when Hardy Island was owned by a Seattle financier named LeRoy Macomber. He owned the island from 1930 to 1951, during which time his caretaker turned it into a deer sanctuary. The island was later logged extensively by a series of owners and present timber growth is about 20 years old.

Harmony Islands 12

This picturesque cluster of four islets lies along the eastern shores of Hotham Sound, where forest-clad mountains provide a stunning backdrop. A small anchorage known locally as Kipling Cove lies amid the three northernmost islets, one of which is part of **Harmony Islands Marine Park**. (The two other islets are privately owned.) A rock lies at the entrance to this tiny cove with less than 6 feet (2 m), and there is no room to swing, so a stern line to shore is required. If the cove is filled with boats, there is additional anchorage in 15 to 30 feet along the east side of the islands and also opposite, along the mainland shore. In settled conditions there is also anchorage behind the islets near Syren Point in 90' and using a stern line to shore. The pass between the southernmost of the Harmony Islands and the mainland has less than 3 feet (1 m) at LW.

Opposite, aerial view of Hotham Sound and Harmony Islands. Inset, pretty Kipling Cove.

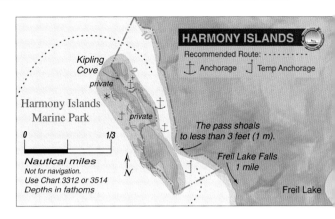

The winds that funnel up and down the reaches leading to Princess Louisa Inlet tend to dissipate in Hotham Sound, and on a calm night at the Harmony Islands, the only sound is the distant roar of Freil Lake Falls, which tumble 1,400' into the still water. Holding in the anchorage is good in mud and shell.

The Harmony Islands were named by Dr. Campbell Balmer, a Vancouver dentist who, with two friends, bought the four islands in 1932 for $248. His son, Jack Balmer, recounted in an article he wrote for *Pacific Yachting* in 1995 that each summer his family would travel to the Harmony Islands aboard their cabin cruiser and tie up to the small dock his father and friends had built out of beach logs. Their nearest neighbour was a hermit living up from the beach on St. Vincent Bay, for whom they would bring fresh bread and pipe tobacco whenever they visited. During World War II, fuel rationing and other restrictions took the pleasure out of boating for Dr. Balmer and he sold both his boat and his island. His two friends also sold their ownership in the other three Harmony Islands.

According to veteran cruiser and writer Sven Donaldson, it is possible to hike up to spectacular Freil Lake. His interesting story on this, in the July 2002 issue of *Pacific Yachting*, describes hiking up forested slopes to the base of the prominent rocky knob that's about 1500 feet north of the falls and from here skirting around its northern flank to follow a 40-degree slope up its backside to the summit. This very challenging hike takes over 2 hours, requires backcountry experience and should only be undertaken in dry conditions.

Princess Louisa Inlet 13

Erle Stanley Gardner, the American writer who created Perry Mason, was deeply moved when he first laid eyes on Princess Louisa Inlet. "One views the scenery with bared head and choking feeling of the throat," he wrote in *Log of a Landlubber*. "It is more than beautiful. It is sacred."

Anyone who has guided a boat to the head of a breathtaking fjord such as Princess Louisa Inlet has no doubt shared Gardner's sense of reverence. Deepwater fjords flanked by mighty peaks are nature's cathedrals, their humbling presence a reminder that we are mere mortals whose time amid these earthly paradises is a gift to be cherished. These are places so serenely beautiful, a person can't help but believe that some omnipotent force had a hand in their creation.

Most B.C. boaters sooner or later make the pilgrimage to Princess Louisa, one of the most stunning fjords on our coast. For sailboats, afternoon inflow winds often help when heading up Prince of Wales Reach, the first of three steep-sided reaches that twist inland from Jervis Inlet. Combined with a flood tide, boaters can make good time travelling the 35 miles to the inlet, passing beneath the cliffs of Marlborough Heights and into Princess Royal Reach. Winds usually die in Queens Reach.

The entrance to Princess Louisa Inlet lies halfway along this reach, where **Malibu Rapids**, with currents up to 9 knots, should be traversed close to slack water. Although there are no obstructions in the pass, there can be impressive turbulence and other boat traffic to deal with – skippers should ensure they keep their vessels on the starboard side of the channel. Malibu Islet presents a blind corner for northbound vessels and in poor visibility it might be a good idea to alert southbound traffic via radio or airhorn of your approach.

Sailing up Prince of Wales Reach with a nice inflow wind taking us to Princess Louisa.

PRINCESS LOUISA AT A GLANCE

CHARTS: 3312, 3514
LAT LONG: Chtbx Falls, 50°12.04'N 123°46.35'W
PROS: This spectacular marine park includes mooring buoys, stern pins, a boat dock and a dinghy dock. For boaters who want to disembark passengers there are a number of campsites, a picnic shelter and toilets. Beautiful scenery, perhaps unsurpassed on the southern B.C. coast. Good (and challenging) hiking.
CONS: Can be busy, dock use limited. Well off the major routes and a long drive each way. Sometimes a battle to get through Malibu Rapids if timed wrong.
MUST DO: Enjoy the sublime setting and go for a hike.

Top, view of Chatterbox Falls and anchorage at Princess Louisa Inlet. Above, Macdonald Island anchorage. Right, Malibu Rapids.

Just inside the rapids, on the north shore, is an impressive lodge with an outdoor swimming pool. It was built in the 1930s as an exclusive retreat for Hollywood movie stars and moguls. Today it is a summer youth camp.

Once through the pass, mariners witness one of nature's grandest glories, their vessels dwarfed by the lofty mountains and chalky white waterfalls that plunge into the still water. A narrow gorge carved by glaciers, Princess Louisa Inlet's sheer rock walls rise to heights in excess of 6,000 feet. At its head you will find the Chatterbox Falls tumbling 1,800 feet down tiers of granite into the turquoise water.

It was here, in the 1920s, that a Nevada prospector named James (Mac) Macdonald, obtained land and built a log cabin. After years of welcoming mariners to his own piece of paradise, Mac donated his property in 1953 to the Princess Louisa International Society, and it became a provincial marine park in 1965. He wanted the inlet preserved "as God created it, unspoiled by the hand of man" so that "all may enjoy its peace and beauty." To this end, BC Parks and the Society play a joint role in preserving the inlet in its natural state and maintaining the park's facilities,

which include a picnic shelter, a dinghy dock and a large float where boaters can moor for up to three days.

Anchoring is possible on the shelf at the base of Chatterbox Falls, where current from the falls will keep your vessel from swinging into shallow water at LW. Mooring rings for stern lines have been installed a few hundred yards west of Chatterbox Falls. On shore, a loop trail leads to Chatterbox Falls where signs warn visitors to be cautious on the slippery rocks. A much more strenuous hike can be made along a very rough trail that climbs up the mountainside to an old trapper's cabin. This is a hard 2-hour climb but worth it for views of the inlet.

In 1972 a special campaign resulted in the Princess Louisa International Society raising sufficient money to build a shelter for boaters (James Macdonald Memorial Lodge). That same year, the Society acquired Hamilton Island (situated about midway up the inlet) and 30 acres of low land east of the island, as well as a couple of other small islands. The island has been renamed **Macdonald Island** and boaters can tie to one of six mooring buoys installed E of the island or anchor in about 20-30 feet with a stern line to either shore (look for stern rings). A dinghy dock serves the park's mainland shore.

In 2001, the Society secured options to purchase the remaining freehold land in the inlet from Weyerhaeuser Canada. Two years later, the Society, in partnership with the Nature Conservancy of Canada and with the generous support of the Tula Foundation, Weyerhaeuser and Society members, purchased the 2,221 acres immediately surrounding Mac's original lands and added it to the marine park. For more information, visit www.princesslouisa. bc.ca.

Copeland Islands 14

The Copeland Islands have long been a popular roadstead for commercial vessels, and log booms are still regularly secured to concrete abutments on the east side of Thulin Passage, which runs between the mainland and these picturesque islands. Now a popular marine park conveniently situated en route to Desolation Sound, the Copeland Islands are enjoyed by pleasure boaters as both a day stop and, in settled conditions, an overnight anchorage.

We have anchored in several spots, including the anchorage halfway along the island chain where the marine park sign is posted. This

---

Map:

F G

Thulin Passage

0   1/2

Nautical miles
Not for Navigation.
Use Chart 3311 or 3513
Depths in fathoms

N

Copeland Islands (Ragged Islands)

stern-tie

stern-tie

Copeland Islands Marine Park

stern-tie

W

stern-tie

FI

COPELAND ISLANDS
Recommended Route: ----------
⚓ Anchorage   ⚓ Temp Anchorage

scenic cove, accessed off Thulin Passage, is some-what protected by an islet from the wash of passing vessels but not from southeasterlies. When these are forecast, we have moved around to the other side of the island where the view of the sunsets are lovely, but swell from the Strait of Georgia can make the anchorage uncomfortable.

One of our favourite spots for anchoring is the passage running between the two southernmost islands. There is good protection along the southern shore of this passage in the lee of the island marked '73'. You can either use a stern line to stay clear of the reefs in the bay or ride freely in the area clear of the rocks to the N. We sometimes anchor inside the nook on the northern shore where we tie a line to a tree on the bluff that rises above the anchorage. The channel with deeper water is east of the drying rock. Although this is a good place to anchor, you can

Above, the anchorage off Thulin Passage. Below, anchored in the cove between the two southern islands. (Keep drying rock to port when entering.)

COPELAND ISLANDS AT A GLANCE

CHARTS: 3311, 3538 3513
LAT LONG: 50˚00.04'N 124˚47.8'W
PROS: Marine park; undeveloped; adequate protection from moderate winds with generally good holding. A miniature archipelago which is excellent for dinghy or kayak exploring and has several spots for swimming and hiking. Good views on west side of islands.
CONS: Some anchorages open to wind and swell. Can be busy. Anchorage on Thulin Passage side gets some wake from passing vessels. Current throughout.
MUST DO: Explore islands by dinghy or kayak.

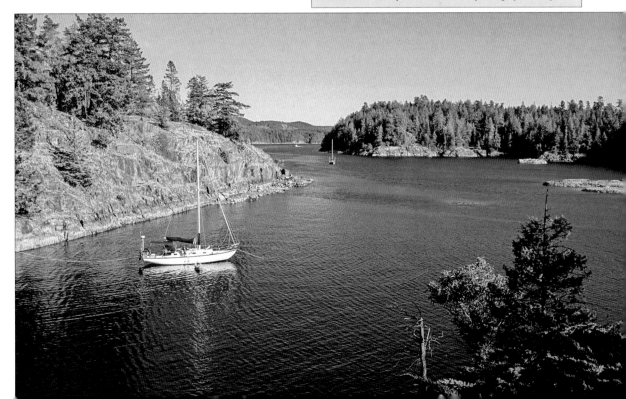

expect some swell and gusts will come around the corner of the western point during NW winds. If such winds are predicted, tuck yourself as far as possible into this small cove. At the western entrance to this anchorage is a foreshore of pink granite that forms tiered steps into the water. On sunny summer days, as the rising tide laps across this smooth stone, the water is warmed by the sun-baked rock, making it a lovely place to ease into the water for a swim.

The Copeland Islands are also ideal for exploring by dinghy or by kayak, and the hiking is easy through thin forests of arbutus and spruce. There are a few wilderness campsites on these pristine islands but no facilities except two pit toilets.

Known locally as the Ragged Islands, the islands' name was changed by the Canadian Hydrographic Service in 1945 to honour Joe Copeland, an American trapper and handlogger who came to the area in 1900 and settled at Portage Cove. Copeland was one of several colourful characters living in the vicinity of Desolation Sound in the early 1900s. He served as a Confederate soldier during the American Civil War and afterwards, according to Jim Spilsbury in his book *Spilsbury's Coast*, he became an outlaw, joining a renegade gang that robbed stagecoaches. Upon escaping to Canada and the remote B.C. coast, 'Old Joe' relived his war years by meeting the steamboat dressed in full Confederate army uniform.

Hernando Island & Area 15

One of the most beautiful beaches of the Sunshine Coast lies at the north end of Hernando Island, extending in both directions from Spilsbury Point.

On several trips north we have dropped anchor either west of the point in about 60 feet in a sand/mud bottom or around the corner in Stag Bay, between Spilsbury and Hidalgo Points. It's a short row ashore for lunch from either location to this lovely stretch of tan-coloured sand on the west side of the point.

The views from here are sweeping. To the west is barren Mitlenatch Island, a nesting and breeding site for thousands of birds, especially glaucous-winged gulls. The island, a provincial nature park, receives relatively little rain (the prickly pear cactus grows here) and, because of the long swim, few predatory mammals threaten the young nesting birds.

Directly across from Stag Bay, on the north side of Baker Passage, lie the **Twin Islands** with anchorage in settled conditions only in Echo Bay. In 1940 a mining engineer named Dick Andrews bought the Twin Islands and had a 14-bedroom log house built on the neck between the two islands.

In 1961 a German aristocrat (and nephew of Britain's Prince Philip) bought the Twin Islands. The Prince and Queen Elizabeth, accompanied on board the Royal Yacht Britannia by their daughter Princess Anne, anchored off these islands in 1971 and spent a day ashore at the log lodge.

Hernando and Cortes Islands were named for Hernando Cortes, conqueror of Mexico, by the Spanish explorers Galiano and Valdes while surveying these waters in June 1792. The *Sutil* and

Spilsbury Point has a great beach and is a perfect stop in settled weather. The bottom shelves quickly here but the holding is good in sand and mud.

Mexicana had sailed up the Strait of Georgia with the *Discovery* and *Chatham*, commanded by Captain George Vancouver, after the two survey parties chanced upon one another off Point Grey. Vancouver was himself busy bestowing place names on the islands and channels in the vicinity, including **Savary Island** which, like Hernando Island, is a remnant of a retreating glacier. The north side of Savary Island also makes for a pleasant beach stop in settled weather, with the added advantage of local roads for those wanting to go for a walk. We've found the holding to be only fair with a loose sand/mud/gravel bottom. The anchorage is completely exposed to the north and west, so close attention should be paid to weather forecasts.

Stag Bay on Hernando Island is a fair-weather anchorage, open to the north, but the sandy holding ground is good and there is decent protection from southerly winds. Keep an eye on the depth sounder to find a spot close to Spilsbury Point. There is fairly constant current between Spilsbury Point and Sutil Point.

On a couple of occasions we've noticed the weather come up quite suddenly in this area between Vancouver Island and the mainland. If menacing clouds start collecting to the south, it may be time to head for the protection of Cortes Bay or Gorge Harbour on Cortes Island. After a sunny afternoon spent on the beach at Spilsbury Point, it's a quick run to either bay for sheltered overnight moorage.

Above right, anchored west of Spilsbury Point.

Below, the view toward Desolation Sound.

CHAPTER FOUR

DESOLATION SOUND

Roffey Island

Desolation Sound is one of the B.C. coast's most scenic cruising areas. There are few sights more thrilling than rounding Sarah Point on Malaspina Peninsula to the view of Homfray Channel winding its way through the massive green and grey portals of the Coast Mountains. To port looms mile-high Mount Addenbroke on East Redonda Island, its eastern slope plunging into the deep waters of Homfray Channel. To starboard is Mount Denman, rising over 6,590 feet (2,000 m). Perpetual snowfields crown distant mainland mountains and a wide variety of vegetation cling to the rugged slopes, from light patches of alpine lichen to dark stands of spruce, fir and cedar. At the base of these mountains lie anchorages of outstanding beauty, their wilderness preserved by their park status but tested each summer when boats arrive by the hundreds.

The unique recreational appeal of this area was recognized in 1973, when the provincial government established Desolation Sound Marine Park. It became British Columbia's largest marine park, with 40 miles of shoreline and over 20,000 acres of upland. As Bill Wolferstan notes in his seminal book *A Cruising Guide to Desolation Sound*, there are so many anchorages in this area that a cruiser could spend over two months here without anchoring more than one night in the same location.

There are uncrowded spots to be found in the Desolation Sound area, and even the most popular anchorages are relatively quiet in the shoulder seasons of early June and mid-to-late September. However, at the height of summer Desolation Sound is one of busiest cruising grounds on the B.C. coast and many anchorages require stern lines to shore.

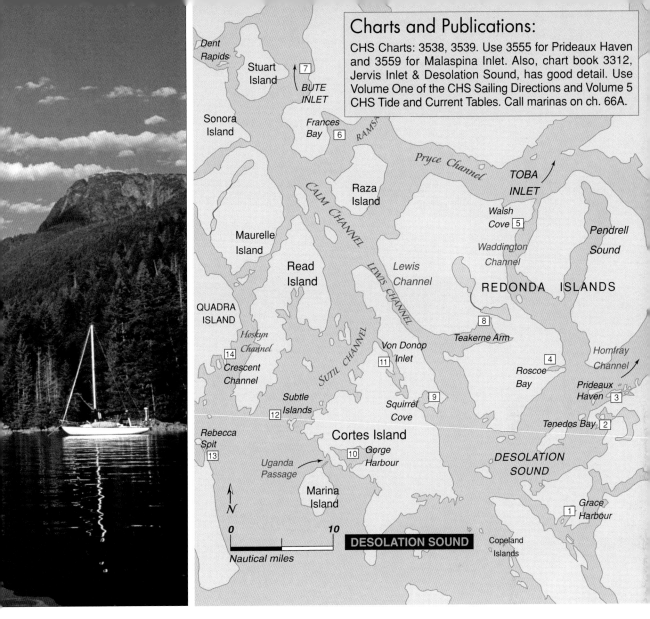

Charts and Publications:

CHS Charts: 3538, 3539. Use 3555 for Prideaux Haven and 3559 for Malaspina Inlet. Also, chart book 3312, Jervis Inlet & Desolation Sound, has good detail. Use Volume One of the CHS Sailing Directions and Volume 5 CHS Tide and Current Tables. Call marinas on ch. 66A.

Dent Rapids

Stuart Island

7

BUTE INLET

Sonora Island

Frances Bay 6

RAMS

Pryce Channel

TOBA INLET

CALM CHANNEL

Raza Island

Walsh Cove 5

Pendrell Sound

Maurelle Island

Waddington Channel

Read Island

Lewis Channel

REDONDA ISLANDS

LEWIS CHANNEL

QUADRA ISLAND

8

Hoskyn Channel

Teakerne Arm

14

Von Donop

Homfray Channel

Crescent Channel

SUTIL CHANNEL

11 Inlet

Roscoe Bay

4

Prideaux Haven 3

Subtle Islands

12

Squirrel Cove

9

Tenedos Bay 2

Rebecca Spit

13

Cortes Island

10 Gorge Harbour

DESOLATION SOUND

Uganda Passage

Marina Island

N

Grace Harbour 1

0   10

DESOLATION SOUND

Copeland Islands

Nautical miles

The topography of the area is such that anchorages run perpendicular to the dominant wind directions in the Strait of Georgia, and most winds are muted by the time they reach the anchorages in Desolation Sound.

Some of the best swimming on the B.C. coast is found in the vicinity of Desolation Sound, where tidal currents are weak and the complex topography is ideal for surface waters to rise in temperature. Good swimming spots are usually found in protected bays and coves where surface water isn't disrupted by tidal mixing and may be further warmed by a sandy beach or rock foreshore during a rising tide. And then there are the lakes. Numerous anchorages in and around Desolation Sound have forested uplands offering a shaded refuge of trails leading to small lakes in which you can take a dip. More marine parks lie immediately north and west of Desolation Sound amid the Discovery Islands – a maze of islands lying between the mainland and Vancouver Island. Those parks located south of the tidal passes are easily accessible and offer scenic anchorages. A few coastal communities are also found in this area, along with an array of marinas that welcome summertime boaters.

Tides and Currents

Flood currents from Johnstone and Georgia Straits meet in this area, resulting in weak and inconsistent tidal streams in Desolation Sound, seldom exceeding 2 knots. This will vary as a result of wind which may be noticeable in Homfray and Lewis Channels. The very last vestiges of flood current from the Strait of Georgia flow N past Kinghorn Island, turn east along the north side of the island and flow NE into Desolation Sound where they dissipate.

Ample fresh water and a sheltered anchorage kept Captain Vancouver in Teakerne Arm for weeks.

GRACE HARBOUR

Recommended Route: ··········

⚓ Anchorage   ⌐ Temp Anchorage

GIFFORD

PENINSULA

0   1/4

Nautical miles
Not for navigation.
Use Chart 3559 or 3312
Depths in fathoms

swimming area

IR

GRACE HARBOUR

Jean I.

Scott Pt

Desolation Sound Marine Park

It's understandable, if somewhat ironic, that Captain George Vancouver chose the name Desolation Sound for what is now one of B.C.'s busiest boating destinations. In 1792, when Vancouver was surveying the Inside Passage, the shores of Desolation Sound probably did seem desolate, their overwhelming impression one of inhospitable wilderness. Arriving on a dark and rainy night in June 1792, unable to gain soundings close to shore, his ship drifting about in light and variable winds as if "it were blindfolded in this labyrinth," Vancouver was finally able to anchor just before midnight on the north side of Kinghorn Island "in company with the *Chatham* and the Spanish vessels, in 32 fathoms."

After dragging anchor the next day in heavy squalls, the ships moved to **Teakerne Arm** and remained there for about two weeks while survey parties set off in the ships' boats. Meanwhile, Vancouver wrote in grim terms of the surrounding countryside – the forests were gloomy, the deep water yielded no fish and the precipitous mountainsides offered little in the way of useable foreshore. There were a few native villages in the vicinity, including one at Prideaux Haven, but this was deserted when visited by one of Vancouver's survey parties. A smallpox epidemic had struck 10 years earlier, devastating the local native population.

By the early 1900s, the quiet solitude of Prideaux Haven made it an appealing place for hermits. Muriel Wylie Blanchet describes in her book *The Curve of Time* the two resident hermits she would visit there – one living in a cabin at Melanie Cove, the other at Laura Cove. The local population took a dramatic upswing whenever Blanchet arrived in her 25-foot cabin cruiser with her five children aboard and a dog in tow. There was no room on board for their Gordon setter, who slept in the dinghy. In wet weather the dog would sleep on shore, under shelter of some sort, and one night she was driven by a cougar into the water where she stood chest deep until morning. Prideaux Haven is now part of Desolation Sound Marine Park, the two other major anchorages within the park being Tenedos Bay and Grace Harbour.

Grace Harbour   1

Located off Malaspina Inlet, this large anchorage is usually less crowded than the other major anchorages in Desolation Sound. It offers excellent shelter and can accommodate several dozen boats. A good spot to anchor is at the harbour's head, where sticky mud provides good holding. Another sheltered spot to drop the hook is north of **Jean Island**. A major

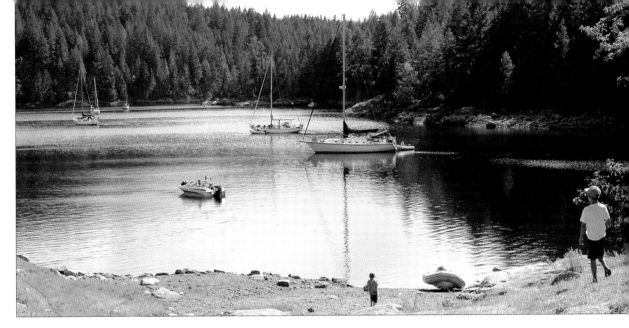

Above, the head of Grace Harbour viewed from the trail head. Below right, a pleasant trail leads to the lake near Grace Harbour. Bottom, summer winds are usually light in Malaspina Inlet.

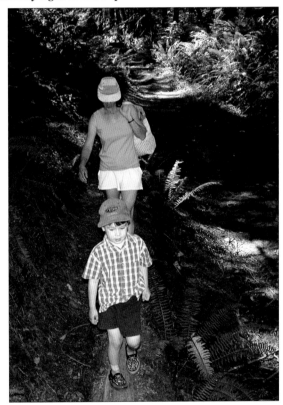

village of the Sliammon First Nation used to occupy the shores of Grace Harbour and some midden stretches of beach are in this anchorage.

At the head of Grace Harbour is a forest trail that leads to a nearby lake (an easy 15-minute walk). The turn-off to the lake veers left from the main trail and winds a short distance through thin forest to the lake's edge. There's a grassy clearing and some wide flat rocks providing access into the water, which is slightly murky from a peat and mud bottom. Garter snakes thrive along the trails and lakeshore, where we've seen them slip into the water for a swim.

Several overnight anchorages can be found on the southwest shore of **Malaspina Inlet**, along the approach to Grace Harbour. The anchorage behind the **Cochrane Islands** lies within the boundaries of Desolation Sound Marine Park and provides access to park trails. The anchorage south of the island marked '53' on Charts 3559 and 3312 of the **Josephine Islands** is outside the park but provides good shelter. Around the corner from Grace Harbour are a number of inlets and bays to explore, including Lancelot Inlet and Okeover Inlet, the latter being where The Laughing Oyster restaurant overlooks the public docks.

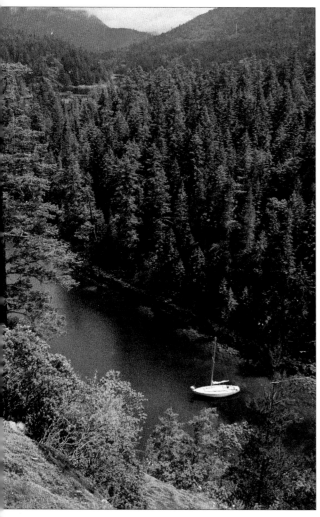

Tenedos Bay   2

This anchorage, when surveyed by Vancouver's officers, was described as 'the deep bay' by Archibald Menzies, the expedition's botanist. Tenedos Bay had everything Vancouver disliked about the area – deep water (over 300 feet/100 metres in the central part of the bay) and steep slopes which provided no extensive foreshore for recreation or the picking of edible vegetation. Recreational boaters, on the other hand, find much to approve of in Tenedos Bay, including its dramatic anchorages, excellent shelter and the lovely hike to Unwin Lake for a freshwater swim.

There are several spots to anchor in Tenedos Bay, including the popular bay just west of Unwin Lake that provides shelter from SE winds. Although fairly deep – 60 to 100 feet, the advantage of this spot is its proximity to the lake, a short hike along a sometimes muddy trail taking about 15 minutes. Some logs along shore provide a platform for swimmers.

Tenedos Bay's westernmost cove, known locally as **Three Fathom Cove** (for its depth), lies between the large unnamed island and the mainland shore. This cove is avoided by many because of the shallow entrance (a shoal extends from the SW tip of the island) but the holding here is good in soft mud and the cove offers superb protection. A drying tombolo, connecting the island with the mainland, separates Three Fathom Cove from the more popular spot that

Left, looking down from our lofty perch on the west side of Tenedos Bay. Below, the bay's east arm provides good, although deep, anchorage.

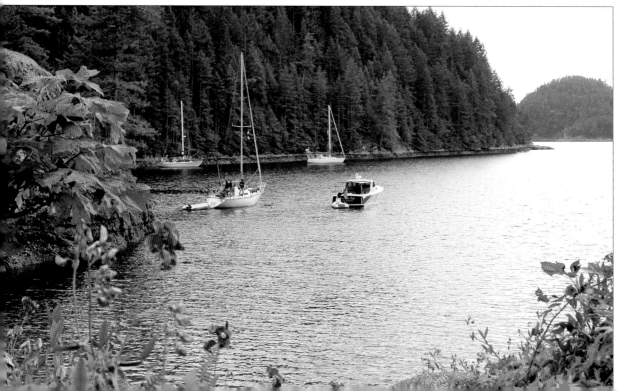

TENEDOS BAY AT A GLANCE

CHARTS: 3312, 3538
LAT LONG: 50°06.9N 124°42.24'W
PROS: All-round great anchorage with many places to safely drop the hook and relax. Good swimming nearby and some hiking.
CONS: Often busy, but with a little searching you can find a quiet spot.
MUST DO: Take a dinghy ride to the tombolo. Go for a swim in Unwin Lake.

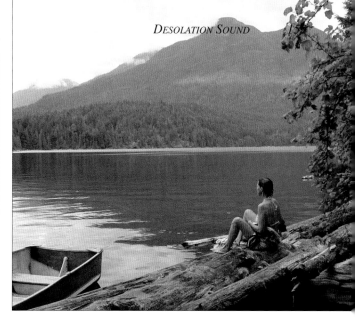

lies along the NW side of the island and opens up to a fairly large bay. This area is also well protected. We often tuck ourselves fairly close to the tombolo end in about 13 feet (4 m) of water with a line to shore. We once anchored here and climbed up the bluff overlooking this nook where we enjoyed an eagle eye's view of our boat at anchor. The sun felt warm that June day, the summer crowds had not yet arrived, and we lingered on our lofty perch, enjoying the surrounding wilderness in all its desolate glory.

Vessels can also anchor with sternlines along the north shore opposite the large island. This is protected from most winds but is exposed to strong southerlies which often bring a chop right into the bay. Another spot that provides good shelter lies south of the island in the area west of a reef and where a stern line will be needed.

Above right, the swimming is good at Unwin Lake. Below, peaceful Three Fathom Cove.

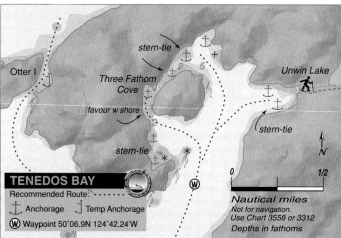

Otter I

stern-tie

Three Fathom Cove

Unwin Lake

favour w shore

stern-tie

stern-tie

TENEDOS BAY
Recommended Route:
Anchorage Temp Anchorage
W Waypoint 50°06.9N 124°42.24'W

Nautical miles
Not for navigation.
Use Chart 3558 or 3312
Depths in fathoms

0   1/2

N

Prideaux Haven

Nestled along the mainland shore is a collection of coves, islands and lagoons referred to as Prideaux Haven – one of the most popular anchoring areas on the B.C. coast. Yet, busy as Prideaux Haven becomes in summer, you can always find a spot to drop the hook. We've often arrived late in the day and always found room. The holding in sticky mud is very good throughout the various anchorages, which are well-protected.

The Prideaux Haven anchorage is the largest and can easily accommodate a dozen boats in depths ranging from 22 to 60 feet (6.7 m to 18 m). Although vessels stern-tie along the north and south shores, this puts them broadside to west winds which occasionally gust through the gap from **Eveleigh Anchorage**. We've seen large boats let go of their stern lines in such winds.

The entrance to Prideaux Haven lies between Eveleigh Island and Oriel Rocks, along a channel less daunting than it looks on a chart. If entering at HW, we maintain a parallel course along Eveleigh Island and into the anchorage. At LW the hazards are visible and easy to navigate around.

Large yachts favour Prideaux Haven for its depth and size, while smaller vessels are found in Melanie or Laura Coves. **Melanie Cove** seems to be the wallflower anchorage and is often relatively quiet when the other bays are packed. Melanie Cove offers the best protection in strong NW winds; favour the Melanie Point shore when entering. **Laura Cove** is perhaps the prettiest anchorage of the group, with pleasing vistas of islets and mainland mountains. A trail runs between the east end of Laura Cove and the parks information shelter at Melanie Point.

In addition to the main anchorages of Prideaux Haven, Melanie Cove and Laura Cove, boats can tuck into various bights along the outside of **Copplestone Island** and along the north side of Eveleigh Anchorage. Boats also anchor with a stern lines along the north shore of the peninsula protecting Melanie Cove. This passage is popular with small powerboats which often raft here in large numbers.

Above, anchorage north of Copplestone Island. Left, aerial view looking across Eveleigh Anchorage to Prideaux Haven. Opposite, aerial view of Prideaux Haven.

'Haystack Bay', east and south of Roffey Island, offers stunning views of mainland mountains.

If the main anchorages are too busy for your liking, a quieter spot can usually be found east or south of **Roffey Island** at the far end of the marine park. Reefs, capped with small islets, extend east from Roffey Island and north from the mainland. They resemble a series of haystacks for which regulars have named this cove. The extent of the reef from Roffey Island can be difficult to identify (we saw a large powerboat go merrily right over it at HW) and the main cove east of the island is more easily entered from the north. There is some current through the anchorage, about a knot at most, so setting a stern line can be a little tricky. Anchoring south of the island affords a better view of Homfray Channel and the mainland mountains.

There are several quiet nooks in which to anchor on both sides of **Homfray Channel**, including a small horseshoe-shaped cove near the southern tip of East Redonda Island which is well sheltered from prevailing summer westerlies. Homfray Channel is named after Robert Homfray, a civil engineer from Worcestershire, who arrived in Victoria in 1860 and worked as a surveyor. In *British Columbia Coast*

Names, Their Origin and History, Captain John Walbran states Homfray "was of an eccentric disposition, and for some years before his death had his tombstone erected in Ross Bay cemetery, with all particulars on it with the exception of the date of his decease" which was added after his death in 1902.

When Captain Vancouver was surveying local waters, the expedition's botanist Archibald Menzies and some crewmembers were exploring the entrance to Laura Cove when they came upon a fortified village perched on an islet. The British seamen were fascinated with this small citadel, "built on a rock, whose perpendicular cliffs were nearly inaccessible

PRIDEAUX HAVEN AT A GLANCE

CHARTS: 3555, 3312,
LAT LONG: entrance: 50°08.75'N 124°40.95'W
PROS: An outstanding series of anchorages with good protection from wind and good holding ground. Numerous opportunities for swimming, hiking and exploring by dinghy.
CONS: During peak season of July and August it is busy, but with a little exploring you can usually find a quiet spot.
MUST DO: Explore the reefs of Laura Cove and Copplestone Island by dinghy. Find a quiet nook in Homfray Channel to go for a swim.

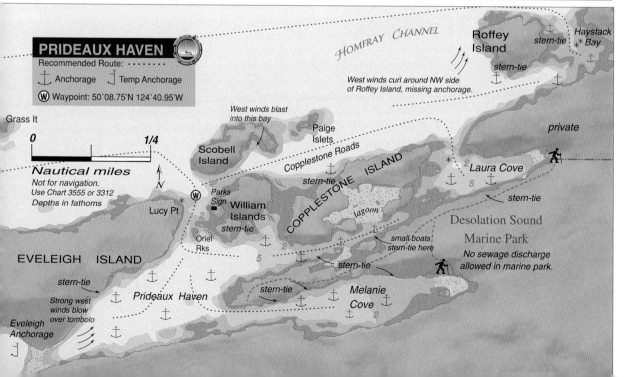

on every side; and connected with the main, by a low narrow neck of land." As Menzies and the others wandered through the recently deserted village, they were suddenly pounced upon by a horde of fleas. The men rushed into the water up to their necks, but the fleas refused to drown, so the men towed their clothes back to the ship and boiled them to get rid of the vermin.

A hermit named Phil Lavine lived in Laura Cove in the early 1930s, near another hermit named Mike over at Melanie Cove. Mike was a philosophical fellow, his cabin lined with books, and when he died the old Frenchman Phil, who couldn't read, built shelves around his bed to hold Mike's library.

Roscoe Bay, West Redonda Island 4

This marine park is extremely popular in the summer months and tying a line ashore has become standard practice for this long, enclosed anchorage to accommodate the number of boats that squeeze in. And squeeze in, they do, through the narrow entrance where a drying bar can be crossed by keelboats only at or near HW. At high neap tides, there is about 12 feet (3.5 m) of water. Inside, this well-protected anchorage is usually like a millpond although occasionally NW gales will gust through the bay.

Logging used to take place on the shores of Black Lake, and a channel was dug the short distance between the lake and the head of Roscoe Bay for floating out the logs. Today a trail traces the remnants of this flume and leads to the north side of Black Lake where some smooth rocks are ideal for summer sunbathing and for a freshwater swim. A dinghy or kayak could be portaged to the lake, and it's also possible to hike up a trail overlooking the lake. There is camping near the lake.

The shores of the anchorage itself are also good for exploring. One sunny afternoon in early June we climbed to the knob on its north side, then returned to the water's edge to lounge on the smooth sandstone. Our reverie was broken only briefly when another boat entered the cove, motored around, then left us to our private paradise.

ROSCOE BAY AT A GLANCE
CHARTS: 3312, 3538
LAT LONG: 50°9.74'W 124°45.01'W
PROS: Well sheltered, with freshwater swimming nearby. Good holding.
CONS: Often busy in summer and can resemble a parking lot with everyone tied to shore.
MUST DO: Go for a swim in Black Lake. Investigate the bar at the entrance by dinghy.

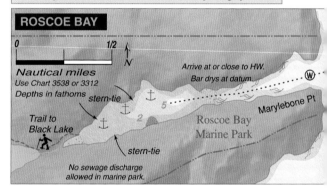

Entering Roscoe Bay requires high water.

Like many marine parks, Roscoe Bay is closed to sewage discharge and vessels are required to keep sewage in holding tanks while at anchor. Because of the restricted entrance, Roscoe Bay has especially poor tidal flushing.

Walsh Cove Marine Park, West Redonda Island 5

This small but sheltered anchorage on the east side of West Redonda Island provides a safe and scenic anchorage for boaters looking to get away from the Desolation Sound area. This a good spot to spend the night, with the Gorge Islets acting as a breakwater to wake from vessels passing in Waddington Channel, and the surrounding islands blocking most winds. The recommended approach into the anchorage is from the south, west of Bluff Point.

Pictographs can be viewed at Walsh Cove on the rock face just inside Butler Point. The Gorge Islets, which are part of the park, are very scenic and offer a great spot for picnicking with a view over the anchorage. There is also excellent swimming at mid-to-high tide along the reefs just west of these islets. Good prawn fishing is reported just south of the Gorge Islets and in Toba Inlet, west of Double Island. If you're passing Walsh Cove in the evening and there is room here, it's a good decision to stay the night rather than have to jockey for a spot at Prideaux Haven or Roscoe Bay.

Frances Bay and the Channels   6

The head of this expansive bay off Raza Passage is well sheltered from all winds but strong southeasterlies. Situated at a crossroads of scenic channels, the anchorage's magnificent vista is of Raza Passage flowing eastward into Pryce Channel which disappears into the distant folds of forested mountains.

Below, Walsh Cove anchorage provides good shelter from W winds but loses the sun quickly.

The west end of Raza Passage connects with Calm Channel, which leads north to the mouth of Bute Inlet. Along the way, overlooking Calm Channel on the mainland side, is the tiny village of Church House, established here by the Homalco First Nation after a gale in 1900 destroyed most of their village across the channel on Maurelle Island. By the end of the 20th century, the Homalco had abandoned their villages in Bute Inlet and many were living at the village of Sliammon (north of Powell River) and at Campbell River. Church House was still occupied (now abandoned) when we pulled up to the dock in the mid-1980s and asked if we could look inside the small wooden church, built by missionaries, for which the village was named.

Bute Inlet   7

Flanked by tall mountains, 35-mile long Bute Inlet is one of the longest fjords on the B.C. coast. Its milky colour is the result of glacial meltwater from the Homathko Icefield which, along with other nearby glaciers, drains into the Homathko River, which empties into the head of Bute Inlet. Strong outflow winds often sweep down from Mt. Waddington (at 13,177 feet, it is the highest peak entirely in B.C.) and funnel past the fjord's steep sides. Temperatures at the head of the inlet are cooler than the Desolation Sound area by about 5° C. Anchorages are limited along the inlet with depths often over 200 feet (65 m) close to shore (see charts 3542 or 3312). Mountain goats can sometimes be seen along the cliffsides lining the inlet and bears are often sighted in the Waddington Harbour area.

Originally occupied by the Homalco Nation, Bute Inlet also became home to a handful of trappers, loggers and fishermen. It was considered as a terminus for the transcontinental railway and, before that, the British entrepreneur Alfred Waddington (for whom the mountain was named) attempted to build a road from the Chilcotin interior to Bute Inlet. However, the Tsilhqot'in who lived there objected to a work

Above, the vista looking up Bute Inlet.
Right, Seattle boaters Kris and Bob Ridenour.

crew cutting a road through their territory and a confrontation erupted in violence with 19 people killed.

One of the most popular anchorages in Bute Inlet is the small cove adjacent to Leask Creek which drains nearby Leask Lake. Although a private residence has taken up land at the head of the cove, a hike along the creek bed is still possible.

A HONEYMOON CRUISE TO BUTE INLET

For most boaters, cruising beyond Desolation Sound means heading north of Dent Rapids, but Bob and Kris Ridenour of Seattle couldn't resist a special detour which took them north without the rapids. For years they had cruised Desolation Sound. However, in 1994, on their honeymoon, they wanted a destination that was remote yet within the two-week time frame required to get back to their business. They had explored Toba Inlet the previous year and enjoyed the beauty and tranquility of the inlet, so they fixed their sights on 40-mile-long Bute Inlet for their honeymoon. With their C&C 30 they made it as far as Orford Bay on their first day and anchored in front of Orford River.

"There was almost no wind, it was very still," Kris recalls. "We passed a beautiful waterfall opposite Clipper Point and felt we had got away."

The next day's destination was the head of Waddington Harbour with a lunch stop to explore the foreshore near Bear Bay. All along the inlet, towering mountains dwarfed their small boat as they made their way north. They tied up to a log boom on the west side of the 3-mile-wide bay and headed ashore with their mountain bikes after spotting a nearby logging road. It was to be a short ride.

"After about 15 minutes we came around a bend and saw a small black bear sitting on a stump," says Bob. "We didn't think too much about it, so we continued on for a few more minutes, then saw the sow crashing about in the underbrush. It took us just minutes to get back to the bottom of the hill."

They jettisoned the bikes in favour of the dinghy to explore two miles up the Homathko River, enjoying the view of mountains and glaciers.

Horseflies forced their departure the next day but they found another gem of an anchorage at Leask Creek, where they hiked to the lake and went swimming. Since then the anchorage has been taken over by a private float and mooring that were installed when a mansion was built on shore. This luxury compound is said to be a Hollywood celebrity's secluded retreat.

Bob and Kris now have a Taswell 43 named *Luna* and cruise extensively along the Inside Passage. But their trip up Bute Inlet "was a cruise we always remember vividly," says Kris.

Homath.

⚓

WADDINGTON
HARBOUR

Southgate

⚓
Bear
Bay   Purcell Pt

Boyd Pt

⚓ Orford
waterfall   Bay

Clipper
Point

0   5

Fawn
Bluff
waterfall   ⚓   Leask
Lake

Nautical miles
Not for navigation.
Use Chart 3542 or 331?
©OCEAN CRUISE GUID

Lots of room in Teakerne Arm anchorage.

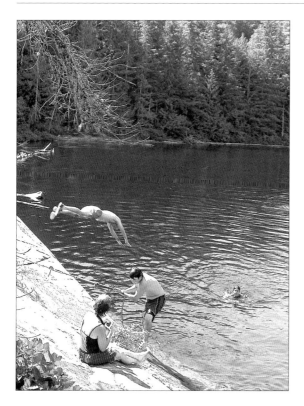

Teakerne Arm Marine Park, West Redonda Island 8

This popular anchorage, considered one of the best swimming spots in the area, is well known for its 100-feet-high Cassel Falls and the hiking trails to Cassel Lake. A dinghy dock provides access to the half-mile (1 km) park trail which ascends past the falls to the lake, where several good spots can be found along shore for swimming.

Most boats anchor in the bight west of the falls with a stern line to shore where eyebolts have been installed. You may find the water deep here (usually 100 feet or more), but setting a stern line to shore and ensuring the anchor digs into the upslope of the steep bottom will keep you secure in the black thick mud. Further west is another excellent spot in a bight near a small reef outcropping. East of the falls, larger vessels sometimes anchor in this deeper water while

Above, swimming in the warm water of Cassel Lake. Below, a waterfall flows from Cassel Lake into the head of Teakerne Arm.

TEAKERNE ARM AT A GLANCE

CHARTS: 3312, 3538
LAT LONG: 50 11.00'N 124°52.04'W
PROS: Beautiful location, dramatic scenery and fair to good anchorage in entire arm. Excellent swimming at nearby Cassel Lake. Some hiking.
CONS: Can be a little crowded at lake. SE winds will be a problem for those in N arm.
MUST DO: Go for a swim in warm fresh water!

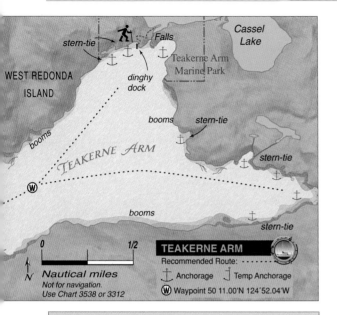

TEAKERNE ARM

Recommended Route: ·······

⚓ Anchorage   ⚓ Temp Anchorage

Ⓦ Waypoint 50 11.00'N 124˚52.04'W

Nautical miles
Not for navigation.
Use Chart 3538 or 3312

0 —— 1/2

WHERE THE WALRUS MIGHT BE FOUND

In Pendrell Sound, near the mouth of Toba Inlet, the top 15 feet (5 m) of surface water can reach temperatures of 70 degrees F (21 degrees C) in early August. These calm, stable conditions are also required for the Pacific oyster to spawn, and Pendrell Sound is one of the few places on the B.C. coast where the water remains consistently warm enough for this to occur. The cultivated oyster larvae are then shipped to other locations in Georgia Strait and grown to an edible size.

other vessels can be seen tied to booms or to shore along the arm's east shore. Summer NW winds can curl around the arm's north shore but are not usually strong – southerlies also are weak here.

If the anchorage near the park is full, nearby alternatives include the east arm where many vessels stern-tie along the shore. Two prime spots include a small bight along the N shore of this arm and, opposite, in the lee of a small islet on the S shore. Talbot Cove and the bight immediately to the west also have shelter and, although more open to the northwest, provide good anchorage in settled weather. The cove north of Joyce Point is occupied with an aquaculture operation. Tying to a log boom along the shore south of Cassel Falls is also acceptable to many boaters – just be prepared to move if a tug arrives.

Teakerne Arm was a busy anchorage in late June and early July 1792 when it was shared by four sailing ships: two under the command of Captain Vancouver and two under the command of the Spanish naval officers Galiano and Valdes. They anchored here off the north shore, a little east of the arm's entrance, and remained at anchor for over two

weeks while survey parties set off in small boats to explore the surrounding waterways.

The weather was wet and gloomy, and Vancouver felt hemmed in by "the dreary rocks and precipices that compose these desolate shores." When he parted company with the Spanish on July 13 and headed toward the open waters off Cape Mudge, his final comment concerning "the station we had just quitted" was "to state the general satisfaction that prevailed on leaving a region so truly desolate and inhospitable." The weather can certainly colour our perception of an anchorage.

Squirrel Cove, Cortes Island 9

A good anchorage, able to accommodate dozens of boats, Squirrel Cove is well sheltered with good holding in mud – unless you happen to snag your anchor on a sunken log or logging cable in the inner cove. This anchorage has been popular with boaters for years and its location just off Lewis Channel makes it a convenient stopover for those making long legs heading north or south. This is a common layover for northbound vessels planning to catch slack at Dent Rapids, which is about 20 miles away. Although strong winds can send gusts through the anchorage, the holding ground is good, making it a very secure anchorage.

We often anchor with a line ashore to the knob of land lying south of the small, bare islet marked '5' on Charts 3555 and 3312. Although Squirrel Cove has a bit of reputation for a cluttered bottom, the result of logging activity years ago, we've stopped here many times and haven't hooked onto anything other than sticky mud. According to published reports, however, the bay east of the little island, as well as the area between it and the larger island to the north, do have logging debris, so a trip line would be prudent in this area.

While Captain Vancouver's two ships were anchored across Lewis Channel in Teakerne Arm, a boat party explored Squirrel Cove. At the head of its inner cove the seamen discovered, as described by Archibald Menzies, "a large stream of water rushing down out of the woods." They assumed it was fresh water until they tasted it and found it was salty. The saltwater lagoon they discovered is now a source of recreation for boaters who, depending on the state of the tide, can ride these rapids by dinghy along a straight, boulder-free passage.

A trail leads from the Klahoose Nation dock in Squirrel Cove to Von Donop Inlet, and wolves have been encountered along this trail, so dog owners are well advised to keep their pets leashed. Most of the SW shoreline of Squirrel Cove is Klahoose Nation land and a proposal is underway by the Klahoose to build a marina and resort in the southwest area of the cove. Objections to this proposed development have been filed by the BC Marine Parks Forever Society and the Council of BC Yacht Clubs. Outside the entrance to Squirrel Cove is a public dock with a general store and restaurant with a waterfront patio.

Above left, aerial view of Squirrel Cove and upper reaches of Von Donop Inlet. Left, Squirrel Cove anchorage. Below, entrance to Gorge Harbour.

Gorge Harbour, Cortes Island 10

The name of this harbour, surrounded by hills, derives from its narrow steep-sided entrance – called The Gorge – which is less than 200 feet wide in places. Along the west wall of the entrance you can still see the outline of aboriginal rock paintings. These pictograghs apparently were completed about 200 years ago and executed by individuals lowered by cedar ropes from the top of the cliff. On the east side of the entrance are huge boulders that formed burial caverns. Although the entrance into the harbour is narrow, it is clear of obstructions. Currents can attain 4 knots in the entrance. Because of these currents, there can be a bad chop south of the Guide Islets in strong south winds. Conditions improve north of the islets.

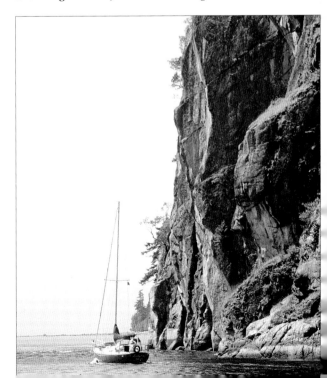

Although shellfish aquaculture takes place in Gorge Harbour, there are a number of sheltered nooks along the south shore of the harbour. These include the one east of a knob of land that lies south of Tan Island, where you can find a secure spot with a line ashore. We like the area east of Ring Islet in about 20 feet (6 m) of water. Many boats anchor south of the marina or west of Bee Islets. We often go to the extreme west end of the harbour (beyond a lone rock) which is very protected if strong NW winds come up. Holding is good in soft mud and sand.

The marina's facilities include a fuel dock, well-stocked store, restaurant (open June through August), laundromat, showers and an outdoor swimming pool. The resort's 7.5 acres include a campground, pond and playground. The various islets that lie within Gorge Harbour are very pleasant for explor-

ing by dinghy. There is also good fishing south of the Marina Reef buoy Q16 and Q20, south of Sutil Point. See charts 3312 or 3538

Uganda Passage

Uganda Passage, encumbered by rocks and shoals, makes a turn of more than 90 degrees around the end of Shark Spit. However, its tidal streams are weak and the channel is well marked with a starboard-hand buoy and two port-hand buoys, marking the upstream direction for boats proceeding N through the passage. Shark Spit – aptly named for its fin shape jutting from the north end of Marina Island – is a good spot to swim and do some beachcombing for clams, sand dollars and moon shells. A lunch stop lies opposite the tip of **Shark Spit**, behind an islet which forms its southern shore, from where you can watch other boats thread their way through Uganda Passage. See charts 3311 or 3312 for detail.

Von Donop Inlet / Hathayim [11] Marine Park, Cortes I

This undeveloped marine park, a joint venture between the Klahoose First Nation band and BC Parks, offers well-sheltered anchorage in several spots along its length of nearly three miles. Thanks to the inlet's narrowness (150 feet / 50 metres at its narrowest) and twisting shape, little wind is able to find its way inside, where the holding ground is good. A mid-channel rock with less than 6 feet (2 m) of water over it lies in the narrowest part of the inlet. Usually marked with kelp and visible at LW, it should be passed by favouring the SW side of the channel, keeping the rock to port. There is a large saltwater lagoon on the east side of the inlet just past this point which can be explored by dinghy, but be aware that currents will run swiftly during mid-tide. Use Charts 3538 or 3312.

Von Donop Inlet (named after Victor Von Donop, a midshipman in the Royal Navy in the 1860s) is normally a very calm anchorage with numerous bights and coves where you can tuck away and think of nothing or everything. There is rarely a stir of wind even when a tempest may be brewing outside. The anchorage's foreshore is a rare blend of Douglas fir, hemlock, red cedar and patches of Sitka spruce, mixed with maple and red alder. It is also home to flying squirrels, river otter and mink, while seals and sea lions can often be spotted near the entrance.

Von Donop Inlet is a good anchorage for exploring by dinghy and kayak.

0 _____ 1/2

Nautical miles
Not for navigation.
Depths in fathoms
Use Chart 3538 or 3312

marina

GORGE HARBOUR

Pill I

Tan I

Ring I

Bee Its

N

Neck I

2-3 kn.
Uganda
Passage

Heather Its

GORGE HARBOUR

Recommended Route: ··········
⚓ Anchorage   ⚓ Temp Anchorage

Marina I

Guide Its

No sewage discharge
allowed in Gorge Harbour

Aerial view looking north over Von Donop Inlet.

B.C. Parks notes that during spring and summer, visitors can hear the calls of varied thrush and Swainson's thrush, a variety of flycatchers as well as yellow-rumped Townsend's and black-throated grey warblers. Bald eagles are often seen soaring above the inlet while the ubiquitous kingfisher is often in the small coves.

In our view, the best anchorage in Von Donop is at the head, which opens into a small arrow-shaped basin. We have pulled into the small 2-fathom (4-m) cove on the north side and stayed for several days. On shore, at the head, there are small camping areas and trails leading to Squirrel Cove. As mentioned in the Squirrel Cove section of this book, be aware there are wolves on Cortes Island and that dogs should be leashed when you're hiking the trails.

Subtle Islands 12

A sand-and-gravel tombolo joins these two private islands, and the anchorage on their east side, off Plunger Passage, provides shelter from NW winds. A private dock takes up much of the south part of the anchorage. The islands' northern anchorage is the prettier bay and one where we have anchored overnight several times in settled weather. It is, however, open to the northwest. A treed bluff graces the western shoreline and near the entrance to the cove, between outcroppings, is a secluded pebble beach.

Robertson Lake

Wiley Lake

min depth 15 feet; keep to sw shore

Hathayim (Von Donop) Marine Park

CORTES ISLAND

VON DONOP INLET

Reversing tidal falls

Saltwater Lagoon

Cork Lake

good picnic spots

0   1/2   N

Nautical miles
Not for navigation.
Use Chart 3538 or 3312
Depths in fathoms

Trail to Squirrel Cove

VON DONOP INLET

CRUISE ROUTES

Recommended Route: ----------
⚓ Anchorage   ⚓ Temp Anchorage

Rebecca Spit, Quadra Island 13

Beaches always draw boaters in summer, and beautiful Rebecca Spit Marine Park is no exception. Forming a natural breakwater that shelters Drew Harbour, this park is a striking example of a West Coast spit. It has formed over thousands of years and is comprised of eroded sand and gravel carried by currents from the cliffs at Cape Mudge and deposited along the southeast shore of Quadra Island.

The flood tide flows north along this shoreline, so boaters approaching from the south can ride a favourable current right up to the harbour entrance, where shelter awaits in a bight just inside the spit's northern tip. If that spot is taken, anchorage can be obtained along the mile length of the spit, as close to the shore of the spit as your keel and tide will allow. The band of shallow water is very narrow, after which the depth drops off quickly. (Note that although the depths inside the spit are fairly con-

Above, small boats can anchor near shore. Below, aerial view of Rebecca Spit and Drew Harbour.

stant, there is one bulge of shoal water about a third of the way along the spit.) Tying a line to shore does not work well anywhere along the spit because of an almost constant current and because of the long distance over the beach to the trees.

The shallower area allows boats to anchor in 30 feet (10 m) or less of depth but in summer is often taken by other boats unless you arrive early in the day. We usually anchor outside the shallow band, in 75 feet (23 m) or more, which suits us as there is more room to let out scope. The holding throughout this anchorage is fair at best, with the bottom a mix of hard sand and gravel. The spit provides little protection from S winds and is subject to strong squalls during gales.

Rebecca Spit was named after the British trading schooner *Rebecca* which sailed this coast in the 1860s when sloops and schooners dominated the coasting trade. The crews of these vessels faced various occupational hazards, including attacks by natives which Captain John Walbran, author of *British Columbia Coast Names*, blamed on "the ardent spirits which some of the coasters traded to them, in spite of all warnings." Harbour pirates were another concern and, while lying in Victoria Harbour one March night in 1861, the *Rebecca* was boarded and some "money and goods were stolen."

Before becoming a park in 1959, Rebecca Spit was owned by local residents James and Mary Clandening who generously allowed visitors access to their stretch of beach, offering it as the site of Quadra Island's annual Victoria Day picnic. A 1946 earthquake caused three acres at the end of the spit to sink beneath sea level, and it left two large cracks in the remaining spit. Long marsh grass and the silver sheen of trees killed by saltwater are evidence of the settling that took place. The park no longer allows overnight camping because of concerns about erosion, but the spit remains popular with locals for daytime outings.

In the 18th century, Coast Salish natives occupied southern Quadra Island, and they built trenches and embankments along Rebecca Spit to fortify their territory against attack from northern tribes. Despite these efforts, however, the Salish were eventually forced south by the Kwakwaka'wakw. Picnic tables and hiking trails have now replaced prehistoric fortifications on Rebecca Spit where the vistas on a clear summer's evening are magnificent. To the east is a sweeping view across the broad waters of Sutil Channel to the mainland peaks rising above Desolation Sound. To the west are the mountains of Vancouver Island, their rugged slopes outlined by the glowing light of a setting sun.

A public dock, full-service marina, hotel and grocery store are located at **Heriot Bay**, while the Taku Resort on the west side of **Drew Harbour** has guest moorage and is a five-minute walk to the grocery store in Heriot Bay.

Crescent Channel, Quadra Island 14

Although Crescent Channel's shoreline has become increasingly developed over the years, its numerous bights occupied by floats and private moorings, the anchorage remains relatively peaceful and is a relaxing place to spend a day or two. The holding ground is good and the anchorage is well protected.

There are a couple of good spots to anchor in the channel's eastern branch. One option is to anchor off the N end of the largest islet with a line to shore. Another is to anchor on the Quadra Island side, in the second bight and pull your stern in close to the steep, treed shoreline in about 15 feet (5 m). The afternoon sun warms the stone cliffs behind this spot, making a swim off its rock ledges a pleasant prospect. The bay to the west at the head of the channel is sometimes used by aquaculture operations but, if clear, can be used for anchoring. The nearby moss-covered islets are pleasant for exploring, their shorelines forming a lagoon that attracts mergansers and river otters while kingfishers chatter above the pines of Bold Island. The salmon fishing at the north entrance is good. See Charts 3538, 3539 or 3312 for detail.

Top, Crescent Channel, looking north. Bottom, stern tied to shore in Crescent Channel.

CHAPTER FIVE

Hole in the Wall

Upper Rapids

ANCHORAGES OF THE PASSES

Boaters who venture into the mountain-bound channels of the Discovery Islands, beyond Desolation Sound, are entering one of our coast's most scenic cruising areas. Access to this labyrinth of forested islands, squeezed between the B.C. mainland and Vancouver Island, is gained by navigating one or more of the area's numerous tidal passes. Because of the speed of these passes, arriving at slack water is the key to a safe transit.

The main commercial route north is Discovery Passage, which entails transiting Seymour Narrows, where currents can reach 16 knots on an ebb. This is an excellent route and our personal favourite. Many northbound pleasure boaters choose the 'back route' around the top of Sonora Island along Cordero Channel. This route – through the Yuculta Rapids, Gillard Passage and the Dent Rapids – is the most direct route north from Desolation Sound.

Another option for northbound boaters is the 'middle route' up the east side of Quadra Island, through Surge Narrows (or Whiterock Passage and Hole in the Wall) and the Upper and Lower Rapids in Okisollo Channel. One advantage to this route is the chance to stop at Octopus Islands Marine Park, where a cluster of islets provides a beautiful and sheltered anchorage accommodating many vessels.

Okisollo Channel

ANCHORAGES OF THE PASSES

This is the easiest route for boaters new to these northern passes. Although Surge Narrows and Okisollo Channel can run fast, these passes have less turbulence and the section of strong current is shorter than the long stretch from Yuculta Rapids to the Dents or along Discovery Passage to Seymour Narrows.

THE BACK ROUTE (aka The Dents)

Transiting the three main passes from the Dents to the Yucultas (Ukes) is normally an easier proposition when southbound because the Dents turn between 15 and 25 minutes sooner than the middle rapids of

CHARTS AND PUBLICATIONS:

Skippers should opt for the large-scale charts showing detail of all the passes. These charts give important information on direction and speed of currents throughout each pass. Use charts 3537, 3539, 3540 (Campbell River) and 3543 (which has an excellent large-scale inset of Dent Rapids). Also, the CHS book of Charts 3312 covers all passes of this chapter with good detail.

Use Volume One of the CHS Sailing Directions for the B.C. Coast South Portion and Volume 6 of the Tide and Current Tables. Call marinas on 66A.

Gillard Passage, and the flood stream at this early stage presents few difficulties.

Because of the high level of turbulence in this set of passes (particularly off Whirlpool Point), accurate tidal research and predictions were difficult to obtain and it was only in the late 1980s that the Canadian Hydrographic Service discovered, through the research of Mike Woodward and his colleagues, that currents were actually much faster than originally thought.

Slow or low-powered vessels may find they are battling more current than they can handle and should keep in mind that there are numerous spots to pull into and wait for the next slack, or spend the night and carry on the next day. This includes Big Bay public dock on Stuart Island, the Dent Island Lodge Resort on the small islands east of Dent Island (a reservation for overnight moorage is recommended) or the anchorage in Mermaid Bay.

Yuculta Rapids

If you are northbound, the Yucultas (pronounced uke-la-taws) will be the first challenge. The predominant characteristic of these rapids is the choppy water and turbulence which starts south of Kellsey Point and continues to Gillard Passage. Although this passage is deep and fairly wide, the middle of the pass usually has the least turbulence right up to Whirlpool Point.

Slow vessels arriving at the tail end of a flood can take advantage of a back eddy along the Stuart Island shore up to Kellsey Point. From there, if conditions are safe, cross over to the Sonora Island side

---

Pass Tip Sheet – Dent Rapids

Yuculta Rapids, Gillard Passage, Dent Rapids and Arran Rapids use Chart 3543 or 3312
Location: 18 miles N of Squirrel Cove
Reference Station: Gillard Passage for Dents and for Yuculta Rapids.
Maximum Flow: Arran – 14 knots (flood) Gillard – 13 knots (ebb); Dent – 11 knots (flood); Yucultas – 10 knots flood
Slack: less than 10 minutes on large tides.
Nearby Anchorages: Stuart Island public dock at Big Bay, Mermaid Bay, Horn Bay, Shoal Bay.
Direction of Flood: Southeast
Key to Safe Transits: Northbound – Calculate time to travel four mile stretch of passes at your vessel's normal speed to be at Dents as close to slack as possible. Southbound – Arrive at Dent Rapids in the last hour of a flood or at the beginning of a flood.

---

of the channel (where the northerly ebb current kicks in early) and continue to Gillard Passage.

The Yuculta Rapids are a sort of catch-basin for debris flowing from the other passes. Some of the bits of wood may be submerged below the top layer of fresh water that flows from Bute Inlet. Debris not buoyant enough to be supported by this freshwater layer can sink to the denser salt water 3 to 6 feet (1 to 2 m) down, so keep a sharp eye for deadheads and other wood bobbing just below the surface.

A northbound powerboat proceeds against five knots of current in Gillard Passage.

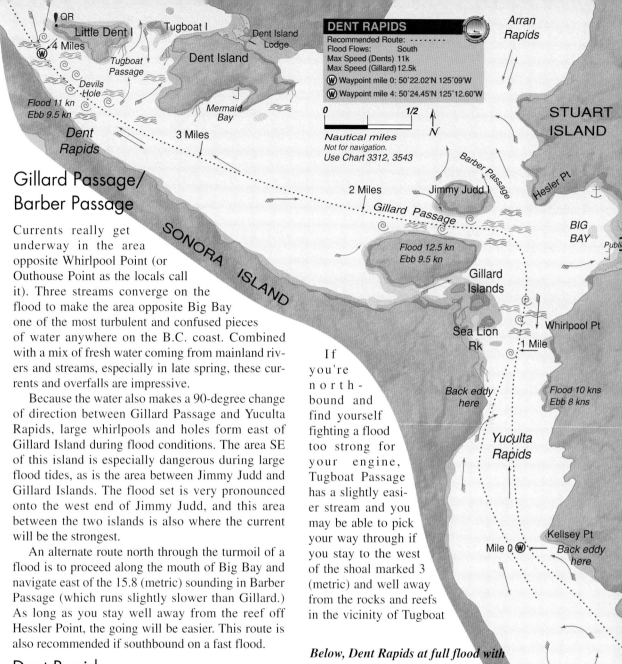

Map labels:

QR
Little Dent I
Tugboat I
Dent Island Lodge
Arran Rapids
4 Miles
Tugboat Passage
Dent Island
Devils Hole
Flood 11 kn
Ebb 9.5 kn
Mermaid Bay
STUART ISLAND
Dent Rapids
3 Miles

DENT RAPIDS
Recommended Route: - - - - - - - -
Flood Flows: South
Max Speed (Dents) 11k
Max Speed (Gillard) 12.5k
W Waypoint mile 0: 50°22.02'N 125°09'W
W Waypoint mile 4: 50°24.45'N 125°12.60'W

0   1/2
Nautical miles
Not for navigation.
Use Chart 3312, 3543
N

SONORA ISLAND

2 Miles
Jimmy Judd I
Gillard Passage
Barber Passage
Hesler Pt
BIG BAY
Public
Flood 12.5 kn
Ebb 9.5 kn
Gillard Islands
Sea Lion Rk
Whirlpool Pt
1 Mile
Back eddy here
Flood 10 kns
Ebb 8 kns
Yuculta Rapids
Kellsey Pt
Mile 0 W
Back eddy here

Gillard Passage/ Barber Passage

Currents really get underway in the area opposite Whirlpool Point (or Outhouse Point as the locals call it). Three streams converge on the flood to make the area opposite Big Bay one of the most turbulent and confused pieces of water anywhere on the B.C. coast. Combined with a mix of fresh water coming from mainland rivers and streams, especially in late spring, these currents and overfalls are impressive.

Because the water also makes a 90-degree change of direction between Gillard Passage and Yuculta Rapids, large whirlpools and holes form east of Gillard Island during flood conditions. The area SE of this island is especially dangerous during large flood tides, as is the area between Jimmy Judd and Gillard Islands. The flood set is very pronounced onto the west end of Jimmy Judd, and this area between the two islands is also where the current will be the strongest.

An alternate route north through the turmoil of a flood is to proceed along the mouth of Big Bay and navigate east of the 15.8 (metric) sounding in Barber Passage (which runs slightly slower than Gillard.) As long as you stay well away from the reef off Hessler Point, the going will be easier. This route is also recommended if southbound on a fast flood.

Dent Rapids

Proceeding north from Jimmy Judd Island, arrive at Little Dent Island near slack or with the beginning of the ebb. Arriving at Devils Hole (a turbulent and aerated section of water) an hour into a strong flood can be, says Woodward, "quite horrendous."

The main problem with the Dent Rapids occurs during the flood as a result of the wrenching Little Dent Island gives the tidal stream at the NW tip of the island. This forces a major deflection of current over to Sonora Island. In a large tide, the deflection has the appearance, for tardy southbound boaters, of the edge of a waterfall as it actually drops onto the back eddy east of the QR light. If you are going with the flood, arrive at slack and favour Sonora Island.

If you're northbound and find yourself fighting a flood too strong for your engine, Tugboat Passage has a slightly easier stream and you may be able to pick your way through if you stay to the west of the shoal marked 3 (metric) and well away from the rocks and reefs in the vicinity of Tugboat

Below, Dent Rapids at full flood with current deflecting to Sonora Island. Devils Hole is at top centre.

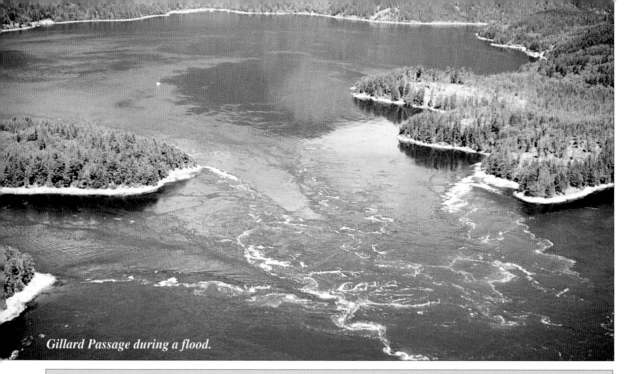

Gillard Passage during a flood.

GILLARD PASSAGE –
by Mike Woodward

Gillard Passage has traditionally been the route favoured by tugs towing log booms, in preference to the rougher waters of Discovery Passage. However, for decades there were no reliable predictions for Gillard Passage, prompting veteran skippers to develop their own formulas based on predicted times at Seymour Narrows.

Early measurement work from shore by the Canadian Hydrographic Service in Gillard Pass included a 'Mast and Boom' setup that held a small paddlewheel boat out in the current. Later, the use of traditional gas launches resulted in near swampings, preventing surveyors from finding the locations of faster water.

In 1987, as part of a project to obtain modern tidal-stream data for the narrow passes in this general area, high-quality data was collected using boats built to work at Nakwakto Rapids and Sechelt Rapids.

We soon found that the fastest speeds occur well to the east of the narrowest geographic section of the channel. We had heard reports of vessels struggling to make way against predicted currents that were supposed to be considerably less than their actual speed through the water, and we now understood why the predicted speeds were all too low.

In the above photo of the flood tidal stream through Gillard and Barber, note the confluence of the eastern jet of Barber Pass with the jet from Gillard. The turbulence and eddies that result from this interaction should be avoided, and a transit into the main flood through Gillard Passage may best be made along a track from the centre of Yuculta Rapids aiming for, or close to, the eastern tip of Gillard Island.

We spent many long days out in the launches, and one day we decided to pay a visit to a tug that was tied up against its log boom in Mermaid Bay. We were greeted by Lee Hollingsworth and his crew, who invited us aboard for lunch. It turned out that Lee was in his fiftieth year of pulling logs through Gillard Pass and we spent a little extra time in his nice, warm galley. Lee was happy to share his well-honed practical knowledge of the business of getting booms through Gillard in one piece – or not.

Hollingsworth recommends always waiting for slack, staying south of Kellsey Point when northbound or, if southbound, pulling into Denham Bay (the bay just north of Horn Point). And he also warns powerboats not to go through the pass too fast: "There's still lots of deadheads out there." After more than 40 years spent working the passes, Hollingsworth retired from the bridge of a RivTow tug in 1992.

Left – Mike Woodward setting a current meter in Discovery Passage.

"Don't Cut The Tow!"

The 'Dents' present special problems for tug skippers. Because of the tugs' slow speeds, especially when towing booms, two-holing (doing the Dents and Gillard Passage at one go) is not an easy task. Skippers often wait at Mermaid Bay for slack to continue south.

Lee Hollingsworth, a tug skipper for 50 years, has heard lots of stories about the rapids – one of the most humorous from his father who once described an episode from the days of steam tugs when manila towline was used.

"The skip on the southbound tug's getting kinda nervous taking a flood, see. It's a big tide and lots of drift in the water as there was in those days. So he gives his mate an axe and tells him to stand by in case the tow has to be cut. The skip said he would toot the steam whistle as a signal to cut the tow.

"Well, they've just got by the tricky part where the flood sets strong over to Jimmy Judd Island and the skip is relaxing when he sees a friend turning into Gillard Passage from the Ukes. So the friend toots his whistle, which is what they did in those days to passing tugs, and the skip, before he knows what he's doing, toots his whistle too. As soon as it happened he ran out on deck and yelled to the mate "No – don't cut the tow!" but he saw that the mate, who was pretty nervous too, had just finished doing the job. They had to turn around pretty quick in that current and managed to pick up the tow and save it from washing up on Gillard Island.

Island (between Little Dent and Dent Islands). Also, as mentioned, Mermaid Bay and the Dent Island Lodge are good spots to wait out the flood.

On the ebb, the stream at Dent Rapids is much more consistent because there is nothing to deflect the flowing water. If you find yourself riding a faster ebb than planned, stay in the middle of the pass as there is a set to Tugboat Passage and the rocks therein. Once clear of Little Dent, steer well to the N of the shoal patch – the 6/4 sounding (metric) about a half-mile NW of the QR light on Little Dent.

Good view of deflection caused by Little Dent Island during a flood, looking south.

Arran Rapids

Although Arran Rapids (which turn to flood and ebb at the same time as the Dent Rapids) would not normally be used for a direct route north, you might want to use this pass after exploring Bute Inlet or after fishing on the east side of Stuart Island.

These rapids are, in a word, bizarre. The Spanish explorers Valdes and Galiano, while braving these rapids in 1792, were spun around three times and came very close to going down, as it is locally known, 'The Drain.' At 14 knots on the flood, 10 on the ebb, Arran Rapids is an extremely energetic and violent pass. The dangers are caused by air. On a flood tide, salt water rushes toward Arran Point and

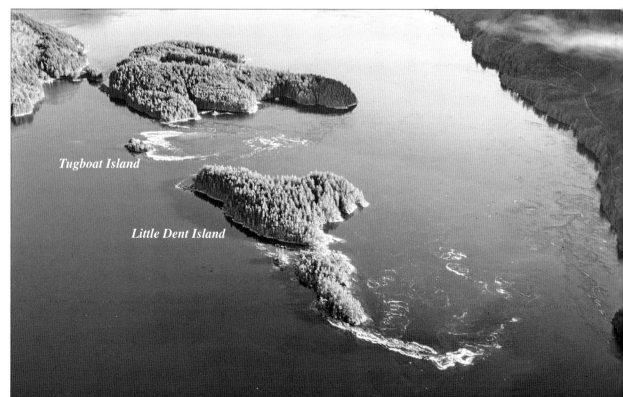

Tugboat Island

Little Dent Island

ARRAN RAPIDS – FIRST TRANSITS!

In the summer of 1792, both British and Spanish naval explorers transited these rapids with the help of local natives – the Euclataws – who lived at a nearby village. A survey party commanded by Lieutenant James Johnstone of HMS Chatham tried to row through the rapids but had to resort to pulling their boat through with ropes. The Euclataws, watching the action from shore, lent a hand with the ropes.

The Spanish showed up a short time later with their two ships – 50' schooners – and despite warnings from the Euclataws, decided to proceed through the rapids. One of the ships was seized by a whirlpool and was turned right around three times – a surprising experience that caused the crew on both vessels to burst into laughter.

meets a foil-shaped cove that accelerates and strongly deflects the water halfway across the channel. Because of the turbulence of the water, air is trapped inside and creates a froth which doesn't give props a lot to bite and also doesn't support displacement hulls very well. Conditions in the pass are further complicated by the large amount of fresh water flowing into it in spring and summer months. The flooding saltwater stream, as witnessed by Mike Woodward who surveyed this pass for CHS, will often just disappear under the quiet and still freshwater from Bute Inlet.

"I've been east of the pass, absolutely still on a layer of green freshwater, watching a 10-knot saltwater stream vanish a few yards away," he recalls.

The pass does not present the same problems on an ebb flow but there can be strong turbulence on the north side of the west entrance as shown on chart 3543. This is a pass that warrants full caution and a close eye to slack water.

THE MIDDLE ROUTE

In many ways the middle route (Surge Narrows to the Okisollo Rapids) is more interesting to use if you plan to continue on to Johnstone Strait. This route connects almost directly with the strait and although currents in these passes can be quite strong, they are not as fearsome as the other two routes because of lighter traffic and less turbulence. The middle route is a good introduction to the northern passes and offers the added bonus of superb scenery and excellent anchorages. The first rapids are Surge Narrows and some 6 miles north are the more turbulent Okisollo Rapids. A couple of miles further northwest are the Lower Rapids, the easiest set to transit.

Aerial view of Arran Rapids during a flood looking north. Current in the pass reaches 14 knots on large tides.

Surge Narrows (Beazley Passage)

Surge Narrows is the fastest-flowing pass of the middle route and currents here can be turbulent, especially on the south-setting flood. Fortunately there is only one stream. This passage actually begins at Welsford Island at the SE end and extends NW through Beazley Passage, where the current is strongest, and then to Surge Narrows, which is the passage between Antonio Point and Quadra Island.

Beazley Passage is the only safe channel through the Settlers Group of islands, although it does present certain difficulties on both the flood and the ebb. On the flood there is a strong deflection off the SW part of Sturt Island. This generates tremendous turbulence in the shear zone which crosses the pass. Working the back eddy off Sturt Island and crossing the shear zone (as we once vainly attempted) is not an option because it is too easy to lose control in this turbulent area and, because the pass is narrow, you have little room to recover.

The ebb produces less turbulence, but there is the hazard of Tusko Rock, which dries at LW and is located just west of Sturt Island in line with the ebb set from the pass. Boaters should favour the west side of the passage until well clear of Peck Island.

The west side of Peck Island is not recommended because of strong turbulence. "A nightmare," says Woodward. The route north of Sturt Island is not recommended either because of its numerous rocks and reefs, and strong, turbulent currents that can set you onto danger very quickly.

A provincial marine park encompasses most of the Surge Narrows shoreline and several of the Settlers Group islands, including Peck but not Sturt and Goepel, which are private. This particular park is of more interest to kayakers and scuba divers than to boaters – none of the anchorages are recommended because of strong currents and poor holding ground (this area is kelp heaven). The park is best visited by inflatable at slack.

Above, Looking north at Beazley Passage during flood. Below, during slack at same pass.

Pass Tip Sheet – Surge Narrows

Chart: 3537
Location: 10 miles N of Heriot Bay
Maximum Flows: Flood 12 knots
Slack: 15-20 minutes. The window on this pass during big tides is just a few minutes.
Direction of Flood: South
Nearby Anchorages: Northbound boaters can wait in Hjorth Bay or at the public wharf opposite the narrows. Southbound boaters can wait at the Octopus Islands or Yeatman Bay.
Key to Safe Transits: Arrive at or close to slack and give Tusko Rock lots of room.

Whiterock Passage

For boaters with experience and confidence in reading one-up range markers, Whiterock Passage is a real treat. It is one of the prettiest channels on the coast, with forested cliffs giving way to low, grassy banks dotted with large deciduous trees.

Whiterock Passage runs between Read and Maurelle Islands, and offers an alternative – albeit

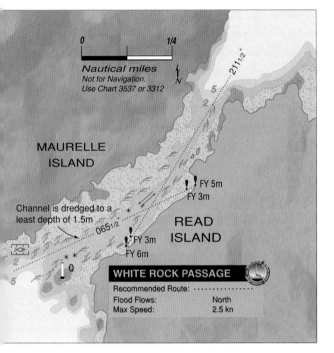

longer – route to the Octopus Islands. This narrow, slow-stream channel is a good example of a pass encouraging various types of weed to grow along the sea bed. It has rock outcroppings, reefs and a rock-strewn bottom with plenty of long-flowing kelp. Currents in Whiterock Passage rarely exceed 2 knots (flood is north) but the real challenge is the narrowness of the pass and the numerous rocks and ledges. At its narrowest point the width is about 70 feet.

A set of range markers makes the approach to the elbow of the pass easy enough, but the problem comes after making the turn and piloting out of the pass. Because the markers are now behind your boat and disappearing astern, the perspective is reversed. So between twisting around to keep the markers aligned and looking ahead to make sure you are avoiding debris and other boats, you will be busy. But it is excellent piloting practice for further travels up the coast, where you will encounter more of these range markers in passes.

Hole in the Wall

One of the useful functions of Whiterock Passage is leading your boat to Hole in the Wall and if one good pass deserves another, then this circular route to the Octopus Islands will be a day well spent among some of the most beautiful scenery on the B.C. coast.

Of all the passes in this area, Hole in the Wall – which cuts between Sonora and Maurelle Islands – is certainly one of the most dramatic. The water flowing past the steep shorelines is a deep green colour typical of glacial run-off and there are two good lunch stops along the way. Florence Cove is on the channel's south shore, and we've anchored in its west side using a lunch hook. About a mile to the west is a wide bight on the channel's north side where, in 40 feet (12 m) of water, you can drop the hook and enjoy the view up the channel.

Currents in Hole in the Wall are strongest at the western entrance in the vicinity of the light marked 'QR', reaching 12 knots on a flood and 10 knots on an ebb. The area of greatest turbulence is the shoal area farther west – a spot to avoid on large tides. We normally set a course south of these shoals. Despite this area requiring caution, Hole in the Wall is a fairly predictable stream with no obstructions within the pass and is twice as wide as Beazley Passage.

During the north-flowing flood at the west entrance, two well-defined shear zones converge to form a broad area of turbulence, and there is a fairly strong set toward the bluffs on the north side. When the flood is especially strong it creates a lot of air

An aerial view of Hole in the Wall looking east.

bubbles in the water, both in the shear zones and downstream, which can cause serious cavitation.

The flow on the ebb is weaker and less confined, and the fastest flow dissipates quickly in the more open waters of Okisollo Channel. If you are going with the ebb, the main stream is easy to ride out into the larger channel.

At the east end of the passage, the current at Bassett Point will be about half that found at the west entrance near Springer Point. Floating and submerged debris is one hazard to be aware of at the east entrance, where the stratification between fresh and salt water can sometimes result in bits of wood floating just below the water's surface.

Okisollo Channel
(Upper and Lower Rapids)

Currents in the Upper Rapids, the first set of rapids encountered when northbound, are considerably stronger (up to 11 knots) than those in the Lower Rapids, which usually run less than 6 knots. The Upper Rapids passage is also encumbered with reefs and rock outcroppings that generate strong deflection. Seas can be quite turbulent in the area near Bentley Rock during large tides.

On the south-flowing flood, the strongest deflection is just south of two small islets (one of which is marked '10' on Chart 3537) on the E side of the channel below Owen Bay. The safest route through this pass is a course favouring the E side of the channel, giving Bentley Rock a wide berth. The ebb in the Upper Rapids is even more confused, especially in the area downstream of Bentley Rock. Be careful to avoid the strong set to Bentley Rock by crossing to the E side of the channel well upstream. Currents in Okisollo are strongest around this rock and the forces of water here are very hazardous.

Although Okisollo's Upper Rapids can be turbulent, the pass is fairly wide and there are opportunities to pull out and assess the situation if conditions are uncomfortable. Owen Bay is a good anchorage to wait out strong tides. The Lower Rapids are more benign, with currents rarely exceeding 5 knots in the channel S of Gypsy Shoal. The channel N of Okis Islands is free of hazards with less current.

Okisollo Channel enters Discovery Passage about 4 miles south of Chatham Point, which marks the eastern entrance to Johnstone Strait.

Right, Okisollo Channel's Lower Rapids at the start of a flood.

Pass tip Sheet – Okisollo Rapids

Chart: 3537
Location: Upper Rapids 2 miles north of Octopus Islands Marine Park.
Reference Station: Seymour Narrows.
Maximum Flow: Upper Rapids, max 11 knots. Lower Rapids, 5 knots
Slack: 15 – 20 minutes
Nearby Anchorages: Octopus Islands Marine Park, Owen Bay, Barnes Bay (open to the west).
Key To Safe Transit: Be at Upper Rapids close to slack and keep to the east side of the channel.

Above, Sailing to Cape Mudge with a 25 knot south wind. Left, Cape Mudge lighthouse.

Discovery Passage

There's something exciting about making a voyage along Discovery Passage. Hemmed in by the steep slopes of Vancouver Island and the forested shores of Quadra Island, this wide ribbon of cold, swift-flowing water bustles with commercial traffic all summer long. Discovery Passage was once the domain of native peoples who plied its waters by dugout canoe, and it was not until the Klondike Gold Rush in 1898 that steamships started flooding north along this major route of the Inside Passage. The steamships have been replaced by cruise ships, but the flow of traffic in Discovery Passage remains under the control of that great gatekeeper, Seymour Narrows. Even the leviathan liners are very careful about timing their transit for slack water at this pass, which is one of the most formidable on our coast with currents reaching 16 knots.

From May through September cruise ships on the Vancouver-Alaska run regularly use this pass, most heavily on weekends during nightime transits. The captains of these ubiquitous cruise ships have great respect for Seymour Narrows, for their flat-bottomed ships tend to slide stern-out in sharp turns – such as the blind corner in this pass.

"Everything hinges on Seymour Narrows. It tells us how fast to go from Sitka all the way down the Inside Passage," Captain Ympa Ercka of a Holland America Line cruise ship confirmed. Asked about other hair-raising passes or navigational hazards of the coast, Ercka shook his head: "There is only Seymour Narrows. Nothing compares."

For the northbound boater, this passage really starts a few miles south of Cape Mudge, where the first effects of currents from far-off Johnstone Strait are felt north of Mitlenatch Island. Even in calm conditions, the waters here can be choppy and rolling. During strong S winds of 25 knots or more

against a flood stream, the seas here can be dangerous and over the years numerous vessels have been
lost in this area, usually during winter storms. In
summer, southeasterlies are not as common, but
seas can still be rough and currents strong in the
area 3 to 4 miles south of Wilby Shoals. Also note,
during a strong ebb there is a significant set toward
Sutil Channel.

If you're bucking a flood tide, the best route for
avoiding current is to pass close by the red buoy at
Wilby Shoals (stand off a mile to avoid the set) and
follow the 20-metre line to the Cape Mudge lighthouse. This will keep you away from the rough
water coming out of Discovery Passage and inside
the back eddy which starts south of Cape Mudge.
Once past the lighthouse, follow the Quadra Island
shoreline until you're near Whiskey Point, then
either cross over to Campbell River or travel along
the Quadra shore to the anchorage of your choice.

Discovery Channel between Campbell River and
Quadra Island is a busy place so, in addition to the
constant current, be prepared for heavy traffic. There
are the hourly crossings of the Quadra Island car
ferry, the comings and goings of tugs (often with
booms or barges), fishboats, numerous pleasure craft
and the cruise ships, which usually transit the pass
during evening or night-time slack. On weekends
there can be four or five lined up from Seymour
Narrows to Campbell River. However, Discovery
Passage is fairly wide and straight, and you can easily pick a clear spot if you need to cross the channel.
Keep your VHF on Channel 16 if you need to clarify
a situation with another vessel.

Seymour Narrows at end of flood looking north.

Seymour Narrows

Back in the 1950s, the currents of Seymour Narrows
were measured using drift poles (8-foot-long two-
by-two's with lead at either end and a flag stick) and
a transit mounted on a cairn of Maud Island. CHS
surveyors would measure the time the pole needed
to travel at given angles on the transit to determine
current speed. CHS staff eventually used a 25-foot
inflatable dinghy with plenty of horsepower to stay
in one position in the pass while a probe, three feet
below the surface, measured current.

Hydrographers say the strongest currents at the
narrows are in the vicinity of Ripple Rock (slightly
west of mid-channel, directly beneath the hydro
lines strung between Vancouver and Maud Islands).
On a flood, the strongest turbulence will be along
the west wall and in the area south of Ripple Rock.
On an ebb, the turbulence – and the set – start
between Maud Island and Ripple Rock. The current
sets northwest to the west wall.

Northbound vessels should arrive off the Maud
Island light within an hour of the ebb finishing or
beginning. Once into the narrows, steer toward the
tongue of the current stream (east of mid-channel) to
avoid the whirlpools and eddies north of Maud
Island up to North Bluff. On large tides in low-powered vessels it's prudent to be at the Maud Island
light at slack or just a few minutes into the north
-flowing ebb. If the slack is LW, be sure to arrive at
the pass before the end of the ebb because slack here
on large tides is not very long – 5 to 10 minutes at
most – and you'll want to be past Brown Bay before
the south-flowing flood gets underway, which can be
brutal in a slow-moving boat. On a large flood,

Above, Ripple Rock being blown up in 1958. Below, during an earlier attempt to remove Ripple Rock, nine men returning from this barge were lost in a whirlpool.

REMOVING RIPPLE ROCK

Captain George Vancouver described Seymour Narrows as a pass that "rushes with some impetuosity" but one of his officers more boldly declared that the pass was "the most nightmarish spectacle his eyes had ever beheld." No doubt this response came from seeing the frightening whirlpools around submerged Ripple Rock. Until the top of this two-headed pinnacle rock was removed in 1958, transiting Seymour Narrows at low water was extremely hazardous. Ripple Rock used to lie less than 9 feet (3 m) below chart datum, where it created dangerous turbulence. Vessels would get caught in the suction around the rock and be pulled under. More than 20 large vessels and over 100 lives were lost before the government was able to remove this terrible hazard.

In 1955 work began on a tunnel – 8 feet wide by 8 feet high – dug under the seabed of Seymour Narrows from Maud Island to the base of Ripple Rock. Chambers were carved into its double heads and stuffed with 1,400 tons of Niramex explosive. On April 5, 1958, scientists from around the world gathered to watch the largest non-nuclear explosion to date. At 9:31 a.m. the plunger went down and a huge bubble rose in the water, then burst skyward like a fountain that sent chunks of rock flying hundreds of feet into the air. Within minutes the debris had settled. When measurements were taken, it was determined that 35 feet of the rock had been blown off with minimum depth at the south head now being 45 feet (14 m) below low water. The twin heads of Ripple Rock were gone and Seymour Narrows was free of the 'killer' rock.

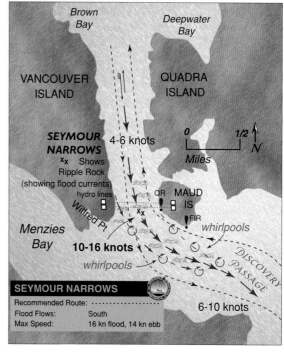

Pass Tip Sheet – Seymour Narrows

Chart: 3539 or 3312
Location: (50°08'N, 125°21'W) 6 miles north of Campbell River, 7 miles south of Kanish Inlet.
Direction of Flood: South
Maximum Flow: Flood 16 knots, Ebb 14 knots.
Slack: 5 minutes on large tides.
Nearby Anchorages: N bound, small bay NE side Maud Island. S bound, Deepwater Bay, Brown Bay.
Key to Safe Transits: Northbound, arrive off Maud Island light at slack or just as current is turning in your favour. Southbound, be opposite Brown Bay as flood is ending or beginning.

Seymour Narrows can reach 16 knots – no place to be in any kind of boat.

Southbound boats should be opposite Brown Bay within the hour of a neap flood ending or beginning. If a large spring flood is underway, it would be wise to be here within a half hour of its end or beginning. The worst turbulence is often south of Ripple Rock, especially if wind is against current. If you stay on the starboard side of the channel throughout the transit, but not too close to the west shore, you'll be out of harm's way in the event you're sharing the narrows with a boom-towing tug or large ship. The good news about Seymour Narrows is that there are no obstructions and just one strong, main stream.

When reading current tables, boaters often assume that the speed of the ebb or flood is like a sine wave, and that being one hour late for slack means the current should be only a fraction of the maximum flow. However, there are surges of flow as water backed up at one end of the pass is suddenly released at slack and rushes through the pass to temporarily equalize with the water level on the other side.

"In some passes – and this is quite pronounced in Seymour Narrows – the flow is non-linear," Mike Woodward relates. "So the flow is not comparable to a sine wave – slowly building to maximum flow, but is more like a saw-tooth wave. In other words, the current can come on strong very quickly."

Woodward has seen many boats trying to buck a big flood at the Narrows – a hazardous practise for this particular pass. "If you try to use the Maud Island back eddy, which is about 3 knots in a north direction, and your boat has a hull speed of 10 knots, that means you are travelling at 13 knots over ground. When your boat crosses over the flooding jet – which it has to do right near the beacon – it could be hit with 15 knots of current. Suddenly the hull is being forced to go at 28 knots for a brief time and the bow wave can go over the prow or perhaps cause the vessel to roll. As well, you run the risk of overheating your engine, which could happen just as a large tug and barge are coming on you."

Woodward says he has motored up to a number of boaters trying to beat Seymour Narrows and they rarely listen. "They sit for a half-hour or more going nowhere when they could just as easily go around the corner and anchor behind Maud Island and have a cup of tea and save all that fuel."

Campbell River

If any part of B.C.'s coastline can lay claim to being the heart of the Inside Passage, it might well be the waters off Campbell River. A steady stream of vessels, from kayaks to cruise ships, passes by Campbell River throughout the summer, travelling this main artery of the Inside Passage. They are following the route first charted by Captain George Vancouver in 1792 as they pass beneath the white cliffs of Cape Mudge at the southern entrance to Discovery Passage, named for Vancouver's ship.

A full century later, a rush of steamships carrying Klondike-bound prospectors headed north up Discovery Passage, past the mouth of the Campbell River. Passing beneath their keels were huge runs of salmon, which thrive in the cold, swift-flowing waters of Discovery Passage and have earned Campbell River the right to proclaim itself 'Salmon Capital of the World.' Five species of salmon migrate up the Campbell River, but it's the prized chinook that first caught the world's attention when, in 1896,

FAMOUS FISHING

Campbell River's fame as a sportfishing destination began with the arrival in 1924 of a boatbuilder named Ned Painter, who rented and sold his wooden rowboats. This enterprise evolved into a fishing camp he and his wife operated at the mouth of the river, followed by a cottage resort. In 1938 they opened Painter's Lodge and this historic resort (replaced with a modern facility after a fire in 1985) achieved worldwide fame as a sportfishing retreat, attracting celebrities such as Bing Crosby and Bob Hope.

This tradition continues today, with luxury yachts arriving in Campbell River each summer to await the arrival of their owners. Some come 'north' to spend time fishing local waters, while others simply want to relax in a wilderness setting. Julie Andrews and her husband, movie director Blake Edwards, have often flown by Learjet to Campbell River to board their yacht for a few weeks of cruising. Ms. Andrews has been heard exercising her vocal chords on the stern deck, her beautiful singing voice wafting across the water.

Sir Richard Musgrave wrote an article for Field magazine in which he praised his native guides' simple but skillful method of catching these large fish from dugout canoes.

Campbell River grew into a logging and pulp mill town, where visiting pleasure boats jostled with commercial fishboats for space at the public docks. In recent years, however, Campbell River has successfully transformed itself from a working town into a base for all kinds of tourism, including sport-

Above, kids enjoy watching the crabs at Patti Finn's fresh seafood market at the Discovery Harbour Marina (below).

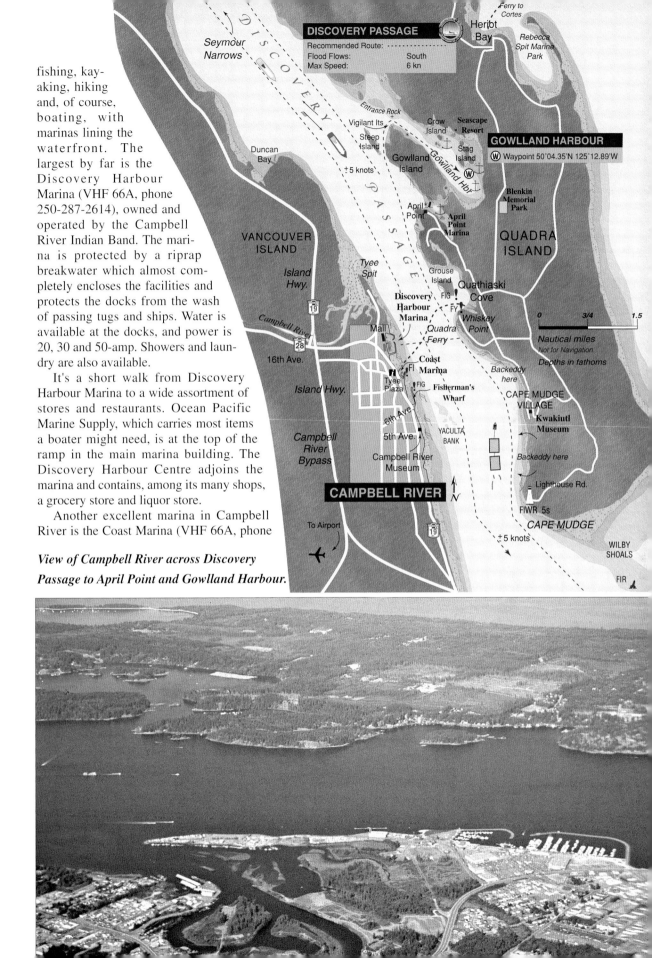

fishing, kay-aking, hiking and, of course, boating, with marinas lining the waterfront. The largest by far is the Discovery Harbour Marina (VHF 66A, phone 250-287-2614), owned and operated by the Campbell River Indian Band. The marina is protected by a riprap breakwater which almost completely encloses the facilities and protects the docks from the wash of passing tugs and ships. Water is available at the docks, and power is 20, 30 and 50-amp. Showers and laundry are also available.

It's a short walk from Discovery Harbour Marina to a wide assortment of stores and restaurants. Ocean Pacific Marine Supply, which carries most items a boater might need, is at the top of the ramp in the main marina building. The Discovery Harbour Centre adjoins the marina and contains, among its many shops, a grocery store and liquor store.

Another excellent marina in Campbell River is the Coast Marina (VHF 66A, phone

View of Campbell River across Discovery Passage to April Point and Gowlland Harbour.

DISCOVERY PASSAGE
Recommended Route: ....
Flood Flows: South
Max Speed: 6 kn

Seymour Narrows

Heriot Bay

Rebecca Spit Marine Park

Ferry to Cortes

Duncan Bay

Entrance Rock

Vigilant Its.

Steep Island

Crow Island

Seascape Resort

Stag Island

Gowlland Island

±5 knots

GOWLLAND HARBOUR
Ⓦ Waypoint 50°04.35'N 125°12.89'W

Blenkin Memorial Park

VANCOUVER ISLAND

QUADRA ISLAND

April Point

April Point Marina

Island Hwy.

Tyee Spit

Grouse Island

Quathiaski Cove

Discovery Harbour Marina

Campbell River

16th Ave.

Mall

Quadra Ferry

Whiskey Point

Coast Marina

Tyee Plaza

Fisherman's Wharf

Island Hwy.

Campbell River Bypass

5th Ave.

6th Ave.

YACULTA BANK

Campbell River Museum

Backeddy here

CAPE MUDGE VILLAGE

Kwakiutl Museum

Backeddy here

Lighthouse Rd.

CAMPBELL RIVER

N

0   3/4   1.5

Nautical miles
Not for Navigation.
Depths in fathoms

Fl WR 5s

CAPE MUDGE

±5 knots

WILBY SHOALS

FlR

To Airport

The anchorage southeast of April Point is well protected with very good holding ground.

250-287-7455). Owned by the Coast Discovery Inn, the marina's guests have access to the hotel facilities. The marina was rebuilt in 1998, when improved concrete docks and new power and water outlets were installed. This marina has the advantage of being right opposite the downtown area and Tyee Plaza, and is just north of the very pleasant Foreshore Park. Just south of Coast Marina is the Fisherman's Wharf, which also welcomes visiting pleasure boats. This marina is a good place to buy fresh fish rigt on the dock.

There are numerous attractions in and around Campbell River, and the visitor information kiosk in Tyee Plaza has details about local sights and transportation. Elk Falls Provincial Park is just outside Campbell River's city limits on Highway 28 and is named after an impressive 80-foot waterfall that plunges into the Campbell River canyon. Vancouver Island has thousands of caves, many close to Campbell River, such as the Horne Lakes Caves. NorthernVancouver Island is also home to the highest concentration of black bears in the world.

South of the marinas is the Museum at Campbell River, a contemporary facility overlooking Discovery Passage on Oceanside Route 19A near the south entrance to town. The museum's permanent exhibits feature a pioneer settlement, float homes, salmon fishing and First Nations' history. You can also watch a documentary video about the record-setting detonation of Ripple Rock.

Over on Quadra Island, in Cape Mudge Village, the Potlatch Collection at the Kwagiulth Museum and Cultural Centre features sacred ceremonial objects such as masks, headdresses, coppers and other regalia used in Kwagiulth (Kwakwaka'wakw) winter ceremonies. There is also a vintage photograph collection, gift shop and, on a nearby beach, over 50 petroglyphs.

THE ANCHORAGES
April Point ☐1

The bay southeast of April Point is a convenient place to pull into before or after transiting Seymour Narrows, where boaters will find sheltered anchorage and good holding. We often drop anchor beside the April Point Marina, or tie up if the weather is poor and there's a slip available. Entrance to the bay is obstructed by kelp and a rock which has a red spar buoy marking its location. Leave this to starboard.

The April Point Marina is part of the sportfishing lodge and resort (and restaurant) located on the point. This well-known lodge was built in 1945 by Phil and Phyllis Peterson, an American couple under whose management, and that of their sons Warren and Eric, the lodge developed into a leading sportfishing resort visited by guests from all walks of life, including politicians and entertainment celebrities. In 1998, the Petersons sold their lodge to the Oak Bay Marine Group.

In September, the off-season descends and the slips normally filled with mega-yachts throughout the summer start to empty. One misty afternoon in October we pulled into this bay for the night and sat outside in the cockpit, enjoying the peace and pine-scented air until the dampness of early evening drove us below decks. That night we could hear a pod of killer whales in the bay, followed by an owl hooting back, in perfect time, at a foghorn.

Gowlland Harbour ☐2

Located 5 miles south of Seymour Narrows, Gowlland Harbour is a nearly land-locked anchorage of wooded islets and hidden passages awaiting exploration by dinghy or kayak. Entry is made between Entrance Rock and Vigilant Islets at the harbour entrance – favour the Vigilant Islets side of the channel.

There are often log booms lining the harbour's western (and sometimes southern) shoreline but there is plenty of room to anchor. Best shelter from south winds is at the south end of the harbour in 40 feet. The east side of **Stag Island** is good in NW winds. Our CQR has no problem penetrating the sticky mud/sand combination here but there may some debris close to shore with the amount of booming taking place. Patience with setting the anchor will usually work.

Tucked close to **Stag Island**, you are sheltered from all but the strongest northwesterlies funnelling into Gowlland Harbour. And funnel they do. In December 2000 a winter 'bomb' tore the Seascape Resort docks from their moorings and sent them a quarter-mile east. With a dozen boats attached to the

GOWLLAND HARBOUR AT A GLANCE

CHARTS: 3540, 3312, 3539
LAT LONG: 50°04.30'N 125°12.89'W
PROS: Fair to good protection with good holding in sand and mud. Scenic setting with pretty sunsets. Marina nearby with showers, laundry. Good spot to anchor before or after transiting Seymour Narrows.
CONS: Northwesterlies can whistle through the harbour. Some anchors have difficulty setting in hard mud-and-sand bottom.
MUST DO: Explore the area by dinghy or kayak.

docks, the ensemble somehow managed to pass over a reef before coming to rest. Miraculously, only a few boats sustained damage. If winds from the northwest are very strong, the gusts are weaker just inside the SE corner of Stag Island.

Northwest winds from Discovery Passage can push moderate swells right up to Doe Islet and N gusts will be keenly felt throughout the small 'animal' islets north of Stag Island. The small bight south of **Vigilant Islets** is suitable only as a temporary lunch stop because of the regular wash from tugs working the bay. The bight is also exposed to southeasterlies and experiences a constant current stream.

Several of the 'animal' islets, namely Wren, Crow, Fawn and Mouse, are protected as provincial park reserves, as are the Vigilant Islets, where seals and sea lions regularly haul out. Private homes dot much of the shoreline but don't detract from the pleasant setting, and road access to the harbour offers boaters the opportunity to explore some of the nearby parks and trail systems. Closest, about 2 miles (3 km) away, is Blenkin Memorial Park, behind the community centre on West Road.

Top, anchorage south of Stag Island and, above, anchorage near Seascape Resort. Below, aerial view of Gowlland Harbour.

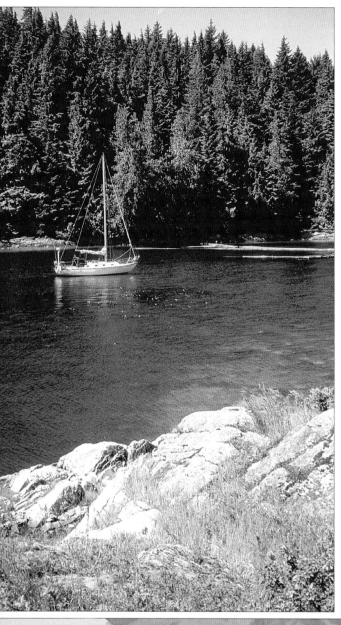

The passage connecting Gowlland Harbour with the April Point anchorage requires local knowledge and no small amount of nerve to safely pilot a keel boat through at HW slack, but is interesting to explore by dinghy.

Kanish Bay/Small Inlet, Quadra Island 3

For years, when southbound in Discovery Passage, we would pull into Kanish Bay for the night and depart the next morning in time to catch slack water at Seymour Narrows. We invariably motored to Small Inlet, at the head of Kanish Bay, where we anchored behind the two small islets in the easternmost part in 2 fathoms (4 m). This is a snug spot and although strong northwesterlies can funnel through Kanish Bay with the odd gust whistling past the islets, the holding is good. We've also anchored west of these islets. The bight on the S shore just E of the inlet entrance also provides some shelter from W winds.

The **Small Inlet** anchorage provides access to forest trails on land recently acquired by BC Parks (thanks to fundraising efforts by a Quadra-based campaign and BC Marine Parks Forever Society). The trail crosses the neck of land separating Small Inlet from Waiatt Bay and connects with a trail leading to Newton Lake and its fresh-water swimming.

Another spot to anchor in Kanish Bay is among the **Chained Islands**, just inside Bodega Point. There are several approaches to this small cove, situated south of the islet marked '4' on metric chart 3312. We follow the thread of deep water that runs between the island marked '58' and the islet lying off Bodega Point, keeping close to the larger island to port, and then swing

Left, beautiful anchorage in Chained Islands.

Nixon Rk

Chatham Point
W

Waiatt Bay
1/2 mile

40
43

Newton Lake
1 mi

KANISH

Granite Bay
3 mi

Chained Islands

BAY

Small Inlet

Strong west winds
can gust into inlet

46

58

66

Newton
Lake

5

102

0   1/2

Bodega Pt

Nautical miles
Not for Navigation.
Use Chart 3539 or 3312

Strong west winds blow
straight into Granite Bay

KANISH BAY
Recommended Route: - - - - - -
⚓ Anchorage   ⚓ Temp Anchorage
W Waypoint 50˚15.52'N 125˚22.00'W

in a wide arc around the islet marked '4', dropping the hook between the islet and the Quadra Island shore in about 40 feet (12 m). Although somewhat open to strong NW winds, which come in muted gusts, this anchorage is otherwise well protected and the holding is very good in sticky mud. Farther into the cove is a small derelict dock which is unsafe for tying up. The islet marked '4' is a small grassy knoll which affords a tranquil morning view of the anchorage. There is another decent anchorage SE of the island marked '66' which fishboats like also.

Granite Bay was the site of a logging and fishing community with a population of some 500 in the early part of the last century. Reclaimed by nature for many years, the bay's shoreline is now dotted with houses. As a result, numerous moored vessels are at the head of the bay, diminishing its appeal as an anchorage. NW winds howl through here keenly.

Kanish Bay was once inhabited by Coast Salish natives who shared their northern frontier with a confederation of Kwakwaka'wakw (Kwakiutl) tribes called the Lekwiltok, later dubbed the 'Vikings of Vancouver Island' for their skill as mariners. About two centuries ago, not long after Captain Vancouver made his historic voyage through local waters, the Kwakwaka'wakw of Salmon River began moving southward to occupy strategic sites along the channels that weave through the Discovery Islands. The Coast Salish villages that had long thrived in Kanish Bay were eventually abandoned after repeated raids.

Right, anchored west of the islets in Small Inlet.

Below, aerial showing the head of Small Inlet.

KANISH BAY AT A GLANCE

CHARTS: 3539, 3312
LAT LONG: entrance, 50°15.52'N 125°22'W
PROS: Selection of good to excellent anchorages with fair to good holding in various mud bottoms. Small Inlet offers best protection. Good hikes from Small Inlet to Waiatt Bay and Newton Lake. Good swimming there and off islet near entrance to Granite Bay. Chained Islands anchorage convenient for northbound yachts.
CONS: Northwesterlies can penetrate most bays. Granite Bay gets strong westerly gusts.
MUST DO: Explore the bays, go swimming!

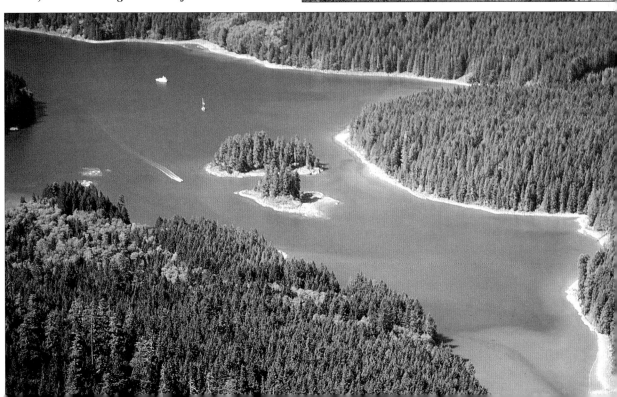

Octopus Islands/Waiatt Bay 4

If it weren't for the tidal passes to the south, the Octopus Islands and adjacent Waiatt Bay would no doubt be as busy as Desolation Sound each summer. This park, at the mouth of Waiatt Bay, contains several scenic anchorages separated by small islands and islets. Its boundaries were extended in 1996 to include the south shore of Waiatt Bay, but the two largest of the Octopus Islands (marked '50' and '71') remain private. An undeveloped park, it's a boater's haven with protected coves, picturesque islets and scenic vistas. Wildlife abounds here, and while poking about in our dinghy we have spotted deer, loons, clam-digging raccoons and a merganser with her chicks.

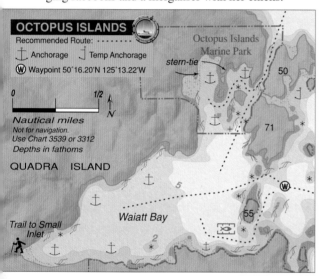

The easiest entry into the anchorage is through the narrow channel that traces the Quadra Island shoreline south from Bodega Anchorage (which is really a tug or commercial waiting area for tide turns at the passes). Entry can also be made south of the Octopus Islands but this is a bit trickier because of islets, shoals and drying reefs clogging the entrance. With someone at the bow, however, and proceeding slowly, this entrance is fairly straightforward. When northbound, coming from Surge Narrows, we go above the small islet N of island '55'. The reef is easy to see and the channel has over 20 feet (6 m) at LW. Another approach to the anchorage is to pass close alongside island '55' and either turn tightly around the island or proceed to the Quadra Island shore before turning west.

Inside Waiatt Bay, you have a myriad of choices. Most people like to anchor in the Octopus Islands and set a stern line because of the limited swinging room.

OCTOPUS ISLANDS AT A GLANCE

CHARTS: 3539, 3312
LAT LONG: 50°16.20'N 125°13.22'W
PROS: Marine park, one of the best. Good protection with very good holding in mud, sand and shell bottoms. Lots to do here.
CONS: Main part of anchorage can be busy. Access can be a little tricky for first-timers.
MUST DO: Relax at one of the finest anchorages of the B.C. coast. Explore islets and reefs by dinghy. Swim at Newton Lake.

When the marine park is too busy, we sometimes anchor at the head of Waiatt Bay, where there is a lovely trail that winds for a half-mile past streams, ferns and evergreens to Small Inlet on the other side of Quadra Island. The trail also branches off to Newton Lake where you can enjoy a refreshing swim. This latter trail ascends some fairly steep terrain but is groomed and signposted. (See map, page 192.)

Waiatt Bay is well protected from most winds. Westerlies will sometimes scoot through the main bay but the holding, in mud and sand, is very good.

Frederick Arm / Estero Basin 5

The head of Frederick Arm is a unique destination for boaters, offering stunning scenery and access to a large uncharted basin. Where the charts end at the top of the arm, a partly hidden gut leads to magnificent Estero Basin. Before dropping anchor in Frederick Arm, we take soundings off the basin's entrance, where depths are uneven and the sandy bottom shoals quickly. We've dropped the hook in the arm's NE corner in 65 feet of water, reversed into 50 feet, and later swung into 25. In settled conditions, we've stayed overnight here but if conditions are unstable you can stern tie in the small bight along the east shore of Frederick Arm, or motor the 6 miles to Shoal Bay or a little further to Bickley Bay.

The waters of land-locked Estero Basin spill across a drying flat into the inlet, and few boats enter Estero Basin because of this shallow entrance channel. When we entered Estero Basin by dinghy one summer afternoon, a family of four was riding rubber air mattresses in the rapids, known locally as 'the Gut.' The father called out to us to take our bathing suits because the swimming was great. We should have heeded his advice because, after making little headway against a rushing ebb current, the three of us (our dog included) climbed out of the dinghy and proceeded on foot. While Bill hauled the dinghy through the Gut, Anne and Tuck walked along the adjacent sand-and-gravel flats. Once through the narrowest part of the channel, we climbed back in and motored the short distance into the basin where we found a flat rock ledge on the north side and sat there awhile, enjoying the stillness, the sun and the solitude.

Estero Basin, which is about 4 miles long and remains uncharted, was named in 1792 by the explorers Galiano and Valdes who explored this basin by small boat after anchoring their ships in Frederick Arm. Estero means *estuary* or *lagoon* in Spanish, but this basin is more like a huge gorge carved out of the mountains, its deep water enclosed by a precipitous shoreline of forested slopes and sheer cliffs.

Opposite, an aerial view of Octopus Islands Marine Park. Below, uncharted Estero Basin.

Aerial view of Handfield Bay looking north.

Handfield Bay, Cameleon Harbour

Thurston Bay Marine Park 6 ⛵🏊🚶

Thurston Bay Marine Park is comprised of two sections – one encompasses the northern part of Thurston Bay and its surrounding shores, the other takes in Handfield Bay and much of the land lying between this bay and Thurston Bay. **Handfield Bay**, inside Cameleon Harbour, is at a popular crossroads just north of the major passes and presents a truly bucolic picture with its islets, pale green water and deciduous trees thriving amongst the evergreens. There is good swimming near the islets at the head

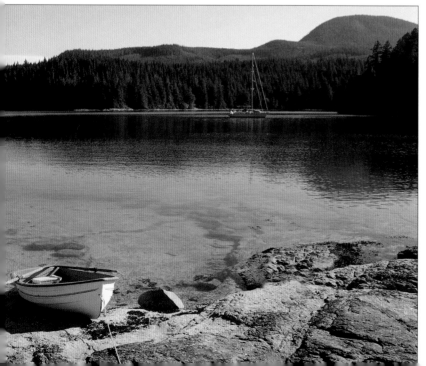

of the bay (the water is warmish) and plenty to explore by dinghy or kayak. Well sheltered, the anchorage is a great spot to rest after the arduous journey north through the passes and is well worth spending a few days to enjoy the scenery.

The entrance to Cameleon Harbour is the narrow gap presented by the sharp end of Bruce Point and the reef off Greetham Point. Swing wide when entering to avoid Douglas Rock, which extends a bit further west than shown on charts.

Inside, there are numerous spots to anchor. One of our favourites is north of the two wooded islets in Handfield Bay with a line to a tall cedar on the northernmost islet. On warm sunny days, this part of the bay can get quite hot. The holding is excellent in a bottom of mud, sand and shell, and provides shelter if strong winds are expected from the south. During strong northwesterlies however, gusts from the lagoon can blast through the entire bay and into Cameleon Harbour. A better spot in such conditions is south of Tully Island with a line ashore to Bruce Point peninsula. Black bears still appear regularly at the head of the bay, picking the fallen fruit from the large cherry tree.

Tully Island is mostly dried grass in summer and is a lovely spot to have a picnic lunch. We have enjoyed many a sunny afternoon here amid the clusters of pink wild onion that bloom each spring.

The park is undeveloped except for an overgrown trail linking Handfield Bay with **Anchorage Lagoon** at the south end of Thurston Bay. The lagoon is a one- or two-boat spot and the entrance is very shallow (less than 2 feet) with boulders. The anchorage has a minimum depth of about 12 feet (3.7 m). Northwesterlies gust through this anchorage but a line to the north shore helps.

The north end of **Thurston Bay** is fun to explore by dinghy where, behind some islets, a stream feeds into the head of the bay. Near the stream is an overgrown trail which leads inland past an old forestry station to Florence Lake (1.5 miles/2.5 km NE). Cut throat trout fishing is reportedly good there. Thurston Bay is deep and somewhat exposed to both westerlies and south winds, but the anchorage is large with good holding.

The SE end of **Cameleon Harbour** is popular with large boats and has a beautiful view to the west. Although it's more exposed if Johnstone Strait kicks up a westerly gale, the holding in sticky mud is good.

HANDFIELD BAY AT A GLANCE

CHARTS: 3543, 3312
LAT LONG: 50°20.60'N 125°19.20'W
PROS: Marine park. Generally good protection with good-to-excellent holding in sticky mud with sand. Beautiful setting with lots of dinghy exploring. Some hiking available.
CONS: Northwesterlies can whistle through NE side of Handfield Bay and through Cameleon Harbour. Some anchors have difficulty setting in the hard mud-and-sand bottom.
MUST DO: Picnic on Tully Island.

Above, anchorage at the head of Handfield Bay and (opposite page, lower left) south of Tully Island.

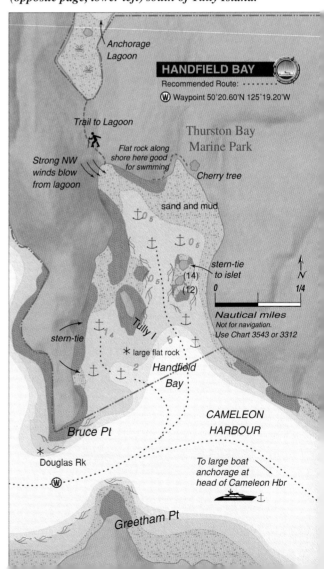

Anchorage Lagoon

HANDFIELD BAY
Recommended Route: - - - - - - - -
W Waypoint 50°20.60'N 125°19.20'W

Trail to Lagoon

Thurston Bay
Marine Park

Flat rock along shore here good for swmming

Strong NW winds blow from lagoon

Cherry tree

sand and mud

stern-tie to islet

(14)

(12)

N

0   1/4

Nautical miles
Not for navigation.
Use Chart 3543 or 3312

stern-tie

Tully I

large flat rock

Handfield Bay

CAMELEON HARBOUR

Bruce Pt

Douglas Rk

To large boat anchorage at head of Cameleon Hbr

Greetham Pt

Hemming Bay 7

If you've had it with westerlies, a good spot to get out of the wind is Hemming Bay. This anchorage will make you forget what it's like out in Johnstone Strait once you're tucked beside the islets near the head of the bay.

There are numerous spots to anchor along the bay's north and northwest shores that provide good shelter. A good spot is north of the island marked '44' (Charts 3543 and 3312) and its satellite islet, with a view through the narrow entrance into a pretty saltwater lagoon. This spot is well sheltered from most winds although strong westerlies sometimes gust out of the mouth of the lagoon. Anchor here in about 40 feet in good holding in sticky mud. The very head of the bay, in front of the low shoreline with a cabin, provides better protection in NW gales. Vessels can also anchor SE of island '44' or SW of the island marked '3' being very careful to avoid the rocks.

A small islet southeast of '44' is a great spot to relax and enjoy a picnic or go for a swim off one of the granite ledges leading into the water. For those wanting to test the waters of Hemming Lake, there are two access points. One is from the north shore of the saltwater lagoon, along a small drainage creek. Follow the creek and cross the old logging road until you're walking parallel with a lagoon filled with old logs. Continue for about a quarter mile to the lake proper where you'll find a rock outcropping to swim from. Another access point is from the north arm of the bay, where an old logging road leads west to the creek. (The small waterfall and creek at the west end of the saltwater lagoon connect with the lake, but the path and road along the creek are private property.)

The saltwater lagoon is a beautiful spot to drift around in a dinghy and watch birdlife. Numerous heron make this bay their home and loud squawking from these modern pterodactyls is the greeting meted out to interlopers.

Of note when entering Hemming Bay north of the Lee Islands: there appears to be less water than charted south of Jackson Point, with depths of less than 13 feet (4 m). If taking this pass, proceed with caution. Kelp can be expected across the pass.

Below, saltwater lagoon at head of Hemming Bay.
Opposite, enjoying the islets in Hemming Bay.

Map:

To Hemming Lake
Logging road
Private
Lagoon
Private
Lagoon
44

0 — 1/4 N
Nautical miles
Not for navigation.
Use Chart 3543 or 3312

Pinhorn It
Menace Rk
Depth less than 10 ft ((3 m)
Jackson Pt
Lee Islands

HEMMING BAY
Recommended Route: ·········
⚓ Anchorage   ⚓ Temp Anchorage

CHAPTER SIX

JOHNSTONE STRAIT

It took Captain Vancouver four days to transit the entire length of Johnstone Strait in the summer of 1792. His two ships rounded Chatham Point in a northwesterly and began tacking their way along this 54-mile-long channel, taking soundings near shore. When the current turned against them, they anchored in various bights to await a change in the tide. On reaching the western entrance to Johnstone Strait, near Telegraph Cove, Vancouver noted they had "beat to windward every foot of the channel."

Modern mariners are well-advised to approach Johnstone Strait with the same determination as Captain Vancouver. Today, we have the advantage of engine power, but it takes a pretty big engine to buck contrary winds and current in Johnstone Strait. In summer, to avoid the predominant afternoon northwesterlies, most northbound boaters travel the strait in the morning, before the wind kicks up, or in the evening, when the wind begins to die down.

In addition, Johnstone Strait carries much of the freshwater runoff that flows from mainland rivers to the Pacific Ocean, resulting in an almost constant north-flowing ebb. So, along with the NW wind, a steep chop can be expected, especially at the intersections with Mayne Passage and Sunderland Channel.

WEST CRACROFT ISLAND

Forward Bay

Chatham Channel

MAINLAND

KNIGHT INLET

5 Port Harvey

Broken Islands

6 Matilpi

JOHNSTONE STRAIT

Port Neville

4

strong ebb here

VANCOUVER ISLAND

MAINLAND

Yorke I

3

Sunderland Channel

this area of strait has heavy chop in NW wind

HARDWICKE ISLAND

Kelsey Bay

Race Passage

Current Passage

Whirlpool Rapids

Forward Hbr

2

Helmcken I

Wellbore Channel

Camp Pt

Chancellor Channel

Tyee Pt

Prince of Wales Range

Vansittart Pt

West Thurlow Island

CORDERO ISLAND

Greene Pt. Rapids

Knox Bay

Blind Channel

1

Mayne Passage

Cordero Channel

Ripple Pt

Edith Pt.

strong flood & ebb currents here

Walkem Is

Rock Bay

Turn Is

Chatham Point

JOHNSTONE STRAIT

Charts & Publications:

Use CHS Charts 3543, 3544, 3545 and 3564 (detail of Chatham Channel). Use 3546 if proceeding west to Blackfish Sound and Alert Bay. Chart book 3312 includes Cordero Islands. Use CHS Canadian Tide and Current Tables Volume 6 and CHS Sailing Directions Volume One. Call marinas on channel 66A.

0   5

Nautical miles

Currents are complex in this strait, its deep waters in continual motion and always cold, causing frequent fog in summer when warm air comes into contact with its frigid surface. At the height of summer, the deep and swift-flowing waters of Johnstone Strait are the coldest on our coast, with surface temperatures rarely exceeding 10° C (50° F). Even the surface waters of Queen Charlotte Sound are warmer during summertime heating than those in Johnstone Strait.

Although flood currents flow east and ebb currents flow west in Johnstone Strait, their speed and times of turn can vary considerably from one side of the channel to the other, with surface waters temporarily flowing in opposite directions, depending on the state of the tide. Generally, flood currents flow strongest on the Vancouver Island side, and ebb currents are strongest along the mainland side of the strait. However, there can be many days when tides are small and there is no appreciable flood current on the surface. As noted in the Sailing Directions, "if the prediction for lower HW at Alert Bay is less than 3.7 m, there generally will be no flood current for that period" west of Yorke Island. The Sailing Directions includes an excellent series of charts that show currents in Johnstone Strait at various stages of tide which can be of some help. The exact timing and predictions by the Canadian Hydrographic Service of the currents in the various channels and for some passes around Johnstone Strait, however, remain largely guesswork, taken from years of CHS and fishing fleet observations.

Estuarine currents, fed by freshwater runoff which flows on top of the heavier saltwater, contributes to the strait's dominant ebb currents. Slow-moving boats are advised to keep well to starboard when travelling in either direction, taking advantage of this current when heading westward and staying out of its path when heading eastward.

Getting used to the constant flow of current is an important aspect of cruising the Johnstone Strait area. The biggest hurdle when northbound is getting

Above, Chatham Point Lighthouse. Below, a westward view over Otter Cove to Johnstone Strait.

from Chatham Point to Port Harvey. Many boaters opt to stay on the 'back route' as long as possible, taking Cordero Channel to Chancellor Channel, then turning off at Wellbore Channel and entering Johnstone Strait via Sunderland Channel, avoiding Current and Race Passages. Anchorages and harbours to stop at along the way include the **Cordero Islands**, **Blind Channel** and **Forward Harbour**.

For boaters who choose the main route along Johnstone Strait, there are numerous bights and bays on both sides of the strait that offer temporary shelter while you wait for a change in the tide or wind.

TIDES AND CURRENTS
Chatham Point to Edith Point

Rock Bay Provincial Marine Park encompasses the two bays on either side of Chatham Point. Otter Cove offers sheltered anchorage at its head, with entry between Rocky Islets and Limestone Island.

The area around Chatham Point can be deceptively calm, while a mile or two west of the lighthouse a strong westerly can be blowing. We have experienced all kinds of localized weather – 40-knot winds, fog, lightning storms and sudden downpours – between Chatham Point and Edith Point, the latter a good place to bail out if the strait is too rough.

The safest route along this part of Johnstone Strait is in the middle of the strait, but be prepared for tough conditions if there is strong wind against current. The area from Walkem Islands to Ripple Point has current up to 5 knots, which against wind can produce quite a nasty chop. If conditions are too challenging, turn into Mayne Passage and take the back route. Here, west winds calm down east of Mayne Point and, while gusts persist for a mile or two into the passage, there is rarely much of a swell or chop. The flood sets north in this channel and can reach 5 knots.

Sometimes if we are battling the conditions south of Walkem Islands we take cover from the wind behind these islands and work our way through them to get to Mayne Passage. This can be a little dicey in large tides – we have sometimes found ourselves barely moving against a west wind and 3 knots of flood current in the midst of the islands and reefs. One option is to pull into the cove between the large island marked '98' and the smaller island marked '64' (Chart 3543) and wait for conditions to improve. There is lots of kelp here so you'll have to find a clear spot to drop the hook while you wait and rest.

Edith Point to Race and Current Passages

From Edith Point, currents in Johnstone Strait are not obvious until the vicinity of Vansittart Point. From here to Race and Current Passages, the ebb especially will be felt although backeddies can sometimes be encountered close along West Thurlow Island. Strong current and turbulence can be expected west of Tyee Point, with patches of whirlpools and upwelling between Ripple Shoal and Speaker Rock.

Between a rock and a hard place: Johnstone Strait in a westerly near Walkem Islands.

If you're early for slack at Current Passage, Knox Bay serves as a temporary anchorage, as do several bights on the south shore of Johnstone Strait, including one opposite the western end of West Thurlow Island. We anchored here one May in 30 feet (10 m) off a gravel beach backed by the Prince of Wales Range, then hiked up the hillside for a picnic lunch overlooking the strait. Afterward we realized this was where Vancouver's two ships anchored in July 1792 after making little progress against a fresh westerly gale. Fortunately we had no headwinds to contend with when we raised anchor later that afternoon and continued our voyage along the restless waters of Johnstone Strait.

Race and Current Passages

These passes mark the last set of rapids for westbound boaters in Johnstone Strait before reaching safe havens further north. Helmcken Island forms a natural obstacle for traffic separation: westbound vessels use Current Passage, eastbound vessels use Race Passage. Although current speeds in the two channels rarely exceed 6 knots, conditions can be turbulent, especially around Ripple Shoal and Earl Ledge – both of which have a strong set onto them.

Also, the hazards of commercial traffic – especially at night or in foggy conditions – should not be underestimated. Tugs with tows that are unable to turn into Current Passage may continue westbound into Race Passage. Fog will hang in this pass long after it has burned off in the rest of the strait.

Trying to arrive here at slack is also a challenge. Part of the difficulty in predicting the turn and speed

Pass Tip Sheet – Race & Current Passages

Chart: 3544
Location: E Entrance: 50°24.10'N 125°55.42'W (15 miles west of Chatham Point).
Maximum Flow: 6 knots (flood).
Slack: 15-35 minutes.
Nearby anchorages: Westbound – Vere Cove, Knox Bay. Eastbound – Port Neville, Yorke Island, north side of Helmcken Island.

of current is the daily wind variation of Johnstone Strait. Tide and current tables may not be accurate on days when a strong wind is affecting current, and predictions can be out by an hour or more. If strong westerlies are predicted, you should try to get through the passages as early in the day as possible.

Anchorages on the N side of **Helmcken Island** include an open bay east of the island's small peninsula, which is suitable only for waiting out wind or

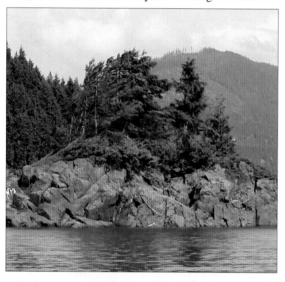

tide for a few hours because the holding ground is poor and the anchorage is open to vessel wash and SE winds. Billygoat Bay, the larger bay south and east, is indented well into the island and more sheltered, serving well as an overnight anchorage, but the mud is soft and the holding is only fair. If you spend the night, set the hook carefully so it buries deep. The Sailing Directions goes as far as to recommend mooring lines to shore. The safest entrance to this anchorage is between islands '43' and '42' (Chart 3544). This is the island with a prominent white storage tank and red-and-white radio mast.

Westbound boaters approaching Current Passage have two areas of concern. The first is from Tyee Point to Ripple Shoal, where currents can be strong and heavy tide rips will be expected if wind is against tide. The area near Earl Ledge at the west end of Current Passage also requires close attention as there is a pronounced set onto this ledge during ebbs. If proceeding on an ebb during strong W winds, you may be better off avoiding these passes and instead use Wellbore Channel.

Sector lights on both Hardwicke and Helmcken Islands mark the preferred route to pass east of Ripple Shoal and then north of (above) Ripple Shoal when westbound. Keep an eye for overtaking commercial traffic, as you proceed along Current Passage and favour the south side of the channel, which is especially important when leaving the passage for the aforementioned danger of Earl Ledge.

At the west end of Helmcken Island, you should be able to discern conditions in the remainder of the passage and into Johnstone Strait. If a west wind is producing a heavy line of whitecaps from Vancouver Island across to Hardwicke Point, it may be wise for

The prevailing westerlies in Johnstone Strait leave many trees permanently bent to the east.

smaller vessels to anchor for a few hours in one of the two bays on the north side of Helmcken Island. Ebb current against a westerly wind can produce a brutal 3- to 4-foot chop, heavy tide rips and standing waves from Kelsey Bay to Hickey Point opposite Port Neville. Winds usually die down in late afternoon, providing better conditions to round this point.

However, if you proceed and get caught in these tide rips, stay clear of Earl Ledge and once past the ledge (50°25'N, 125°55'W, marked with a flashing red light), favour Hardwicke Island because conditions are usually worse on the Vancouver Island side of the channel. Vessels can pull into Kelsey Bay where moorage is available; however, there can be considerable chop in the vicinity of the breakwater, and in strong SE winds there is a set onto the wharfs. Winds from Brasseau Bay to Hickey Point are known to accelerate strongly and can be double the strength of those in the middle of the strait. We were knocked down here once under sail.

Eastbound boaters should try to be east of Kelsey Bay before noon and be wary of entering these passes when strong west winds blow against an ebb current. If such conditions exist, it is prudent to bypass these passes altogether and proceed along Sunderland Channel to either Forward Harbour or Blind Channel. Eastbound boaters can get a jump on the passes by spending the night in Port Harvey or Port Neville and getting away early enough to clear the rapids before westerlies pick up. When approaching Race Passage, we normally favour the Hardwicke Island side of the channel until we are about a mile from Earl Ledge, then cross over into Race Passage, staying in the middle of the pass until east of Helmcken Island. Favour the Vancouver Island side after this until you are well past Camp Point. If you are battling an ebb, there is little relief until well beyond Vansittart Point on West Thurlow Island.

Travelling east, at least in a sailboat, can be exhilarating when a flood tide and westerly wind are in the same direction, although the area around Race Passage is still, for most recreational vessels, quite a challenge in such conditions.

Johnstone Strait West: Hardwicke Point to Cracroft Point

North of Race Passage, boaters can find several bays on the mainland side of Johnstone Strait to escape strong W winds. These include Blenkinsop Bay and the small bay just east of Tuna Point, which offer easy access, good holding and shelter from westerlies. These two bays make acceptable overnight stops if westerlies are predicted to persist through the evening but they are open to the southeast, making Port Neville or Port Harvey better bets if such winds are expected.

Taking Johnstone Strait beyond Port Harvey is the direct route to Blackfish Sound and the towns of Alert Bay and Port McNeill. Although there are no

Johnstone Strait, looking east to Mayne Passage and the Walkem Islands.

well-protected anchorages in the 15-mile stretch to Blackney and Baronet Passages, there are a few bights and hooks on the N (Cracroft Island) side of the strait to anchor in during settled or strong W conditions. Keep an ear to the weather if overnighting along the strait and consider either **Boat Bay** or **Forward Bay** if conditions are favourable. These two anchorages are open to the east but both have islets providing some protection from the wash of passing vessels in the strait. Both anchorages will also provide good shelter if a W breeze comes on early in the morning. We have been caught in Forward Bay when the wind unexpectedly turned SE with force during the night and we anxiously waited for hours in our heaving boat for dawn before raising anchor and finding refuge in another bight along the strait. If the day is cloudy and a southeasterly is expected, **Growler Cove** is reported to be a good, although there you could be sharing this spot with commercial fishboats in late July or August.

Early-morning travellers heading west from Forward Harbour usually enjoy a good ebb ride from the south end of Sunderland Channel right to the entrance of Havannah Channel.

Greene Point Rapids during a flood with current about five knots. Looking east to Mayne Passage.

Greene Point Rapids

Greene Point Rapids is far less daunting than the major passes to the south. Although the maximum current is 7 knots, the current stream is fairly straight and wide. Depths are well marked on the chart, the only danger being the reef extending east from Griffiths Island with the QR light. There is a pronounced set onto this reef, so stay well clear. Also, there can be a set onto the rock at the east side of Edsall Islets on the flood. There is a suitable shortcut between the island marked '27' (Chart 3543) and West Thurlow Island for small craft going to Mayne Passage (known also as Blind Channel) however it may be quite thick with kelp.

Currents in this area's interconnecting channels are strongest in the middle, and slightly slower along shorelines. Charts indicate the flood direction in

Pass Tip Sheet – Greene Pt Rapids

Location: 1/2 mile west of Cordero Islands.
Direction of flood: East
Reference Station: Seymour Narrows
Maximum Flow: 7 knots
Slack: 15-30 minutes
Nearby Anchorages: Westbound boaters can wait at Cordero Islands; eastbound vessels in the open bay northwest of the pass.

most of the channels. Mayne Passage floods north. Sometimes a bay or large bight will produce a back eddy, providing a short burst of positive current. The channels around East and West Thurlow islands are greatly influenced by freshwater runoff from nearby mountains and by Johnstone Strait.

Strong summer westerlies from Johnstone Strait are common, and will push water into the back channels, delaying and diminishing the onset of the ebb. It is worth noting that over a period of hours, wind can push water at a rate of up to 3 per cent of the air speed; thus a 30-knot wind can produce, for example, a one-knot current. If winds die off in early evening during the onset of the ebb, the current may come on very strong in these channels. Occasionally the effects of a flood may be non-existent as it slides under an outgoing layer of fresh water.

Ebbs along Cordero and Chancellor Channels are helped by the freshwater outflow from the coastal mountains. Currents often reach 2 to 3 knots, and up to 5 knots in places during strong spring tides.

The distance from Dent Rapids to Forward Harbour is 25 miles and the scenery is sublime. Fjord-like channels intersect with inlets and other channels, and the milky-emerald water mirrors the forested mountainsides. There is a magnificent view just west of Lyall Islet, looking north up Loughborough Inlet where its numerous steep points disappear into the mauve haze.

However, if a westerly is blowing, the calm water ends at Lyall Islet because Chancellor Channel will be a bear. During strong westerlies, which can start early in this channel, there can be a white line extending from West Thurlow Island across to Lyall Island. If so, the winds will be at least 20 knots. In such conditions, the distance from Lyall Island to the entrance to Wellbore Channel will seem interminable. Still, it makes arrival at Forward Harbour or Port Neville all the more satisfying because there are no more big passes to face.

Wellbore Channel/ Whirlpool Rapids

Wellbore Channel is a straightforward channel about 4 miles in length from D'Arcy Point to Althorp Point off Sunderland Channel. The current sets up near D'Arcy Point and builds to considerable strength at Whirlpool Rapids. However, the channel is deep and free of obstructions.

Heading up Wellbore Channel against a westerly. Current can be 7 knots at Whirlpool Rapids at north end of this channel.

Although there can be impressive whirlpools at the rapids, especially opposite the light on the small island near the north end, turbulence or overfalls are not excessive at most stages of tide. As you clear the small island, the worst of the current is over and turbulence rarely extends beyond the entrance to Forward Harbour.

The current is reported to be 7 knots at maximum. The shores of the pass, particularly on the east side, can be quite thick with bull kelp, so if you're bucking a tide along the edge of the channel, take care to avoid catching your prop on kelp which may lie just below the surface.

Wellbore Channel is a preferred route to Johnstone Strait when wind-against-current conditions are creating heavy tide-rips in Current and Race Passages. The former was the route followed by British and Spanish explorers in the summer of 1792. The Spanish, whose two ships were smaller than those under the command of Captain Vancouver, anchored opposite the entrance to Forward Harbour in late July. Three weeks earlier, Lieutenant James Johnstone had explored Wellbore Channel by longboat. He knew that an opening to the ocean lay ahead after he and his men were swamped while camping on shore one night, soggy proof that the flood tide was no longer flowing from the south, but from the north.

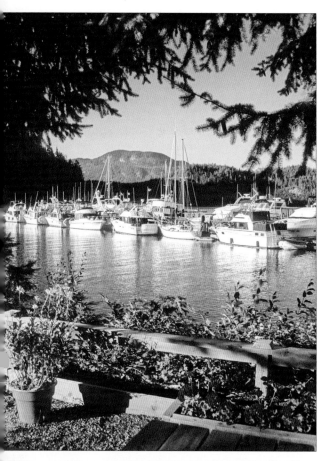

Blind Channel Resort, West Thurlow Island

The Blind Channel Resort, with its first-rate facilities, has been owned and operated by the Richter family since 1969. Younger members of the extended family arrive each summer to help out, and one of them is often waiting by an empty slip to take your bowline, because currents in Mayne Passage can make docking a challenge. On shore, the facilities include a general store stocked with fresh produce and bread baked on the premises, as well as a liquor store, post office, showers, laundromat and licensed restaurant. Pub lunches are served on the resort's seaside patio, and dinner (by reservation) is always excellent at the Cedar Post Restaurant.

Adjacent to the marina resort are the Blind Channel hiking trails. These lie within a tree farm license and were first cleared in the late '80s, when Fletcher Challenge began logging the eastern end of the island. At that time, Edgar and Annemarie Richter voiced their concerns to a forester employed by Fletcher Challenge. The Richters told him that visitors to their marina liked hiking into the nearby woods to view a huge, 800-year-old cedar, 16 feet in diameter, which had been left standing when the area was hand-logged at the turn of the century.

The forester listened, then approached his managers with a proposal (which was approved) to create a buffer strip next to the Richters' property and build hiking trails to acquaint the public with the multiple uses of a forest. A crew of men soon began clearing the first of what are now called the Blind Channel Hiking Trails, which are mapped and explained in a company pamphlet available at the marina's general store. Wooden footbridges span streams and a bench provides a resting spot for hikers beside the Big Cedar. On a hot summer day the trails are a refreshing respite from the blazing sun as soft light filters through the forest's canopy of second-growth timber. (For a history of Blind Channel, see Part One's 'A Storied Coastline'.)

Nearby anchorages, in addition to the Cordero Islands, include a decent spot almost directly across from Blind Channel in **Charles Bay** which can accommodate two or three boats. The best part of the bay, to get out of the current, is north of small Eclipse Island in about 15 feet (4.5 m) minimum depth. Westerlies gust a bit into the anchorage but the bottom is soft mud and the holding quite good.

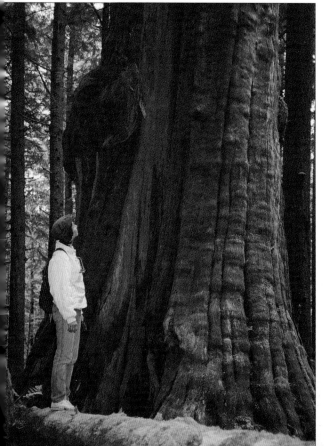

Top left, Blind Channel floats. Bottom left, a cedar snag left standing by turn-of-the century hand loggers on the Blind Channel forest trails.

THE ANCHORAGES
Cordero Islands 1

Many times we have travelled Cordero Channel, intent on getting through Greene Point Rapids, and motored right past the Cordero Islands without a second glance. Then, one sunny July afternoon while westbound in Cordero Channel under a balmy blue sky, we noticed a boat anchored in this cluster of islands. Because we were, for once, in no hurry to go anywhere as we slid past steep shores thickly treed with evergreens and gazed up at distant peaks with pockets of snow clinging to their crowns, we decided to stop at the Cordero Islands for a closer look. We ended up anchoring here for the night and since then have returned several times.

The anchorage is ringed by three small islands, each of which is corralled with bull kelp. Protection from wind is good in most conditions. Southerlies usually get lost when they show up at the intersection just below Cordero Islands, and most northwest breezes from Johnstone Strait will blow down Chancellor Channel into Loughborough Inlet. Strong northwesterly winds (above 25 knots), however, will gust throughout the anchorage.

Aerial view of Mayne Passage showing Blind Channel marina at left and Cordero Islands top.

Cordero Islands

81

7 knots

Griffiths It

QR

current sets into pass — Min depth 6 ft

GREENE POINT RAPIDS

calmer side of pass

strong set to reef on ebb

37

59

0 — 1/4

↑ N

Nautical miles
Not for navigation.
Use Chart 3312 or 3543
Depths in fathoms

Vest Thurlow Island

CORDERO ISLANDS
Recommended Route: ·········
⚓ Anchorage ⌐ Temp Anchorage
Ⓦ Waypoint: 50'26.45N 125'30.45'W

The holding is good in a bottom of mud and sand, although sometimes big wads of kelp will come up with the anchoring gear. The anchorage has some current but nothing like that which will be on the outside of the surrounding islands. One spot to avoid when anchoring is in front of the gap between the islands marked '81' and '59' on chart 3312. When the tide turns to ebb, there's a strong set into the gap as the current rushes into the rapids. This area would also be dicey in a dinghy. We've used this gap at high tide as a shortcut leaving the anchorage, but it should be noted this pass has less depth than shown on charts 3543 and 3312, with a minimum depth of less than 6 feet (2 m) at LW and not the 18 feet on the chart. On big ebbs the set to the reef extending east from Griffiths Islet is considerable.

Cordero Islands anchorage offers a peaceful and pretty setting with good protection.

The Cordero Islands anchorage is a beautiful setting. The islands make for a fun day of exploration by dinghy or kayak, with foreshores of smooth flat stone which are warm to sit on during a sunny afternoon. A house stands on the mainland shore, backed by tall cedars and fronted by a dock, but its presence is unobtrusive.

The anchorage offers views of busy Cordero Channel and, as this is a major junction for recreational vessels, there is a parade of boats during the slack. There are often flocks of birds hovering over the Greene Point Rapids – loons, eagles and herons all frequent this anchorage. The salmon fishing is good south of the islands, while bottom fish, such as ling cod, can sometimes be caught in the kelp along the arm west of the rapids.

Forward Harbour 2

For northbound boaters, there are few decent anchorages beyond the Cordero Islands until you get past Whirlpool Rapids and set the hook in Forward Harbour, some 15 miles distant. Currents dimish quickly at the entrance, opposite Horace Point, and the channel into the anchorage is clear.

This scenic and spacious harbour affords sheltered anchorage off a fine pebble beach in **Douglas Bay**, and is especially peaceful when a westerly is howling just a few hundred yards away in Sunderland Channel. The anchorage can sometimes be busy with a dozen or more boats anchored near the beach and north shoreline. We usually find ourselves anchoring in 55 feet (17 m) or more while smaller boats tend to snuggle up to the beach. There is current throughout the anchorage so it makes sense to give other vessels lots of room. The holding is very good in thick mud. Although shelter from the west is good, strong east winds can be a problem and may force you to move to the head of the bay to find shelter. Another option is to tie off if booms are lying along the south shore and of course keep a watchful eye for attending tugs Our experience in Douglas Bay has been that easterlies are about half the strength of what's blowing out in Johnstone Strait. Small vessels sometimes anchor in the nook of the channel leading into Forward Harbour and this appears to be a quiet spot during SE winds. Some logging has taken place on the NE slopes of the harbour but the snowcapped mountain at its head remains a beautiful vista.

A lovely forest trail leads from the pebble beach at Douglas Bay across a neck of land to the shores of Bessborough Bay on the other side. Black bears are sometimes spotted in the vicinity, so be sure to make plenty of noise when hiking this trail.

FORWARD HARBOUR AT A GLANCE

CHARTS: 3544
LAT LONG: 50˚28.20'N 125˚46.60'W
PROS: Good protection from west winds with good holding in sticky mud. Lots of room, deep harbour. Good hiking, nice pebble beach.
CONS: Can be busy. The harbour has current, so be careful how you pick your anchoring spot.
MUST DO: Hike across peninsula to Bessborough Bay.

Above, looking toward head of Forward Harbour.
Below, enjoying the pebble beach in Douglas Bay.

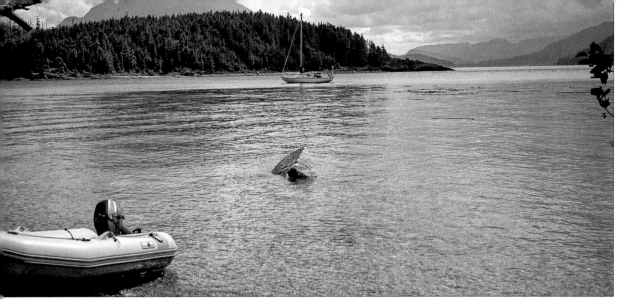

Above, Yorke Island anchorage has plenty of kelp and current. Keep an eye on the wind while on shore. Bottom, underground tunnels on Yorke Island fed ammunition to the main guns, below.

Yorke Island 3

This uninhabited island at the junction of Johnstone Strait and Sunderland Channel makes an interesting day stop for anyone interested in World War II history, for it was here that the Canadian government built a gun emplacement to protect the country's west coast from enemy invasion. The island's overgrown trails received a major clean-up effort by volunteers after the island became a conservancy managed by BC Parks in 2007.

Morning is generally the best time to pull into the kelp-strewn bight at the island's southeast end, before the prevailing northwesterly in Johnstone Strait has time to intensify and make departure a difficult exercise. When anchoring here, we try to find an area free of kelp and ensure the anchor is well set before leaving the vessel. Although this bight provides surprisingly good protection from northwesterlies, it's open to the south and there is usually some current flowing. See Chart 3544.

After landing our dinghy on the pocket beach facing the bight, we scramble up the hillside past the crumbling officers quarters and hike along what is left of a road that continues uphill in a northerly direction, then turns west. The terrain is moss-covered ground dotted with colourful clumps of foxglove and thin stands of forest. At a steady pace, it takes about 20 minutes to reach the deserted bunker and gun emplacement situated on a cliff overlooking Johnstone Strait on the island's western edge.

Construction of this military outpost began in 1937 when Yorke Island was placed under the reserve of the Department of National Defence. The site was chosen for its strategic location: any enemy ships approaching Vancouver from the north would have to pass this island sentinel where two turret guns and a searchlight were waiting. Lead shielding protected the 6-inch guns, which swivelled inside well installations and could fire seven 100-lb rounds per minute. The ammunition bunker, connected by a tunnel and pathway to the guns, was camouflaged with cement and rock to make the structure appear part of the cliff.

Yorke Island never came under attack and the last firing practice took place on August 10, 1945, by which time 62 buildings stood on the island, including the officers' quarters, barracks, canteen and drill hall overlooking the old wharf at the island's southeast end. During the war, both naval and fishing vessels were employed to monitor ship movements in the passes and straits leading from Yorke Island.

Port Neville 4

Port Neville marks the end of the major obstacles encountered by northbound boaters. In fact, the main pilotage challenges of the entire Inside Passage, from Vancouver to Skagway, are the series of passes that start at Seymour Narrows or Yuculta Rapids and end at Race Passage or Whirlpool Rapids. There are other difficult areas and other passes, certainly, but the main route of the Inside Passage lies open once you reach Port Neville. Completing the transits of these passes is an accomplishment, and once you're in the beautiful cruising grounds north of Port Neville, you'll be in no hurry to return to the busier waters of the Strait of Georgia. In fact, you may not want to go back at all.

Port Neville is a convenient port, offering easy access off Johnstone Strait and secure anchorage or

Right, the historic wharf at Port Neville. Below, a cruise ship southbound in Johnstone Strait glides past the anchorage at Port Neville.

moorage at the public float. Popular with both plea-sure boats and fishboats, the small float at the inlet's mouth is often full and boats regularly raft, especial-ly during commercial fishery openings. There is no water or electric power at the docks and the old store at the head of the dock is closed.

The long sandy beach that stretches below the pilings is a good place to take a cruising dog for a walk or let the children roam. If the float is crowded, we anchor along the west shore opposite the Port Neville docks. Although kelp and current can be a hindrance, the holding ground is good once the hook has been firmly set. Current can flow up to 3 knots at the entrance to the inlet but is a bit less inside.

This long, sheltered inlet was the site of several Kwakwakw'waka villages long before its forested shores of prime timber began attracting hand loggers in the late 1800s. When a 32-year-old Norwegian named Sven Hans Hansen arrived at Port Neville in 1891, several hand loggers already lived in and around the inlet, but Hansen soon became the com-munity leader. His homestead, where he planted a garden and orchard, became a local gathering place and in 1895 he was the first postmaster for Port Neville. With no wharf yet built, Hans had to trans-fer all steamship-delivered mail and freight by row-boat. After his first wife died, Hansen voyaged back to Norway and returned with his 18-year-old bride

Above left, deer (and black bears) are often spotted on the shores of Port Neville. Below, a view up Port Neville inlet. Public dock is at lower right.

Kathinka. Together they raised a family while living off the land. Their growing family soon needed more living space, so in 1923 Hans built the two-storey house that still stands at the top of the wharf.

The Hansen home became a full-scale store and in 1928, with construction of a wharf, Port Neville became a regular port of call for the Union Steamships. Meanwhile, local logging operations were making Port Neville a thriving settlement, with float homes and logging camps hugging the inlet's shoreline, its waters busy with tugs and barges while farmland was cultivated at the head of the inlet.

The children living in Port Neville enjoyed birthday picnics at Robbers Nob, complete with ice cream shipped by steamer in wooden barrels surrounded with ice. During the hippie movement in the 1960s, a commune (now abandoned) was established at Robbers Nob. Petroglyphs can be viewed on foreshore rocks on the west side of the knob along level sandstone near the HW mark.

Hans passed away in 1939 at the age of 80. His son Olaf remained at Port Neville, settling with his bride Lilly into a log home where he lived until his death in 1997 at the age of 87. Their daughter, Lorna Chesluk, raised her daughter, Erica, at Port Neville but moved to Campbell River in 2010, at which time the Port Neville post office was closed. Although the local population has dwindled and few people now live around the inlet, it is still used for the booming and storage of logs. Forested Milly Island was for years a landmark for northbound vessels until it was extensively logged and a house built on it in the mid-1990s. Much of Hardy Peak, just south of Port Neville, has also been logged and the large spar tree used for the logging operation still stands.

Port Harvey [5]

Conveniently located just two miles off Johnstone Strait where it intersects with Havannah Channel, this scenic inlet lies between East and West Cracroft Islands and offers good anchorage in several spots. Many boaters like the anchorage north of Range Island opposite the marina at the head of the inlet. Although the holding in soft mud is good, westerlies can really blast into this part of the anchorage from Cracroft Inlet. This normally shouldn't be problem in summer when W winds die out in the evening, but if a gale is in the offing for overnight, a better spot is north of the largest of the Mist Islets (marked '78' on Charts 3564 and 3545). This is a favourite spot of ours. We've also anchored in the middle of the moss-covered **Mist Islets**, between islets '49' and '78' in about 20 feet (6 m) of water. With a stern line bringing us close to shore, we can pull out of the chop from Johnstone Strait.

PORT NEVILLE AT A GLANCE

CHARTS: 3564, 3545
LAT LONG: 50°28.95N 126°05.25'W
PROS: Good overnight or extended stop for transient vessels with a public dock and good anchoring opportunities. Inlet well worth exploring. Some wildlife (bear, deer).
CONS: Dock can often be full. Anchoring opposite dock requires care to ensure set due to kelp. Current throughout inlot.
MUST DO: Visit tho old dock and Robbers Nob

Below, a petroglyph at Robbers Knob.

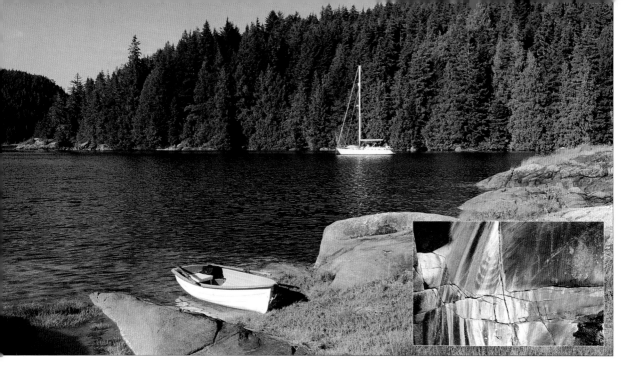

Above, anchored north of the Mist Islets in Port Harvey. Inset, pictograph on west facing bluff.

Port Harvey Marine Resort has a general store, licenced restaurant and access to hiking trails. A lovely shell midden backed by low bush lies at the head of the inlet. The Kwakwaka'wakw (Kwakiutl) natives who once lived here used the drying gorge connecting Port Harvey with Cracroft Inlet as a canoe route. Port Harvey was once a hand-logging centre called Cracroft and lively times were known here when the settlement boasted a store, hotel and beer parlor that catered to local loggers. A few private homes and floats now occupy the west side of the inlet.

Matilpi 6

Located opposite the midden of an ancient Kwakwaka'wakw settlement, this anchorage lies between the mainland and the northernmost of the two Indian Islands. Matilpi is an easy distance from Port Neville (about 15 miles) and close to Chatham Channel. The anchorage is marked by a lovely shell midden which fringes the mainland shore, and the two islets providing shelter from Havannah Channel. After anchoring behind the Indian Islands in 30 feet (10 m), we often go ashore and enjoy the shell beach which is good for swimming although you have to watch for bits of old glass while being mindful that black bears sometimes wander the shoreline at LW.

Holding ground in Matilpi, in mud and shell, is good and the anchorage is protected from most winds. We've also anchored between the islands when the main anchorage has been filled.

Apart from the midden, nothing remains of the Kwakwaka'wakw village that stood here before it was abandoned in the last century when its residents joined the band at Karlukwees on nearby Turnour Island. There's a haunted feel to the place, which only adds to its beauty. Although the village may be gone, the animals depicted in Kwakwaka'wakw crests remain. We've seen red-throated loons swim past the islets and we've listened to a raven cluck vociferously at its neighbours in the forest. On one visit, we watched a black bear thrash its way onto the beach to check out the berry bushes and another time a mink poked its nose out of the brush to take a quick look at us. When night draws in and the forest becomes dark and still, the midden lying along the water's edge remains ghostly white.

Nearby anchorages include Burial Cove, which can be busy with local traffic and not a great anchorage because of poor protection from south winds. A better bet, if Matilpi is busy, is in the lee of **Triangle Island** in about 30 feet (10 m). **Warren Islands** are worth exploring if you're waiting for a tide change but are too exposed to E winds for overnight. Detail on Chatham Channel is found in Chapter Seven.

Matilpi anchorage

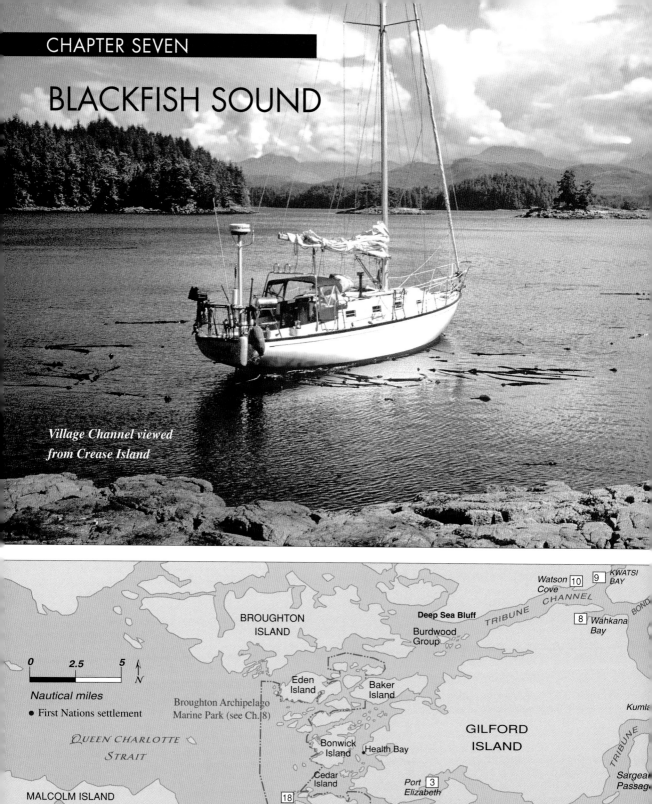

Village Channel viewed from Crease Island

Watson Cove 10 9 KWATSI BAY

Deep Sea Bluff

TRIBUNE CHANNEL

8 Wahkana Bay

BOND

BROUGHTON ISLAND

Burdwood Group

Eden Island

Baker Island

Broughton Archipelago Marine Park (see Ch.8)

GILFORD ISLAND

Kumla

QUEEN CHARLOTTE STRAIT

Bonwick Island   Health Bay

Cedar Island

Port Elizabeth 3

Sargea Passage

MALCOLM ISLAND

Sointula

18

BLACKFISH SOUND

Swanson Island

Crease Island

15

Village Island

14

KNIGHT INLET

TRIBUNE

Minstrel 2 Cutter Cove

Stubbs

Mamalilaculla

Turnour Island

1

Ferry

Alert Bay 20

Pearse Islands

Spout I

Berry I

16 17

Dead Pt

13

New Vancouver

12 Beware Cove

Beware Passage

Karlukwees

Lagoon Cove

East Cracroft Island

21

BROUGHTON STRAIT

19

Blackney Passage

Hanson Island

Harbledown Island

11 Potts Lagoon

Port Harvey

Port McNeill

Weynton Passage

Weynton

West Cracroft Island

See Ch.6

VANCOUVER ISLAND

Telegraph Cove

JOHNSTONE STRAIT

Baronet Passage

0   2.5   5

N

Nautical miles

● First Nations settlement

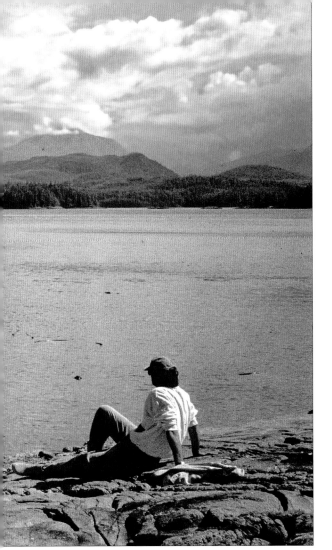

The fragrant islands and green waters of Blackfish Sound await boaters sailing clear of Johnstone Strait. In this area you will find a heady mix of stunning scenery, prolific wildlife and a palpable atmosphere of the past. Heavy cedars draped with shawls of cat-tail moss stand along shorelines, where they seem to be forever waiting. And the tree-top utterings of ravens sound as unsettling today as when they were first heard thousands of years ago by the local Kwakiutl. Many boaters agree there's something about Blackfish Sound that takes hold of you and never lets go.

Getting to Blackfish Sound and Queen Charlotte Strait, though, can seem like *The Seven Voyages of Sinbad*, what with westerly winds, the currents in Johnstone Strait and the prevalence of fog in mid-to-late summer. And then there are the passes still to be transited.

Blackney Passage & Weynton Passage

These passes receive considerable current – at least 6 knots – and can have impressive rips, especially in wind-against-current conditions. They are used extensively by commercial traffic, including cruise ships, and are major routes for killer whales.

Bill Mackay, a pioneer of the local whale watching industry (who today runs Mackay Whale Watching out of Port McNeill), has seen killer whales work against a large flood (which sets southeast) in Weynton Passage, by swimming close to Weynton Island and threading through the Plumper Islands.

At first glance, both Weynton and Blackney appear to be straightforward passes that are fairly wide and without major obstructions. However, because of their orientation to Queen Charlotte and Johnstone Straits, difficulties can arise for small craft during windy conditions. Weynton Passage, especially, can be deceptive. Although it is fairly wide and bound by numerous islands, the current is not errant and diffused (as you might assume) but is surprisingly strong, especially between Stubbs Island and the top end of the Plumper Islands. On a couple of occasions we have felt as if we were towing Stubbs Island for hours. More than anything, be wary of a strong wind against current.

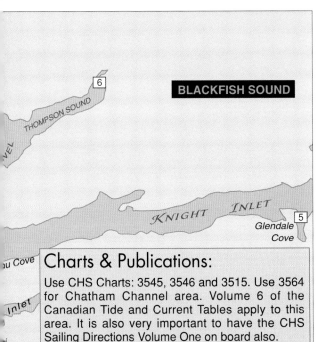

BLACKFISH SOUND

THOMPSON SOUND

6

KNIGHT INLET

5

Glendale Cove

u Cove

Inlet

NLAND

Charts & Publications:

Use CHS Charts: 3545, 3546 and 3515. Use 3564 for Chatham Channel area. Volume 6 of the Canadian Tide and Current Tables apply to this area. It is also very important to have the CHS Sailing Directions Volume One on board also.

"A big flood against a southeaster is bad. You'll see haystacks from Stubbs Island to Donegal Head (on Malcolm Island)," Mackay says. Of concern in these conditions is a pronounced set onto Stephenson Islets where the worst turbulence can occur. Stubbs Island, as John Chappell warns in *Cruising Beyond Desolation Sound*, is to be avoided – locals call this island ' Sinkhole' and the Sailing Directions advise of heavy tide-rips in the vicinity. There is also a strong set onto Donegal Head during an ebb.

Weynton Passage underwent extensive monitoring by Mike Woodward of CHS. In 1981 he installed a current meter southeast of Stubbs Island on top of the 18-metre shoal on the southeast side and gathered months of current data, which was incorporated in the 1986 Tide & Current Tables.

Blackney Passage is assigned as a secondary station on Johnstone Strait and is also somewhat difficult to predict. The maximum current is reported to be 4 knots but Bill Mackay says he has seen up to 10 knots in sheer zones near Cracroft Point. Tide rips can be strong off this point during flood-against-wind conditions. Because this is a busy pass, be very careful when approaching in reduced visibility and stay well to your side of the channel. For us, Blackney is the preferred pass over Weynton.

Blackfish Sound, from the north side of Hanson Island to a line between Bold Head on Swanson Island and Donegal Head on Malcolm Island, can

Blackney Passage is a busy commercial route but only poses a problem when wind is against current.

also be a challenge for small craft during large tides and strong winds. Currents can be 3- to 5-knots and because of the sound's openness to wind from Queen Charlotte Strait, the seas here can build to 4 to 5 feet and form dangerous tide rips – especially over Egeria Shoal. If you are caught in such conditions, look for a haven. The north side of Hanson Island is quite foul, and during strong westerlies the only bay providing easy access and protection from most winds lies south of **Spout Islet**. The southwest end of this bay provides good shelter from wind and swell off the sound. Other options include the anchorage behind Mound Island or, in south winds, Farewell Harbour.

There is still much that is unkown about the currents around Malcolm Island and Alert Bay. Currents for Alert Bay and Pulteney Point are referenced for Johnstone Strait which, as any gillnetter will confirm, is as predictable as next week's weather. There's a lack of research into the currents in this entire area, so the tide predictions of Weynton Passage are not always an accurate indicator for the nearby channels.

Pass Tip Sheet – Blackney Passage

Blackney Pass: (Off Licka Point) 50°34'N, 126°41'W, 4-5 knots – more in strong winds.
Weynton Pass: 50°35'N, 126°49'W, 6 knots
Blackfish Sound: 50°35'N, 126°42'W, 3 knots
Slack: 10-25 minutes. **Flood:** East
Nearby Anchorages: – W, Growler Cove, E, Sprout Island or north side of Hanson Island.

KILLER WHALES AND YOU

Blackfish Sound, the body of water that lends its name to the general area, is one of the best places on our coast to view killer whales – once known as 'blackfish'. Their species name is *orcinus orca*, and these sociable marine mammals frequent the swift-flowing waters of Johnstone Strait and the nearby passes where salmon often collect waiting for a tide change. Here the orca feed on salmon, and often stay long periods in Robson Bight to rub against rounded pebbles in the bight's rocky shallows. In 1982 this bight was protected as an ecological reserve to prevent vessels from entering and disturbing the killer whales. When noted marine mammalogist Michael Bigg died in 1990, the reserve was renamed the Robson Bight/Michael Bigg Ecological Reserve to honour his pioneering research on killer whales along the B.C. coast.

The nearby boardwalk community of Telegraph Cove, founded in 1912 as a one-room telegraph station, has become a popular base for whale-watching tours in Johnstone Strait, while serious students of whale behaviour set up camp on West Cracroft Island, at Swaine Point, directly opposite Robson Bight. The whales often travel between Johnstone Strait and Blackfish Sound via Blackney Passage, and the Pacific Killer Whale Foundation monitors underwater whale vocalizations from Hanson Island.

The best time to sight orcas in Johnstone Strait is from July to October, when sightings are frequent. Keep in mind a few guidelines as set out by the Department of Fisheries and Oceans:

1) Do not split groups of whales.
2) Do not disturb whales while they are resting on the surface.
3) Do not chase whales.
4) Slow down and move carefully when within 1,000 feet (300 m).
5) Do not come any closer than 300 feet (100 m).

Generally, we try to maintain a distance of 1,000 feet (300 m) from orcas. Occasionally a pod will surface close to your vessel and if this occurs, maintain your speed and direction until the pod moves away.

A male orca

Above, fin whale exhibit in museum. Below, view across Telegraph Cove to Johnstone Strait.

Telegraph Cove

This cove is home to a number of companies offering tours for travellers wanting to see whales, bears and other wildlife. If such tours are of interest, you can temporarily tie up at the main front-facing dock (below the red building) and inquire about whale-watching at Stubbs Island Charters at the top of the dock or about bear watching at Tide Rip Tours.

Telegraph Cove is an authentic boardwalk community that harks back to the days when the Union Steamships ruled Broughton Archipelago. This small community has good restaurants, souvenir and craft shops, and a general store. A tour along the boardwalk presents great views of this cove and of Johnstone Strait. One of the best reasons to visit Telegraph Cove is the whale museum that displays skeletons of numerous species of whale. The museum has a killer whale interpretive centre and also features a 66-foot-long (20 m) fin whale skeleton discovered on top of the bow bulb of the *MS Galaxy* cruise ship in the summer of 1999. Boaters wanting to have lunch and spend a few hours enjoying this unique port can usually tie up at the front dock but be sure to either call ahead or check with the Stubbs Island office.

Vessels wanting to stay overnight should call ahead to either Telegraph Cove Marina at (250) 928-3163 or to Telegraph Cove Resorts at (250) 928-3131. Limited moorage is available for boats 30 to 50 feet. Water is available as well as power, laundry and showers. Although there is a gas dock, there is **no diesel** available here. Stubbs Island Charters (250) 928-3185, run by Jim and Mary Borrowman, has regular whale-watching tours departing from Telegraph Cove aboard their vessel *Lukwa*.

Other channels and passes:
Baronet Passage

Baronet Passage is not often used by recreational boaters but it does offer a different approach to Potts Lagoon and Clio Channel. Currents are in the 3 to 4 knot range at springs in the vicinity of Walden Island and about 2 knots at most other times. Amazingly, the flood sets west in this pass – as it does in Clio Channel. Baronet Passage is a secondary station referenced on Seymour Narrows. There is no suitable anchorage in this 7-mile passage, but there are several bights for lunch stops.

This is a good channel in which to catch spring salmon, and the experts advise fishing close to shore during LW slack and fishing through the rising tide. The waters off Cracroft Point at the western entrance to Baronet Passage are a gathering point for salmon during an ebb tide, as they wait for the next flood to push them eastward. Parson Bay is also reputed to be a hot spot at times in summer months.

When the west-flowing flood in Baronet Passage meets a south-flowing flood in Blackney Passage the waters can be very turbulent. Currents here attain 5 knots or more and create heavy races off Cracroft Point. In strong winds, from the southeast or west, this pass can be dangerous for a small boat.

Whitebeach Passage

Whitebeach Passage is a narrow pass that connects Blackfish Sound with Indian Channel and the Carey Group of islands. A summer village thrived on Compton Island back in the 1940s when houses overlooked the white beach which was often lined with dugout canoes and is today used by kayakers. Currents in the pass rarely exceed 2 knots and vessels should favour the N side of the pass at the narrowest part to avoid the drying outcrop and shoal water. Bull kelp thrives along both sides of the pass.

Indian and Village Channels

Indian Channel and Village Channel are the main thoroughfares, and the safest routes, of the Carey and Indian groups of islands. Because of currents, numerous reefs and unmarked rocks throughout this area, you should stick with the main channels and anchorages. Currents in these channels are surprisingly swift and can run up to 3 knots (flood flows east). The Sailing Directions warn, in bold type, that these channels are sprinkled with unmarked rocks and shoals, so keep your depth sounder on all the time and navigate very carefully in this area.

Eastbound in Chatham Channel

Chatham Channel

Chatham Channel is a narrow gorge-like channel with a constricted kelp-laden pass at its east end. The pass itself is pretty and home to much bird life, including herons and eagles. The main piloting challenge is the 2-mile stretch from Root Point westward where currents can be up to 5 knots but are usually not turbulent. Range markers at each end of the narrows greatly assist with staying in the middle of the channel. Although the flood sets east, the times of maximum current can change depending on freshet outflow from Knight Inlet (especially in May and June) or after large rains, which can delay the onset of the flood. Just west of the pass is a large scar on the mountainside from a 1975 slide.

Chatham Channel received its name from the extraordinary pilotage and survey of this shallow narrows by Lieutenant Broughton while in command of the 90-ton *Chatham* in 1792. Broughton guided his ship along Havannah Channel, then proceeded into Chatham Channel and made a similar survey of Tribune Channel.

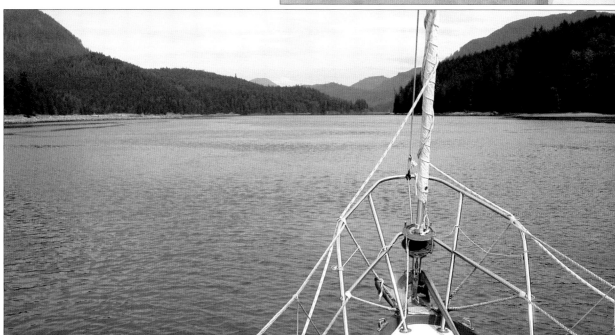

Be especially careful if you're bucking a flood near the day beacon on the small island just south of Bowers Island (the route north of Bowers Island should not be attempted because of shoal water.) Another tricky spot is close to the west end of the pass, at its narrowest point, where the current is strongest, with accompanying upwellings and whirlpools. These difficulties are compounded by large masses of bull kelp which grow almost entirely across the channel in this area during the summer. Fog is also common and will persist in this pass after it has burned off elsewhere.

Boaters have many choices at the junction of Chatham and Clio Channels with Knight Inlet. You can turn southwest into Clio Channel to explore Potts Lagoon and Beware Passage, go west to Village Island and the Carey Group, head north up Tribune Channel, or turn east into Knight Inlet to see the bears at Glendale Cove.

Beware Passage

This pass has earned its name from the proliferation of rocks, reefs and bull kelp throughout its length. Transiting the pass at LW slack offers the advantage of being able to see the dangers, especially Beware Rock – which dries about 5 feet. Fortunately, current is not an issue as the stream is only 2 to 3 knots at springs. The flood current flows east.

This pass should not be attempted if visibility is poor – you must be able to see at least half a mile to ensure your position on one of the two most common routes through the pass. Chart 3545 provides excellent detail of the routes and their hazards. As mentioned, Beware Rock, lying in the middle of the pass at the west end, is the major navigational challenge and, as is the case in all rock-strewn passes, the rule is to go dead slow throughout the transit.

If transiting the pass at HW, the safest approach is along the bottom route (going below Care Rock). If westbound, this route is along the channel between Kamano Island and an islet marked '15'. Steer 266° to the open water north of the island marked '44' near Harbledown Island and pick your way along the channel between two small islets to the north and Harbledown Island to the south. The last dangers involve getting past the drying reefs of Beware Rock and another rock to the south that dries 3 feet. This will be more difficult at HW if these rocks cannot be seen, but using the small islet marked '12' south of Care Island and the east end of Dead Point as a reference for a danger bearing will assure a safe transit. This bearing is about 270° when westbound – GPS is a helpful back-up to pinpoint position. We often use the route above Care Rock at LW, turning north from Kamano Island and then turning west, staying close to Care Island. We like the fact this channel is deep and, during summer months, the location of most reefs can be identified by the presence of bull kelp.

The numerous islets in Beware Passage are a pretty sight in spring with wildflowers along the shores. We've sighted dolphins in this passage. Near the passage's eastern entrance, on the shores of Turnour Island, is the overgrown site of Karlukwees village and is where an old government wharf stands in disrepair. It's a beautiful scene and sad to see this once-busy village abandoned. We've seen six boats rafted to the dilapidated pilings of this old wharf, which seems like tempting fate. The foreshore consists of a clamshell midden, and some petroglyphs can be found in the vicinity. Visiting beyond the foreshore should not be done without permission of the local band office. Anchorages in Beware Pass include Beware Cove and Dead Point Bay (see pages 236 and 237).

Yvonne Maximchuk, of Echo Bay, painted this view of Karlukwees from early photographs.

Map: Beware Passage

TURNOUR ISLAND

Mink Pt

Dead Pt

logging here

Beware Cove

lots of kelp

Cook I

"Monks Wall"

westbound 270° to Dead Pt.
eastbound 90° to islet "12"

BEWARE PASSAGE

Turnour Pt

*Beware Rk

Caution Rk

Caution Cove

Care Island

BEWARE PASSAGE

Low Water Route: ············
High Water Route: — — — — —
Flood Flows: South
Max Speed   2 kn

2-3 knots

HW route   (12)   Care Rk

(17)

Karlukwees
Ru Aband
IR

**HARBLEDOWN
ISLAND**

0   1/2   N

Nautical miles
Not for Navigation.
Depths in fathoms

(44)

(15)

Kamano I

*good spot in strong
NW wind*

HW route

Beware
Passage is a
good way to sidestep the
stronger passes of Blackfish
Sound when northbound, and is a
more direct route to the spectacular anchorages further north – especially to Village Island and
the Indian Group. If southbound, Beware Passage
connects with Clio Channel, which is relatively free
of hazards, apart from a rock that lies between Jolife
and Klaoitsis Islands. The tide floods west in Clio
Channel, producing about one knot of current. Good
fishing is reported at LW along Turnour Island.

*Below, Beware Passage is pretty but filled with
dangers. Right, the old dock at Karlukwees is in
poor shape but some boaters still tie-up.*

THE ANCHORAGES:
Lagoon Cove 1

Near the western entrance of Chatham Channel is the popular Lagoon Cove Marina, operated since the early 1990s by Bill and Jean Barber. We were very sad to hear that Bill passed away in early 2013. The Barbers cruised this area for years before transforming Lagoon Cove into a successful marine resort with a sociable atmosphere. For boaters wanting to drop the hook, there is good anchorage south of the marina in about 60 feet (19 m) of water; however, it is open to strong NW winds.

Above, Lagoon Cove Marina and anchorage.
Below, a calm evening at Cutter Cove.

Cutter Cove 2

This anchorage has received a bit of a bad reputation because the holding is fair at best, the winds blow through almost uninhibited, and the bottom is littered with rocks. Yet, it remains one of the busiest anchorages in Blackfish Sound due to its proximity to great cruising, fishing and the popular marina nearby at Lagoon Cove.

John Chappell (*Cruising Beyond Desolation Sound*) had this anchorage right 25 years ago when he said if a westerly is predicted, anchor on the north side of the cove, and if an easterly is predicted, go to the south side. But the holding ground takes some getting used to – it feels like soft mud or ooze on top of rock or the other way around. Whatever anchoring tackle you employ, be alert if the wind comes up strongly in the night – if your vessel isn't dragging, someone else's may be. The cove is fairly level for the first two thirds of its length and shelves near the head. We like to anchor near the old snag just past the bluff on the north side in about 30 feet (9 m).

We've been here several times with never a problem. Granted, we've not been here in a howling wind but that is the luck of the draw when cruising. We've enjoyed the peaceful views, the sunsets and exploring the head of the bay. Still, Cutter Cove has that bad rep!

Port Elizabeth 3

Situated in lower Knight Inlet, Port Elizabeth lies on the north side, between Minstrel Island and Village Island. Fair protection can be gained from west winds in Duck Cove, north of the island marked '47' on Chart 3545. During easterlies and southerlies, we've anchored in the SE corner of the harbour and found it secure, although gusts come over the low shoreline. The setting in Port Elizabeth is uninteresting (there are log dump sites in the harbour and an aquaculture operation) but the anchorage is useful to get out of the weather in Knight Inlet. There is a good lunch stop at the entrance to Port Elizabeth, off Gifford Point, where two islets and a clamshell beach look appealing.

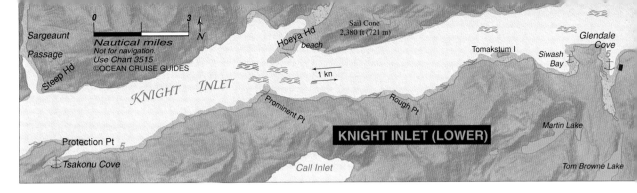

Sargeaunt
Passage

Steep Hd

0   Nautical miles   3   N
Not for navigation.
Use Chart 3515.
©OCEAN CRUISE GUIDES

Hoeya Hd
beach

Sail Cone
2,380 ft (721 m)

Glendale
Cove

Tomakstum I

Siwash
Bay

1 kn

KNIGHT   INLET

Prominent Pt

Rough Pt

KNIGHT INLET (LOWER)

Martin Lake

Protection Pt   5

Tsakonu Cove

Call Inlet

Tom Browne Lake

KNIGHT INLET

The longest inlet on the British Columbia coast, Knight Inlet (named by Lieut. Broughton) cleaves its way for nearly 70 miles into the Coast Mountains. No wider than one-and-a-half miles, the inlet winds past snow-clad summits and numerous waterfalls before reaching the glacier-fed rivers at its head. There, the massive peak of Mount Waddington rises more than 13,000 feet. Exploring this wild and remote channel can be formidable in any vessel.

The entrance to Knight Inlet lies between Warr Bluff (Village Island) and Slope Point. From its entrance to Glendale Cove, the inlet is quite open to the west, and afternoon summer winds funnel into this area with force – often 20 to 25 knots. Currents from Village Island to Steep Head at Sargeaunt Passage can be 3 knots on an ebb and against a strong westerly will produce a rough 4- to 5-foot chop. The Sailing Directions caution that wind has a considerable effect on the rate of tidal currents and an increase of 2 knots of current can be expected when strong winds are blowing with the tidal stream. The turn of current occurs 1 to 2 hours after high or low water at Alert Bay.

Pacific white-sided dolphins are often sighted in Knight Inlet in the reach up to Glendale Cove.

East of Tribune Channel, the current is about one knot, but conditions can be quite rough from Protection Point to Sallie Point when westerlies are blowing against an ebb. On big ebbs, a bad tide rip is reported south of Hoeya Head which can produce a dangerous swell during strong west winds. Late afternoon inflow winds are common in summer in many stretches of water right to the inlet's head. Pacific white-sided dolphins are common in Knight Inlet, so don't be surprised to find a troupe tagging along on your journey up the inlet. The only chart available for this area is 3515.

Tsakonu Cove 4

Farther east up Knight Inlet, Tsakonu Cove lies below Sargeaunt Passage and is a pretty spot offering overnight anchorage during settled weather, but is completely open to the east. Strong W winds can come over from Cutter Cove and some anchors may drag in the mud-and-pebble bottom, as Muriel Wylie Blanchet noted in *The Curve of Time*. Despite recent logging activity at the head of the cove, this anchorage still has a wild and remote feel and is a beautiful spot at night when the moon is full. Further up the inlet, Hoeya Sound is open to the west and too deep for small boats to anchor. (There's a nice beach east of Hoeya Head.) There is really no decent anchorage until Glendale Cove, 18 miles from Tsakonu Cove.

Above, a grizzly known as "Sargeaunt" lurks in grass by shoreline. Below, a view of Glendale Cove anchorage looking north.

Glendale Cove [5]

After the long trip up Knight Inlet, this pretty cove offers a welcome respite from westerlies in the lee of the bight south of Macdonald Point. Anchor in about 50 to 70 feet (15 to 20 m) as close to the west shore and the beach as possible. The anchorage is suitable for most vessels however it shelves more than indicated on the chart and although the bottom is sticky mud, make sure you are well anchored before shutting off the engine. If you are spending extended time here, a line to the west shore is a good idea if strong west winds are expected. Even in summer, westerlies can reach 30 knots and may blast right over the headland. If conditions are severe, consider retreating to one of the bights along the west shore north of Naena Point or behind Adeane Point. Glendale Cove is also open to NE winds, although these are not common in summer months. If strong SE winds are called for, the east shore of **Siwash Bay**, just around the corner, provides better shelter.

Grizzly bears can be seen in the cove from spring until mid-July, at which time they move up the hillsides to feed on berries. By late August they return to

Glendale Cove at a glance:

CHARTS: 3515
LAT LONG: 50°41.32'N 125°44.08'W
PROS: Beautiful remote location, stunning views and wildlife make this a special destination. Anchorage has good holding, protection only fair.
CONS: Long drive in and out of inlet. Sudden wind change can result in having to move your vessel.
MUST DO: Spot a grizzly! Go to Cascade Falls.

the south end of the estuary and Glendale Creek to feed on spawning salmon. Black bears can be seen throughout the summer months near the lodge and in Siwash Bay. Glendale Cove attracts both grizzly and black bears because of the salmon stream and the LW buffet available on the beach and estuary. For early-summer visitors, mornings are a good time to venture by dinghy, slowly making your way to the west side of the cove where you'll soon spot a bear. Grizzlies are often seen along the beach near Macdonald Point, so be careful if venturing on shore. If you want to observe bears throughout the day, anchor opposite the pilings of the old pier where usually two or three bears can be seen along the beach. The bottom shelves steeply here so be careful how your vessel is swinging.

For wildlife buffs, it is hard to beat this anchorage. Knight Inlet has become world renowned for sighting bears, seals, porpoises, killer whales and eagles. Knight Inlet Lodge, located south of Duncan Point, exists for the sole purpose of offering such sightings to its guests. Although it has no moorage, supplies or restaurant facilities for visiting boaters, the lodge employees are very friendly in offering information about the cove and bear watching.

The viewing of bears that feed in Glendale Creek each fall is regulated by a local conservancy group. The Knight Inlet Lodge (as well as tour companies located in Telegraph Cove) use viewing stands along the creek for their clients. Boaters who are keen to actually spend a few days at the lodge with guides can contact the lodge at by phone at (250) 337-1953.

Also in Glendale Cove are reports of naturally occuring obsidian (volcanic) glass being found at the head of the bay. This is one of only three locations of obsidian glass on the B.C. coast, the other sites being in Dean Channel and Haida Gwaii.

In settled conditions Knight Inlet is well worth exploring and most boats can travel much of the inlet in a day and return to Glendale Cove. There are few overnight anchorages in the inlet, or you might consider using a fisherman's mooring (see sidebar). Keep in mind conditions in the inlet can change rapidly.

Six miles north of Glendale Cove is a trail accessed at the mouth of **Kwalate Creek**. The trail follows this boisterous creek for a few miles, then turns to ascend the hillside to a viewpoint. Be aware that bears can be along the creek in summer. Keep an eye for fresh tracks or scat indicating recent bear traffic – an airhorn is a must. Fishing at the creek mouth is good in summer months. Although suitable as a lunch stop, the creek mouth is open to inflow winds and anchoring overnight is not secure.

For real adventure cruising, the upper reaches of Knight Inlet offer spectacular views of glaciers,

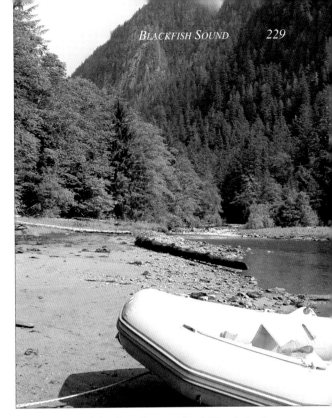

Kwalate Creek is six miles north of Glendale Cove.

KNIGHT INLET (UPPER)

Left, our boat with a fisherman's mooring at Spire Peaks. The slope behind appears unstable and this bight would not be suitable for overnight. Below, the view across Knight Inlet to Cascade Falls.

Fisherman's Mooring

Fishing vessels travelling in Knight Inlet sometimes employ a mooring tactic which works well in small bights when there is nowhere else to drop the hook. The method is to find a suitable spot such as an indentation in the shoreline with deep water. For overnight mooring, avoid slopes where there is evidence of recent slides. Point your bow into the wind and tie lines fore and aft to each shore so that you are lying parallel with the inlet. You can add a third line amidships to pull yourself as close to shore as you like. Pick a bight that has enough lee to provide shelter from the wind and, ideally, where the shore is deflecting any waves.

hanging waterfalls and frequent wildlife sightings. There are anchorage possibilities opposite **Glacier Bay** (15 miles from Glendale Cove) and at **Wahshihlas Bay** (25 miles distant) where log booms are sometimes tied up. Although the sighting of wildlife at the head of Knight Inlet is an exciting prospect – bear, moose and wolves frequent the river flats – the area is quite open and evening williwaws can occur if a north wind pipes up. The Klinaklini and Franklin Rivers meet opposite Dutchman Head.

One of two beautiful waterfalls in the vicinity is **Rainbows Falls**, about 5 miles from Glendale Cove on the east side of the inlet. The mist from the falls, falling hundreds of feet, produces a beautiful rainbow in the afternoon and early evening. Perhaps the most dramatic of waterfalls along the southern B.C. coast is **Cascade Falls**, about 14 miles from Glendale Cove. This waterfall drops an amazing volume of water from about a 100 feet, generating a constant cool breeze. Opposite this waterfall are **Spire Peaks**, one of the most impressive ridges along Knight Inlet.

Around the corner from these peaks is an anchoring possibility at the mouth of the **Ahnuhati River**. Another is the bay north of Ahnuhati Point. The mouth of the Ahnuhati River was once the site of a native village, but no evidence of this remains today. In his book *Full Moon, Flood Tide*, Bill Proctor talks about cannonballs being found on the beach here and speculates that either the village was bombarded or the cannonballs were traded for furs. The anchorage is along the southwest shore and requires a stern line. Another recommended anchorage is at the mouth of the Sim River in Wahshihlas Bay.

TRIBUNE CHANNEL

If you are heading north into Tribune Channel from Chatham Channel or Knight Inlet, Sargeaunt Passage provides a scenic and sheltered route. The channel shallows to less than 20 feet (7 m) depth and, as shown on Chart 3515, vessels should stay fairly close to Viscount Island when transiting the passage. Current in the pass ranges from 2 to 3 knots depending on the tide. Tribune Channel, north of Sargeaunt Passage, is truly spectacular with steep sides and, in spring, beautiful cascading waterfalls.

Thompson Sound 6

This beautiful inlet has an extensive mud flat on its north side from the large Kakweiken River and is a fascinating area to explore. Anchorage is possible in settled weather at the head of the sound opposite Sackville Island. Depths are over 100 feet (30 m) well into the anchorage where the bottom shoals rapidly. Favour the SE shore when approaching this pocket of deep water and keep the white X scar in the granite rock hillside off your port bow (11 o'clock). Anchor in 60 to 80 feet (19 to 24 m) with mud and sand providing good holding. If a big westerly is coming up, you should retreat to the anchorage west of Kumlah Island or head for Kwatsi Bay.

An old steam donkey as well as numerous bits of old logging equipment lie rusting along the head of the beach on the east side. Logging operations sometimes locate at the mouth of McAlister Creek.

On a rising tide, you can explore for some distance (2 miles) up the river and really get a feel for the remote wilderness of this sound. There are bears in this area and you should be extremely careful if setting out on foot into the brush. During late summer, grizzlies will be feeding along this river.

Above, the dramatic sheer cliffs of Spire Peaks. Below, Cascade Falls create a cool mist falling from Glacier Peak. Bottom, heading up Kakweiken River.

Bond Sound 7

This is another beautiful inlet along Tribune Channel with interesting river valleys; the Ahta River empties here. If exploring the river by dinghy, be sure to arrive at HW as the mud flats are extensive and at LW the boulders in the river will stop most dinghies. There is no real anchorage in the sound but there is a bight near the head along the east side where anchoring with a line ashore will keep you away from inflow winds. Any kind of a westerly blows keenly into Bond Sound.

The Ahta River has undergone extensive cleaning and rejuvenating for salmon stock, thanks to the

Bond Sound with Ahta Valley in background.

Mainland Enhancement of Salmonid Species Society (MESSS). According to Bill Proctor, the stream supports all five of the West Coast salmon stocks as well as steelhead and trout. The valley is home to several species of mammals including cougar, bear (black and grizzly), river otter, wolverine and deer.

Wahkana Bay, Gilford Island 8

A sac-like anchorage opposite Bond Sound, this bay provides good anchorage in most conditions. A stream at the SW head of the bay is also the site of extensive work by MESSS to try to bring back coho salmon runs after the creek was severely damaged by logging and a landslide in the 1960s. After years of work cleaning up the stream, salmon are starting to return and with them the kingfishers and eagles. A partial trail along the stream leads to a small lake and makes for a good hike, but be careful not to knock debris into the creek. Black bear inhabit Gilford Island, so taking along an airhorn is a good idea.

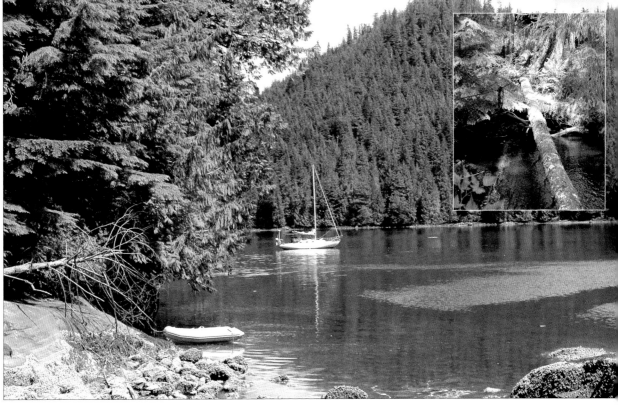

Wahkana Bay and local salmon stream (inset).
Right, scenic anchorage at head of Kwatsi Bay.

The anchorage itself is quite deep, showing about 100 feet (35 m) on chart 3515 but there are shallower areas along the south and east shore where depths are between 35 and 65 feet (10 and 20 m). This is the preferred part of the bay to duck out of the west winds which can gust through from Viner Sound. The drop-off is quite steep and the shelving is narrow so it may be a good idea to tie a line to shore. Holding in sand and mud is good. This is usually a very quiet bay, rich with birdlife.

Kwatsi Bay, Tribune Channel 9

Near the bend where Tribune Channel turns west is a friendly marina and good anchorage at the head of Kwatsi Bay, a 2-mile detour off the main channel. The marina (once the site of a shingle mill) is owned and operated by Max Knierim and Anca Fraser. Services include potable water and showers on the dock but no power. A small store sells local products (including honey and jams) and souvenirs. On alternating nights there are happy-hour gatherings or pot-luck dinners on the dock at which visiting boaters share anchorage stories and ideas on the world.

It's a short dinghy ride from the marina to a trail leading up to a beautiful tumbling waterfall. Good fishing, especially for snapper and cod, is also nearby along the shores of the mouth of the bay.

Kwatsi Bay Marina (above and below) and (inset) Russell Knierim catches a red snapper.

Kwatsi Bay at a Glance:

CHARTS: 3515
LAT LONG: 50°50.75'N 126°16.12'W
PROS: Beautiful setting, waterfalls, forests and sheer clifts of granite. Good marina nearby with friendly ambiance. Close to other anchorages. Protection from wind quite good.
CONS: Deep anchorage with limited room.
MUST DO: Go fishing, take the hike to the nearby waterfall. Stay at least a night at the marina.

One of the main attractions at Kwatsi Bay is the beautiful scenery at the head of the bay – a stunning vista of clouds and trees and soaring smooth granite. The steep rock sides of the bay give the feeling you are floating in a lake very high in the mountains.

Westerly winds diminish at the entrance to Kwatsi Bay, and the inner bay, especially on the east side, is sheltered and peaceful. The recommended anchorage is this eastern side of the bay in about 100 feet in good holding. (A slide in the fall of 2005 dumped debris in the extreme NE corner of the bay.) The sheer sides may produce williwaws, but the nights we've anchored here have been absolutely still. According to Max and Anca, northeasterlies produce the strongest winds in the bay but these are rare in summer. The west part of the bay is reputed to have an uneven and rocky bottom but provides the best shelter if a hard westerly is kicking up. The marina may be the best choice if W winds are quite strong.

Watson Cove 10

This is a deep anchorage with good shelter from SE winds but it is quite exposed to west winds. However, the cove is a good lunch stop as there are two waterfalls nearby. The most spectacular one is about half a mile west of the cove and consists of large cascading falls sliding down hundreds of feet of granite before reaching the sea. According to Bill Proctor the locals call it simply 'The Falls' as there is no other one in the area that's quite this large. He says the nearby fish farm workers refer to it as 'Glacier Falls' and tourists call it 'Lacy Falls,' so take your pick. Another, much smaller waterfall is at the head of Watson Cove, hidden among the thick forest and rock outcropping on the north side. On the south side, also at the head of the bay and about a hundred-yard walk from the shore, is a huge cedar measuring about 15 feet across. Aquaculture operations are sometimes located in this cove.

Beyond Watson Cove to the west, just beyond Rainy Point, is a large scar in the hillside from a slide in 2000. Deep Sea Bluff marks the western terminus of Tribune Channel. Just beyond lies the Burdwood Group and Broughton Archipelago, another great cruising area covered in Chapter Eight.

Potts Lagoon 11

Lagoons are tempting to visit, but many along our coast are very dangerous to enter. Those that can cause trouble are typified by a large elliptical basin with a small neck opening. One lagoon, however, that offers safe anchorage for boats heading to or from Blackfish Sound is Potts Lagoon.

With its fairly wide and deep entrance leading into a relatively small basin, Potts Lagoon presents no threat to boats seeking shelter. Good, all-weather

Above, "The Falls" outside of Watson Cove.
Below, Potts Lagoon provides good shelter.

Potts Lagoon

while making quite a racket, eventually land at the far end of the lagoon on a marsh flat. In summer months black bears feed among the berry bushes near the old logging camp on the southwest side of the anchorage, so be careful and take an air horn and a stout stick if you decide to hike along the logging road. Also, if exploring the lagoon, keep an eye on the state of the tide, for the lagoon nearly dries at LW and there can be a 4- to 5-knot stream at the neck during spring tides.

Several floathomes are moored along the SW side of the anchorage. The first person to homestead in Potts Lagoon was a man named Murray Potts, who lived at the head of the lagoon where he kept cows at his creekside farm and had a horse for plowing. Potts lived in his namesake lagoon until 1946, when he left to accept the job of Indian Agent at Alert Bay.

Beware Cove, Turnour Island [12]

This cove is a good spot to wait for a tide change or to find overnight anchorage in settled weather. Two or three boats can anchor north of the two small islets on the south side of the cove and this is really where the best protection is found. Most northwesterlies die out just outside of Cook Island, but the anchorage is fairly open to south winds. The holding is in soft mud and sand, and there is a lot of kelp along the edges of the anchorage so be sure you are well set before turning in for the night.

The safest approach to Beware Cove is along the west entrance on the north side of Cook Island. We

anchorage can be found inside the entrance, behind the small island marked '41' on Chart 3545. This scenic anchorage is well protected and safe in all winds – although westerlies can occasionally sneak around the small island. Another option is to anchor in the cove outside the entrance.

If the weather is fine, plan on spending an extra day or two at Potts Lagoon. The upper reaches of the lagoon, reached via a narrow set of rapids, are very interesting to explore by dinghy. One September we saw a flock of sandhill cranes circle overhead and,

Beware Cove has fair protection from the west but gets hit by wind from the south.

found the pass south and east of Cook Island has less depth than shown on the chart, with a least depth of about 10 feet (3 m). It is almost choked with kelp. John Chappell noted in his book that the original Kwakiutl name of the cove was "bad smell coming up from beach" in reference to the large expanse of tidal flat that takes up the east end of the cove.

Dead Point Bay 13

At Beware Passage's western entrance is an unnamed bay southwest of Dead Point, which has a straightforward entrance and good holding ground in sand and mud. This is a fair-weather anchorage, providing shelter from northwesterlies but not from southwesterlies, which apparently blow with force over the low hills. We've used this anchorage when southbound from Village Island and have always enjoyed the beautiful sunsets. See Chart 3545.

A shallow cove indents the bay's southern shore and hidden in the brush along its west side (see map) is a stone wall that was built by William and Mary Anne Galley in the late 1800s when they homesteaded here with their three sons. They built this rock wall on the site of an abandoned Catholic Mission (established in 1864), but the structure came to be known as Monks' Wall because of an unverified report that Buddhist monks had built a temple on Harbledown Island.

Another early settler was a Kanaka named George Kamano who cleared 20 acres at the head of the cove and planted fruit trees. He and his wife raised a large family, and one of their daughters, Maria, married Jim Joliffe. They homesteaded on land next to the Kamano farm where they also cultivated a fruit orchard.

Above, Dead Point Bay offers shelter in settled conditions. Below, pioneers built Monks' Wall.

Village Island at a Glance:

CHARTS: 3545, 3546
LAT LONG: 50°37.34'N 126°35.02'W
PROS: An important stop for native culture. Good holding in thick mud, and safe from most winds. Wildlife (black bears) can sometimes be spotted along the beach.
CONS: Anchorage is somewhat exposed during strong westerlies.
MUST DO: Spend a day exploring the village and take the tour if available. Walk along the midden.

MAMALILACULLA

Recommended Route: ·············
⚓ Anchorage ⏛ Temp Anchorage

Warr Bluff

0   1/2

Nautical miles
Not for navigation.
Use Chart 3545
Depths in fathoms

Pearl I

Eliot Passage Ⓦ

VILLAGE
ISLAND
IR
Mamalilaculla
(aband)

Scrub It

5

5

Chart It

Native
Anchorage

Hail Its

Turnour
Island

Mamalilaculla, Village Island [14]

For years boaters have anchored off Village Island to visit the abandoned and slowly deteriorating Kwakiutl village of Mamalilaculla. The anchorage providing access to the village site lies on the west side of the island, where a reef and string of islets extends from the anchorage's northern point and creates a natural breakwater to NW winds and sea. The swinging room is limited but the holding ground is good and the anchorage is fairly well sheltered, except during strong northwesterlies.

Native Anchorage on the SW side of Village Island is another spot to consider if the weather is settled – it has a pretty view to the south. Over half of the bay is a drying mudflat so you should anchor as close to the entrance of the bay as possible. Holding is good in sand, shell and mud, but this bay is open to the south and east, and provides only limited protection from westerlies. East winds can funnel along Canoe Passage into the anchorage.

If staying overnight, we usually anchor on the west side of the island. When heading ashore, we beach the dinghy near the old wharf and scramble up the hillside trail. At the top, the path leads past a dilapidated wooden building where a missionary nurse named Kathleen O'Brien once ran a school and a small tuberculosis sanatorium for the local children. She came to Village Island in 1920 and was named to the Order of the British Empire for her years of missionary work before she retired to England in 1945.

Just beyond the abandoned schoolhouse is the village site, situated atop a low bluff overlooking a shallow cove dotted with islets. At the base of the bluff, along the water's edge, is an extensive midden. During our first visit to the village in the fall of 1989 the village's last totem pole was still standing, but by the following spring it had toppled toward the sea. That was also the year Tom Sewid began acting as a guardian for the traditional territory of the Mamalaleqala. Under his direction, members of the Qwe'Qwa'Sot' Enox Band based in Campbell River started maintaining the village site and providing tours to visitors for a small fee. Mark Puglas, whose grandparents once lived on Village Island, was our guide when we took a tour in 1993.

On a subsequent visit in 2003, we tied to the temporary floats that had been installed by Village Island Tours adjacent to the old wharf. We were greeted by Tom Sewid, who donned traditional regalia and stood in front of the existing long house frame to deliver his eloquent speech about his ancestors and their beliefs, which are passed down orally from generation to generation in the form of myths. The role of storyteller comes naturally to Tom, whose grandfather was Chief James Aul Sewid,

Above, fallen totem with sea wolf. Below, Tom Sewid, a guardian of the village. Opposite page, a view looking eastward of Mamalilaculla.

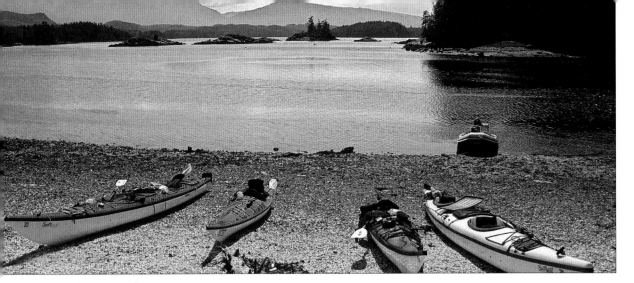

A midden beach, popular with kayakers, lies below the village site at Mamalilaculla.

author of *Guests Never Leave Hungry* and recipient of the Order of Canada for his work at improving the lives of his people. Recent developments at Village Island include the construction of traditional cedar cabins to accommodate guests of Adventure Village Island, which operates cultural tours and sea kayaking expeditions to view whales and other wildlife.

Village Island was the scene of a famous potlatch that took place in the winter of 1921, an event that resulted in a mass arrest and confiscation of regalia, including masks and rattles. In 1884, the Canadian government had placed a ban on potlatches. This decision was based on a lack of understanding of nature culture and an attempt to assimilate the Kwakwaka'wakw people, as well as a growing alarm at the destruction of property (as a display of wealth and power) that was taking place at these gatherings. Yet, these celebrations were central to their culture and were still being held in secret. At Mamalilaculla a long house was built with no crests engraved on the house posts, so that different clans in the area could come and hold secret potlatches here. The large potlatch gathering of December 1921 resulted in 49 people being charged and 26 eventually sent to jail for several months. Hence the village came to be known as Mamalillaculla, which means 'village of the last potlatch', although its true name is Meem Quam Leese – 'the village with the rocks and islands in front.'

In the early 1960s the village was still thriving, but by the end of the decade everyone had left. A wooden sea wolf lying in the grass had once protected a home's entrance. The sea wolf crest is also found on a toppled totem pole, which had landed on its back with the sea wolf pointed seaward. The orca and eagle on the very top of the pole are gone because (according to legend) the whale swam out to sea and the eagle flew into the sky. Set back from the fallen pole are the massive corner posts and cross beams of the village's long house. Up to 300 men were required to lift these log beams. Cedar siding and roofing were then added, but these could be removed and towed by canoe to a summer fishing village in Knight Inlet.

Goat Island anchorage, Crease Island / Carey Group 15

The Carey Group contains several one-boat anchorages, including one on the east side of Leone Island and another along the SE shore of **Madrona Island**. The best overnight anchorage in Village Channel, however, is a small bay on the SE side of Crease

Map

Raleigh Pt

CREASE ISLAND

Recommended Route: - - - - - - -

⚓ Anchorage   ⚓ Temp Anchorage

Ⓦ Waypoint 50°36.89'N 126°38.25'W

0   1/3

Nautical miles
Not for navigation.
Use Chart 3546
Depths in fathoms

Fern I

CREASE ISLAND

Goat I

VILLAGE CHANNEL

Carey Group

Madrona I

1-3 kn

Leone I

Chief's Bathtub

Island opposite **Goat Island** (sometimes called Goat Island Anchorage) which can accommodate a dozen boats. Sheltered from moderate westerlies, the anchorage offers good holding in mud, although there is some kelp along the rim of the anchorage and patches of eel grass throughout. Set your anchor well, for evening W winds can gust through this bay. The approach to the anchorage is on either side of Goat Island – the north side is better because it is clear of underwater obstacles. Some current is noticeable throughout the anchorage.

A scenic lunch spot can be found on the northeast side of Crease Island, off the shoreline's granite ledge, with a splendid view of Village Channel and its avenue of islands.

Crease Island was named in 1905 by the Geographic Board of Canada to honour Sir Henry Pering Pellew Crease, the father of the Bar of British

Columbia. Born in Cornwall, England, the son of a naval captain, Crease emigrated to the Crown colony of Vancouver Island in 1858 where, as a judge, he travelled to distant parts of the province. On one occasion, while in northern British Columbia, Judge Crease was seriously injured but continued trying cases from a stretcher. When his condition worsened, his native bearers were tempted to desert him but, according to John Walbran in *British Columbia Coast Names*, Crease "made them carry him down the steep trails not 'feet foremost like a dead man,' as he said, 'but head foremost', by which means he persuaded them to bring him out."

The Crease Island anchorage makes a very good base from which to explore the area's numerous islands. There is plenty to see and do nearby, between visiting the various native sites and enjoying the good fishing in Knight Inlet.

If you are looking for a lunch spot in the immediate area, there is a pretty anchorage just east of **Leone Island** in about 20 feet (6 m) of water. Although there is a fish farm a few hundred yards south, the view to the east is scenic. Also, decent anchorage in settled weather can be found on the northeast side of **Alder Island** but it is somewhat exposed to daytime westerlies.

CREASE ISLAND AT A GLANCE

CHARTS: 3546
LAT LONG: 50°36.89'N 126°38.25'W
PROS: Good holding, fair protection from most winds. Close to native sites, lots of nearby beachcombing and dinghy exploring. (Native sites include: Karlukwees, Mamalilaculla, Chief's Bathtub). Beautiful passes and intricate waterways make this an excellent spot for a few days' stay.
CONS: Wind out of NW can gust over low hillsides. Open to easterlies. Some aquaculture.
MUST DO: Explore area by dinghy or kayak.

Aerial view of 'Goat Island Anchorage' at Crease Island. This anchorage can accommodate a dozen vessels and is safe in most summer conditions.

Above, view of Chief's Bathtub and pictograph on Berry Island. Below, Farewell Harbour.

Farewell Harbour 16

The islands and islets clustered around Blackfish Sound form a gunkholer's paradise. Several of these islands lie within the convoluted boundary of Broughton Archipelago Marine Park. One of these is Berry Island, with a popular anchorage called Farewell Harbour on its west side. The harbour got its name from officers of the surveying vessel *Beaver* in 1870 because it was the last place surveyed as the ship departed the area.

Although the holding ground is quite good, in sand and sticky mud, the harbour experiences healthy current during large tides and the anchorage can be uncomfortable when strong westerlies blast over West Passage. This is, however, a good place to be during easterlies, in the lee of Berry Island. The best spot to anchor, away from most of the current, is between Kamux Island and the reef due south which is marked by kelp. Depths in this part of the anchorage are about 30 feet (10 m).

The entrance through West Passage should not be attempted during a strong westerly and a large flood tide because of the very dangerous reefs, especially Punt Rock. The better approach during such conditions is from the south between Compton and Sarah Islands. Currents during springs in West Passage are easily in the 4-knot range so be careful here.

Luxury yachts drop anchor here during the summer months and on shore is a former sportfishing lodge, called the Farewell Harbour Resort, built in 1982 on a private acreage before the rest of the island became part of the marine park. The resort eventually closed for personal use under new ownership. There are rough trails on Berry Island, which used to be accessed from the resort's floats. It's possible to beach a dinghy on the foreshore north of this parcel of private land.

The fishing is good around Berry Island and halibut can be caught right in Farewell Harbour. On the north side of Berry Island, just below the HW mark, is an eroded depression in the side of a cliff known as the **Chief's Bathtub**, for it fills with water at high tide. This rock formation and its adjacent pictographs can be viewed from Village Channel.

Mound Island

A popular alternative to Farewell Harbour is the large anchorage south of Mound Island. Clear of aquaculture operations, the bay is quiet with a nice view of the mountains to the east. This is a good anchorage from which to explore the many nearby middens, such as the one at the SW end of Mound Island. Holding in mud with sand and shell is good. Anchor within the 30 feet (10 m) line, keeping a healthy distance from the rocks along both shores.

There is another anchorage for one or two boats farther east along the north shore of **Harbledown Island**, behind a small islet in front of a mud-and-shell beach. This is a pretty spot with a great view across Indian Channel to the islands of the Carey Group. Farther east still is **New Vancouver** where First Nations people have built a new dock and a long house dedicated in 2003.

Cedar Island

This beautiful anchorage is located in a cluster of islets to the west of Cedar Island at the north end of Providence Passage. The entrance is narrow but hazard-free, allowing entry for most mid-sized vessels.

Although open to north winds, it makes an excellent lunch stop or, in very settled weather, an overnight anchorage. The main drawback, especially for sailboats, is the lack of depth with only 4 feet (1.2 m) during zero tides. With our boat drawing over 6 feet, this anchorage is usually a temporary stop. Although exposed to west winds, the islets divert the swell coming from Queen Charlotte Strait. The anchorage east of Cedar Island is deeper but gets some current, and strong west winds can come in unwelcome gusts through the gut facing Providence Passage.

Aerial view of Mound Island anchorage, looking east to New Vancouver on Harbledown Island.

The foreshores of the surrounding islets consist of smooth stone, their slopes blanketed with mosses and gentle crowns covered with salal, cedar and spruce. Nearby are a number of interesting islands to explore by dinghy including White Cliff Islets – a popular nesting area for oystercatchers. Pick your weather carefully if visiting these islets.

In 1912, a man named George Nelson began camping on Cedar Island so he could fish the 'Merry-Go-Round' in Providence Pass. This was a popular spot for the local fishermen who trolled with handlines from rowboats along the kelp beds where, as Bill Proctor explains in his book *Full Moon, Flood Tide*, "the big springs like to lie." He recounts how the Merry-Go-Round was discovered by a Japanese troller in 1918 when a flood tide pushed him into the pass where he caught dozens of coho in one day. He promptly told his pals about this hot spot, and the next day about 20 boats joined him, drifting around in a big circle and catching coho.

Cormorant Channel Marine Park (Pearse Islands) 19

This beautiful undeveloped marine park consists of a number of islands of the Pearse and Plumper archipelagos, situated at the northwestern end of Johnstone Strait between Hanson Island and Cormorant Island. In addition to the eastern portion of the Pearse Islands and most of the Plumper Islands, the park takes in Stephenson Islet and Stubbs Island. Safe overnight anchorage in most conditions can be gained in the Pearse Islands.

Running through the middle of the park is impressive Weynton Passage, which carries a large part of the water flowing from Johnstone Strait to the Pacific Ocean. Currents in Weynton Passage can reach 6 knots. (See pages 219-220 for more detail.)

The Cormorant Channel area (from Johnstone Strait north to Queen Charlotte Strait) is part of the core habitat of the northern resident killer whale population. Both Weynton Passage and, more often, Blackney Passage are excellent viewing spots. In summer, humpback whales are also frequently sighted in these waters.

Salmon fishing in the area is very good and the waters adjacent to this marine park are rich in wildlife. Both the Pearse and Plumper Islands are renowned for their world-class scuba diving, enhanced by the superb visibility of the water – you can often see the set of your anchor at these islands.

Cedar Island anchorage is a sublime hideaway.

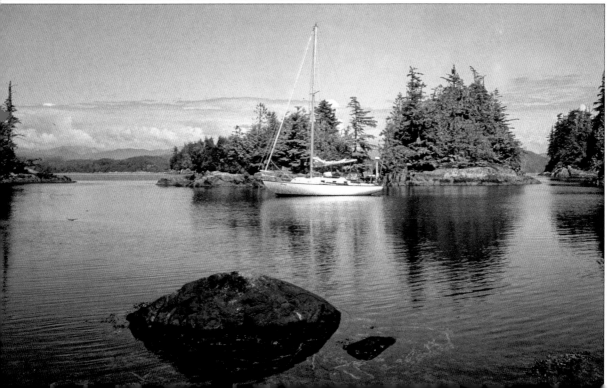

Currents are ever-present in these islands (in the one- to 3-knot range, setting your vessel either NW or SE) but there are some pretty spots with enough swinging room to ease a boater's concern. The best anchorage is inside the long narrows between the largest island marked '104' and a smaller island marked '75' on Chart 3546. Although the entrance from the south is tight with lots of kelp streaming along the edges of the shoreline, it is clear of obstructions with a depth of about 20 feet (6 m). Entrance from the north is also hazard-free and is wider. We like to anchor about halfway along, opposite a small gut, in about 25 feet with good holding in sand and mud. Although this anchorage is oriented in a NW-SE line, winds from these directions usually enter only in diminished gusts. The anchorage is also free of swell from the outside straits.

Locals sometimes use these narrows as a pass, so have an anchor light on in the evening. Also during the night, bull kelp carried along with current may foul your rode and although this doesn't normally present a problem, you may hear the kelp bulbs continuously thumping against the hull. Current may also start spinning your prop; to avoid it fouling on kelp, leave the engine in gear. This anchorage is a good base for exploring the entire group of islands which are home to an abundance of birdlife and sealife. If venturing by dinghy to the outer islands, be very careful of currents and winds.

Just SE of this anchorage is a small one-boat nook and although it is a tight spot and open to the southeast, it is quite safe in west winds or settled conditions, and provides southbound boaters a quick access to Johnstone Strait. We've anchored at the widest spot, opposite a small bight in the island marked '72'. The anchorage provides a great view south to the strait and a peaceful setting. At the head of this cove lies a drying reef which, although a barrier to boats, does not prevent the movement of water between this anchorage and the larger anchorage. The steady flow of water will normally keep your bow pointed in or out of the anchorage.

Another anchorage possibility lies south of the island marked '44' but in settled conditions only. This cove is quite open to the north and seems to get the most current of all these islands.

Below, narrow and quiet Pearse Islands. Bottom, an aerial view (looking east) of the main anchorage at Pearse Islands.

PEARSE ISLANDS AT A GLANCE

CHARTS: 3546
LAT LONG: 50°34.6'N 126°50.6'W
PROS: Good protection from most winds with good holding. Excellent visibility in water. Quiet anchorage, good fishing nearby. Good kayaking area.
CONS: Regular current will swing your vessel around but strength is under 2 knots. Entrances are tricky in poor visibility. Kelp in anchorage.
MUST DO: Explore islands by dinghy.

The Pearse Islands are ringed by reefs and shoal water, especially on the north and east sides, requiring the full concentration of boaters entering these islands. Because of their proximity to a large pass, strong currents and breaking seas are a common hazard. If arriving from the SE on an ebb, be careful of the set to Stephenson Islands and give this area a wide berth. Arriving from the north can be even more challenging as both the Pearse Reefs and Stubbs Island can generate dangerous waves during big tides and wind. **Close reading of the Sailing Directions is essential for cruising in these waters.**

In the late 1800s, steamboats would take on wood fuel at the Pearse Islands where a camp of mostly Chinese workers would cut and split Douglas fir. Although the steamers burned mostly coal to fire their boilers, they sometimes used wood. The Pearse Islands and Alert Bay were among the last places the northbound steamers could get Douglas fir, which burns hotter and slower than other wood.

Compared to the Pearse Islands, the Plumper Islands get more current, owing to their parallel orientation to Weynton Passage, and really have no safe anchorages. One anchorage that is popular with divers, is between the two most northerly islands marked '70' and '69'. Currents during HW come over the tombolo with some strength. Navigating through these islands is dangerous because of the ever-present current.

Alert Bay 20

Alert Bay is a bustling port with an excellent small-boat harbour protected by a stone breakwater. There is secure overnight anchorage SW of the breakwater in about 40 feet in mud and sand. Overnight and temporary **moorage** is available, with visiting boats allowed 4 hours free moorage – just time enough to take on water and provisions (the local grocery store provides transportation back to the docks), then set off on a walking tour of this interesting town rich in native culture. However, an overnight visit would give you time to linger at some of the town's attractions and enjoy one of the local restaurants.

A Visitor Information Centre is located on the waterfront, and across the street is the Old Customs House, built in 1917, its upper floor now a charming restaurant. A short distance past the InfoCentre along the waterfront is the 'Namgis Burial Grounds where the first of its totem poles was raised in the late 19th century.

A pamphlet identifying each pole is available at the Infocentre. Of note is Pole #9, carved in 1970 by Henry Hunt and Tony Hunt with assistance from John Livingston and Lawrence Bell (Haida) at the Royal British Columbia Museum in Victoria. This pole is a memorial to Mungo Martin of Fort Rupert, a high-ranking chief and renowned carver who was the first leader to openly host a potlatch when its prohibition ended.

The two shorter poles at the front of the grounds, representing Thunderbird and Giant Halibut, were carved in 1995 to commemorate the resolution of a land claim between the 'Namgis First Nation and the government. The burial grounds are sacred and visitors are asked to honour the 'No Trespassing' sign by viewing the totem poles from the roadside.

In 1870, the 'Namgis moved their main village at the mouth of the Nimpkish River across Broughton Strait to Alert Bay on Cormorant Island (named for the British naval survey ships *Alert* and *Cormorant*). Here some white settlers had established a store and saltery. Natives from other villages also moved to Alert Bay, which became a major port for the commercial fishery and remains a cultural and commercial centre of the Kwakwaka'wakw.

A hike up the hillside behind the town will take you to Gator Gardens Ecological Park, a natural swamp fed by an underground spring which supplies the island's water system. When the early white settlers built a dam halfway up the hill to store water for their cannery, the surrounding area was flooded and the trees died, their tall trunks and craggy limbs now devoid of vegetation. These dead trees, which can be viewed from a boardwalk, make ideal perches for bald eagles and ravens. Nature trails wind through the surrounding forest.

There are more sights to see on the other side of town, past the boat harbour. Follow the main road along the waterfront and you will pass the Historical Anglican Church – constructed in 1892 under the supervision of Reverend James Hall who relocated his mission from Fort Rupert to Alert Bay in 1880. The church's stained glass window depicts scenes of that era, including the mission ship *Columbia* and a 'Namgis canoe.

A short distance farther along the road is the U'mista Cultural Centre, a modern museum built in the traditional plank-and-beam style. Housed inside is a collection of elaborate masks, rattles and whistles that were used at potlatch celebrations of feasting, dancing and gift-giving. Many of these items were seized by the Canadian government following a mass arrest at Village Island in 1921, then returned in 1979 for display in the U'mista Cultural Centre. Many of these artifacts suffered soot and water damage from an arson fire in July 2013, but curators from other museums (including the Royal B.C. Museum and University of British Columbia's Museum of Anthropology) rushed to Alert Bay to help restore these cultural treasures.

A 10-minute hike up the hillside behind the museum, along residential streets, will take you to the Big House, originally built in 1963 and modeled on the traditional residences of the Kwakiutl people. A community centre, it is primarily used for potlatches. A two-day potlatch was underway when Oprah Winfrey arrived by private yacht at Alert Bay and paid a visit to the Big House, where she was given the honourary name Noxsalaga ,which means 'wise woman.'

Native public art greets visitors to Alert Bay's small boat harbour.

Not far from the Big House is the world's tallest totem pole, which stands 173' high. Raised in 1973, the pole displays the crests of various tribes and is crowned with Sun Man, crest of the Quatsino. This pole has become a point of interest for passing cruise ships which glide slowly past Cormorant Island before entering Johnstone Strait.

The last operating fuel dock in Alert Bay was closed in 2005 and, at present, Port McNeill is now the closest location for fuel.

Port McNeill 21

This prosperous logging and fishing town is an ideal port in which to reprovision, do laundry, and take on fuel and water. Inland are the rivers, lakes and forests of the Nimpkish Valley, while local waters offer excellent fishing, especially near the entrance of Mitchell Bay on Malcolm Island and along the east side of Cormorant Island.

Port McNeill is a busy port during the summer boating season, but if you call the harbourmaster on Channel 66A (or call 250-956-3881), an empty slip can usually be found (try to call before noon). Port McNeill Fuel Dock & Marina also accommodates visiting vessels (phone 250-902-8128). If both marinas are full, good anchorage in about 35 feet can be had across the bay, SW of **Ledge Point**. There is plenty of room here to accommodate numerous boats and although the bay is somewhat open to both N and S winds, there is good protection from seas and the holding is excellent in sticky mud.

Top, 'Namgis Burial Grounds. Left, Alert Bay's Big House. Below, U'mista Cultural Centre.

Above, a BC ferry pulls away from Port McNeill where the small boat harbour (also shown below) accommodates visiting boats.

We like to spend a day or two in Port McNeill. The municipal docks (with showers) are well run and maintained, and the town's facilities are an easy walk away. Two grocery stores and a liquor store are located a short walk up Campbell Way, and a medical clinic is located farther up the hill on the same street. An excellent restaurant is located in Haida Way Inn, also on Campbell Way.

The hub of town is the harbour, with its ferry dock, marinas, fuel dock, log-loading facility and local fleet of floatplanes. At the seaward end of the municipal pier we have seen people catch coho by throwing a line in the water. A fish-cleaning station near the ramp is well utilized.

Although there are small-boat facilities in both Sointula and Alert Bay, visiting by ferry as a foot passenger is another option. While in Port McNeill it's easy to hop aboard the inter-island ferry which runs all day between the three ports.

Sointula – a Finnish word meaning harmony – was founded at the turn of the last century by pioneer farmers from Finland who wanted to create a utopia of co-operative rural living in a scenic seaside setting. They were granted government land and today visitors can stroll the town's tidy streets and visit the local museum, shops and restaurants. Free bicycles can be borrowed from the Paddlin' Dragon Grill & Bar beside the ferry terminal.

CHAPTER EIGHT

BROUGHTON ARCHIPELAGO

▲ Mt. Stephens

21 Turnbull
Cove

20
Claydon
Bay

Hopetown
Passage

22 Mackenzie Sound

0   2.5   5
Nautical miles
N

Drury
Inlet
23

Davis
Bay

19

SUTLEJ CHANNEL

KINGCOME INLET

16
Moore
Bay

Wells Passage

N. BROUGHTON
ISLAND

Tracey 24
Harbour   26

25

Dickson I

Carter Passage

Greenway 18
Sound

Shawl 15
Bay

13
Simoom
Sound

▲ Mt Ick

17

Laura
Bay
14

Deep Sea
Bluff

Tribune
Channel

QUEEN CHARLOTTE STRAIT

Polkinghorne
27 Islands

Booker
Lagoon

12

Cullen
Hbr

11

BROUGHTON
ISLAND

FIFE   SOUND

Ladyboot
Cove

Eden
Island

8

Joe Cove

9

7

John I 10

Baker
Island

Tracey I

1
Burdwood
Group

2

● Echo Bay

3 Proctor Bay

4

Shoal Hbr

BROUGHTON ARCHIPELAGO

Recommended Route
To Cape Caution: · · · · · · · · · · · · ·

Broughton Archipelago
Marine Park

Mars I

5

Bonwick
Island

Waddington
Bay

Bootleg 6
Bay

GILFORD
ISLAND

I n rainy weather, the remote islands of
Broughton Archipelago seem shrouded in
the past, when hand loggers worked the
coast and small settlements clustered around
sawmills. This sense of bygone days prevails
while anchored beside a deserted midden or
motoring past the rotting remains of a wharf
where people once awaited a Union Steamship,
its whistle piercing the foggy silence to
announce the arrival of mail and supplies.

When the sun breaks through the mist and such
musings dissipate, a mariner's contemplations may
turn to the present reality: interesting passes, pristine
anchorages and the sublime scenery of Broughton
Archipelago, where low islands front a backdrop of
snow-capped mountains. Marina resorts are tucked
into various bays and coves, and their operators
appreciate each and every visitor. Boaters arriving
for fuel or supplies often succumb to the charm of
these upcoast mini-communities, pausing to

Charts & Publications:

Use CHS Charts: 3546, 3547, 3515. Canadian Tide
and Current Tables Volume 6 applies to this area.
Also be sure to have the CHS Sailing Directions
Volume One for the British Columbia south coast.

exchange yarns with fellow cruisers and spend a few
days before setting off for new anchorages.

Broughton Archipelago is a term loosely used to
describe the area in and around the extensive marine
park named for it. This undeveloped park's meandering boundary encompasses some 300 islands and
islets lying between Fife Sound and Blackfish
Sound. (Anchorages south of Bonwick Island are
covered in Ch. 7, Blackfish Sound.) The Broughton
area in general has dozens of intriguing anchorages,
some quite busy at the height of summer but others
offering the seclusion and remoteness boaters expect
along the east side of Queen Charlotte Strait.

Logging camps still exist in some of the area's inlets, but aquaculture and fish farms are now a more common sight, their presence hotly opposed by many of the area's residents because the proliferation of sea lice on penned fish is viewed as a threat to the region's wild salmon stocks. Clamshell middens are plentiful throughout this traditional territory of the Kwakwaka'wakw (Kwakuitl). Villages once dotted the shores of these islands, which are interconnected with narrow, maze-like passages.

Summer weather among the islands is dominated by Queen Charlotte Strait, with morning cloud or fog usually clearing by mid-day as the prevailing summer northwesterly sets in and blows through the channels. This sea breeze usually dies out in the evening, while at night a land breeze often funnels down the mainland inlets. Fog is a common occurrence from late July right through September, but it usually burns off by noon.

Tides and Currents

Booker Lagoon Passage, Carter Passage and Hopetown Passage are shallow passes with streams in the 4- to 8-knot range and should be attempted only at HW slack. Hopetown Passage is perhaps best transited by dinghy – the drying reef at the east entrance has snared more than a few boats. The passes are described in detail in The Anchorages section of this chapter.

Stuart Narrows, located at the entrance to Drury Inlet, has fairly strong currents with an ebb of 7 knots and a flood of 6 knots, referenced to Alert Bay. The normal route through the pass is south of Welde

Rising over 400 feet, Deep Sea Bluff marks the west entrance of Tribune Channel.

Rock, favouring the S side of the passage. Current streams are fairly smooth without much turbulence. However, large whirlpools can form downstream of Welde Rock and, as a result, the pass should be navigated near slack. Current is found in many of the small passages and channels, but usually reaches no more than 2 knots. Indian Passage, Old Passage and Cramer Passage have slightly stronger streams (up to 3 knots).

Deep Sea Bluff

This well-known landmark was named by Captain Vancouver when he and his officers explored and charted these waters in 1792. As Vancouver noted in his journals, while his ship *Discovery* lay at anchor off Hanson Island in late July, any investigation of the area's multitude of islands was unnecessary until he determined "how far the *Chatham* had been able to succeed in fixing the continuation of the continental shore." Under the command of Lieutenant Broughton, the *Chatham* had exited Johnstone Strait via Havannah Channel, picked her way along narrow and shallow Chatham Channel, then followed the twists and turns of Tribune Channel to its western entrance. By the time Broughton arrived at Deep Sea Bluff, he and his men had safely piloted their ship through a watery labyrinth in an impressive test of seamanship. Broughton then entered Queen Charlotte Strait via Fife Sound and made a beeline south to rendezvous with the *Discovery*, passing to port an "extensive cluster of islands, rocky islets and rocks" which Vancouver, in commemoration of his lieutenant's discovery, named Broughton's Archipelago, a reference that was revived two centuries later with the establishment of Broughton Archipelago Marine Park.

THE ANCHORAGES

Burdwood Group 1

This group of small islands and islets lies at the entrance to Tribune Channel where it intersects with Fife Sound and Penphrase Passage. For about 5,000 years, native fishing camps were located on these islands. Today summertime kayakers often set up camp at these former sites, one of which is marked by a beautiful midden where the clear water shimmers turquoise-green over a clean white crescent of crushed clamshells. This stunning midden lies at the east end of the islet north of the island marked '110' on Chart 3515.

Access is fairly clear into the Burdwood Group from either Tribune Channel (keeping island '85' off the port) or Hornet Passage (keeping island '85' to starboard). Gunkholing around these islands is a sheer delight with plenty of wildlife reported both on the islands (deer, cougar and wolves often swim to the islands) and in the surrounding waters. We've seen killer whales and humpback whales within a mile and a half of these islands. Many species of birds make the Burdwood Group their home, including eagles and numerous sea ducks.

Above, the Burdwood Group is a good lunch stop with a beautiful midden beach, right.

Above, the east side of Scott Cove is a good bet in SE winds. Below, the beautiful Burdwood Group.

Although there is no obvious protected overnight anchorage, there are one or two locations to drop the hook for the day south of island '85'. Several small islets are adjacent to the island with the midden and these provide some protection from W winds. We anchor either just NE of the midden in about 70 feet (21 m) or between the two islets that line up with the midden in about 30 feet (9 m). Current can flow through the islands at a knot or more. You can anchor right in the middle of the islets and this might be the safest bet for overnight, if you don't mind the 120-foot depth. West and S winds can pipe through here, but in settled weather this anchorage would be fine. Although we have stayed overnight here, we usually treat the islands as a day stop, enjoying the beautiful beach and exploring the area before retreating to a more secure spot for the night.

The closest overnight anchorage is **Scott Cove**, in either the south arm or, in settled weather, the bight behind an islet. Most of this cove is being used for forestry and salmon hatchery operations. The small pretty cove at the head of **Viner Sound** is another option, although strong westerlies find their way into this anchorage.

BURDWOOD GROUP AT A GLANCE

CHARTS: 3515
LAT LONG: 50˚47.79'N 126˚27.39'W
PROS: A beautiful oasis with clean midden beach.
CONS: Anchorage area quite deep.
MUST DO: Have a picnic on the beautiful midden and definitely go for a swim.

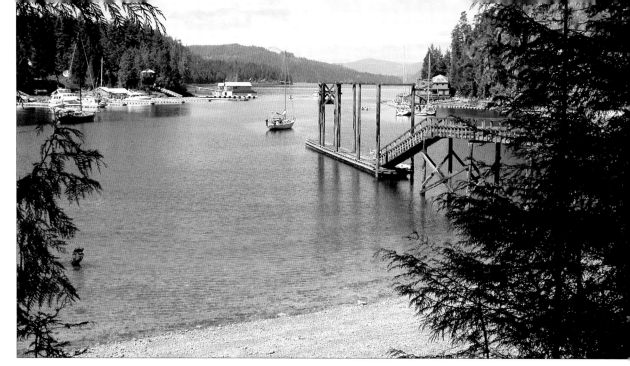

Echo Bay, Gilford Island 2

The midden and anchorage at the head of Echo Bay.

Echo Bay, on the northwest side of Gilford Island, is a year-round floathome community with two marinas just inside its entrance and a scenic anchorage at its head where the open uplands of Echo Bay Marine Park provide access to good trails. The anchorage is sheltered from all winds and the holding ground is good, but swinging room is limited. The marine park's small wharf is used by the school boat, and on shore is a shell beach edged by a seawall that was built by the BC Forest Service in 1958 to stop the bank from eroding. A schoolyard is located above the open uplands of the park, and behind the school is a lovely stream called Ranger Creek. Old logging trails lead deep into the woods. One of these trails leads east to a lake and others lead south to 'Proctor Bay' and Shoal Harbour.

Like most isolated villages, Echo Bay clings tenaciously to a way of life that began at the turn of the last century when hand loggers moved from cove to cove working their claims. Camps consisted of two or three families, their individual floathomes rafted together and moored to shore with long logs holding them off the beach at low tide.

The white-shell midden at the head of Echo Bay once marked the location of the largest First Nations village in the area. Now Echo Bay is home to one of the last one-room schools in Canada. Children come to school by boat, but in other ways it is a normal school complete with computers and teeter-totters. Between 1920 and 1960, about 40 families lived in and around Echo Bay. Today about a dozen children attend the local school.

Back in 1910 Louie McCay bought land around Echo Bay, clearing room for a garden where the park is now, and built a store on a large float, as well as a fuel float and fish-buying camp. In the 1930s a shingle mill was built where the community hall now stands, and a camp and cookhouse were built where the one-room school, constructed in 1961, now stands. Children living in floathomes in Echo Bay would haul themselves to the school dock on a pulley float.

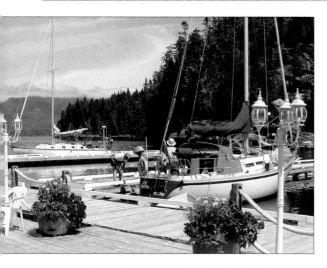

Above, the main marina at Echo Bay has been expanded since its acquisition by Pierre and Tove Landry. Below, The Cliffside's floats. Bottom, Echo Bay's colourful floathomes.

Summer is the make-or-break season for most resort operators in this area, and Echo Bay's two marinas welcome visiting boaters who can tie up and enjoy one of the B.C. coast's prettiest floathome settings. Both marinas are located at the entrance to this small bay and are owned by Pierre and Tove Landry, who used to operate Pierre's Bay Lodge & Marina in Scott Cove before taking over the Echo Bay Resort. The Landrys moved most of their docks and structures from Scott Cove to Echo Bay, and they continue to develop the facilities at Pierre's Echo Bay Lodge & Marina. Services here include fuel, power, water, showers, laundry and a grocery store.

Echo Bay's other marina, also run by the Landrys, is The Cliffside (formerly called the Windsong Sea Village), and is located opposite at the base of a rock bluff. Sounds echo clearly off its face, giving the bay its name. The evening sun lingers on this side of the bay, bathing the floathomes and moored vessels in sunlight. A trail leads from The Cliffside's floats to the head of Echo Bay and onward to Billy's Museum in 'Proctor Bay.'

Just north of Echo Bay is the abandoned settlement of Little Simoom Sound, where a floating village (originally located in Simoom Sound) once served loggers and various logging outfits in the area. Today there are a few floathomes and tour operators located in Little Simoom Sound. The old Simoom Sound Post Office building was towed to Echo Bay and is part of the Echo Bay Resort.

'Proctor Bay'   3

A neck of land separates Echo Bay from the bay directly south, known locally as Proctor Bay. This small bay is home to three well-known writers and environmentalists. Boaters anchored in Echo Bay can follow the short trail through the woods to arrive at the museum and homestead of Bill Proctor. If you arrive by boat, you can tie to Proctor's dock on the north side of the bay, or you can anchor off in about 60 feet (20 m). Bill Proctor, who grew up on Swanson Island, has long been known as a fighter for the preservation of wild salmon stocks and has received an even wider audience with the publication of his bestselling book *Full Moon, Flood Tide*.

Co-written with artist Yvonne Maximchuk, the book is filled with fascinating recollections of life in this area over the past century along with tips on local anchorages and wildlife viewing.

A lifelong resident of this area and an avid collector, Proctor built a museum on his property in 1999 to house all of the artifacts he has acquired over the years – his own memorabilia and that of various individuals who have homesteaded and worked in the area at fishing, hand logging and trapping. His museum charges no admission fee but accepts donations for local salmon enhancement. Over 3,000 vistors come to see his museum each summer.

Across the bay from the Proctor homestead is the home of marine biologist Alexandra Morton, renowned for her work studying orcas and the complexity of the language of these whales. Morton has also been instrumental in researching the impact of fish farms on wild salmon stocks and works with various organizations to restore salmon-bearing creeks in the Broughton Archipelago.

Local author and artist Yvonne Maximchuk lives at the SW end of Proctor Bay where she operates an artist retreat from her home. Maximchuk paints canvases of local scenes, past and present, and created the cover and inside art for *Full Moon, Flood Tide*. Yvonne is also well known for her superb pottery and ceramic work. Her art is displayed in Victoria, Campbell River and Port McNeill. Yvonne's husband, Albert, is a prawner (and potter) who has fished Broughton Archipelago for many years.

Shoal Harbour   4

This is a well-protected and pretty anchorage that provides shelter from west winds but not from easterlies, which funnel strongly throughout the harbour. Used for years as a logging base with booms along the SE side, Shoal Harbour's eastern arm continues

Above, Bill Proctor in his gift shop. Below, artist Yvonne Maximchuk with her husband, Albert. Bottom, Shoal Harbour, looking southeast.

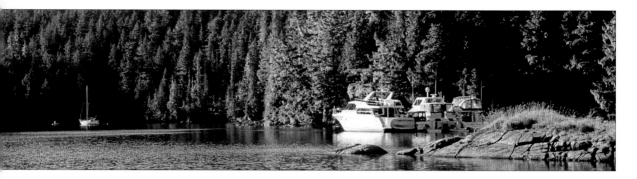

,to be busy with forestry operations. Several log booms may be moored along this part of the harbour.

Good anchorage is available in the western arm but depths can be a little shallow – about 7 to 10 feet (2-3 m) feet at very low tides. The area west of the small islet, outside this arm, offers more depth and plenty of swinging room. Anchorage south of this islet is also good but be aware that there could be a satellite cable running from shore out to the islet. If you see a satellite dish on the small islet, stay clear. Farther into the harbour, there is an anchorage east of an islet located on the north side. Anchor in soft mud with good holding. Use Chart 3515.

Waddington Bay 5

Waddington Bay, at the NE end of Bonwick Island, is an all-weather anchorage that provides fairly good protection from most winds brewing out in Queen Charlotte Strait. Not only is it sheltered with good holding in thick mud, but the cluster of islets at its entrance is perfect for birdwatching, picnicking or simply exploring by dinghy, while the near-

by channels offer good fishing. A maze of small islands – the Fox Group – clogs the entrance but careful attention to Chart 3546 and a slow approach will get you safely inside.

Entry from the north and northeast is made between the two islands marked '46' and '52'. If you're approaching from the south, the conservative entry is to keep islands '66' and '41' to port, then proceed in between the two above-mentioned islands. An alternative approach is to proceed west of island '66' and thread your way slowly through the reefs, which are fairly easy to spot.

Most boats anchor in the main part of the bay, east of the small islet guarding the inner and more shallow part of Waddington Bay. Afternoon wester-lies can be expected throughout the bay and some-times the gusts are strong. A good way to escape these west winds is to tie a stern line on the east shore of the small island and, with your anchor well

Above, the anchorage west of central islet in Shoal Harbour. Below, aerial view of Waddington Bay.

WADDINGTON BAY AT A GLANCE:

CHARTS: 3546, 3515
LAT LONG: Waypoint 50°42.84'N 126°36"W
PROS: The central anchorage in Broughton Archipelago, with numerous anchorages and marinas nearby. Fairly well protected with good holding. Good fishing, crabbing and birdwatching nearby.
CONS: Occasionally busy, can receive gusty summer west winds. As in most northern anchorages, there is limited hiking.
MUST DO: Explore nearby islets and reefs.

set, pull yourself snug up to the island. Yours will be the only barbecue that isn't flaming out. We usually anchor in the small inner bay in a minimum depth of about 12 feet (4 m). This is more protected from SE winds, but westerlies still pipe through smartly. The holding in this part of the bay is also good in thick mud. On shore are a few short trails.

Grebe Cove, next door, has decent anchorage near the head. Few boats venture into this long narrow anchorage, so it is usually quiet. It gets some west winds coming over from Sedgley Cove and is exposed to the east, as the Sailing Directions warns. Holding, though, is good. Carrie Bay, further south, has a better reputation for protection from W winds, but its shoreline is not as interesting.

'Bootleg Bay' 6

An alternative to Waddington Bay is the unnamed, L-shaped cove that lies about a mile due east on Gilford Island. Known locally as Bootleg Bay, this anchorage has a fairly clear entrance but has lots of kelp along this stretch of the shoreline. The anchorage is small and holds only one or two boats, but it's serene and not often visited by recreational vessels. It is also well protected, with a forested shore blocking most wind, although southeasterlies sometimes

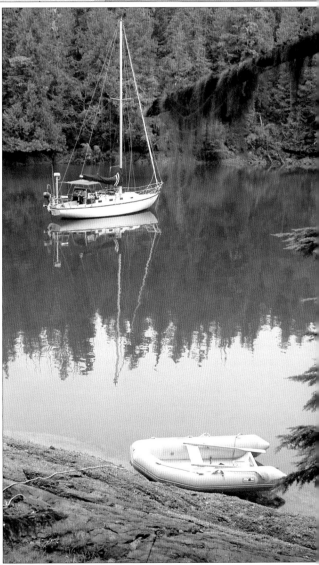

Bootleg Bay offers cozy anchorage.

The midden on the east side of Eden Island is a perfect picnicking spot with great views.

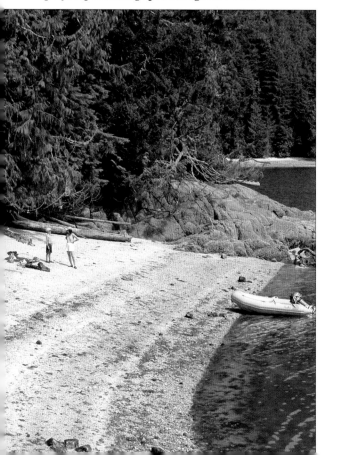

gust through. In summer mosquitoes like it also, so have nets in place at night. Holding is good in soft mud in 12 feet (4 m) at the end of the leg; beyond this the bay dries. We usually tie a line to a tree at the small knob on the west shore where there is a clearing for campers and some short trails. This is a very good alternative if Waddington Bay is full for the night. A fellow named Johnny Card lived and hand logged in this bay from the mid- to late-1920s and this anchorage is still sometimes referred to by locals as Johnny Card's Bay.

Old Passage / 7 Misty Passage / Indian Passage

At the southwest corner of Insect Island is an inter-section of channels which just begs for exploration. This is a beautiful area and was the location of at least four native villages in the past. The intersection takes in five islands, including Baker, Tracey and Eden Islands. The only anchorage lies at the north-west end of Blunden Passage, where it intersects with the three other channels. Two middens, mark-ing old village sites, overlook this marine cross-roads, one gracing the southeast shore of Eden Island, the other lying opposite on Insect Island.

We've motored or drifted through these passes many times en route to the many nearby anchorages and have always thought the anchorage noted above would make a good spot to stay overnight, even though summer westerlies tend to gust through the intersection. Our friends Fred and Rita Vitringa of Quadra Island anchored their 35-foot sailboat many times over the years off the Eden Island beach during summer months and were well tucked out of west winds. We explored this anchorage by dinghy one summer while our boat was anchored at John Island, and not a single boat or kayak passed by as we lazed on the beaches for several hours.

Nearby is another beautiful channel – Old Passage – which is a pretty route to take if you're going from the Burdwood Group to Joe Cove, or taking Insect Island Pass to Ladyboot Cove. Standing along the shorelines are cedars canted over the water and draped with cat-tail moss. With the current pulling your vessel and the breeze lifting the moss like an exotic veil, the visual effect is quite transporting. However, between the kelp, currents and strong afternoon winds that blow throughout the pass, the small basin here is not a relaxing place to anchor. Minimum depth in the pass is 10 feet (3 m) at the west end. The northern section of Blunden Passage, between Insect Island and Eden Island, is one of the most sublime passages anywhere.

Joe Cove, Eden Island 8

Joe Cove is nestled on the south side of Eden Island, its shoreline forming the northern boundary of Broughton Archipelago Marine Park. This anchorage is a pretty haven during the best and worst of weather coming from Queen Charlotte Strait. Its setting is pristine, with a tree-draped shoreline and a stream near the head on the NW shore. This stream leads to a lagoon that can be explored by dinghy at high water.

There are several spots to anchor in sheltered Joe Cove and the holding throughout in thick mud is very good. At the head is a small basin with room for three or four boats. This anchorage is fairly sheltered from W winds, which diminish by the time they reach this part of the cove.

Many mid-size and smaller vessels like the narrow east arm, where a derelict float is located. Boats used to tie up to the float, but now anchor off with a

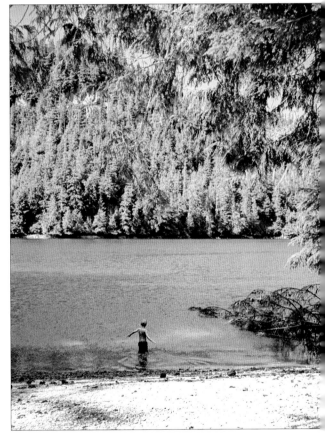

Top, the inner anchorage at Joe Cove where a float (upper left) used to be a convenient tie-up but is now derelict. Above, a nearby midden beach.

Aerial view of Joe Cove showing north arm and east arm, where vessels can anchor and stern tie. Float is now derelict and no longer useable.

line to shore. This inner anchorage provides complete protection from all winds, although occasional W gusts are felt. The rocks lying west of the islet at the entrance to this pocket anchorage are shown on Chart 3547 and the usual entry is between these rocks and the islet – staying closer to this islet. Minimum depth in this channel is about 15 feet. Entry is also possible close along Eden Island and the very small islet (really just a large rock). Favour the Eden shore with channel minimum depth of about 10 feet (3 m).

Billy Proctor, who grew up in this area, recounts in *Full Moon, Flood Tide* that a native trapper from Alert Bay named Joe Jack used to spend his winters in Joe Cove, where he and his wife lived in a shake shack. They also dug clams for a living, something their ancestors did in great numbers as evidenced by the numerous clamshell middens in the immediate area. One of these pocket beaches lies at the mouth of Joe Cove, overlooking the entrance channel.

Southwest of Joe Cove is a sac-like bay, also on Eden Island, known locally as **Mud Bay**, which offers good protection from W winds although it is quite open to SE winds. This wide bay would be especially useful for larger yachts. **Monday Anchorage** is another possibility although the entire bay receives unimpeded west winds. There is some shelter behind the east islet on the N shore. **Sunday Harbour** is also open to west winds, which reach every corner.

'Ladyboot Cove',aka 9 'Tombstone Bay' or 'East of Eden'

This bay, unnamed on the charts but locally known by the names listed above, lies on the NE side of Eden Island. The heel of the boot, which is the small cove with a drying foreshore, has room for two or three boats and is sheltered from northwesterlies and light southwesterlies but provides little protection from strong E winds. The smaller inner bay to the west (the toe of the boot) offers better shelter from most winds, except strong easterlies, in depths of over 20 feet (6 m) with a mud-and-shell bottom. The holding ground here is quite good and if an easterly is forecast, you can tuck yourself up to the north shore in the lee of the small hook of land and get out of some of the gusts. Depths here at LW are about 10 feet (3 m). There was once a small settlement and logging operation on this side of the cove.

This is a popular cove with locals, and rafts of small boats from Port McNeill often appear here on weekends. Good fishing is reported just outside the cove, along the Eden Island shoreline and off the north tip of Fly Island. Another good fishing spot is from the Walkem Cone bluffs to Gordon Point on Broughton Island.

Due north of Ladyboot Cove is another small cove, known locally as **Little Tombstone Bay**, where a loner named Matt Rose once lived and operated a small sawmill. He built a boat grid right beside his sawmill so he could use his boat engine to power the mill, constantly moving the engine from boat to mill and back again. This is quite a tight little cove – requiring a line ashore – but it is well protected from most winds and the holding is good.

Misty Passage, between Eden Island and Tracey Island, gets one or 2 knots of current and is a safe pass, although a westerly blowing against an east-flowing ebb can produce a surprisingly stiff chop, at least for dinghies. There is a small bight halfway along the pass, with a drying lagoon directly north, which makes for a pleasant lunch stop and is tucked out of most of the afternoon W wind.

John Island anchorage is a good one-boat bight shared only with a large colony of sea stars.

John Island 10

If Ladyboot Cove is full, this bight on the SE side of John Island is an idyllic, one-boat anchorage and will provide excellent overnight shelter in almost all conditions. Part of the Benjamin Group of islands, which lie within the boundaries of Broughton Archipelago Marine Park, this sheltered spot can be entered off Indian Passage through a small collection of islands with about 20 feet (6 m) of water, or via the deeper channel a little further to the west.

The small cove has lots of kelp around the sides of the entrance but there is usually a large clear area in the middle to get the hook down. We anchor in 20 feet (6 m on Chart 3547) in mud and shell, and point our bow southwest with the stern tied to the east side of the bight. Westerlies may gust through Indian Pass, but this bight is out of almost all wind. The NE side of the cove shelves quickly but the visibility is good and the shoal water can be easily seen. At low water the shoreline and tidal pools make for an interesting morning's exploration. This cove seems to be a sea star city with dozens of these colourful creatures easily visible in the shallows.

Evening sunlight pours into this secluded spot, nestled amongst low-lying islands. The small island opposite was once used for raising goats by a man named Louie McCay. He and his family lived in a cabin he built in 1925 near Twin Lagoon on Broughton Island, a short boat trip across Fife Sound. The narrow bay on Davis Island is open to west wind and chop.

Cullen Harbour, 11 Broughton Island

When travelling from Fife Sound to anchorages north, boaters are faced with a dilemma. Do you turn east through Raleigh Passage and explore Simoom

CULLEN HARBOUR AT A GLANCE

CHARTS: 3547
LAT LONG: Entrance 50°45.93'N 126°44.57'W
PROS: Unusual anchorage on the edge of Queen Charlotte Strait with lots of room. Secure from wind with good holding.
CONS: Gets some swell from strait and some current from Booker Passage.
MUST DO: Explore islets and Booker Passage.

Above, Inukshuk at entrance to Booker Passage.

Below, view of Cullen Harbour, looking north.

Sound, Penphrase Passage and Kingcome Inlet, or turn west and find an anchorage near Queen Charlotte Strait for further explorations north? Either way is a win for cruisers and, if westbound, Cullen Harbour on Broughton Island is an excellent anchorage for overnighting.

The entrance to Cullen Harbour from the south is between Gordon Point and Nelly Islet, staying in the middle of the channel until you are past Ben Rock and the peninsula on the opposite shore. We sometimes enter the anchorage from the west, coming close along Olden Island (the reef shown at the SW end of this island extends a little further south than shown on the chart, with a rock at 50°46.08'N and 126°45.17'W). The passage east of Long Island has numerous obstacles and hazards, and kelp grows nearly across the passage.

There is plenty of room in Cullen Harbour, and boats often anchor in a line along the east side to the small islet that marks the entrance to Booker Lagoon.

Boats also anchor just east of Long Island, where protection from W winds is better. Westerlies (which normally die out in early evening) can enter the harbour during gusts, and S gusts can also find their way well into the harbour. During HW, remnants of swell from Queen Charlotte Strait will be felt, especially along the S side of the harbour. Holding is very good in the mud-and-sand mix and most of the current from Booker Lagoon will be avoided inside the 30-foot (10 m) line. If you are staying for a few days, there are many small islets and passes to explore by dinghy, but beware of strong currents in Booker Lagoon (see pass info below) and swells from Queen Charlotte Strait breaking on the outer reefs.

Several shell middens mark the site of former native villages, and a retired sea captain once homesteaded in this harbour. Good fishing is reported along the outer shoreline SW of Wicklow Point.

Top, view of pass looking east. Above, facing 5 knots of ebb current at Booker Passage.

Booker Passage
Booker Lagoon 12

Just beyond Cullen Harbour is one of the most beautiful lagoons of the Inside Passage. However, entering this lagoon must be timed correctly as the lagoon is guarded by a very swift little pass. We tried to enter it on one occasion 15 minutes after LW at Alert Bay and were greeted with 5 knots of current ebbing out of the lagoon. Maximum current in the passage is at least 7 to 8 knots – some local fishermen say it is more like 10 to 12 knots. At full flood or ebb on big tides, the pass is a cauldron of white and turquoise water with whirlpools for hundreds of yards leading to and from the narrows.

In our observations of the pass, slack times on large tides are about 25 minutes after HW at Alert Bay and 35 minutes after LW. Slack period is about 10 minutes. During neap tides, the period of slack is about 25 minutes and during these smaller tides it should be safe to transit this pass up to one hour after Alert Bay. There is good depth, about 20 feet (6 m), throughout the pass.

If you are **westbound**, be sure to give the reef at the E end of Long Island a wide berth. Kelp will be present along the length of this reef and there may be an Inukshuk showing the HW side of the reef. We aim for the centre of the small bight on Broughton Island and make our turn once we have rounded the kelp and have a clear view up the pass. Be careful to stay right in the middle of this pass as it is very narrow (perhaps 50 or 60 feet at HW) and there are rock outcroppings off Long Island and along the N shore. At

The anchorage on the north side of Booker Lagoon is well sheltered with a lovely islet for exploring and swimming.

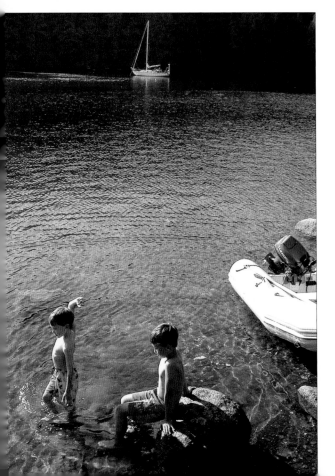

the passage's W entrance, favour the island marked '56' to avoid the marked rock to the south.

If **eastbound**, the pass can be hard to pick out from across the bay, but the small islet north of Long Island indicates the entrance. We come near the island marked '56' and check that no other boat has entered the pass. If there is another vessel in the pass, it is best to turn around as this is a one-boat pass. (The passage west of Long Island might be attempted at HW slack, but the entire entrance area to the south is kelp-infested, as is the pass itself, which is quite shallow.)

Inside the lagoon, you are presented with a myriad of anchoring possiblities – especially now that all aquaculture operations (although they are still shown on recent editions of Chart 3547) have been removed. During normal summer weather with daytime westerlies, the two NW bays offer good shelter and have nearby scenic islets. Drying lagoons with nearby middens are adjacent to these anchorages and make for interesting areas to explore by dinghy. Bears are reported in the area so be sure to take along an air horn if hiking into the bush.

The small cove due north of the pass is also quite good and although west winds do curl around the steep rock shoreline, the gusts are not strong by the time they make it into the anchorage. This cove is also well protected in south winds. There is a pretty islet in this anchorage which is ideal for picnics or for swimming from the granite shoreline. Seals and kingfishers also seem to like this cove and will likely

Above, Booker Lagoon, with westernmost anchorage in foreground. Right and bottom, a small drying lagoon and nearby western anchorage.

be the only sounds you hear while anchored here. The remains of a log dump can be seen on the north side of the anchorage; logging took place in this area up to the late 1960s. There is reported to be an old logging road here.

The bay at the extreme E end offers good protection during SE winds, and during settled conditions it is a good spot to enjoy the sunsets. There is another small cove S of this, with the island marked '56' to the west, which also provides shelter in SE winds.

The holding ground is good throughout the lagoon – soft mud in the bays to the east, and sticky mud and sand in the western bays. There may be discarded logging gear near the shore of the north and west bays. The head of the south arm is also an anchoring possibility, but it seems to get more breeze when a westerly is blowing.

BOOKER LAGOON AT A GLANCE

CHARTS: 3547
LAT LONG: Entrance: 50°46.67'N 126°44.50'W
PROS: A beautiful destination with many safe overnight anchorages. Lots of things to do here – swim, hike, explore and picnic. Good fishing and prawning nearby.
CONS: Access is through a tricky pass.
MUST DO: Explore lagoons and islets.

Above, entrance to Simoom Sound. Left, a hump-back whale feeds in Penphrase Passage.

50 feet (15 m) in soft mud at the extreme NW end of the bay. If you tuck behind the knob of land extending from the N shore, you will gain good protection from an E wind. We've also found good protection from SE winds in McIntosh Bay, in the the cove north of Hannant Point in about 25 feet (8 m). Be careful to avoid this spot's numerous rocks and shoal water, especially to the south.

In the last century, Simoom Sound was home to a major logging camp which evolved into a floating village complete with store, community hall, post office and school. A large empty float served as a tennis court/baseball diamond. From 1908 to 1936, a man named Jack Dunseith ran a post office out of his general store, which sat on floats inside the entrance. According to some reports, Dunseith also ran a floating casino and saloon. In 1936, the entire village was moved to Little Simoom Sound (the small bay N of Echo Bay) where Dunseith's daughter Irene and son-in-law Dan Sutherland ran the store and post office for nearly forty years. In 1973 the store and fuel dock was moved to Echo Bay where it remains and the post office still retains its Simoom Sound name.

Simoom Sound 13

This large, dog-leg inlet is where Captain Vancouver anchored his two ships in the summer of 1792 while survey parties set out in boats to examine the continental shoreline west of Deep Sea Bluff. By ship's boat Vancouver explored Simoom Sound to O'Brien Bay its head, where he walked across the narrow isthmus that separates it from Shawl Bay. Standing on the edge of the lagoon there, Vancouver could see the entrance to Sutlej Channel.

Simoom Sound's two popular anchorages, offering good protection from the west, are **McIntosh Bay** and **O'Brien Bay**. For the latter, anchor in about

Laura Bay, Broughton Island 14

The small inner bay of this anchorage has become a favourite with boaters over the years for, although it has limited room, it offers a pretty setting with excellent shelter in most winds. The main part of the bay is open to SE winds which die out near the western point of Trivett Island, although gusts from this direction do enter the inner bay.

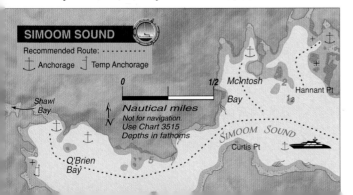

SIMOOM SOUND

Recommended Route: ·········
⚓ Anchorage ⚓ Temp Anchorage

0   1/2

Nautical miles
Not for navigation.
Use Chart 3515
Depths in fathoms

Shawl Bay

O'Brien Bay

McIntosh Bay

Hannant Pt

SIMOOM SOUND

Curtis Pt

Above, aerial view of Laura Bay's inner anchorage where stern-ties are often necessary (right). Bottom right, Shawl Bay Marina.

Vessels tuck in behind the small island north of this point and normally tie a stern line to the peninsula jutting out from Broughton Island. The only chart available for this anchorage is 3515 which has little detail of this anchorage. There is shoal water and a rock awash NE of the small island. Further E, a drying tombolo connects Trivett and Broughton Islands. Anchoring NE of the small island provides only about 10 feet (3 m) of water and this depth carries almost to the E end of the small peninsula. NW of the small island the depth is about 18 feet (6 m). Holding is good in thick mud and sand.

Shawl Bay 15

Tucked in a bight on the bay's SE shore, the Shawl Bay Marina is a popular stop for boaters, where overnight moorage includes a pancake breakfast. Brown family members, who have owned the marina for several decades, serve visitors breakfast on a large float sheltered by a pavilion roof. The general store is stocked with dry and canned goods, as well as freshly baked bread and cinnamon buns.

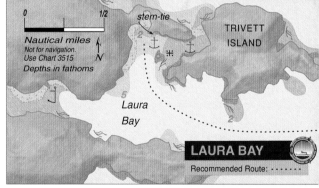

A narrow neck of water, with a minimum reported depth of about 2 feet, connects the north end of Shawl Bay with Moore Bay. With depths of about 10 feet (3 m) and little current, this passage can be piloted by most keel boats at mid-tide. Shoals extend partially into the pass at two locations from Gregory Island, and kelp thrives along the edges.

Just outside of Shawl Bay we have twice seen a humpback whale, which locals say has been visiting this area for some years.

Above, Thief Island anchorage in Moore Bay and, below, view of Kingcome Inlet from anchorage.

MOORE BAY AT A GLANCE:

CHARTS: 3515
LAT LONG: 50°52.80'N 126°34.12'W
PROS: Wide bay with lots of anchoring sites, good views to Kingcome Inlet, lots to explore by dinghy. Swimming in E side of bay or by gravel beach.
CONS: Quite deep in spots. E side of bay is open to west wind.
MUST DO: Swim near forest service dock. Visit Shawl Bay.

Moore Bay 16

Lying at the entrance to stunning Kingcome Inlet, this large bay offers several good anchorages and great views of the surrounding mountains and inlets. One of the most protected anchorages lies at the NE end of arrowhead-shaped **Gregory Island**, SW of Thief Island, where you can anchor in the crux of a bay in 35 feet (10 m). This is well sheltered from westerlies and only a persistent E wind will be a problem. The anchorage has a rocky bottom, however, and some anchors will have to be coaxed in before setting. We have found that once our CQR has dug in, the holding is quite good. There is a superb view of the entrance to Kingcome Inlet from this small bay. Thief Island, to the NE, is quite pretty with a granite shelf on its S side. Rock cod of decent size can be caught near Thief Rocks, about a half-mile north of the anchorage. At low water, there are numerous tidal pools along these reefs to explore.

Farther west along Gregory Island is another cove located behind a peninsular arm, which provides decent shelter from W winds but is open to the east.

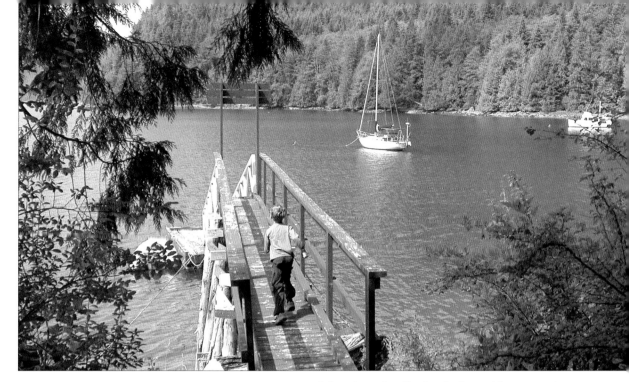

The head of the cove is shoal and the foreshore is low and uninviting.

Good shelter from easterlies can be found on the E side of Moore Bay where there are two spots to spend the night. The first, opposite the Thief Island anchorage, lies behind a small island in about 45 feet (14 m) of depth with a gravel-and-mud beach to the E. The other location, and more sheltered from E winds, is in the bay's NE corner where two BC Forest Service mooring buoys are located near a small dock. On shore is a stream, a few trails and a small campsite overlooking the anchorage. Sunsets are spectacular here and the swimming is very good in cool, clean water.

The two anchorages at the west entrance of Kingcome Inlet – **Reid Bay** and the narrower bay below it W of **Magin Islets** – are both exposed to E winds. In settled weather we've stayed overnight at the head of the smaller bay, anchoring in about 40 feet (13 m). This bay commands a beautiful up-inlet view of snow clinging to the rocky peaks of mainland mountains, but the steep sides of the anchorage are a little gloomy and nearby Moore Bay is a better overnight stop.

Kingcome Inlet

Kingcome Inlet is widely known for its fjord-like beauty and stunning vistas of snowcapped mountains. *I Heard The Owl Call My Name*, a famous novel by Margaret Craven, was set in remote Kingcome Village. The village, unconnected by road to the outside, is located about a mile up the Kingcome River at the head of the inlet and is the

A forest service dinghy dock provides access to shore in the northeast part of scenic Moore Bay.

GREGORY ISLAND

A fellow named Blondy Carlson once tended a garden on Gregory Island. He kept his floathouse tied in Shawl Bay where he had another garden at the head of the lagoon. Blondy, like many of the area's settlers, was a jack of all trades who worked a trapline at the head of Wakeman Sound. He was also a hand logger who, according to Bill Proctor in his book Full Moon, Flood Tide, had a habit of "borrowing" trees from land that wasn't part of his claim. In one instance, Blondy had just finished borrowing a large cedar off the bluff above Steep Point in Penphrase Passage when a Forest Service boat came along. When a tree slides down a steep slope into the water, it will often shoot clear back out of the water and land with an impressive splash. This is what Blondy's tree apparently did, prompting the forestry boat's crew to stop and wait for Blondy as he scrambled down the bluff so they could ask him what he was up to. When Blondy said he needed a firewood log, the forester responded that most people burn fir. Blondy, displaying the resourcefulness required in such a situation, told them he needed kindling.

ancestral village of the Tsawataineuk, "People with Eulachon". This long, silvery fish, also called oolichan, was valued as a food source and for its oil, which could be used as a condiment, preservative and medicine.

The distance is 17 miles from the mouth of Kingcome Inlet to its head, where **Anchorage Cove**

Above, the view looking east up Kingcome Inlet.
Below right, Stopford Bay, Cypress Harbour.

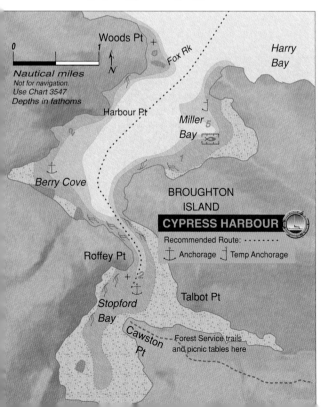

provides anchorage but no shelter from north and west winds. The river is navigable only by small craft, and if you wish to visit the native village, you may want to check with the Browns at Shawl Bay beforehand to find out if visitors are welcome.

Captain Vancouver's crew surveyed Kingcome Inlet by longboat in 1792, but it was named by Captain Pender in 1865 for Rear Admiral John Kingcome, who was commander in chief on this station. In 1895 the Halliday brothers settled along the river flats at the head of the inlet where they established one of British Columbia's most isolated cattle ranches, which stayed in the family until the 1990s. William Halliday also was an Indian agent for the federal government and played a controversial role implementing the official ban on potlatching which was enforced with zeal in the 1920s when several arrests were made.

In 1958 the Edmonton-born Anglican missionary Eric Powell moved to the native village in Kingcome Inlet, where his experiences formed the basis of Craven's bestselling novel. Powell moved away in 1961, serving as a minister in various coastal communities. He died in Victoria in 1997.

Cypress Harbour 17

Several anchorages lie within this harbour although **Miller Bay**, just inside the entrance, is currently occupied by what appears to be a derelict fish farm. Anchorage is also available south of Harbour Point in **Berry Cove**. This spot provides good protection from westerlies but not from east winds. Anchor in 25 feet (8 m) in soft mud. Aquaculture may be taking place in this part of the bay at times.

The best spot we've found for shelter is the inner anchorage of **Stopford Bay**, reached via a narrow

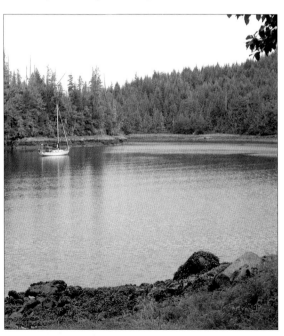

entrance with kelp on either side. This anchorage is a quiet place to spend a day or two but is shallow. Chart 3547 indicates a rock with 6 feet (2 m) or less of depth at LW is located about 100 yards south of Roffey Point. We've anchored southeast of this rock in 14 feet (4 m) with good holding in soft mud. If you arc anchoring during large tides, a line ashore might be a good idea to prevent the possiblity of swinging over the rock.

Inland of Cawston Point is an old logging camp which was considered an eyesore by John Chappell back in the 1970s but is now a pleasant campsite maintained by the BC Forest Service with picnic tables, fire pits and an old logging road which leads to a low marsh where cranberries grow. Good fishing is reported south of Moore Point into Harry Bay.

Great blue herons also like this anchorage. It's a beautiful sight to see these birds lifting on their huge wings high above the treetops, their primordial squawk echoing throughout the forested lands.

Greenway Sound 18 🚶

Most boaters pulling into Greenway Sound are heading to the marina in the bay east of Greenway Point. For large vessels especially, this is an excellent facility with its wide U-shaped docks and 30 amp power. Run for years by Thomas and Ann Taylor of LaConner, the Greenway Sound Resort has a licensed restaurant, store, showers and laundry.

In addition to the facilites at the marina, boaters are also drawn to the nearby BC Forest Service trail leading up to Broughton Lake and Beaver Dam Lake. The trail, which runs beside a creek, starts at a dinghy dock S of the resort at the base of Mount Ick. Hikers can take a turn-off to the right and climb to the viewpoint above Broughton Lake or continue walking farther alongside the lake to an old "corduroy" road made of logs, which leads to Beaver Dam Lake. The trail is about 2 miles each way.

For boaters wanting a quiet gunkhole, there are two good spots at the mouth of Greenway Sound near the SE shore. A fish farm lies at the entrance to Greenway Sound, between Walker Point and Cecil Islet, but this is unseen from the anchorages to the

Above, Cypress Harbour, showing Stopford Bay with Berry Cove in background. Below, a small nook inside the entrance of Greenway Sound.

Sullivan Bay is a good place to reprovision, take on fuel and soak up the ambiance.

south. The innermost anchorage is protected by a small, unnamed islet. The other anchorage is a bight immediately to the north, where a smooth cliff face of rock and shrubs form a grotto-like backdrop. We have been stern-tied in this spot, in about 25 feet (8 m) of depth, when a stiff W breeze was blowing and current was pouring out of Broughton Lagoon, yet the anchorage stayed calm. This anchorage also enjoys the warmth of a western exposure and becomes awash in evening sunlight.

Broughton Lagoon can be explored on foot along a trail leading from the S anchorage. The lagoon can also be explored by dinghy or small powerboat, but you should be very careful at the entrance to ensure you have arrived at slack, reported to be about 2 hours after Alert Bay. Wait at the E end of the small bay N of the lagoon entrance to ensure arrival at slack because the current here is in the 8- to 10-knot range. According to locals, there is anchorage at the extreme southwest side of the lagoon.

Sullivan Bay, 19
North Broughton Island

Sullivan Bay is a classic example of an upcoast resort. Historically located at an important cross-roads for the logging and fishing industries, today its position at the intersection of Wells Passage and Sutlej Channel makes it a good place to reprovision before setting out to new anchorages.

In 1945, the floating village at Claydon Bay was towed to Sullivan Bay, where the string of buildings included a store and post office servicing what was, until the mid-50s, the busiest floatplane base on the coast. Several of the original buildings remain as part of the Sullivan Bay Marine Resort, such as the "Town Hall" which contains a ping-pong table, board games and easy chairs.

This full-service marina has a well-stocked grocery and liquor store, fuel dock, showers, laundromat and licensed restaurant. A happy hour and other social events are held regularly. Many boaters use Sullivan Bay as a base for the area's renowned sport-fishing. Others simply enjoy the lovely setting while strolling the floats, chatting with fellow visitors or lounging in deck chairs.

Claydon Bay 20

This is a popular anchorage close to Sullivan Bay and especially useful if the marina is full for the night. Claydon Bay was an old Union Steamship stop and logging camp where several float camps, now long abandoned, once occupied the bay. In the early 1940s there were 19 families living here in floathouses, as well as dozens of single men living in bunkhouses. Remains of the logging roads and wharves are still visible in the north arm of the anchorage. Enter the anchorage along the SW shore and, if proceeding into the north arm, keep the islets to your starboard side. See Chart 3547.

The two arms of the bay provide decent shelter in most winds with very good holding in a mud bottom. The entire anchorage is susceptible to strong summer westerlies which gust over the surrounding low hills. SE winds also gust strongly into the main part of the bay. The N bay has the better sunsets and is a good spot for a quick swim off the boat – water temperatures in this bay are quite warm. Deer flies can be persistent and come in swarms – which seems to be the case throughout Mackenzie Sound.

The NE arm of Claydon Bay has the best sunsets. Holding is good throughout the anchorage.

Turnbull Cove 21

This roomy anchorage provides good shelter from all winds except strong southeasterlies. It was once busy with log booms and floathomes, and the last old-time logger to live here (from 1960 to 1985) was Owen Lane, who operated a logging camp at Huaskin Lake. The old steam donkey displayed on the Port McNeill waterfront was used by Lanc to pull logs out of Huaskin Lake. In July 2005, a fairly large slide pushed some debris to the shoreline on the north side of the cove W of the two small points. Boaters should be careful if anchoring here as the slope could still be unstable and the bottom foul with debris. The west side of the cove provides the best shelter and holding is good in thick mud. The SD cautions "SE gales circle the cove at full force."

A Forest Service trail leads from the NE side of the cove (there is a sign at the trailhead) over a high hill to Huaskin Lake, where there is a swimming float and a cleared area with picnic tables. The hike is about three-quarters of a mile and takes about 30 minutes. Large and scenic, Huaskin Lake stretches in numerous directions but visitors reaching the lake from Turnbull Cove are looking north up the E arm of the lake, which extends about 4 miles north to within 2 miles of Seymour Inlet. Part of the lake also splits off to the west where it travels over 7 miles and almost touches Actaeon Sound off Drury Inlet.

West of Turnbull Cove, beside Watson Point, is an abandoned sawmill operated from 1930 to 1965 by Charles and Ivy Kilbourne. North of Watson Point is a large bay with Embley Lagoon on the E side, an inviting lagoon to explore at HW. East of Turnbull Cove is the entrance to the 5-mile long Nepah Lagoon. This lagoon is reported to be quite pretty. We haven't ventured inside, but the entrance at Roaringhole Rapids looks like it lives up to its name. With a shoal depth of 3 feet (1 m) and a huge lagoon behind it, this would be a dangerous pass at anything other than HW slack. Chart 3547, however, shows excellent detail of the entrance with a detailed note on slack times for the pass – 2 hours after HW at Alert Bay for HW slack. The chart doesn't note the current, but it would no doubt be well above 7 knots. The only useable anchorage within the lagoon is in Yuki Bay along the northeast shore.

Turnbull Cove is serene and well sheltered. However slides, as shown above, happen.

TURNBULL COVE AT A GLANCE

CHARTS: 3547
LAT LONG: Entrance, 50°57.32'N 126°49.64'W
PROS: Remote, peaceful anchorage. Good hiking and fishing nearby.
CONS: Can become a wind bowl in S winds.
MUST DO: Hike to Huaskin Lake.

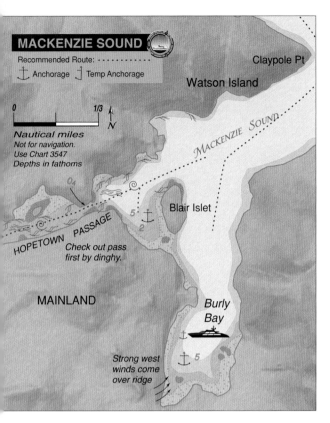

A boat waits for slack at Hopetown Passage, with Claypole Point and Mt. Stephens in background.

Mackenzie Sound 22

Mackenzie Sound, a watery chasm carved into the mountains, is best entered via **Kenneth Passage**. Captain Vancouver observed that "this channel is excessively dangerous, owing to the number of rocky islets, sunken rocks, and, by the tides setting through it with great rapidity and irregularity." Currents in Kenneth Passage are strongest opposite the island marked '70' and Jessie Point, and are perhaps 3 to 4 knots at large tides. Chart 3547 clearly shows all dangers. Wide languid whirlpools extend from this area well into **Steamboat Bay**, which is a pretty anchorage for a lunch stop but receives a bit too much current to our liking for an overnight stay. Proceeding through the pass, the safer route is N of the island marked '79' where the water stays deep.

There are few hazards in the deep waters of Mackenzie Sound, its entrance marked by the sheer cliffs of Claypole Point, but there are few good anchorages as well. Three miles east of Claypole Point is the entrance, encumbered with rocks, to **Nimmo Bay**. A scenic anchorage lies near the E end of Little Nimmo Bay with reported good holding. A fishing lodge is located on the bay's north shore.

At the head of Mackenzie Sound is a small anchorage, useable in calm weather, along the N shore. A creek leads to Mackenzie Lake from this anchorage, but keep in mind that grizzly bears are often sighted in this area.

Turning back to the west, **Burly Bay** has a dramatic granite hill on its E side and affords a great view to Claypole Point and the mountains beyond. However, with the steep hills on either side and a low foreshore in the middle, strong W and S winds would enter the bay easily. Blair Islet Bay, SW of Blair Islet, is better protected and also has a pretty view to Hopetown Passage. Some current from Hopetown Passage comes into this anchorage.

Hopetown Passage is a good shortcut for vessels wanting to get quickly from Mackenzie Sound to Sullivan Bay. While tracing the mainland shore northbound in the ship's boats, Captain Vancouver and his men transited this passage, noting afterward that it was admissable only for boats. The Sailing Directions further qualifies this pass as suitable only for shallow-draft boats at HW. It is quite shoal at the E end with a large drying rock covering all but the north side of the pass. Numerous vessels have struck this rock over the years and this is a pass a skipper should reconnoiter first at LW in a dinghy before taking the mother ship through. We transited this pass at an Alert Bay HW of 13.6 feet (4 m) and had about 8 feet (3 m) of water at the shallowest point. We made it through by favouring the Watson Island shore, and perhaps we were lucky. Currents can be swift here also, and are likely in the range of 4 knots. If using this pass, arrive at the very tail end of a flood to be safe.

Overlooking Hopetown Passage is Hoy Bay, where the Kwawwaineuk band still has a small settlement on the E side of the bay. A shell midden graces the foreshore and a totem pole stands in front of a house overlooking the beach. On a point of land due west of the settlement there is a tiny graveyard. The W side of the bay is often used as a log dump and sorting area.

Drury Inlet 23

Like nearly all the mainland inlets, Drury Inlet was surveyed by Captain Vancouver and his officers. Unlike the others, however, this inlet does not penetrate the mainland mountains but runs parallel to them. Its shores are low-lying rather than steep, their rock formations prompting gold prospectors to stake claims in this area. One fellow back in the 1920s claimed to have discovered oil in Sutherland Bay and, after moving a small rig into the bay, drilling a few test wells, and selling shares in his company, he promptly vanished with the shareholders' money.

Vancouver and his men proceeded through **Stuart Narrows** and traced the mainland shore for several miles before "landing to dine about the time of high water." They "soon perceived a rapid ebb tide coming from the west" and surmised that this was yet another inlet. Tidal currents in Stuart Narrows, at the entrance to Drury Inlet, can reach 7 knots on a ebb and 6 knots on a flood, but are generally weaker, attaining about 2 knots on a 6-foot (2 m) tide.

Captain Vancouver returned to his ships in Simoom Sound, leaving Second Lieutenant Puget and Master Whidbey to continue the survey of this

11-mile-long inlet. When they reached its head, they followed Actress Passage into Actaeon Sound, past overfalls and sunken rocks, before reaching the tidal rapids at the entrance to Tsibass Lagoon. Whidbey ascended the falls here at LW to find a small lake branching in various directions through a "low, swampy, woodland country."

Extensive logging has taken place in this area since Vancouver's survey, but Drury Inlet remains for the most part a sparsely inhabited inlet offering numerous anchorages, including well-sheltered **Richmond Bay** and **Jennis Bay** – where a marina provides access to miles of logging roads and trails leading to freshwater lakes. The best anchorages for exploring Actaeon Sound are two sheltered spots on either side of **Muirhead Islands** (one S, the other NW) or the shallower **Sutherland Bay**, further west. Although somewhat open to SE winds, this large bay has good holding in mud and nearby are trails along logging roads that lead inland. The logging roads are NW of the small westernmost part of the bay.

Davis Bay provides good shelter in a pretty setting.

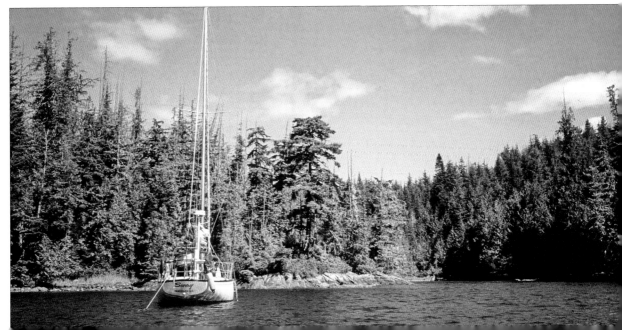

Our favorite anchorage in Drury Inlet is **Davis Bay**, a pretty anchorage offering good shelter and holding in about 24 feet (8 m) in thick mud. Entry is made S of Davis Islet, keeping close to the smaller islet off its SE side while entering the cove. Decent protection for large vessels is just west of Davis Islet in about 60 feet. Everard Islets offer some protection from W winds.

Tracey Harbour   ☐24

This long and well-protected inlet is a favourite with boaters wanting a base for a few days of fishing in Wells Passage. It is a bit of a drive (2 miles) from Wells Passage to the anchorage at **Napier Bay** but the steep hillsides knock down most winds from the strait. At the NE side of the bay, within the entrance to a small cove, the holding is good but the view of the logging operation on the S side of the bay is the trade off. The bay south of Carter Point is prettier and offers good protection from most wind but the bottom is poor with possibly a combination of ooze and rock or a thin layer of mud on rock.

Dickson Island   ☐25

An unattractive but very convenient anchorage lies on the NE side of Dickson Island, an uninhabited Indian Reserve. The shoreline surrounding this cove was extensively logged in the late 1980s and has grown back somewhat since to provide a better buffer from W winds. The topography of the island and nearby islands provide good protection from southeasterlies, but the anchorage is open to the NE) which is a rare wind in summer). Most boaters tie a stern line to the south shore since there is limited swinging room. We often go well into the anchorage and tie a stern line to the small island inside the cove, anchoring in about 20 feet (6 m) in soft mud.

We've stayed at this anchorage many times as a stopover before heading north to Blunden Harbour or Miles Inlet, and have found the protection good. A short dinghy ride away in Wells Passage off Bourmaster Point there is excellent fishing. In the

Above left, a minke whale feeds near Dickson Island while birds dive for the crumbs. Below, Dickson Island anchorage isn't pretty but it works.

Above, Tracey Harbour is secure in most winds.
Right, the anchorage at Dickson Island. Bottom,
conning the entrance to Carter Passage.

first half of the last century, the cove was used by floating logging camps as well as a fish-buying camp run by a man named Tommy Badger who bought salmon from the trollers working Wells Pass.

If you want to make this area a base for a few days, there are many other good anchorages nearby, including Tracey Harbour and, one of our favourites, Carter Passage. Also, there is a good anchorage on the N side of the entrance to **Carter Passage**, just below the steep hillside and E of the collection of reefs. Although the anchorage looks open to the west, winds from this direction are forced up the hill, leaving behind nascent gusts. In a SE wind, this spot is very well protected. Some current from Carter Passage wanders into this anchorage but, otherwise, this is a very quiet spot.

Carter Passage Anchorage 26

Over the years, this anchorage has remained a quiet retreat for boaters wanting to enjoy simple peace and quiet. Its remoteness has been helped by the fact the anchorage can only be accessed for a few minutes each day owing to the impressive tidal rapids at its west entrance.

The anchorage is **not** accessible from the east, except in a dinghy during a high tide of at least 10 feet at Alert Bay. The deeper part of this pass is along the N side but be aware there are numerous large boulders in this pass and that slack water is very short – often 15 minutes or less.

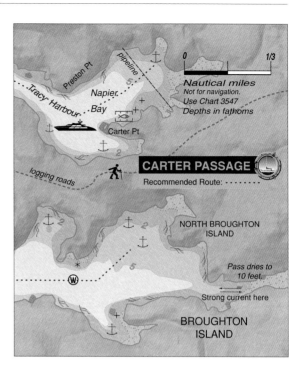

Above, good anchorage can be had in a bight on the north shore at the entrance to Carter Passage. Below, anchorage within the passage is sublime.

Transiting the western entrance of Carter Passage is not difficult at slack HW as the entrance is fairly straight and there are no major obstructions – the two rocks within the pass shown on the chart are well off to the S at the eastern end of the pass. Bull kelp thrives in large patches along the sides of the

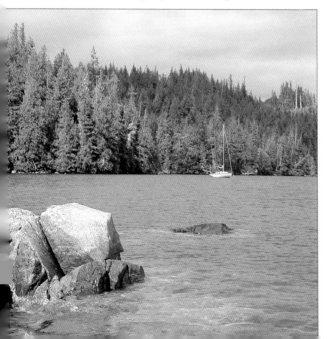

channel, leaving the middle clear. Minimum depth, as indicated on Chart 3547, is indeed 10 feet (3 m) and, since this is a narrow pass, transiting on a HW slack is the safest approach. Current in the pass is reported in the Sailing Directions at 7 knots, and it is all of that. High water slack is very close to Alert Bay HW, perhaps minus 10 or 15 minutes. Low water slack, however, is about one hour after Alert Bay LW. As you transit the pass, be sure to favour the N shore to avoid the aforementioned rocks.

Once you are east of the pass, any leftover current quickly dissipates and you can look ahead to the enjoyable prospect of not one but three excellent anchorages. The two bays along the N side have lots of room and good depth with a flat sticky mud bottom. We prefer the larger second bay as the small peninsula along its west shore deflects W wind coming into the bay. Anchoring depth in this bay is about 40 feet (13 m) and, as noted, holding is superb. There may be another boat or two around but because of the space you don't notice. This is the type of anchorage where solitude can be drunk in great gulps and the only sound breaking the silence is the occasional dignified rattle of a kingfisher.

CARTER PASSAGE AT A GLANCE
CHARTS: 3547
LAT LONG: Anchorage: 50°50.17'N 126°51.65'W
PROS: Serene, well protected and good holding. Remote and peaceful.
CONS: Entrance is through a set of rapids.
MUST DO: Hike logging trails; view E pass at LW.

Polkinghorne Islands 27 🏊 🛶

Boaters leaving Carter Passage or Dickson Island for Queen Charlotte Strait can follow the ethereal passage east of Dickson Island. On a sunny afternoon, threading your way among the numerous small islets is dreamlike. The view is of cat-tail moss hanging from silver snags and little bays with verdant grass crowding the shoreline. This passage has current coming from Carter Passage and during large tides it will exceed 2 knots. The pass can be maze-like, so it's important to verify your correct position throughout the transit. The deepest route is between islet '62' and '58'. Because of the rocks extending west of Drew Islet, we favor Percy Island before turning south.

Just beyond this beautiful collection of islands is another cluster at the Polkinghorne Islands. Named for a commander in the British navy, these islands merit a day of exploration by dinghy among the array of small islets and reefs. The bare rocks in the middle of the islets create striking scenes against the sky over Queen Charlotte Strait. Herons and seals abound throughout the islands. Although the water is cool, there are a couple of good spots to swim opposite the large lagoon in the middle of the biggest island. See Chart 3547.

We have anchored for lunch stops in the bay to the south, in depths of about 40 feet (13 m), and found the bottom to be rocky with only fair holding. The bay to the N may be better; we've seen larger vessels anchored and tied to shore there. Westerlies gust through the entire anchorage but are weaker than winds blowing out in the strait. The anchorage is quite exposed to SE winds.

Polkinghorne Islands are an excellent day stop with numerous islets to explore. Staying overnight is possible only in very settled conditions.

CHAPTER NINE

QUEEN CHARLOTTE STRAIT

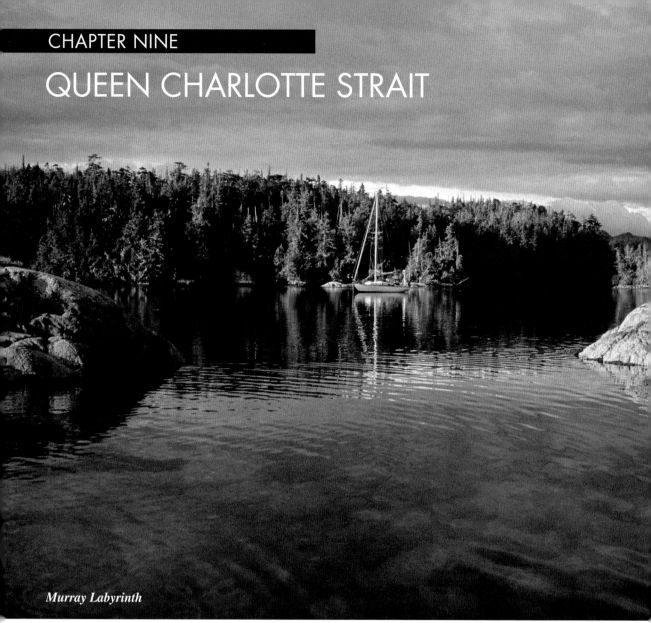

Murray Labyrinth

Between currents, wind and waves, the natural elements are always at play in Queen Charlotte Strait. Remnant ocean swells roll in from Queen Charlotte Sound and sweep onto exposed shorelines. This heavy swell is common in the northwest part of Queen Charlotte Strait, where it's open to the Pacific Ocean, and crossing the strait (about 14 miles wide) will give you a taste of open ocean cruising. Combined swell and wave heights in the strait can be over 12 feet (4 m) when a strong westerly is blowing against an ebbing tide. However in summer, this area can be suprisingly calm with seas no more than a gentle swell.

Tides and Currents

Tide differences in Queen Charlotte Strait are referenced on Alert Bay, with the flood stream setting ESE and the ebb WNW. Currents in adjacent waters of the strait can be surprisingly strong, with streams often 2 knots or more in the vicinity of island groups. In early summer, melting snow along the mainland shore tends to accentuate the ebb current on the northeast side of the strait while afternoon northwest winds can increase the strength of flood current along the Vancouver Island side of the 50-mile long strait.

The large passes, Nakwakto Rapids and Nahwitti Bar, are covered later in this chapter. Other channels and passes requiring vigilance include Bolivar Passage, which can experience up to 4 knots of current, especially at the south end near Alex Rock and Davey Rock. Browning and Christie Passages are also in the 3- to 4-knot range of current. The S end of Shelter Passage during a southeasterly will be turbulent, especially during a south-flowing flood. Ripple

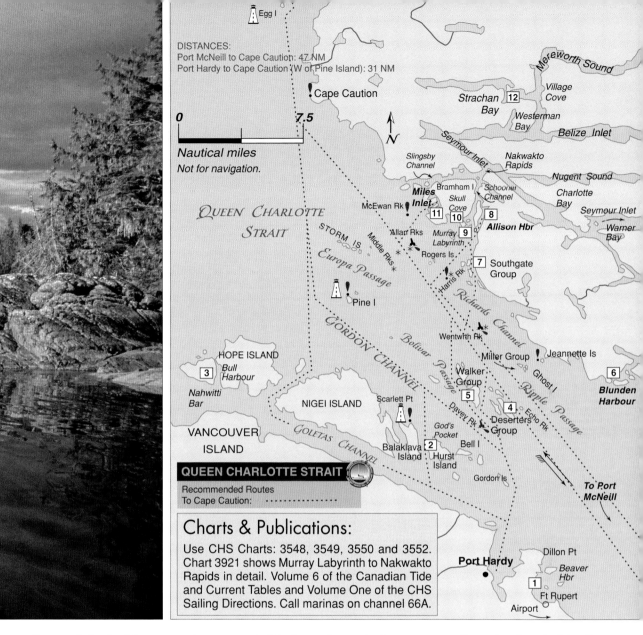

Egg I

Cape Caution

0   7.5

Nautical miles
Not for navigation.

QUEEN CHARLOTTE STRAIT

Strachan Bay 12 Village Cove

Merework Sound

Westerman Bay

Belize Inlet

Seymour Inlet

Slingsby Channel

Nakwakto Rapids

Nugent Sound

Bramham I Schooner Channel Charlotte Bay

Miles Inlet Skull Cove

McEwan Rk 11 10 8 Allison Hbr Seymour Inlet

Allan Rks Murray Labyrinth 9 Warner Bay

Rogers Is.

STORM IS

Middle Rks

Europa Passage

7 Southgate Group

Harris Rk

Richards Channel

Pine I

GORDON CHANNEL

Wentwrth Rk

Miller Group Jeannette Is

Bolivar Passage

Walker Group

Ghost I

Ripple Passage

6

Blunden Harbour

HOPE ISLAND

Bull Harbour 3

Nahwitti Bar

NIGEI ISLAND

Scarlett Pt

Davey Rk

5

Echo Rk

4 Deserters Group

God's Pocket

VANCOUVER ISLAND

GOLETAS CHANNEL

Balaklava Island 2 Bell I

Hurst Island

Gordon Is

To Port McNeill

QUEEN CHARLOTTE STRAIT

Recommended Routes
To Cape Caution: ·············

Dillon Pt

Beaver Hbr

Port Hardy

1

Ft Rupert

Airport

Passage is in the 2-knot range but current is felt for some distance on either side of the Walker and Deserters Groups of islands.

Pine Island

Pine Island stands like a lonely sentinel at the strait's western entrance, where it bears the full brunt of Queen Charlotte Sound's winter storms. Until 1907, when a lighthouse was built here, Pine Island's only visitors were the seabirds who nest here, including the rhinoceros auklet. This nocturnal seabird tends to make awkward landings when flying back from sea after dark, sometimes running into a tree and landing with thud on the ground – which is where this species burrows to make a nest.

The early lighthouse keepers stationed on Pine Island had to endure long winters of isolation, listen-ing to the incessant pounding of surf on the island's rocky foreshore. Sometimes they were marooned for days on end when the seas were too rough for a boat to land safely. Then, in the winter of 1967, on a black February night, hurricane-force winds drove a 50-foot wave onto Pine Island.

This rogue wave demolished outbuildings and washed away fuel tanks, surging right up to the front steps of the lightkeepers' house. Mr. and Mrs. Brown, their two daughters and the assistant light-keeper all scrambled to higher ground where they huddled around a campfire for the rest of the night. Afterwards, demoralized by the wreckage to which their years of hard work had been reduced in a mat-ter of seconds, the Browns left for another posting and the Pine Island light station was rebuilt to stron-ger standards on higher ground.

Above, Pine Island lighthouse. Below, seas can build quickly in Queen Charlotte Strait.

Wind and Fog

On early summer mornings, Queen Charlotte Strait can be surprisingly calm. By late morning, a sea breeze typically develops and, combined with the prevailing summer northwesterly, often produces a heavy swell at the strait's W entrance. These winds regularly increase to 20 or 30 knots before dying out by evening, to be replaced by a weaker land breeze. Northwesterlies are stronger on the W side of the strait (the area around Port Hardy always seems to be blowing over 20 knots).

Pilotage can be a challenge in the shoal-infested waters of Queen Charlotte Strait, especially in late summer when sea fog is a frequent hazard. August is the worst month for fog in Queen Charlotte Strait, and Captain Vancouver noted in his journals that "since the commencement of the month of August (1792), the foggy weather had totally precluded our making any celestial observations." Shoals and drying rocks are especially numerous on the north side of Queen Charlotte Strait, and when Captain Vancouver's two ships were sailing northbound in these waters, the mainland was unshrouded but the islands ahead were obscured by a thick fog. They were transiting Richards Channel, between the Millar Group and the mainland, when *Discovery* "suddenly grounded on a bed of sunken rocks."

A signal was immediately sent to the *Chatham*, under the command of Lieut. Broughton, and her crew promptly dropped anchor and launched their boats to assist the *Discovery*. Her port bow was hard on the rocks while her stern remained afloat. The crew carried out a stream anchor to heave the ship off, but the tide was falling rapidly, causing the ship to swing forward. Drinking water was drained overboard and wood fuel tossed in an attempt to lighten the ship's ballast. Meanwhile, the local natives paddled out in canoes to take a closer look at the stricken vessel. The ship was heeled "very considerably" on its starboard side and, as the tide ebbed, the crew removed upper spars to shore the ship. At low water, the starboard main chains came within 3 inches of the water's surface but, fortunately, the seas were calm and the ship refloated at two o'clock in the morning. Today, a light on the southern Jeannette Island marks the channel's north side, which should be favoured to avoid the drying reefs that lie opposite, off Ghost Island. Tidal currents can reach 3 knots in Richards Channel and heavy overfalls develop if there's a strong wind against tide.

Vancouver's initial survey of these waters was continued in the 1800s by the Royal Navy. After gold was discovered on the Yukon's Klondike River in 1896, steamship traffic along the Inside Passage increased dramatically as prospectors rushed north. Lighthouses were built at strategic points along the main route, including Scarlett Point (1905) and Pulteney Point (1907). The steamships of a century ago have given way to cruise liners that service the Vancouver-Alaska run, following the main route of Gordon Channel.

Port Hardy

A major service centre for pleasure boaters, Port Hardy is also the terminus for BC Ferries, which provides service to Prince Rupert and some of the smaller communties along the Central and North Coast.

The town's public **Seagate Wharf** has a T-shaped float attached on the north side during summer months and accommodates about half a dozen vessels. This wharf extends from the foot of Granville Street in the heart of town and is a good place to tie up for a few hours to reprovision. If the public dock is full, there are four mooring buoys nearby for recreational craft. Although west winds seem to die just outside of the wharf area, it is open to swell from Hardy Bay.

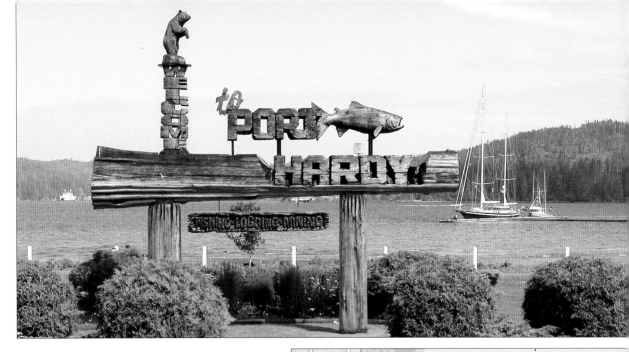

Above, Port Hardy's waterfront park and public wharf. Below, aerial view, looking north.

A better place to tie up overnight is at the **Quarterdeck Marina**, located due south of the town centre near the head of Hardy Bay (see map). Services at the Quarterdeck Marina include power, water, showers, a laundromat, wine and beer store, and a pub-style restaurant. The marina also has a haulout and well-stocked marine store. An airport is located 5 miles (8 km) away, and taxis are available. The public commercial docks to the north can also accommodate visiting boats, but you may have to raft with another vessel.

The town is named in honour of Sir Thomas Hardy who was right-hand man to Lord Horatio Nelson, Britain's greatest naval hero. No naval battles have been staged in the waters off Port Hardy but Britain's Hudson's Bay Company did establish Fort Rupert at nearby Beaver Harbour in 1849 after coal was discovered there.

Permanent settlement of Port Hardy didn't begin until the turn of the last century when it grew slowly along with the local industries of fishing, logging and mining. Today, the population of Port Hardy is about 5,000. Visitors to Port Hardy can enjoy a stroll past Fisherman's Wharf and along Market Street with its selection of shops. The local museum features an exhibit on the excavation site at nearby Bear Cove, which was first occupied more than 8,000 years ago and is the location of the BC Ferries terminal for Port Hardy. The museum also has a video of Edward Curtis's epic film *Land of the War Canoe*, which premiered in New York in 1914.

THE ANCHORAGES

Beaver Harbour [1]

This historic harbour, just around the corner from Port Hardy, provides a good haven for boaters looking to escape a tough westerly. The harbour is ringed with small islands and offers several anchorages that are sheltered from most winds. Strong W winds diminish in the lee of Round Island and easy entry can be made south of Deer Island.

Good anchorages include the SW lee of Cattle Islands, south of the fish farm. Anchor here in 15 to 30 feet (5 to 10 m) in mud. There is a small but nice bight on the S shore of Peel Island which provides very good holding and protection from W winds but is open to south winds. A few hundred yards to the west is Patrician Cove, good also in west winds but open to the south. Basket Eaters' Cove, half a mile to the north, provides good shelter in all winds but from the northeast.

The Spanish explorers Valdes and Galiano anchored their ships *Sutil* and *Mexicana* off Thomas Point in August 1792. They spent a windy, rainy night at this location, taking water over the bow as their schooners pitched in high seas. Next morning the wind eased and, finding their cables damaged, they weighed anchor and left. Had they been able to sail their vessels into the harbour, they would have enjoyed a quieter night at anchor.

Fort Rupert, built by the Hudson's Bay Company in 1849, once stood on Beaver Harbour's south shore, its construction overseen by Captain William McNeill, commander of the HBC steamship *Beaver*. The fort was built to protect the company's coal mining interests in the area after coal was discovered along the beach at the mouth of Suquash Creek, near the western entrance to Broughton Strait. About 10,000 tons of coal were shipped out of Beaver Harbour. The coal was transported in canoes to Beaver Harbour by the local natives, who had abandoned their main villages along the Cluxewe River to establish a new village beside Fort Rupert.

Map

BEAVER HARBOUR

Recommended Route: ----------

Basket Eaters' Cove

Daedalus Passage

Peel Island

Patrician Cove

Twin Rks

Round I

Cattle Islands

Deer Island

Cormorant Rk

Eagle I

Shell I

Tex Lyon Trail

Start at boat ramp

Thomas Pt

0   3/4

N

Nautical miles
Not for navigation.
Use Chart 3548
Depths in fathoms

BEAVER HARBOUR AT A GLANCE:

CHARTS: 3548
LAT LONG: 50°42.76'N 127°24.66'W
PROS: Shelter can be found from most winds. Good haven from westerlies. Usually quiet with good beaches and hikes nearby.
CONS: Aquaculture SW of Cattle Islands.
MUST DO: Walk a leg of the Tex Lyon Trail.

Aerial view of Beaver Harbour showing lee provided by Peel Island during NW winds.

When the HBC abandoned Fort Rupert in 1882, its factor, Scottish-born Robert Hunt, stayed to run the company store with his wife Mary Ebbetts, a Tlingit noblewoman from Alaska. They had 11 children and it's said that most of the area's longtime residents are related to the Hunts. The artist Henry Hunt was born at Fort Rupert in 1923, and worked as a logger and fisherman before apprenticing with his father-in-law Mungo Martin at the Royal British Columbia Museum in Victoria. Hunt eventually succeeded his father-in-law as chief carver. His sons Tony and Richard, born in Alert Bay, also became leading artists. Henry Hunt died in Victoria in 1985.

Little remains of the old fort in Beaver Harbour. More enduring are the petroglyphs carved on the sandstone foreshore. Across the water is Deer Island, where Edward Curtis filmed *Land of the War Canoe* (originally called *In the Land of the Head Hunters*). A self-taught photographer from Seattle, Curtis devoted his life to photographing and filming the aboriginal people of North America.

The 4.5-mile (7-km) **Tex Lyon Trail** traces the shoreline from the boat launch at the SW corner of Beaver Harbour to Dillon Point. The trail starts out easily with a 20-minute hike from the boat launch to the rock bluff opposite Cattle Island, then becomes a more challenging 4-hour hike from the bluff to Dillon Point. Allow 8 hours for the entire round-trip hike, and wear proper attire and footwear.

God's Pocket Marine Park 2

Situated at the south entrance to Goletas Channel, this marine park encompasses Hurst Island, Bell Island and numerous smaller islands and islets. God's Pocket is a local name for the small cove on Hurst Island's W side. This spot provides good shelter and has long been a favoured anchorage for recreational boaters heading north. A small resort here provides overnight moorage, showers, and laundry facilities. Harlequin Bay, on the east side of Hurst Island, is protected from S and W winds.

The small channel between **Bell Island** and Heard Island provides some shelter as an anchorage, with a view of cruise ships in Gordon Channel, but a fish farm takes up most of the west side. The cove formed by two islets off Bell's south shore is protected from swell and S wind but west winds whistle through the cove with surprising strength.

Goletas Channel extends for 23 miles between Vancouver Island and a chain of islands through which several navigable channels lead to Gordon Channel. Northwest and SE winds funnel up and down Goletas Channel, causing local winds along the island points to accelerate with force.

Below, God's Pocket is a haven from all winds.

Bottom, aerial view of God's Pocket, looking SE.

Bull Harbour [3]

Lying off the NE tip of Vancouver Island, Hope Island is a jumping-off point for boaters heading around the top of Vancouver Island to cruise its west coast. Bull Harbour, entered off Goletas Channel, provides protected anchorage at the N end of Hope Island. The harbour was called Ga'ya by the Nahwitty people who had a village-fortress on the rocks at Cape Sutil. In more recent times, a Canadian Coast Guard station was located in Bull Harbour but it was closed in the early 1990s.

While anchored in Bull Harbour, take the opportunity to hike the road leading from the old government dock to the abandoned Coast Guard Station at Roller Bay. At Roller Bay you can stand on the exposed edge of Hope Island and watch the waves crash onto the shore. The beach consists of pebbles

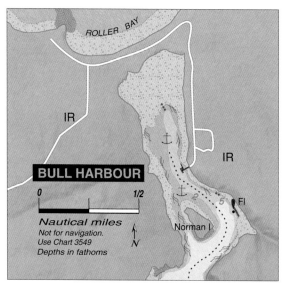

the size of cannonballs. Logs, bleached white by sun and saltwater, have been tossed onto shore where they lie in disarray. The vista is an unobstructed view of Queen Charlotte Sound, where swells roll relentlessly across Cook Bank and release their energy onto shore. It's an exhilarating experience to view such a sight.

Nahwitti Bar

Located at the W end of Hope Island and extending across the entrance of Goletas Channel, this bar is known for its steep waves when an ebbing current is against strong west winds or big ocean swells. When these incessant swells, coming from depths of 30 fathoms, roll into the channel, where the depths off Mexicana Point are 6 to 7 fathoms, the change in depth can result in breaking waves. The bar can be especially dangerous in late afternoon during an ebb if a westerly and large swells are in play.

However, Nahwitti Bar can be traversed safely with a bit of planning. Prudent boaters should try to cross the bar in the early morning, before wind and swell have had a chance to build. This tactic may be preferable to waiting for slack in late morning or afternoon, as the leftover waves may continue breaking for some time. The route to the south, over the Tatnall Reefs close to Vancouver Island, is sometimes used by vessels to avoid the Nahwitti Bar; however, skippers should be very cautious using this passage. This entire stretch of coast becomes a lee shore when a late-morning westerly builds, as is common in summer.

Roller Bay earns it name with a thunderous surf that's constantly moving debris on the beach.

Deserters Group 4

The Deserters Group contains a sheltered, storm-proof anchorage – often used by local boaters – situated near the south end of Wishart Island with Deserters Island as its NE shore. Easiest entry is from the south, favouring the Deserters Island shoreline to avoid a set of drying rock ledges off Wishart Island that are located at the point where the entrance channel opens up to the anchorage. A person at the bow would be a good idea if this is your first visit to the anchorage. Once inside, we usually anchor closer to the Deserters Island shoreline where minimum depth is shown on charts to be about 10 feet (3 m). With openings at either end of the cove, the current (up to about 2 knots) flowing through the anchorage will keep your boat lying parallel to the east shore. The other spot to anchor in this tight cove, which is actually a passage between the two islands, lies closer to Wishart Island and the south entrance, being careful to avoid the shoal water. Holding is very good in firm mud. Although muted gusts may make their way into this cove, the shelter from all winds is otherwise excellent.

There is much to explore by dinghy in this small archipelago, including the fascinating and narrow, twisting passage that leads north from the anchorage, along which a couple of derelict fishboats sit beached on a small midden. At HW, vessels drawing

Above and below, the sheltered Deserters Group anchorage provides good holding.

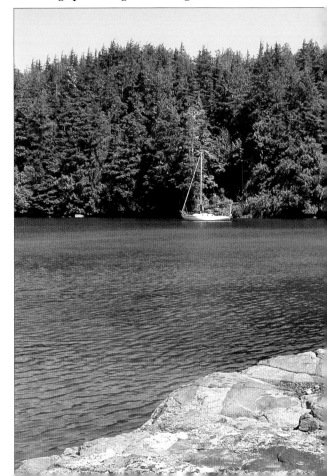

DESERTERS / WALKER GROUPS AT A GLANCE

CHARTS: 3549
LAT LONG: Dsrtr Grp: 50°52.09'N 127°28.18'W
PROS: Two beautiful archipelagos side by side with dozens of islets. Fair to good shelter from most winds, fair to good holding ground. Lots to explore, fishing nearby. A cruiser's paradise.
CONS: Reefs and currents throughout. Lots of kelp. Challenging piloting to access some areas.
MUST DO: Fish off Castle Point, hop in the dinghy for a tour through Deserters Pass.

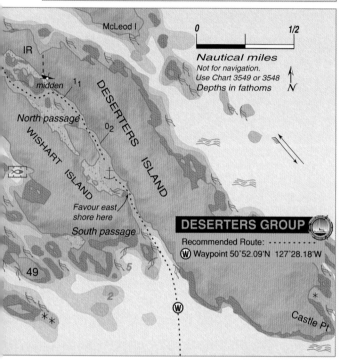

6 feet or less can use the north channel to access or leave this anchorage. This must be carefully done and the pass should be toured at LW in a dinghy if deciding to take your boat through. (See map.) It's a fascinating little pass with lots to see. The salmon fishing is good off Castle Point.

'Shelter Anchorage', Walker Group 5

Situated about 25 miles N of Pulteney Point, this small but intriguing archipelago contains a useable anchorage in the channel between Kent and Staples Islands, known locally as Shelter Anchorage. Chart 3549 provides good detail of the few hazards in the immediate vicinity and the anchorage can be gained with either an E or W approach. The best spot offering protected shelter is on the north side of the channel, just south of the small islet (where a commercial buoy is moored). We usually tie our stern off to the islet with our bow set in a SW direction, then pull ourselves as close to the islet as possible to get out of the NW winds which gust through the anchorage. South winds are muted by Staples Island. The holding, in about 15 to 25 feet (5 to 8 m), is just fair in soft mud and stone with kelp patches throughout. We've seen 40-foot powerboats (using Bruce and CQR anchors) repeatedly re-anchor during persistent 20-knot gusts, each time hauling up large clumps of kelp, but eventually

Below, the north passage out of the Deserters Group anchorage is a pretty channel.

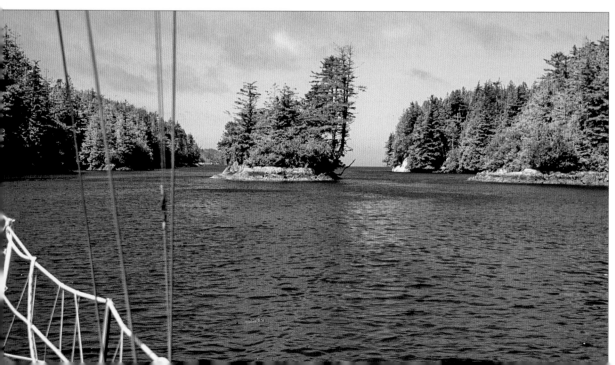

getting their anchors to hold. If there's no room at the islet to stern-tie, the west shore of Kent Island offers shelter from W winds. Bull kelp thrives throughout the anchorage's entrances, which have currents up to 2 knots.

One July morning we arrived at this anchorage from Bolivar Passage in dripping fog with a building SE wind. To our surprise, after we entered from the mist outside, the anchorage was sunny, empty and quite sheltered. With dozens of small islands in the area and two lagoons, there is plenty to explore by dinghy. A beautiful fine sand beach lies between the islands marked '80' and '56' on Chart 3549. This beach, which reveals itself at mid-LW, is entirely surrounded by small islets and is sheltered from most wind and swell. The bay in front (east) of the

Top, aerial view of Kent Island lagoon. Right, beautiful beach at east end of lagoon. Below, aerial view of Shelter Anchorage, looking north.

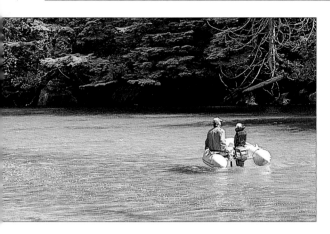

Above, exploring the Kent Island lagoon. Below,
Pacific Grace anchored in Blunden Harbour.
Bottom, aerial of harbour's inner anchorage.

beach is too shallow for most boats to anchor. The lagoon between Shelter Anchorage and the beach is beautiful for exploring and can be safely navigated at a half-tide or better. Less than this, it dries in parts, making passage by dinghy difficult.

You can explore the east sides of Kent and Staples Islands and discover a number of small islets and sand beaches. Be careful in a dinghy if a wind is blowing though, as there can be quite a chop along the outside of the islands.

Blunden Harbour 6

This historic harbour is large and sheltered, with an impressive selection of small islets and passes you can explore by dinghy. The key to finding the harbour's entrance, which lies between Shelf Head and Edgell Point, is to identify Siwiti Rock (named for the hereditary chief of the Nakwakto tribe), which has less than 6 feet (2 m) of water over it and is usually marked by kelp and a breaking swell. Barren Rock, further E, also stands out and helps in navigation. Burgess Island melds too completely into Robinson Island to be of much help when approaching from the south.

Once you are between Edgell and Robinson Islands, sheltered anchorage (especially from W winds) can be obtained in a bight immediately E of Bartlett Point (with a line ashore) or by proceeding to the inner harbour where secure anchorage can be found almost anywhere in depths between 12 feet (3.7 m) and 20 feet (6 m) over a thick mud bottom. Entrance to the inner anchorage is restricted by a drying reef and rock that lie south of the Augustine Islands and by another drying reef off Bartlett Point, but with Chart 3548 pilotage is straightforward.

The inner anchorage is expansive, with several areas to anchor. Westerly winds often penetrate the harbour and a good spot out of the breeze is just inside the narrow opening between Robinson Island and the mainland shore, with a stern line to the W shore. The anchorages just east of Grave Islet and Byrnes Island are also prized for providing protection during westerlies. Wherever you anchor, the inner part of Blunden Harbour is one of the more secure anchorages in Queen Charlotte Strait with very good holding in thick mud and lots of room to let out scope.

Many boaters like to spend days anchored here because there is so much to see and explore. This is an anchorage where you can almost get lost in the maze of islets lying east of Augustine Islands in the passage leading to beautiful Bradley Lagoon. The current can be quite strong (at least 4 to 5 knots during big tides) at the shallow neck entering the lagoon, but the passage is quite safe if transited within an hour of HW slack. The lagoon itself is huge and uncharted, which makes for an exciting day of exploration by dinghy.

The other main attraction at Blunden Harbour is the shell midden marking the former site of a Kwakiutl village that once stood on the N shore, behind the Augustine Islands. This village was depicted in a famous 1930 painting by Emily Carr entitled *Blunden Harbour*. It depicts a boardwalk backed by plank houses and graced with welcoming figures overlooking a tide-covered beach. The several hundred inhabitants of the village, seeking better access to halibut and deep-sea fishing, had moved to Blunden Harbour in the mid-19th century from various villages around Smith and Seymour Inlets.

In 1918, a sawmill and steamship landing called Port Progress were established near the harbour entrance. Abandoned in the early 1930s, the settlement's store and post office were derelict by the time Muriel Wylie Blanchet, author of *The Curve of Time*, pulled into Blunden Harbour one summer in the 1940s and tied to a half-sunken float near the entrance.

The native village, on the north side of the habour, also appeared unoccupied with its main buildings under lock and key. In front of the village there stood a "beautifully spiralled

BLUNDEN HARBOUR AT A GLANCE:

CHARTS: 3548 (has excellent 1:15 000 scale inset)
LAT LONG: Entrance 50°53.87'N 127°16.23'W
PROS: An important and historic location for First Nations people. Fair to good protection from most wind. Excellent holding throughout most of harbour. Lots of channels and islets to investigate by dinghy.
CONS: Westerlies can blow like stink in main anchorage.
MUST DO: Walk beautiful midden at north end of anchorage. Explore Bradley Lagoon.

Below, the midden in Blunden Harbour.

totem pole, on top of which sat a comfortable-look-ing carved eagle with outstretched wings" overlook-ing the white shell beach. Steps led to the village platform where two communal houses, supported by carved interior houseposts, were padlocked. Blanchet and her children entered one of the long houses "by the two loose boards, round at the side, that are always left for departing spirits."

Today, few traces remain of the original village, its residents eventually relocating in the 1960s to the Tsulquate reserve at Port Hardy. Some fallen posts protrude from the grassy bank above the shell mid-den, but the scene depicted by Emily Carr is no more. Time and nature have reclaimed her canvas.

Southgate Group 7

This group of islands has long been used by south-bound tugs waiting for settled weather after depart-ing Seymour Inlet with a log boom. Small vessels will find sheltered anchorage between the mainland and either Southgate or Knight Islands. Both the north channel or the pass between Southgate Island and Knight Island are well protected and safe to nav-igate. The south channel between Tinson Islands and Arm Islands has a few obstacles and is a bit more challenging. Depending on the direction of the wind, shelter can be found E of Knight island in 24 feet (7.6 m) or east of Southgate Island in about 40 feet (12.8 m). We have anchored east of Knight Island in mud and sand, and found the holding very good.

Allison Harbour 8

Numerous bights along the east shore of Allison Harbour provide good anchorage, as does the head, with a mud bottom. A former port of call for the Union Steamships, this harbour – named after Allison Logging Co. – was once a supply centre for nearby logging camps and the site of a sawmill.

In foggy conditions the entrance to Allison Harbour is much easier to negotiate than the one into nearby Murray Labyrinth. From Harris Island (easy

Top, motoring along the passage into Bradley Lagoon. Above, the passage leading to Southgate Group anchorage. Below, spacious anchorage at the head of Allison Harbour.

to identify with its tall white mast) stay to a course keeping the Southgate Group island marked '56' on Chart 3921 (and 3550) close to starboard and aim for Eno Island and City Point. From this point, passage into the harbour is clear of hazards.

In thick fog we keep the harbour's E shoreline within sight if we are headed to the first bight about half a mile from the entrance. This anchorage, a small bay S of an islet, used to be a landing site for logs towed out of Seymour Inlet, and cables once used for binding booms can still be seen rusting on shore. West winds die out near the entrance to the harbour, making this spot secure in most winds. However if you are venturing further into the harbour, stay closer to the west shore as a nasty reef shown on chart 3921 juts into the fairway.

Another islet further N also has good shelter in about 24 feet (7.3 metres) while the main anchorage near the head of the harbour provides ample room for several boats. West winds are stronger on the east side but the holding is good, as it is throughout the harbour. The lagoon to the NE of the head makes for an inviting day of dinghy exploring.

In 2008, a swath of waterfront property in Allison Harbour became parkland after it was purchased with funds raised by The Land Conservancy of B.C., B.C. Marine Parks Forever and the British Columbia government. This wilderness property had been purchased back in 1981 by an international group of environmentalists who sold it at below market value. Located mid-way along the east side of the harbour, it contains three pocket beaches and two creeks.

Murray Labyrinth

Located 12 miles south of Cape Caution, Murray Labyrinth is a pristine anchorage and a rewarding destination for mariners who have learned to navigate intricate shorelines. This particular cove is encircled by islets, rocks and reefs, but safe entry is possible from two directions. The preferred entrance is from the SW, shown clearly on Chart 3921 with detail of the dog-leg entrance channel that cuts between the islets. The other more daunting entrance from the north has ample depth in a narrow channel but is best reconnoitered by dinghy at LW first.

The entrance from the south follows a 9-foot LW (2.7 m) trench clear of kelp in a NE direction to two islands where the first 45-degree turn to port is made. The S island marked '34' has a reef close to its N side which has lots of kelp over it and juts out slightly into the channel. Once past this reef, make another 45-degree turn to port and follow the clear water past a treed islet and a bare islet on the starboard side. Once past these, make a 90 degree turn into the cove.

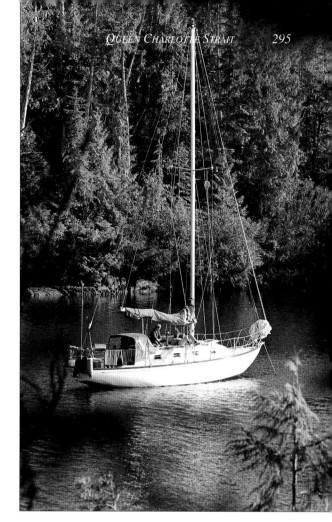

Anchored in small cove on east side of Allison Harbour. Most of the harbour is well sheltered.

MURRAY LABYRINTH AT A GLANCE:

CHARTS: 3921, 3550
LAT LONG: 51°02.56'N 127°32.5'W
PROS: Pristine. Peaceful. Far from the madding crowd feel. A week here goes by all too fast.
MUST DO: Explore the islets, stare at the beauty.

Once inside, the best spot to anchor is on the SE side in about 12 to 18 feet of water, well away from a rock that lies in the middle of the anchorage. The entire cove is quite sheltered, with only the odd northwesterly gust disturbing the serenity of the islands. We have been anchored here when Egg Island was reporting a SE gale and all that ever moved within Murray Labyrinth were the tree tops. Holding is very good in sticky mud and sand. There is little current running through the anchorage or the entrance channels.

This has been a favourite anchorage of ours for many years and we linger here for as long as possible. The anchorages immediately south of Cape Caution are often quiet as most boaters are focused on getting around the cape and often overlook these beautiful islands at the entrance to Seymour Inlet.

It is also a utopia for those who enjoy puttering about in the dinghy, with miles of shoreline, numerous little passages and dozens of islets to explore. Beyond Murray Labyrinth to the west, lie the Deloraine Islands with their tiny coves and rocky islets upon which grow an assortment of ferns and mosses and where bonaparte gulls carve out pieces of blue sky. In the other direction you can explore Allison Harbour and Schooner Channel right to the entrance of the feared Nakwakto Rapids. Local wildlife we have noted in our log in this area include killer whales (actually seen a little further north around the corner from Skull Cove), seals, kingfishers, red-throated loons and various sea ducks.

Skull Cove, Bramham I [10]

The only part of this anchorage which seems to be out of the wind is the SW corner near the spot marked 4.3 m on Chart 3921. Locals and fishboats can often be seen on this side of the anchorage, which also has a great view out to the strait. The north part of Skull Cove, just northwest of the two islets in the middle of the cove, really seems to get the wind – especially when it's out of the south. Although we have found the holding

Above, aerial view of Murray Labyrinth looking east. Left, Murray Labyrinth anchorage.

to be fairly good, gusts throughout this part of the anchorage may cause a sleepless night. In settled weather, though, this is an intriguing cove in which to spend a few days exploring. The inner bay, east of the three islets, is quite pretty but has only enough depth for small, shoal-draft vessels.

Miles Inlet, Bramham I 11

Located 10 miles south of Cape Caution on the north side of Queen Charlotte Strait, T-shaped Miles Inlet offers superb protection from angry winds and seas. The inlet has a straightforward approach, making it an ideal haven if sea fog has started rolling in from Queen Charlotte Sound.

Pale-colored McEwan Rock lies about one mile west of the entrance to Miles Inlet and is marked with a light. The entrance channel, between Bramham Point and McEwan Point, is long, straight and free of hazards, narrowing to 150 feet before reaching the head where the inlet branches into two arms. You can anchor at this junction with a clear view down the entrance channel to Queen Charlotte Strait. Neither westerlies nor southeasterlies seem to make much impact on the anchorage. We have also anchored in the NW arm, in about 25 feet (8 m) of water, its far end bounded by a lagoon with swift currents at its bottleneck entrance. The lagoon beyond with numerous islets and birdlife, makes for an interesting day of exploring by dinghy.

Our favourite spot to drop the hook is in the south arm opposite the entrance to another lagoon. There will be about 6-7 feet (2 m) at LLW in this part of the anchorage with good holding in soft mud. This is a nice area to row about in the din-

Above, anchored in the south arm of Miles Inlet.
Below, the narrow entrance channel into Miles Inlet .

North Lagoon

0   1/4

Nautical miles
Not for navigation.
Use Chart 3550
Depths in fathoms

McEwan Pt

rapids
5 knots

6 foot min
pool

rapids

Bramham Island   South Lagoon

MILES INLET
Recommended Route: ·······
⚓ Anchorage Temp Anchorage

McEwan Rock, near entrance to Miles Inlet

MILES INLET AT A GLANCE:

CHARTS: 3550
LAT LONG: 51°03.60'N 127°36.26'W
PROS: Storm-proof anchorage with lots to explore in area. Convenient haven near Cape Caution.
CONS: A little tight if busy, which is rare.
MUST DO: Explore lagoons at either end of main anchorage. Go for a swim near the south lagoon.

ghy or for swimming – there is an area, almost like a pool, in front of a small reversing falls leading to the lagoon. Yet another lagoon, leading south from the pool area, is accessible by foot at mid-tide.

Nakwakto Rapids

Seymour and Belize Inlets form an almost-land-locked, 85-mile-long basin of water joined to Queen Charlotte Strait by one confined opening called Nakwakto Rapids – one of the world's fastest tidal rapids. Less than a sixth of a mile wide, this dramatic bottleneck creates currents that are extremely turbulent and unpredictable when squeezed through its small, twisting and shallow opening. The flow through the pass, which attains 16 knots on an ebb, is complicated by many factors – water forced to turn more than 130 degrees, obstacles such as Turret Rock, and extremely steep shelving at both the west and east entrances. Use Chart 3921 for the rapids.

An ebb current from the eastern inlets is travelling along a 250-foot trench when it hits a shoaling wall at the pass with depths of only 50 feet off Johnson and Harvell Points. A similar wall exists just off Kitching Point and Butress Island where shoal water creates a venturi effect in the flow. Tremendous turbulence is generated by these dra-

matic changes along the bottom, resulting in large whirlpools and upwellings.

The greatest turbulence, however, is caused by Turret Rock. During a strong ebb, this treed islet appears in aerial photos like a large tug plowing up a bow wave at full steam. The reef to the southwest of Turret Rock is an important factor in making ebb currents faster than floods; the other ingredient is fresh water runoff from the 85 miles of inlets. The turmoil generated by this reef includes an overfall which first rises 3 feet, then drops 5 feet.

In *The Curve of Time*, Muriel Wylie Blanchet relates how – on her way to the pass – she and her children met a fishing inspector in Allison Harbour who had just survived a traumatic experience in the Nakwakto Rapids. Entering the pass 20 minutes after slack water, his 40-foot boat was seized by the current and rammed against a shelving cliff.

Over the years tugboat operators developed their own equations for determining slack at the rapids but, fortunately for us, this complex pass was surveyed by Mike Woodward of the Canadian Hydropgraphic Service in 1983-84 and his findings were first incorporated into daily predictions of the Tide and Current Tables in 1987.

However, with only a 6-minute window at Nakwakto, it's prudent to arrive a half hour early and watch, from a safe distance, for slack. Meteorological conditions will sometimes alter tides slightly, and slack may not always be exactly at the time estimated in the tables. It doesn't coincide with HW and LW, but occurs midway in the cycle when the water level inside the Seymour basin briefly equals that in the strait. Maximum currents develop near HW and LW when water level differences are greatest.

Good anchorages to wait for slack include the west end of **Treadwell Bay**, west of Nakwakto Rapids, and the protected but shallow cove SE of **Goose Point**. The entrance to **Cougar Inlet** at the N end of Schooner Channel is a temporary anchorage to wait for slack but the inlet itself is guarded by a very shallow pass and a healthy patch of kelp.

Butress Island directs most of the current during an ebb into Slingsby Channel, and this results in Schooner Channel receiving much less current. Vessels exiting Slingsby Channel with an ebb during strong west winds will encounter large seas from the Outer Narrows to Lascelles Point. Currents in these narrows can be 9 knots on an ebb (and this is 5 miles from the main set of rapids), and waves over 15 feet (5 m) are not uncommon here. Mariners should be very wary about approaching the narrows during these conditions. If such sea conditions are anticipated, a good option is to take Schooner Channel to Allison Harbour or to Miles Inlet, and avoid the Outer Narrows completely. The channel between Fox Islands and Bramham Island is a possible pull-out lane, but there is lots of kelp in this pass and the currents, with whirlpools, are strong. The basin between the two Fox Islands is almost completely choked with kelp and is not a suitable anchorage.

Schooner Channel is narrow, but free of swell and waves and fairly easy to navigate once south of the rocks opposite Goose Point. Tidal streams can attain 5 knots on the flood and 6 on the ebb, so be sure to monitor your position as you transit the passage. There are numerous protruding reefs, including a rock that lies in the middle of the channel near Murray Labyrinth. However, Schooner Channel is very pretty, its narrowness and overhanging trees evocative of a small river.

Seymour Basin 12

Once you've made it through the Nakwakto Rapids, there are over 85 miles of protected waterways to explore in Seymour and Belize Inlets. Although logging has taken place here for decades, a detailed survey of the area didn't take place until the early 1980s. Chart 3552 now provides mariners with detailed survey information for cruising this maze of long, narrow inlets.

Protected anchorage near the Nakwakto Rapids can be found about 3 miles into Nugent Sound, NW of a mid-channel islet in about 20 feet (6.5 m). Another nearby anchorage is **Charlotte Bay**, about 5 miles SE of the rapids. Back in the days of hand logging, camp boats would converge on Charlotte Bay for summertime gatherings where its flat beach, was the perfect picnic site.

Top, racing the tide to post our boat name on Turret Rock. Above, the same rock at full ebb.

Nakwakto Rapids during an ebb.

Above, early morning in Strachan Bay. Right, area west of Nakwakto Rapids showing Treadwell Bay at left and Slingsby Channel to right. Below right, sailing in Seymour Inlet.

Seymour Inlet extends east for 38 miles before terminating at a glacier-covered plateau, which is a source of Squamish winds in winter. During cold spells, when parts of the Seymour Basin freeze over, people once living at the logging camps would haul their rowboats to the ice-free narrows by sled to get to a port for supplies. The first hand loggers began arriving in "cedar country" in 1885, drawn to the area's abundant shoreside stands of timber where a tall conifer could be felled and slid straight into the water. From the 1920s to the 1960s, as many as 50 camps operated in the Seymour Basin, including a large one run by A.P. Allison at **Warner Bay** in Seymour Inlet, some 18 miles from Nakwakto Rapids. Allison took over the claim in 1926 and used a wheel generator for electricity while the sawmill produced boat lumber and shake bolts.

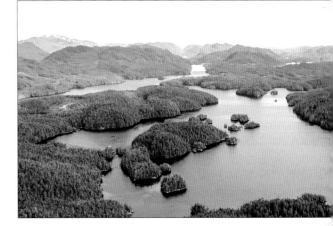

We have anchored near the mouth of Warner Bay, on its east side, where we tied a line ashore to keep us well away from a log boom. A lovely lagoon lies at the bay's head, which we explored by dinghy, and we also hiked along the logging road.

In Belize Inlet, just north of Seymour Inlet, anchorage can be found in **Westerman Bay** near its west end, or farther along in **Mereworth Sound** and **Alison Sound**. **Village Cove**, at the entrance to Mereworth Sound, is sheltered by two wooded islets. In adjacent **Strachan Bay** there is a lovely, secluded cove lying in the bay's SW corner. A creek leading into Pack Lake lies opposite in the bay's NW corner. A logging operation with booms is currently located on the west side of the bay.

The weather was splendid when we anchored in Strachan Bay's southwest cove in 45 feet of depth one September evening. Next morning, under a cloudless sky, the anchorage was, to quote Emily Carr, "in the brilliant sparkle of the morning when everything that was not superlatively blue was superlatively green."

Pack Lake

STRACHAN BAY

Recommended Route: · · · · · · ·

Mereworth Sound

IR

Village Cove

59

0   1/4

Nautical miles
Not for navigation.
Use Chart 3552
Depths in fathoms

N

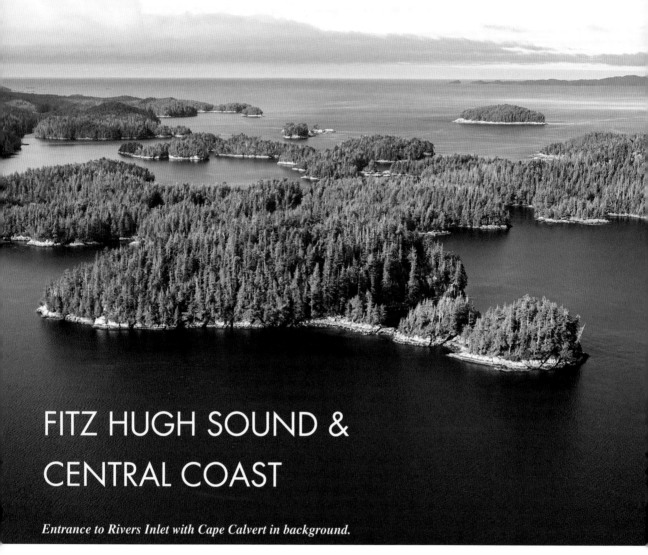

CHAPTER TEN

FITZ HUGH SOUND & CENTRAL COAST

Entrance to Rivers Inlet with Cape Calvert in background.

Of all the boating we've done along the Inside Passage, our favourite cruising area is B.C.'s central coast, just north of Cape Caution. Once past this aptly named cape, you enter some of the best coastal cruising in the world: dozens of deserted islands, secluded anchorages, beautiful beaches and an abundance of wildlife, not to mention some of the best sportfishing anywhere.

Cape Caution, its name bestowed by Captain Vancouver in 1793, marks one of the few exposed legs of the Inside Passage. There's no avoiding the open waters of Queen Charlotte Sound off this cape, and this leg of your voyage up the Inside Passage should be approached with ample preparation (make sure your marine insurance provides coverage north of Cape Caution) and a close eye on the weather. We've rounded Cape Caution many times and only

twice have we had to break off our attempt and wait at a nearby anchorage for conditions to settle. In calm or light-wind conditions, we pass fairly close (within one to two miles) to the white tower upon which the cape's beacon is mounted, but if the seas are at all rough, we'll stand off three or four miles.

Wind accelerates around a cape and this is especially true when southerlies converge at Cape Caution. But the real problem is the bizarre wave action created by a confluence of tidal currents flowing in and out of Queen Charlotte Strait, combined with the almost continual outflow from Smith Sound and Fitz Hugh Sound. Meanwhile, a constant ocean swell shortens and steepens in the shoal waters that extend for more than a mile off the cape. The result is a nasty 4- to 6-foot chop in the vicinity of the cape, especially during an ebb tide. These waves worsen in strong wind-against-current conditions. If you're going with the wind and current, it's not so bad, but once you're around the cape be aware that a southerly will usually shift to the west as it funnels up Smith Sound and the worst bit is between the cape and Egg Island.

The ideal tide and wind conditions for rounding Cape Caution when northbound would be a southerly wind and slack tide. Conversely, for a southbound crossing, a northerly wind with a neap flood tide would be ideal. If possible, make your move during light winds and neap tides.

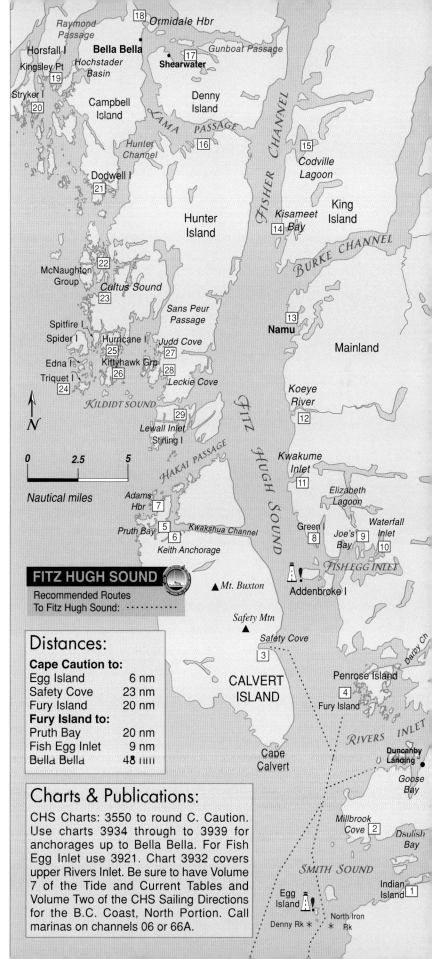

FITZ HUGH SOUND

Recommended Routes
To Fitz Hugh Sound: ·········

Distances:

Cape Caution to:

Egg Island	6 nm
Safety Cove	23 nm
Fury Island	20 nm

Fury Island to:

Pruth Bay	20 nm
Fish Egg Inlet	9 nm
Bella Bella	48 nm

Charts & Publications:

CHS Charts: 3550 to round C. Caution. Use charts 3934 through to 3939 for anchorages up to Bella Bella. For Fish Egg Inlet use 3921. Chart 3932 covers upper Rivers Inlet. Be sure to have Volume 7 of the Tide and Current Tables and Volume Two of the CHS Sailing Directions for the B.C. Coast, North Portion. Call marinas on channels 06 or 66A.

Approaches to Cape Caution
(See map on page 283)

There are a number of approaches for northbound vessels heading past Cape Caution. Some boaters prefer to set out from one of the anchorages on the southern shores of Queen Charlotte Strait, namely Bell Island, God's Pocket or **Cascade Harbour** at the north end of Nigei Island. A heavy swell does enter this last anchorage during prolonged north-westerly winds but this can be avoided by anchoring

View of Egg Island with Egg Rocks in foreground.
Only ten miles to Cape Calvert from here.

on the west side of the anchorage, close to the islet.

From an anchorage on the south side of Queen Charlotte Strait the usual route is toward Pine Island (passing it to starboard), then altering course toward Egg Island (which can be passed on either side depending on conditions). The course continues to South Passage and into Fitz Hugh Sound where you will be out of the swells of Queen Charlotte Sound. The Sailing Directions advises mariners using South Passage to pass W of Egg Island no closer than 0.8 mile and no more than 3 miles to the west of it. This course is important for avoiding the dangerous reefs of the Sea Otter Group lying to the west, and the rocks (especially Denny Rock) to the east.

The route we prefer for rounding Cape Caution is straight up the middle of Queen Charlotte Strait from either Port Hardy or Port McNeill. We have departed Port McNeill at dawn, setting a course from Pulteney Point to go between Deserters Island and Echo Island – then passing to the east of Allan Rocks and straight past the cape. We usually pass east of Egg Island, giving the North and South Iron Rocks lots of room.

If conditions are deteriorating as we approach the western entrance of Queen Charlotte Strait, we will pull into **Miles Inlet** or **Allison Harbour** (both of which are secure overnight anchorages) to wait for more favourable weather. Upon rounding Cape Caution, we take Alexandra Passage to go between North Iron Rock and Egg Rocks. The swells west of Egg Island are notorious, especially in a south wind, but are flatter on the Smith Sound side.

Egg Island Lightkeepers

Egg Island, at the entrance to Smith Sound, is one of the most exposed lighthouses on our coast. The lighthouse keepers on this isolated island have an unobstructed view of Queen Charlotte Sound and the seas it produces – from the gentle swells of summer to the frenzied breakers of a winter storm.

Egg Island's first lighthouse was constructed in 1898, and it stood on an adjacent islet west of the main island, to which it was connected by a footbridge. Huge seas crashed onto Egg

Island during a November storm in 1948 and swept away the lighthouse, which hadn't been bolted to its foundations. The lighthouse keeper and his wife, Bob and Marie Wilkins, were asleep in their bed when the sea crashed through their bedroom window. They woke their nine-year-old son Dennis and hurried out a window on the back side of the house. When they got to the fog alarm building, they found it full of water so they traversed the footbridge that led to the large island even though many of its planks had been washed away. Dennis recalled years later that "the sea was a continuous roar, like a raging waterfall."

The family spent the remainder of the night on the high point of the main island. When the storm had passed, they found shelter in the chicken coop until rescued several days later by a passing fishboat. The lighthouse was later rebuilt on the site of the chicken coop and the site of the original lighthouse is now a helicopter pad.

Stan and Judy Westhaver ran the light on Egg Island from 1977 to 2001 and were well-known to local mariners. Over the years the Westhavers saw their share of bad weather and when Stan was once asked, after an intense September storm had blown through, what 77kn winds looked like at Egg Island, he replied, "Not as bad as 100kn winds."

Stan and Judy Westhaver, former lightkeepers at Egg Island, have seen lots of heavy weather.

Smith Sound

With its funnel-like entrance and no large island to act as a buffer, northwest winds blast unimpeded for several miles into Smith Sound. These winds also bring along significant swells from the Pacific Ocean and Queen Charlotte Sound, convincing most boaters to bypass Smith Sound and focus on getting north to Fitz Hugh Sound and the protection of Calvert Island. However, if you're looking for a place to pull out or simply to explore, there are several adequate-to-good anchorages not too far off the main routes.

Indian Island   1

One year in late September, during the southbound leg of our trip, we were faced with a southeasterly gale coming on fast as we drew near to **Egg Island**. The winds, which later built to storm force, were churning up a large swell so we decided to seek refuge along the south mainland shore of Smith Sound. We had heard Jones Cove, six miles north of Cape Caution, was good but we could see several fish boats heading for this small anchorage. We headed further east, hoping to find a spot near Indian Island.

Both **Anchor Bight** and **Fly Basin** inside **Takush Harbour** looked like good spots to wait things out. We've seen forestry and fishing boats collect here during a southeasterly storm. However, it was getting so windy we decided to first investigate the cove at the SW end of Indian Island where a drying channel connects along the island to Anchor Bight. Although the anchorage is more open to W winds, it appeared to give excellent protection from SE winds.

We dropped the CQR, let out lots of rode and took another line to a big tree on shore, pulling ourselves close to the lee south shore. Here we comfortably sat for two days while SE winds blew overhead at 50 knots and more than 70 at Egg Island. Although our CQR held firm, the stern line was taking most of the load. A fish boat anchored nearby dragged a few times as the wind gusted throughout the anchorage.

On the SE side of Indian Island, anchorage can be found in Anchor Bight opposite a cove where a midden marks the site of a former First Nations village. However, the south winds really gusted through this spot. We later went over to Fly Basin and although it also got some gusts, this anchorage is more protected than Anchor Bight and provides good shelter in strong winds. Holding is very good in thick mud.`

Indian Island anchorage is perfect in SE winds.

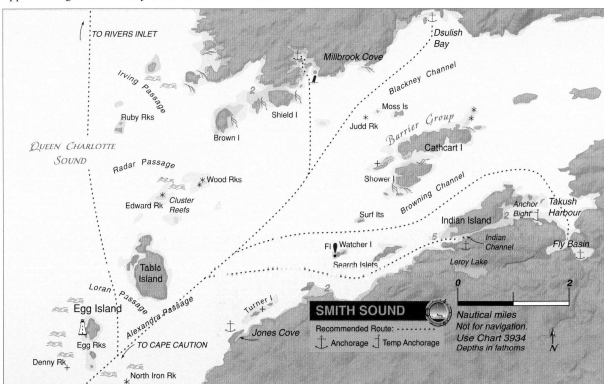

TO RIVERS INLET

Millbrook Cove

Dsulish Bay

Irving Passage

Blackney Channel

Ruby Rks

Shield I

Moss Is

Judd Rk

Barrier Group

QUEEN CHARLOTTE SOUND

Brown I

Cathcart I

Radar Passage

Wood Rks

Shower I

Edward Rk

Cluster Reefs

Surf Its

Browning Channel

Anchor Bight

Takush Harbour

Indian Island

Table Island

Fl ! Watcher I

Indian Channel

Fly Basin

Loran Passage

Search Islets

Leroy Lake

Egg Island

Alexandra Passage

Turner I

Egg Rks

Jones Cove

SMITH SOUND

Recommended Route: ·······

Anchorage   Temp Anchorage

Denny Rk

North Iron Rk

TO CAPE CAUTION

Nautical miles
Not for navigation.
Use Chart 3934
Depths in fathoms

0   2

N

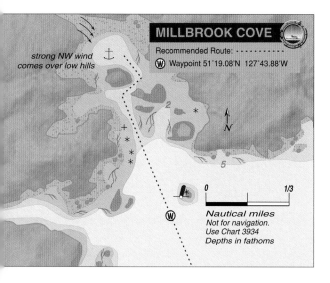

Dsulish Bay has a beautiful golden-coloured beach.

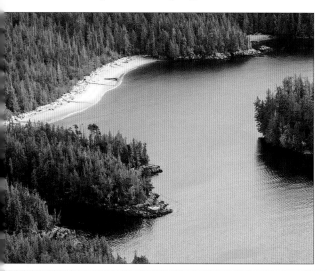

Millbrook Cove 2

Located on the north side of Smith Sound, this is a popular anchorage for fishboats and pleasure craft. Although the entrance is encumbered with rocks, the dangerous one, right in the middle, is marked by a starboard-hand buoy. In a NW blow, Shield Island knocks down the surf and most of the wind, allowing for safe entry. Keep west of the buoy, then remain in mid-channel as you enter the cove, passing between the two islets at its head . Anchor in the northern end in five fathoms over sand. A friend of ours sat out a southeasterly gale here. Because of the low lying terrain, westerlies tend to blast right over the land, but the holding is good.

Entry into Smith Sound from the north can be made through Irving Passage and from the south via Alexandra Passage, keeping North Iron Rock to the south and passing between Wood Rocks and Surf Islets. This passage is deep, but in poor visibility extreme caution is required because soundings give little warning of the drying rocks and other hazards.

If conditions are settled, Dsulish Bay is worth visiting for its beautiful golden beach. Although quite open to the south, it is fairly protected in most north winds, receiving only the remains of leftover swell and the occasional gust. The best anchorage is northeast of Dsulish Island in about 40 feet in mud and sand. Keep an ear and eye to the weather for any wind shift out of the south.

Fitz Hugh Sound

The reward for rounding Cape Caution is the welcoming sight of Fitz Hugh Sound. Cape Calvert marks the south entrance to this broad, 40-mile-long channel. Lined by mainland mountains and inlets to

View of Millbrook Cove's west entrance

the east and by the islands of the vast Hakai Luxvbalis Conservancy to the west, Fitz Hugh Sound offers mariners a bounty of best anchorages. The waters here are rich with marine life, including Pacific white-sided dolphins and killer whales, and in summer are a feeding ground for humpback whales. The sound's fishing banks are good places to catch halibut and lingcod while large runs of salmon, including chinook, coho and sockeye, enter Fitz Hugh Sound through Hakai Passage on their way to the mainland rivers to spawn.

Safety Cove, Calvert Island 3

This anchorage, with its wide entrance, is a popular first stop for northbound pleasure and commercial boats after crossing Queen Charlotte Sound. This is especially true if battling NW or SW winds – conditions in which the anchorage affords its best protection and respite. The cove is situated within the Calvert Island Conservancy, which encompasses the southern half of the island. Although sheltered from north and west winds, any wind from the east will gust into the bay and up the Oatsoalis Valley.

A sand-and-mud drying flat lies at the head of the cove but the rest of the shoreline is steep and the water is deep throughout. Anchor about two-thirds of the way to the head, in the middle of the cove, in 80 to 100 feet with a soft mud-and-sand bottom.

In August of 1792 Capt. Vancouver's two ships – *Discovery* and *Chatham* – pulled into Safety Cove where the Chatham was beached to inspect her hull for damage incurred during her grounding in Queen Charlotte Strait. While the ships remained at anchor, the boats were dispatched on survey expeditions. Capt. Vancouver sent Master Whidbey and Lt. Puget to survey Smith Sound and Rivers Inlet while he and Lt. Johnstone explored Fitz Hugh Sound.

Rivers Inlet

This mainland fjord is famous for its salmon fishing. The first salmon cannery opened here in 1882, followed by more than a dozen others, but by 1950 they had all shut down. Sportfishing still thrives and several of the old canneries have been converted into sportfishing lodges. The inlet's supply centre is **Dawson's Landing** – a floating community tucked among tall cedars in Darby Channel. Facilities here for visiting boaters include moorage, fuel, a post office and a general store selling groceries and liquor. Call ahead on VHF Channel 06. Another marina is located at **Duncanby Landing** in Goose Bay, on the south shore of the entrance to Rivers Inlet. Facilities include moorage, power, fuel and showers.

Top, a humpback whale feeds in Fitz Hugh Sound. Above, Safety Cove is deep but well protected from NW winds. Below, a young sportfisherman displays his catch near Rivers Inlet.

Fury Island / [4]
Penrose Island

Almost without exception, the first anchorage we pull into after rounding Cape Caution northbound is Fury Island at the mouth of Rivers Inlet. This anchorage, part of Penrose Island Marine Park, is partially ringed with dazzling white midden beaches of crushed shell and sand. In sunny weather the setting is reminiscent of a South Seas atoll, especially at high water, when the water lapping ashore turns a brilliant turquoise as it shimmers over the white shore. The cove's outer beaches can be visited by dinghy or kayak, and are a lovely place to have a picnic or a secluded swim.

Top, aerial view of Fury Island. Below and opposite, the anchorage has beautiful midden beaches.

Fury Island is one of a cluster of islands bordering the southwest shores of Penrose Island. The other anchorages, known collectively as Schooner Retreat, include Exposed Anchorage, Secure Anchorage and Frigate Bay. But the best anchorage is the one lying between Penrose and Fury Island – often referred to as Fury Cove.

With numerous islands surrounding the southwest side of Penrose Island, entry to the anchorage might seem a bit challenging for first-time visitors to this beautiful spot. We first identify Rouse Point on the outer islands, then steer to the steep rock cliffs of Cleve Island (marked "200" on most charts) and keep it close to our port side as we enter the deep basin that fronts the cove's entrance. Breaker Pass, to the north, can be used in calm conditions.

Inside the cove there are numerous good spots to drop the hook. The mud-and-shell bottom offers very good holding, and the anchorage is sheltered from most winds except from the southwest which, if strong, can gust through the anchorage with enthusiasm. If a southerly gale is forecast, a good spot to anchor is in the lee of Fury Island with a line ashore. Cinch in your stern and you'll be protected from any gusts that funnel through the entrance.

There is much to see and do while anchored at Fury Island, starting with a stroll on the beautiful shell beaches. These pre-historic middens date back

FURY ISLAND AT A GLANCE

CHARTS: 3934

LAT LONG: Entrance 51°28.70'N 127°45.44'W

PROS: A beautiful anchorage with extensive mid-den beaches. Several islands and islets to explore by dinghy or kayak. Fair to good shelter from most winds, good holding ground. Lots to explore, fishing nearby. A stunning destination.

CONS: Somewhat open to the SW. Can be busy. Challenging piloting to access nearby anchorages.

MUST DO: Fish off Rouse reef; picnic on shore.

FURY ISLAND

Recommended Route: · · · · · · ·
⚓ Anchorage ⊥ Temp Anchorage
Ⓦ Waypoint 51°28.7'N 127°45.44'W

0   1/4   1/2

Nautical miles
Use CHS chart# 3934
Not for Navigation.
Depths in fathoms

N

DARBY CHANNEL

Finn Lake

PENROSE ISLAND

Big Frypan Bay

Fishing here usually good

Rouse Rf.

Southwest winds can blast into anchorage

sea birds here

Rouse Pt.

Fury Cove

135

FURY I

Exposed Anchorage

BAR ISLANDS

Good area to explore by dinghy.

Rocky Bay

Cleve I

Walrus Rk

Fury Pt.

Ⓦ

Breaker Pass avoid in strong south winds

Main entrance to Fury Island anchorage

Heathcote I

Highway I

Secure Anchorage

SCHOONER RETREAT

Sulky Pt

Folly Is

Bird I

Maze Its

Frigate Bay

Stunted Its

Ironside I

Sheltered beach

Fire Its

Sea Bluff

JOACHIM ISLAND

Stormy Point

Safe Entrance

FITZ HUGH SOUND

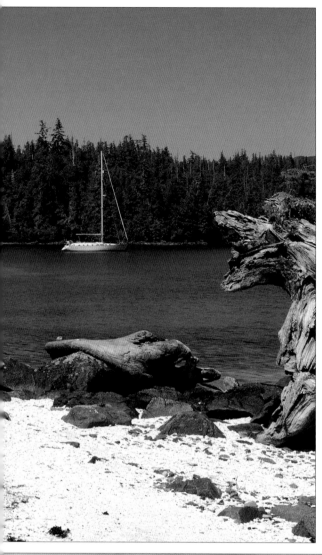

thousands of years when the area was inhabited by the Oweekeno, whose winter villages once stretched along the shores of Rivers Inlet. The stone remains of an ancient fish trap can be seen in the shallow channel leading from the west side of the cove into Darby Channel. Rouse Reef lies a half mile outside and is a good spot for salmon fishing (as is the west side of Penrose Island). There is a beautiful beach at the southwestern tip of Fury Island. All in all, the anchorage is a ten out of ten.

If the Fury Island anchorage is a little too busy, which rarely happens, **Secure Anchorage** contains a couple of good anchoring spots northeast of Bird Island. Best entry is between Ironside and Bird Islands. The east side of Penrose Island has two large and well-sheltered bays – **Frypan Bay** and **Big Frypan Bay** – both deep but with small nooks providing shelter. Ripon Island's west side also has a few anchorages which you may be sharing with one of the many floating fish camps in the area.

Hakai Luxvbalis Conservancy

Called Hakai Recreation Area when established in 1987, this is the largest provincial marine protected area on the B.C. coast and is now called Hakai Luxvbalis (looks-bal-ease) Conservancy. It is managed under an agreement between the Heiltsuk Nation and the Province of British Columbia. The conservancy encompasses more than 120,000 hectares of islands and waterways, including the northern half of Calvert Island, most

Left, anchored at Fury Island. Below, looking north across Kwakshua Channel toward Hakai Passage.

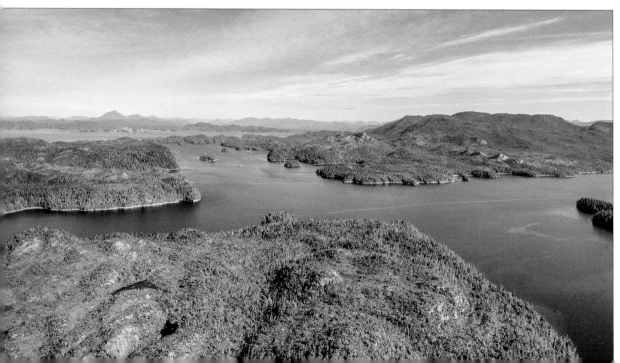

of Hunter Island and dozens of islands and islets bordering Queens Sound.

Reached only by sea or by air, Hakai has long attracted sportfishermen to its salmon-rich waters, with floating lodges operating near Hakai Passage each summer. It was the construction of a permanent, land-based lodge at the head of Pruth Bay on Calvert Island that set off a storm of controversy in 1993. This parcel of private land, previously leased by B.C. Parks from its owner, had been sold and a lodge hurriedly constructed, despite protests by the Heiltsuk people of Bella Bella, who were trying to protect the site of an ancestral winter village. Boaters also joined the protests, writing dozens of angry letters to various government departments.

An uneasy truce descended on Pruth Bay, with boaters allowed access to the lodge property and the trail to West Beach. But tensions intensified when the property was sold in 2003 to a development company that ran the lodge as an exclusive gated resort. Salvation came in 2009 when the property was purchased by the Quadra Island-based Tula Foundation. This family foundation was formed by Eric Peterson and his wife, Christina Munck. A research scientist, Peterson made a fortune when he sold his medical imaging company and is now one of B.C.'s most generous philanthropists. Upon acquiring the Pruth Bay property, the Tula Foundation established the Hakai Beach Institute and transformed the luxury lodge into a research institute for environmental science, with scientists and undergraduates working here throughout the summer months.

Boaters are once again welcome and access to the ocean beaches has never been better.

Above, Hakai Beach Institute's dock in Pruth Bay. Below, an old tree carving near the Institute's headquarters overlooking Pruth Bay (bottom).

Top, former Hakai resort houses university students.
Above and below, the beautiful sands of West Beach.

Pruth Bay 5

Pruth Bay is the centrepiece of the Hakai area. Pacific white-sided dolphins frequently feed at the mouth of this bay, which is popular with boaters for its easy access to beautiful ocean beaches. The approach to Pruth Bay is along Kwakshua Channel.

Although the holding in Pruth Bay is very good, boaters should make sure their anchor is well set in the thick mud and sand before going ashore. The main part of the bay is open to easterlies that can funnel down Kwakshua Channel with force. However, we've seen a dozen boats hold firm here in 30-knot gusts. Westerlies will also gust through the anchorage but are not the same threat. Depths at the head are 35 to 60 feet. The south arm provides better protection in SE winds.

On the western shore at the head of Pruth Bay is property owned by the Hakai Beach Institute, its buildings used for housing up to 100 scientists and university students, whose meals are served in the

PRUTH BAY AT A GLANCE
CHARTS: 3935
LAT LONG: Entrance: 51°39.23'N 128°06.60'W
PROS: Big beach, big sky and big surf. Lucky you if you have arrived at Pruth Bay. A best anchorage with lots to do. Hike, fish, beachcomb, watch the surf, see wildlife or swim.
CONS: Main anchorage is quite exposed to E winds.
MUST DO: Walk along West Beach or take the 30 minute hike to North Beach. Beautiful and extraordinary white sand beaches.

main lodge. The Panabode cabin once used by park rangers was moved to the other side of the dock and is the Institute's headquarters. Nearby is the tree mask, carved by a caretaker when most of Calvert Island was still Crown land.

There are no services or facilities for visiting boaters, such as moorage, fuel, water or supplies. The floats are used by delivery vessels and seaplanes which come and go frequently. Boaters are asked to anchor well away from the docks. The rear fingers are kept free for dinghies and visitors are welcome to tie up here to access trails to the West and North beaches.

It's an easy hike from Pruth Bay to West Beach along a well-marked and maintained trail. The beach is beautiful – a long crescent of soft sand with views of the surf pounding onto distant reefs. Smooth rock formations overlook parts of West Beach and form an appealing backdrop for a picnic lunch while watching the splendid sight of ocean swells rumbling onto shore and of sandpipers skirting the edge of the surf as they flit across the glistening sand.

The hike to North Beach is longer and a bit more strenuous, but the trail is now well-maintained with a sturdy boardwalk bridge straddling a wetland filled with native water lilies (a felled log with a rope handrail used to serve as a footbridge). In 2010, BC Parks, Hakai Beach Institute and Nuxalk Guardians began upgrading the existing trail system and for three summers park rangers and volunteers worked at building boardwalks and stairs.

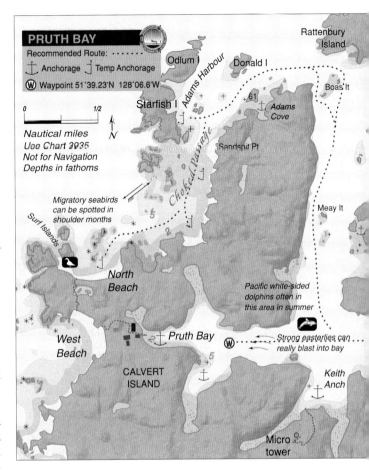

West Beach is a beautiful stretch of beach facing the open Pacific and is an easy hike from Pruth Bay.

The signpost for the North Beach trailhead is near the north end of West Beach, and the trailhead for the Lookout Trail, which climbs to a high point overlooking West Beach, is located at the south end of West Beach.

Keith Anchorage 6

This anchorage is a good alternative to Pruth Bay in settled weather, its main attraction being access to a trail leading up to a telecommunications tower overlooking Kwakshua Channel. We anchor in the west arm in 45 to 50 feet of water. The holding is only fair in loose mud and rock. The trailhead is located on the east side of the anchorage, where a felled log serves as a landing place for dinghies at high water. The trail is rough but well trodden, and it takes 30 minutes at a brisk pace to reach the radio tower where a platform provides an eagle's eye view of Kwakshua Channel and distant islands.

Adams Harbour 7

There are several conditional anchorages in the area bounded by islands to the W and N of Calvert Island. The anchorage SE of Donald Island (**Adams Cove**) is a little tight for large boats, with reefs near the entrance, but this cove is well protected from most winds for an overnight stay and the holding here in mud and sand is good. A popular harbour for floating fish camps, the anchorage may be busy at times with small boats heading out to Hakai Passage. The anchorage we like, in settled weather, is on the lee side of **Starfish Island** at its southeast end. Holding is good in sand and mud. Or, as a temporary stop, you can motor to the bottom of Choked Passage (choked mostly with kelp), anchor in two fathoms and enjoy a sandy beach right off your stern.

Top, a morning visit ashore in Keith Anchorage. Above, anchored off North Beach. Below, an aerial view of Choked Passage looking south.

FISH EGG INLET

This large inlet was surveyed in 1984 but remained undiscovered by most boaters until a CHS chart (Chart 3921) was published in the early '90s. Until then, local knowledge was the main way of getting around this vast assortment of islands and small inlets. Within its scenic shores are several, perhaps dozens, of secluded and snug anchorages. One note of caution: because charting of this area is relatively recent, it's wise to take your time in shallow areas. There have been a few reports of uncharted rocks.

Addenbroke Island, its lighthouse overlooking Fitz Hugh Sound, is one of several islands lying at the entrance to Fish Egg Inlet. Convoy Passage provides entry from the south while Fairmile and Patrol Passage provide entry from the north. To access the inner part of this inlet, use either Souvenir Passage or Patrol Passage into the central part of Fish Egg Inlet, which branches into numerous bays and inlets on either side of the inlet. The entire inlet is fairly protected in all but the most insistent breezes and it's a pleasure just to motor or sail about to the various anchorages.

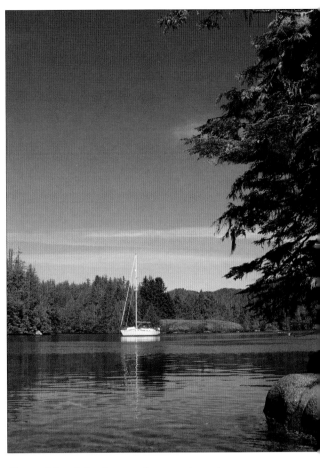

FISH EGG INLET AT A GLANCE:

CHARTS: 3921 (scale 1: 20,000), 3935 entrance
LAT LONG: (Entrance) 51˚37.75'N 127˚50'W
PROS: Numerous anchorages, good fishing and dinghy exploring. Great haven from most winds. Most anchorages quiet with nice scenery.
CONS: Few hiking opportunities.
MUST DO: Explore several anchorages, see the reversing falls at Elizabeth Lagoon in Joe's Bay.

Green Island Anchorage is a scenic and secure harbour with good protection from most winds.

Green Island Anchorage 8

Accessed off Fairmile Passage at the mouth of Fish Egg Inlet, this very sheltered and pretty anchorage is located on the west side of Illahie Inlet. Formed by a cluster of islands, one of which is Green Island, the anchorage is one of the gems of Fitz Hugh Sound. Although four channels lead into the cove, the safest entrance is from the southeast. Currents are negligible. The anchorage can accommodate several boats, although we rarely see more than one or two. Depths throughout the anchorage don't exceed 60 feet and we normally like to anchor in the west side of the basin in about 30 feet. The holding is superb throughout in soft yet sticky mud.

Green Island itself isn't any greener than most treed islands, but the islet lying off its southwest corner is covered in brilliant green bramble. It forms a beautiful backdrop for anchored boats and is one of several islets awaiting exploration by dinghy or kayak.

Joe's Bay 9

This snug anchorage lies midway along the north side of Fish Egg Inlet and includes a dramatic set of reversing falls. We anchor in the deep part of the bay in about 60 feet and usually have the cove to ourselves. If it's busy, take a line to the south shore and you'll be quite secure. The drying rock opposite island "31" and the reef extending from the islet

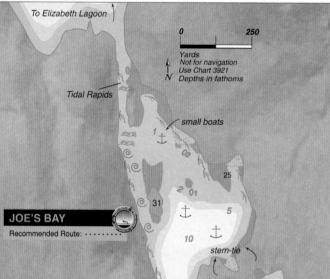

To Elizabeth Lagoon

0   250

Yards
Not for navigation
Use Chart 3921
N   Depths in fathoms

Tidal Rapids

small boats

25

JOE'S BAY
Recommended Route: ....

1

02

2 01

31

5

10

stern-tie

Top, aerial view of Green Island Anchorage.

Below, secluded Joe's Bay.

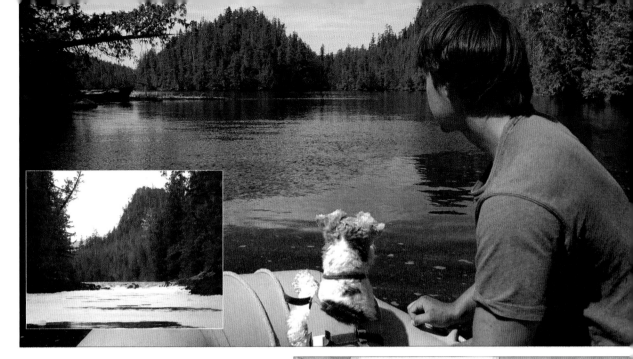

marked '25' must be accounted for before setting the hook. The holding, in a bottom of mud, sand and shell, is very good. The narrow part of the bay to the north gets plenty of current and, with surrounding reefs, is a tight fit suitable for small boats only.

A tidal rapids leading to Elizabeth Lagoon lies at the head of the cove, creating a profusion of foam carried by current into Joe's Bay. Although very interesting, this set of tidal rapids ranks as being one of the more dangerous of lagoon passes on the coast. On ebbs, a significant waterfall is created at the lagoon entrance with up to a 4-foot drop which you only need to see once to be impressed. If you're heading into the lagoon by dinghy, be sure to depart from it within an hour of HW slack. As the Sailing Directions warn, the lagoon water is opaque, making it difficult to see dangers. Tides can be referenced to Wadhams in CHS Volume 7 Tide and Current tables.

Waterfall Inlet 10

This scenic inlet is entered through the small pass north of Island '99' on Chart 3921. Currents in the pass seem to be 2 to 3 knots at most and if you stay in the middle you'll have at least 12 to 16 feet of water. A small waterfall flows into the east side of the inlet at the mouth of a creek which leads, after a short but steep hike along the creek bed, to a lake.

A very pretty anchorage lies in the SE corner of this inlet about half a mile from the waterfall. We've tucked into the bight behind a small peninsula and, with a line ashore, have been completely out of any wind. The holding is good in 35 feet over sticky mud. Good anchorage for larger boats

Above, venturing into Elizabeth Lagoon near HW slack.
Inset, an ebb tide rushing out of Elizabeth Lagoon.
Below, aerial view of Waterfall Inlet looking south.

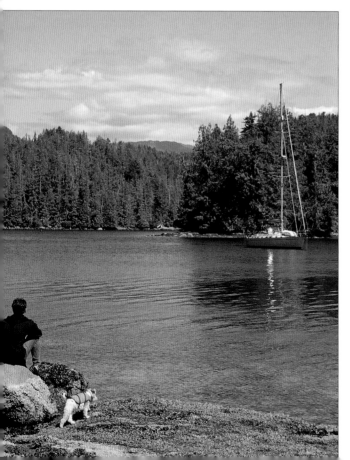

Top, serene and sheltered Waterfall Inlet. Left, entrance into Kwakume Inlet and, bottom, at anchor west of the forested islet.

can be had in the middle of this cove in about 45 feet. There is a small lagoon in this cove's NE corner which makes for an interesting, if short, dinghy trip. To the east of the lagoon is a small lake which you can hike to along the creek bed.

This is one of those remote anchorages where time indeed seems to stop and let you hear the birds and the cedars as the wind, high above, moves through the inlet.

Kwakume Inlet 11

There are many "best" anchorages in Fitz Hugh Sound but Kawakume Inlet ranks as something even better. A spacious inlet with midden beaches, mountain vistas, a couple of small islets and an inner basin with an intriguing pass, it is an ideal all-weather anchorage – well protected with good holding. The entrance, however, is a little tricky with a significant rock lying 200 yards outside the passage. Although there is enough depth on either side of this obstruction to pass, the north side has a small peninsula jutting out from the mainland, which serves as a navigational landmark.

Once inside the inlet, we like to anchor near the head, to the SW or NE of the forested islet. There is a large rock that dries six feet south of this islet and is a favourite spot for seals parking themselves at LW. Keep a close eye to the chart to avoid this hazard. We often drop the hook to the SW of the islet in about 16 to 20 feet. The holding ground – a combination of mud, sand and

---

KWAKUME INLET AT A GLANCE:
CHARTS: 3935
LAT LONG: 51°42.44'N 127°53.39'W
PROS: Pretty anchorage, lots of room. Great view to Calvert Island and good fishing nearby.
CONS:.A dicey entrance in SE winds.
MUST DO: Explore lagoon at east end of inlet.

shell – is good here and throughout the inlet. While anchored in this spot, the view to the west is of the distinctive peak of Mt. Buxton on Calvert Island. The foreshore is a combination of boulders, sand and gravel.

Other spots to anchor include the bight near the inlet's entrance, between a round islet and a pretty midden on the north side of the inlet. This spot provides good shelter from NW winds but less so from the south or east. Fish boats often anchor a short distance further into the inlet, in the small bay to the SE, while pleasure craft gravitate toward the head.

Kwakume Inlet contains a lagoon at its head where some flat rocks at its entrance make an ideal picnicking spot. Although this inner basin can be an anchorage for shallow-draft boats, it does receive significant gusts in strong NW winds. The entrance to the basin has less than a metre (3 feet) at LW.

Koeye River [12]

The mainland lakes and rivers that flow into Fitz Hugh Sound are prime habitat for grizzly bears that come to feed on spawning salmon. Several provincial land conservancies have been established to protect these watersheds, including in 2007 the Koeye Conservancy, which encompasses two freshwater lakes, the river's estuary and extensive wetlands and old-growth forests.

The shallow bay behind Koeye Point at the mouth of the Koeye River provides good temporary anchorage for anyone interested in venturing by dinghy up the Koeye River, which can be navigated all the way to Koeye Lake on a high tide. This bay faces almost due west and a nasty chop

Right, entrance to an abandoned limestone quarry. Below, aerial view of the Koeye River.

*Above, fisheries officers march to waiting skiff
after doing a salmon count at Koeye Lake.
Below, the old boardwalks and buildings at Namu.*

will quickly develop if NW winds come up, so keep
an eye on the weather if anchoring here.

Used by local fishermen and kayakers, this bay
has a sandy beach at its head and is the location of an
educational youth camp run by the non-profit Qqs
Projects Society of Bella Bella. The contentious
sportfishing lodge built here on a private lot in 1996
was bought in 2001 by several conservancy societies
in partnership with the Heiltsuk Nation and became
part of the camp. The lodge was destroyed by fire in
late 2011 and its reconstruction is being done with
lumber milled in Bella Bella and barged to the site.

We learned about the Koeye River in the early
1990s while moored overnight in Namu. Docked
nearby was a fisheries boat, its crew there to monitor
salmon stocks at Koeye Lake. Next morning a floatplane picked up the fisheries officers and flew them
to Koeye Lake. They left armed with rifles for their
hike out along one of the area's busiest grizzly bear
trails. We left that morning too, and arrived at the
mouth of the Koeye River an hour later, anchoring in
the shallow bay behind Koeye Point. Then we
climbed into our small dinghy, armed with a flare kit
and airhorn for our journey into grizzly country.

About a mile upstream we stopped to explore the
site of an abandoned limestone quarry, now in ruins,
and noticed bear scat on the trail. Back on the river,
we continued slowly motoring upstream, our dinghy
pushed along by a 2hp Johnson. At one point a fisheries skiff sped past. Swimming beneath us were
thousands of pink salmon in numbers so thick they
clogged the shallow waters and thumped against the
bottom of our dinghy. The river was literally alive
with leaping fish.

The tide was dropping and we eventually caught
up with the fisheries skiff, which had stopped and
was waiting for the three officers who were hiking
out from the lake. As we bobbed nearby in our
Galleon dinghy, the driver of the skiff warned us we
were in "wild kingdom" and there were a lot of grizzlies about. We thanked him and puttered a bit further upriver and stopped. All was quiet.

Suddenly something came charging out of the
brush. For a split second we thought it was a grizzly,
but it was one of the armed fisheries officers, followed
by the other two. Wearing hip-waders and stoic
expressions, they marched past us in the knee-deep
water, climbed into the waiting skiff and sped away.
We were left rocking gently in their wake. As the
grassy shoreline pressed in on us, we looked at each
other and agreed it was time to turn the dinghy around
and leave the Koeye River to the grizzlies.

Namu 13

An historic cannery town built on pilings, Namu's
weatherbeaten buildings and boardwalks used to
bustle with activity. Namu's first cannery was built
in 1893 and for decades tins of salmon rolled off the
assembly lines during the salmon season. Rebuilt
following a fire in the 1960s, Namu remained in
partial operation until the 1990s with a small staff
running its freezing plant.

Boaters still tie up at Namu, but the boardwalks and buildings are slowly rotting. In the
early 1990s we enjoyed hiking the boardwalk
trail to scenic Namu Lake but the encroaching
wilderness has brought frequent sightings of
wolves and grizzly bears around the abandoned
townsite.

Back in the 1970s and 80s, archaeologists from Simon Fraser University conducted digs at Namu, an important Heiltsuk site that was occupied continuously for 10,000 years. The remains uncovered during these digs were returned to their final resting place in September 2011. The school children of Bella Bella had made dozens of bentwood boxes to hold their ancestors' remains and a ceremony took place in a forest clearing above the Namu townsite at which these boxes were lowered into a cedar-lined chamber.

Kisameet Bay 14

Fitz Hugh Sound ends north of Namu, where it narrows and becomes Fisher Channel. The good anchorages continue however and one of the best is Kisameet Bay on King Island, eight miles SE of Lama Passage. Commercial vessels sometimes anchor in Kisameet Bay, but not always successfully. In May 2008 a small cruise ship (105 feet long and carrying 10 passengers) struck a rock while departing Kisameet Bay and sank in 70 feet of water. No one was hurt but saltwater damage to the salvaged ship, which was raised a week later, was assessed at $3 million. Analysis of the accident determined the ship's master had turned too sharply to starboard leaving the anchorage and the ship's bow rode up onto the rock which dries 6 feet.

For recreational vessels, the anchorage is a little easier to enter and leave. If coming from the south, the obvious approach is between Kipling and King Islands. From the north, Fog Rocks indicate the entrance area between the island marked '131' and the small islet to the south marked '35'. From either N or S, the main navigational hazard to avoid in the bay are the two rocks blocking the way to the snug anchorage at the head. Favour the small football-shaped island on your port side on final approach and anchor anywhere north of this islet or half way along the islet shaped like a dagger to the west. Depth varies between 20 to 60 feet. Holding in soft mud is fair to good and will depend on your anchor getting through the kelp lining the bottom. Being patient should result in a good set plus the anchorage is well sheltered.

Kisameet Bay has good salmon fishing just outside its entrance and on the west side of Kipling Island. An excellent example of a stone fish trap lies at the mouth of the stream flowing into Kisameet Bay, and an overgrown trail traces the stream to Kisameet Lake. This land lies within Heiltsuk First Nations territory and for generations the local natives treated various skin ailments with a putty-like clay they had discovered here. In the 1950s they drew the attention of a geoscientist to this mineral-rich clay and its unique healing properties. A pure colloidal glacial clay called Kisolite, it formed when the glaciers retreated 10,000 years and the minerals in the

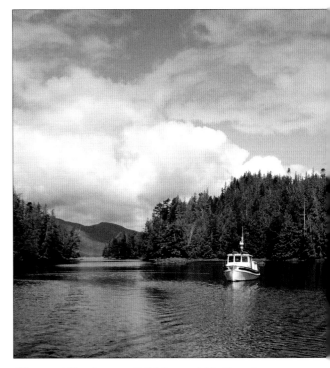

Kisameet Bay has good fishing outside its entrance.

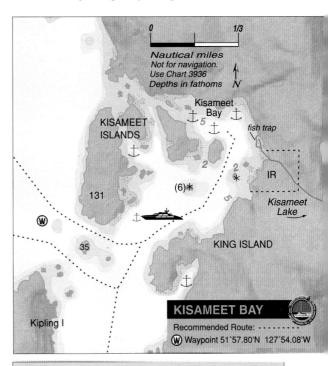

KISAMEET BAY AT A GLANCE:

CHARTS: 3936
LAT LONG: 51°57.80'N 127°54.08'W
PROS: Interesting anchorage with lots of islets to explore. Good protection. Great fishing nearby.
CONS: Anchorage bottom has some kelp.
MUST DO: Explore islets and exceptional fish trap.

Top, aerial view of Codville Lagoon.
Below, Fancy Cove in Lama Passage.

glacial melt collected in a shallow five-acre granite basin about 30 feet about sea level. Now covered by a layer of moss and other vegetation, the 400,000-ton deposit is being hand-harvested and used in the production of skin care products.

Codville Lagoon 15

This small marine park on King Island, established in 1965, is entered from Lagoon Bay opposite Pointer Island at the eastern end of Lama Passage. The entrance is quite narrow with a rock (part of a reef) with less than 6 feet lying north of mid-channel. Favour the south side as you transit the passage and you will have about 25 feet in the fairway.

This all-weather anchorage is well sheltered but it's quite deep throughout most of the lagoon. A recent landslide on the southeast side has, according to B.C. Parks, altered the data shown on some marine charts, presumably with debris and rock.

The best place to anchor, to be near Sagar Lake, is in the basin at the NE end in about 45 feet in soft mud with fair holding. Gusts of W winds are muted. A rough trail, constructed by the Ocean Falls Yacht Club, leads from this anchorage to Sagar Lake where a long sandy beach provides access to the lake's warm water for swimming. The trail can be quite muddy during rainy spells.

Lama Passage 16

If travelling north to **Bella Bella**, boaters can take either the longer scenic route of **Gunboat Passage** (use Chart 3939) or Lama Passage, which includes two good anchorages at which to pull off the highway. Gunboat Passage is fairly sheltered with weak tidal streams that generally set west. The main challenges to the transit are the east entrance, passing south of the rock below Maria Island, and the shoal area SW of Picture Island. There are range markers and a starboard buoy just to the W of this island. A good anchorage within the pass is the west side of **Gosse Bay** in 40 feet. The bottom is good in mud and sand.

Lama Passage, though not as interesting as Gunboat Passage, is the more direct route to Bella Bella, and is wide and safe for any size of vessel. This is the normal route for cruise ships plying the Inside Passage. Two coves we've pulled into are **Fancy Cove** and **Ada Cove**. In Fancy Cove, anchor NE of the small peninsula and islet jutting NW into the bay in depths of 35 feet. Smaller boats can anchor SE of this islet in 12 feet. Ada Cove is a little further west with anchorage just inside the constriction leading to the inner bay and NW of the drying rock on the mud flat.

Bella Bella (Waglisla)

Stretching along the east side of Campbell Island is the Heiltsuk community of New Bella Bella (pop. 1,400) although most people drop the 'New' when referring to the town. The original village was located on Denny Island, but in 1833 the Hudson's Bay Company built a trading post at McLoughlin Bay on Campbell Island and the Heiltsuk moved their village, which they called Waglisla, to its present site. The Bella Bella public docks are often filled with local fishboats, and fuel is not always available in Bella Bella, which suffered a major blow in 2013 when a waterfront building containing the community's general store, library and post office was gutted by fire.

Shearwater 17

This is one of best marinas along the coast with good docking space and extensive facilities. Services at this marina resort include fuel, water, showers, a hardware store (with fishing tackle) and a grocery store which stocks wine and beer. There is also a travel lift and boatyard should you need to make repairs to your boat. You can dock temporarily at the Shearwater Marina while you reprovision or tie up overnight to enjoy the waterfront restaurant. A sea bus runs regularly ($5 per person each way) between Shearwater Marina and Bella Bella.

About 70 residents live year-round in Shearwater. During World War II the Royal Canadian Air Force operated a reconnaissance base at Shearwater, with about 1,000 military personnel stationed here. After the war, Shearwater was developed into a world-class sportfishing resort. Guests fly in from Vancouver on the resort's private aircraft to Denny Island's air strip or take scheduled flights to Bella Bella.

Top, Gunboat Passage is an interesting route to Bella Bella. Above, Shearwater Resort & Marina.

Ormidale Harbour 18

Whether you're northbound or southbound in Seaforth Channel, this is a good overnight anchorage just around the corner from Bella Bella. The main entrance into Ormidale Harbour is west of Nevay Island and you should favour the Nevay Island shore upon entering to avoid foul ground extending from the Campbell Island shoreline (see Chart 3938). We like to set the hook close to the SE shore in about 50 feet of depth. When anchored in Ormidale Harbour, the views past Thorburne and Nevay Islands provide glimpses of Seaforth Channel, where 80,000-ton cruise ships pick their way past Regatta Rocks. The harbour was named for Robert Macfarlane, a Scottish barrister who received the courtesy title Lord Ormidale when raised to the bench in 1862.

Horsfall Island / Campbell Island 19

Heading southbound from Bella Bella, boaters can take one of several routes to Hakai Passage or Fitz Hugh Sound. Lama Pass and Gunboat Passage are obvious options, but for the adventurous with time to explore, there's the route less travelled along Raymond Passage and into Queens Sound.

If you're looking for shelter from NW winds, one possibility can be found at the small second cove

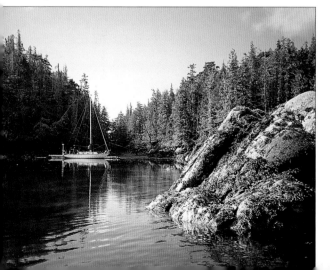

north of Kingsley Point on Horsfall Island. Although open to the south, this cove is easier to enter than the one just south. Anchor in about 25 feet in soft mud and kelp bottom. The tricky entrance to the cove immediately south is often choked with kelp.

A couple of well-protected coves lie nearby across Raymond Passage on Campbell Island. These small coves are south of the entrance to **Hochstader Basin** and about a mile north of Gow Island. Using Chart 3938, keep the island marked '60' on your port side when entering the channel leading to the coves. Turn to the island marked '52' and keep it close to port. The cove straight ahead is the first of the two anchorages. If you prefer a smaller anchorage the basin to the N is also good. Continue along the W shore to the island marked '42' and turn sharp SE. Favour the east side of the pass into the cove to avoid two rocks and anchor in depths between 20 and 30 feet. The holding is very good here in thick mud.

Stryker Island 20

If the light is still with you from Bella Bella heading south, another interesting and attractive cove is the small hurricane hole deep inside Stryker Island. The approach to the anchorage leads along Codfish Passage, which is safe in clear weather with little tide rip (although the south end of this passage can often be fog-wreathed in summer). After you have rounded either the island marked '61' or Alleyne Island (at the sound end of Stryker I) turn N to enter a long narrow bay about a mile and a half in length.

This entrance unfolds into a series of islands and small bays yielding to smaller coves. Near the N end is a small channel on the east side that leads to a tiny cove providing secure anchorage in all winds. This pretty cove, unnamed on the chart, is almost land-locked and, with bright afternoon sun, really captures the mood of the remote anchorages in Queens Sound. While the sun slowly sets and the wine is being poured, you can walk out to the bow and gaze across to the quixotic little island guarding the entrance to yet another secluded cove. "Ne plus ultra!" someone wrote in the log.

When departing from Stryker Island, carefully pick your way out of the coves and bays to safely pass Alleyne Island. It's tempting to take Codfish Passage to pass along the south end of Miles Island to the Tribal Group, as I have done. But this is not to be recommended as the area around these islands is strewn with rocks, choked with kelp and subject to current.

Above left, Shearwater's WWII airforce history and First Nations heritage are commemorated in a waterfront park. Left, Stryker Lagoon anchorage.

This is a complex area of reefs and islands and the safer and more prudent course is to take the short dogleg up Codfish Passage and south through Brown Narrows to the Admiral Group.

QUEENS SOUND

The labyrinth of scrub-forested islands and intricate waterways north of Hakai Passage are part of the Hakai Luxvbalis Conservancy. Queens Sound, the area extending from Hakai Passage to Milbanke Sound, is a boater's feast of archipelagos and anchorages. Its numerous small islands, passes and pocket beaches are also perfect for kayakers.

Surrounded by islands on three sides and Queen Charlotte Sound on the fourth, Queens Sound can be a daunting place during southerly gales. In summer, however, calms prevail for nearly a quarter of the time, although the weather can change quickly in this area, with sea fog frequently blowing in from Queen Charlotte Sound. Throughout this entire area from the Tribal Group south to Hakai Passage, there are a lot of rocks, reefs and small islands. Always keep an eye to your charts, your surroundings and the sounder. Queens Sound is not on every cruiser's itinerary but those prepared to pilot the maze-like channels and kelp-strewn passes will be rewarded with some very unique and pretty anchorages.

Many islands in this area ware given their names by pilots based at Shearwater, near Bella Bella, during World War II. This air strip (still in use) was the site of an air force base from 1938 to 1947. The pilots patrolling the central coast named some of the larger islands after fighter planes for ease of identification. Both Spider and Triquet Islands contain the remains of gun emplacements that were built during WWII to defend the coast. However, getting through the brush to see them can be tough going.

Dodwell Island 21

These interesting anchorages can be approached from either the west via Raymond Passage and Brown Narrows, or from the east side of Campbell Island via Hunter Channel. There are no all-weather anchorages in the Tribal Group or Admiral Group of islands. However there are several nooks above Dodwell Island at the south end of Campbell Island. There are also anchorages just inside Soulsby Point, where a cluster of islets form a small harbour.

The passage above Dodwell Island is quite pretty in sunshine and two small coves present

Temporary anchorage by midden on islet '49'.

lagoon

stern-tie

small boat
anchorage

Campbell
Island

min depth
16 feet
mid-channel

Old
fishing Cabin

61

small boat
anchorage

stern-tie

Soulsby Pt

46

2

5

12

62

47

DODWELL
ISLAND

stern-tie

49

44

5

31

49

0

1/2

49

Nautical miles
Not for navigation.
Use Chart 3937
Depths in fathoms

N

midden

DODWELL ISLAND

Recommended Route: - - - - - - - -
Anchorage Temp Anchorage

Hunter Channel

Stubbs Pt

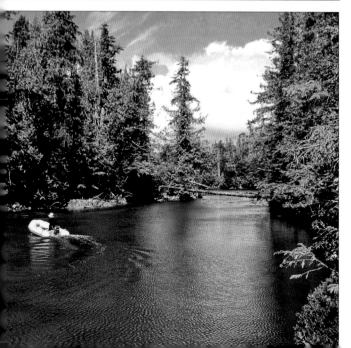

Above, midden beach on islet near Soulsby Point.
Bottom, exploring nearby lagoons.

themselves at the middle part of the pass. The first has 12 feet of depth with numerous small islets on either side. This anchorage requires a stern line. The next cove to the east should be accessed between a small islet and the larger island marked '61' on chart 3937. This is a very secure spot with room for only one or two boats. Anchor in 16 feet with a soft mud bottom with good holding.

If the cove is full (as we found to our surprise one time in late July) you can motor further along to the anchorages inside Soulsby Point. Along the way, there's a small white midden beach, popular with kayakers, on the islet marked '49'.

The entrance to the Soulsby Point anchorages requires a careful approach as numerous rocks and reefs are poised on either side of the channel. Just past these reefs, a good one-boat anchorage lies to the southwest between the islands marked '47' and '49' below the islet containing an old cabin. This is a good spot in almost any wind but, with limited swinging room, a stern line would be wise. Beyond the channel between Campbell Island and the island marked '47' is a larger anchorage but is blemished with several reefs. There is ample depth in the centre of the channel but watch for the reef at the NW tip of island '47'. Once into the larger anchorage, proceed to the deep part of the bay to anchor in about 30 feet. The bottom of soft mud is uneven but a patient pull on the rode will get a good set. The basin collects a lot of drift so a log or two may brush by in the night. Holding is fair in soft mud. This basin is open to

S winds and gets significant gusts during strong westerlies. However, in settled weather it's a great spot to access the nearby lagoons and labyrinth of islets, and offers a great view for miles to the south. A more protected anchorage suitable for small boats is between islands '61' and '62' to the SW in 15 feet. Depth is a little uneven in the approach to this spot.

Sans Peur Passage

Sans Peur (Without Fear) Passage leads from Dodwell Island to Cultus Sound. Although strewn with rocks and kelp (especially on its east side) and with noticeable current, this passage is the recommended route north or south. The trickiest part of the passage is the bottleneck created by a cluster of rocks and islets near mid-channel. Steer to the centre of the channel, allowing ample room around this small reef and shoal area formed beside the west island. Current in the pass is weak and usually not more than 2-3 knots.

McNaughton Group 22

Sounding more like an investment firm than a group of islands, there are numerous anchorages within the McNaughton Group providing good shelter depending on the wind direction. Safest approach is from the south – the N pass is quite encumbered with rocks. Protection from NW winds is good in the bay made by the two islands marked '98' and '84'. Gusts will whistle through the pass between them but not with great conviction. To get away from S winds, the gut between island '98' and the large island to the south provides very good protection in the small bay at the mid point of the channel. The anchorage is also fairly good in W winds, but in strong winds, gusts can really blast through the channel. A good suggestion from the Hamiltons' book *Cruising the Secret Coast* points out that the bight halfway along the gut on the north side makes a good wind blind with a line to the W shore (see map next page).

From the anchorages of the McNaughton Group, there are numerous islets, beaches and lagoons to explore by dinghy or kayak. South of Lane Rock is a pretty bay, too deep to be useful as an anchorage, which contains a reversing waterfall. Nearby is Kinsman Inlet, where two-mile-long Kinsman Lagoon offers hours of exploration by dinghy.

Cultus Sound 23

At the south end of Cultus Sound, along the Hunter Island shore, is a small bay with a sand beach, popular with kayakers. This anchorage provides shelter from the east and south, but is exposed to northwesterlies and the attendant swell coming off Queen Charlotte Sound. Nonetheless, you could spend a blissful afternoon here on the beach or exploring the

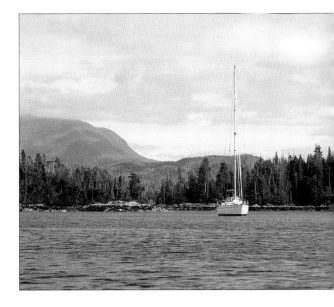

Above, Large anchorage west of Soulsby Pt. Below, entering cut in McNaughton Group. Bottom, the beach at Cultus Sound anchorage.

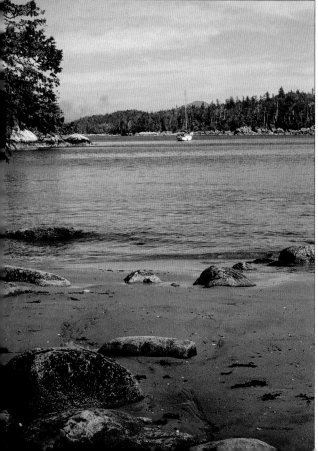

area by dinghy. There is a trail from the anchorage to a cove to the immediate south. If the weather looks at all dicey, motor a few miles north to one of the anchorages in the McNaughton Group.

We've anchored just south of the islet in the centre of the bay in about 30 feet with a mud-and-sand bottom. There is, as with many anchorages in this area, lots of kelp nearby, so find a clear spot.

Spider Anchorage

Proceeding south from Cultus Sound, a vessel is exposed briefly to ocean swell and outer-coast conditions before entering Spider Channel. If those conditions include fog, stand off well to the west to give Superstition Ledge a wide berth. This is a nasty reef which breaks on the smallest swell and will have some tide rip. The light (Fl 4s) at the N end of Spider Island signals the way for boaters into the pass, staying clear of the reef to the NE. In clear weather, the channel east of the island marked '42 ' is safe and a shorter route. If conditions are very clear and calm, and you want to avoid Spider Channel, use Fulton Passage at the S end of Spider Island (Chart 3937).

Spider Channel, between Spider and Spitfire islands is cluttered with rocks at its south end but is a deeper route than either **Spitfire Channel**, which has a minimum depth of 6 feet, or the channel **east** of Spitfire Island which shallows to about 10 feet. (This channel is made more difficult because its almost impossible to see bottom for the thick kelp.) Spider Channel's main challenge is the appropriately named Stopper Group. We transit this channel between islands '48' and '40' at the south end (see map) staying closer to '48' until exiting the pass. The reef just S of this islet can be passed, dead slow, on either side.

Edna Islands Anchorage

The water is deep in the middle of Spider Anchorage but there are several nooks you can pull into among the dozens of islands, including two fairweather anchorages between Edna Islands and Anne Islands. One is the small bight north of the island marked '27' and another, for small boats, is just off the beach in the gap between the Edna Islands. Both of these have about two fathoms of depth with holding in mud and sand. Another anchorage at the SE side of the larger island also would make a good conditional anchorage in sand and mud bottom.

Triquet Island 24

Several narrow but navigable channels lead south from Spider Anchorage to Triquet Island, with the easiest route being the one between Edna and Anne Islands passing E of the Lyte Group.

At the north end of Triquet Island there is a fair-weather anchorage situated beside a small sand-and-shell beach. The anchorage is just NW of the small islet in the bay; anchor in 25 feet in soft mud and sand with good holding. Although the anchorage is partially open to the west, the swells from Queen Charlotte Sound are fairly tame by the time they make their way into the anchorage.

A campsite used by kayakers is on shore, and a beautiful saltwater lagoon lying east of the anchorage is frequented by seabirds. A nice sandy beach lies on the west side of Triquet Island and can be reached by dinghy.

Hurricane Island 25

One of the most popular and secure anchorages in the area around Spider Anchorage is the harbour-like bay at the south end of Hurricane Island. Access with deepest water is to the west of the islet marked '39', keeping the reef and small islet on your starboard as you enter. Anchor in 50 feet in thick mud and clay with great holding. This anchorage can accommodate several vessels, including large boats.

This is an all-weather anchorage and a base from which to explore the surrounding area by dinghy. A wide rock ledge on the NE side of the bay is a good spot for a picnic on a sunny day.

Top, granite ledge at Hurricane Island anchorage,
secure in all weather with good holding (right).
Opposite page, anchorage on N side of Triquet I.

Kittyhawk Group anchorage

Name That Cove

Many of the anchorages in the Queens Sound area, although charted, are unnamed. And just as wartime pilots who patrolled these waters took it upon themselves to name some of the islands for ease of reference, peacetime boating authors have taken it upon themselves to do likewise with the area's anchorages. We too have done the same, but only once. It was while visiting an unnamed cove in Watt Bay in the early 1990s that we called Judd Cove, after Bill's great-great-great grandfather, Robert Hayley Judd, who had been a captain in the Royal Navy in the time of Lord Nelson. When we submitted this name to the BC Geographical Names Office, we were told, understandably, that Capt. Judd's naval career wasn't relevant to the BC coast and that we should propose another name. We have yet to come up with another suggestion. Meanwhile, until an official name is bestowed on the anchorage, we'll keep calling it Judd Cove.

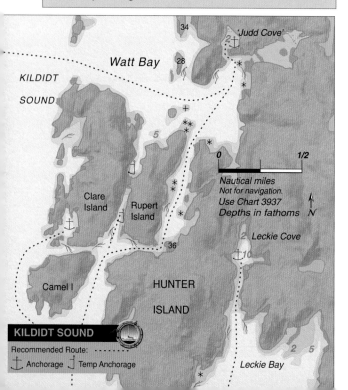

KILDIDT SOUND
Kittyhawk Group 26

Located on the west side of Kildidt Sound, this cluster of islands contains a couple of small and secure anchorages. One small-boat anchorage is at the NW tip of the island marked '79' while a larger anchorage is in the basin south of the island marked '72' (Chart 3937). There is easy access to Kittyhawk Group from either Brydon Channel or Kildidt Sound, watching for the reef N of the island marked '50'. The holding in the larger anchorage is in soft mud with fair holding in about 50 feet.

Brydon Channel, which leads around the top end of the Kittyhawk Group to Spider Anchorage, is best transited at mid-tide (preferably a flood) to easily spot reefs and drying rocks.

South of the Kittyhawk Group is a small but beautiful beach within the Serpent Group of islets lying near the mouth of Kildidt Sound. A white shell beach lies at the head of the small cove on the northeast side of the middle islet, which makes for a good afternoon stop in settled, sunny conditions.

Kildidt Lagoon

Many boaters enjoy the thrill of transiting a set of rapids to explore hidden lagoons, and we are not the exception. However, after many years of boating, the thrill has been replaced by caution when it comes to lagoons. It may be from clutching the tiller in a death grip while our little diesel tried its best to get us out of a dire pass or perhaps it was seeing a badly damaged 40-foot boat that got caught in one of these lagoon passes. Although we have transited Kildidt Narrows into its lagoon without incident, it is a very narrow and rocky pass and can be dangerous if any current is running. If you really want to see this lagoon, exploring in a fast dinghy might be safest way.

'Judd Cove', Watt Bay 27

It will be time well spent if you decide to sample a few anchorages along the east side of Hunter Island. Within the large and encompassing Watt Bay is Bremner Bay, which the Sailing Directions recommend but we found to be quite deep (about 70 feet close to shore). However, due south of Bremner Bay is a nameless bay that contains a small, enclosed cove on its north side which is entered between a drying reef and a narrow point of land. Once through the tight entrance, make a sharp turn to starboard around the point and into the anchorage, which we referred to as 'Judd Cove' in our logbook (see sidebar).

The holding is very good in soft mud and after anchoring in the middle of the cove in 30 feet, we have reversed toward the eastern shore and tied a stern line to a tree. The depth remains almost constant as you pull your stern close to a grassy shoreline bordered by a garden-like wall of angular, rose-hued stones. A perfect hideaway, its shores thick with cedar and salal, the anchorage can be as still as a millpond. We have enjoyed this secluded spot for several days and it's one of those special anchorages you think about as time slips away and you ponder the places you'd really like to see again, if just one more time.

The pass between Rupert Island and Hunter Island is a good shortcut in or out of Watt Bay and for avoiding the swell in the sound. It's easy to navigate and has a least depth of 20 feet. There also are a few nooks to drop the anchor between Clare and Rupert Island and one very secure spot on the west side of Clare Island. (See the Hamilton's *Cruising the Secret Coast* for an excellent report on this area.)

Leckie Bay, Hunter Island 28

An anchorage at the mouth of Kildidt Sound that we like very much is a small cove on the north side of Leckie Bay. Although the main part of Leckie Bay, facing south and with depths of 300 feet, is not a suitable anchorage, this sword-handle shaped cove lies at the end of a narrow channel and is a great spot to drop the hook. Anchor in 60 feet in brown mud, favouring the W shore, and you will be sheltered from most winds including those from the south. No swell enters the cove. On the cove's eastern shore is a stream of fresh water, stained a rusty colour from the cedar trees. We once stayed here for three days, enjoying the peace and tranquility of this anchorage and hated to leave.

Lewall Inlet, Stirling I 29

The salmon fishing in Hakai Passage is legendary and we have caught coho off the SW tip of Stirling Island when motoring into Kildidt Sound. If proceeding into the sound from Hakai Passage when a southerly is blowing, a safer route is to go north up Edward Channel and west through the pass above Stirling Island. This protected route has a few nice anchorages on the way, the most popular being Lewall Inlet on Stirling Island. Anchor anywhere in the basin created by the elbow where the inlet turns north. This spot provides excellent protection from most winds. Holding is good in mud in about 20 feet (Chart 3936). Another best anchorage appears to be behind the islets on the east side of Underhill Island. Another anchorage for next time.

Top, 'Judd Cove' lies within Watt Bay. Middle, Leckie Bay. Bottom, aerial view of Underhill Island anchorage with Edward Channel and Lewall Inlet in background.

INDEX

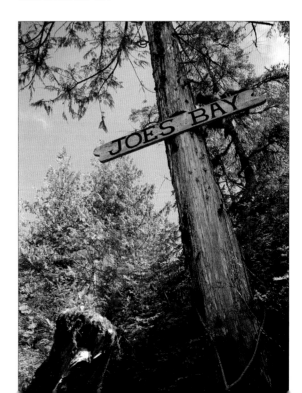

Photo Credits

pg VI, Micheal DeFreitas
pg 8, by permission of Canadian Hydrographic Service
pg 11 top, Mike Woodward
pg 13, Michael DeFreitas
pg 16, 17, Vancouver Archives
pg 18, Poets Cove Resort
pg 24, painting by Alan Nakano of 'Haida Travellers' by permission of the artist
pg 25a, Cartesia
pg 25c, painting by John Horton of 'I Name This Place Desolation Sound' by permission of the artist
pg 27a, painting by John Horton of 'Repairs to Discovery' by permission of the artist
pg 27b, Tourism Vancouver
pg 28, Alan Nakano
pg 29c, Campbell River Museum
pg 30b, Campbell River Museum
pg 30c, painting by Alan Nakano of 'The Buyer and the Fisherman'
pg 34b, Ian Douglas
pg 36a, painting by Emily Carr, 'Kwakiutl House', 1912, oil on card, Collection of the Vancouver Art Gallery, Emily Carr Trust, Photo: Trevor Mills
pg 36b, painting by EJ Hughes, 'Indian Houses at Alert Bay' 1951, by permission of the artist and the National Gallery of Canada
pg 42a, 43, 44b, 47a,c, Michael DeFreitas
pg 48, 58 Russ Heinl

pg 61a, top Chris Cheadle
pg 64, Russ Heinl
pg 68b, Buchart Gardens
pg 74a, 76, 77, 79 Michael DeFreitas
pg 86, Russ Heinl
pg 88b, 89b, 92a, Michael DeFreitas
pg 94, Russ Heinl
pg 95a, 100, Michael DeFreitas
pg 107, 118, Russ Heinl
pg 121, Ian Douglas
pg 129, Fraser River Port Authority
pg 146, Chris Cheadle
pg 149 (all) Phil Hersee
pg 160b, Phil Hersee
pg 161, Chris Cheadle
pg 167b, Ian Douglas
pg 169a, 171, 172b, 173a, Russ Heinl
pg 170, Ian Douglas
pg 174, Russ Heinl
pg 177, 178a, Mike Woodward
pg 179, 180, Russ Heinl
pg 181a, Mike Woodward
pg 181b, 182, 183, 185, 191, Russ Heinl
pg 193, 194, 196, Ian Douglas
pg 202, 206, 209, Russ Heinl
pg 224, painting by Yvonne Maximchuk of 'Karlukwees' by permission of the artist
pg 234 (inset), Arno Andreas
pg 250/251, Russ Heinl
pg 275, Duart Snow
pg 296a, Michael DeFreitas
pg 299b, Mike Woodward
pg 300, Chris Cheadle
pg 301b, 302, 306a, 308a, 310b, 311c, 314c, 316a, 317b, 318b, Michael DeFreitas
pg 319, Sam Beebe, Ecotrust
pg 322a, 323a, Michael DeFreitas
323b, Shearwater Resort & Marina
331c, Michael DeFreitas
Inside Back Cover, Mike Robichaud

All other photography by Anne Vipond & Bill Kelly.